Interdisciplinary perspectives on modern history

Editors
Robert Fogel and Stephan Thernstrom

Working-class Americanism

Working-class Americanism

*The politics of labor in a textile city,
1914–1960*

GARY GERSTLE
Princeton University

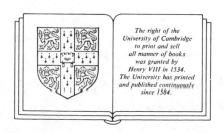

CAMBRIDGE UNIVERSITY PRESS
Cambridge
New York   Port Chester   Melbourne   Sydney

Published by the Press Syndicate of the University of Cambridge
The Pitt Building, Trumpington Street, Cambridge CB2 1RP
40 West 20th Street, New York, NY 10011, USA
10 Stamford Road, Oakleigh, Melbourne 3166, Australia

© Cambridge University Press 1989

First published 1989

Printed in the United States of America

Library of Congress Cataloging-in-Publication Data
Gerstle, Gary, 1954–
Working-class Americanism: the politics of labor in a textile city,
1914–1960/Gary Gerstle.
p.   cm. – (Interdisciplinary perspectives on modern history)
Includes index.
ISBN 0–521–36131–1
1. Textile workers – Rhode Island – Woonsocket – History – 20th century.
2. Textile industry – Rhode Island – Woonsocket – History – 20th century.
I. Title. II. Series.

<table>

HD8039.T42U646 1989	89-9792
331.7′677′0097452 – dc20	CIP

</table>

British Library Cataloguing in Publication Data
Gerstle, Gary
Working-class Americanism: the politics of labor in a textile city,
1914–1960. – (Interdisciplinary perspectives on modern history)
1. United States. Textile industries. Trade Unions, History
I. Title   II. Series
331.88′177′0973

ISBN 0–521–36131–1 hard covers

For my parents and
for Liz

Contents

Illustrations and tables

ix

Acknowledgments

When I began working on this project, virtually nothing had been written on the Independent Textile Union of Woonsocket, once the most powerful of New England's textile unions; worse, virtually none of its records seemed to have survived the union's collapse in the 1950s. This book owes its very existence, then, to scores of individuals – textile workers, union veterans, labor lawyers, labor priests, employers, and Catholic activists – who allowed me to probe their memories and to examine their personal archives. I am deeply grateful for their generosity, and I hope that they will find in these pages an accurate rendering of their remarkable history.

The union archive that I assembled from surviving personal holdings made it possible for me to utilize effectively the union materials that had found their way to various libraries – Harvard University's Littauer Library, the Department of Labor's Library and the National Archives in Washington, D.C., and the Wisconsin State Historical Society. I wish to thank the staffs of these institutions as well as those of the Rhode Island State Archives, Providence Public Library, Providence Superior Court, Slater Mill Historic Site, Rhode Island Historical Society, Providence Diocesan Archives, Mallet Library of the Société St. Jean Baptiste, Museum of American Textile History, Columbia University Library, and Library of Congress, for their invaluable assistance.

Grants from the Harvard University History Department and University Consortium for Research on North America (1980–81) made possible preliminary research trips, and a 1982 William F. Sullivan Research Fellowship from the Museum of American Textile History (then the Merrimack Valley Textile Museum) funded an initial year of writing. Princeton University's Committee on Research in the Humanities and Social Sciences helped me defray the cost of transcribing tapes and of reproducing the illustrations that appear in this book. A 1987 Faculty Research Grant from the Canadian Government sponsored my research for the book's final chapters, and a 1987–88 Charles Warren Center Fellowship allowed me the luxury of an additional year of writing freed from the hectic demands of university teaching. For all this financial assistance, I am most appreciative.

At Cambridge University Press, Frank Smith sure-handedly took hold of this manuscript and expertly guided its transformation into a book. Edith Feinstein supervised with patience, thoroughness, and good cheer the nitty-gritty tasks of production while Ann Finlayson, my copy editor, held me to a high standard of stylistic and historical accuracy. My thanks to them all.

At every point of research and writing I have benefited enormously from the expertise and wisdom of individual scholars. I would like to thank the following in particular: Pierre Anctil, Chris Appy, David Brody, Paul Buhle, David Casey, Stewart Doty, Laurence Gross, Mark Hirsch, David Jaffee, Michael Kazin, Alexander Keyssar, Gary Kulik, Nelson Lichtenstein, Arno Mayer, James McPherson, John Murrin, Joel Perlmann, Daniel Rodgers, David Scobey, and Richard Sorrell.

I owe a very special debt to several friends whose commitment to this project has been long-standing and steadfast. Stephan Thernstrom, who has watched over this project and me for more years than any thesis advisee has a right to expect, has worked hard to curb what he once called my "youthful enthusiasm" and to make my history more precise, mature, and shrewd. I hope he will find his efforts rewarded. Alan Brinkley and Roy Rosenzweig believed that I had important things to say and showed me – through their insightful criticism and through the example of their own important work – how I might say them better. Peter Mandler has argued with me long and hard over many of the vexing issues raised in this book, determined that he – and I – should get them right. Steve Fraser and I, drifting together almost by chance several years ago, struck up a wide-ranging conversation that led to a lot of good times, prompted us to coedit a collection on modern political history, and spurred me to think in new ways about the important themes of this book; those who know Steve's work will recognize its influence upon my own.

That leaves a few familial debts. I thank my parents, Jack and Else Gerstle, who long ago imparted to me a passion for learning and whose own immigrant experience (and my desire to understand it) provided an early and inexhaustible inspiration for this book. Young Daniel Gerstle, with his timely interruptions and provocative suggestions (that I ought to put a fire truck on the book's cover and shift my focus, in my next project, from labor to transportation history) has made the task of writing altogether more delightful. And Liz Lunbeck, in her uniquely talented and spirited way, has made this a far better work of history while filling my life with riches, both large and small. To her go my most heartfelt thanks and the hope that she will share some of my satisfaction in seeing this book, by now nearing the age of adolescence, finally leave home.

Introduction

This book explores the efforts of two groups of twentieth-century workers to build a union and to fashion a class identity for themselves. The first group consisted of secular and modernist radicals, mostly European-born, who brought dreams of social democratic transformation to American shores; the second consisted of devout and traditionalist ethnics, largely French Canadian and American-born, torn between responding to pressures they experienced as workers in an industrial society and reaffirming their fealty to their ancestral culture. In the 1930s these workers came together in the Independent Textile Union. In the process they made the city in which this union emerged, Woonsocket, Rhode Island, into what Fall River and then Lawrence had once been – the bastion of organized labor in New England. Their union movement was also an integral part of the CIO insurgency that erupted in most centers of industrial production in those years; it opposed the principle of industrial unionism to the worn AFL principle of craft unionism, and it viewed unionism not in the practical, bread-and-butter terms of AFL unionists, but in terms of a grand struggle for freedom and independence.

This book uses the story of this union's swift, dramatic rise – and equally precipitous fall – to probe the characters of the modern labor movement and of modern, working-class political culture during their formative, twentieth-century years. The beginning of that formative period lies not, as is often assumed, in the economic collapse of 1929, but in the dramatic changes in American politics and culture World War I brought to a head. Prior to 1917, an ethnic group could choose, if its members desired, to remain separate from the American cultural mainstream and to cultivate its Old World traditions; the American landscape was dotted with insular ethnic communities, whose cultural life remained remarkably autonomous of the Protestant, republican, and commercial culture around them. Prior to the war, political radicals, too, enjoyed a period of unusual independence. The number, size, and influence of radical groups in the prewar period was probably greater than in any other period of American history, and the variety of political languages they spoke was similarly unprecedented: socialism, syndicalism, Bellamyite

1

nationalism, anarchism, populism – most flourishing in multiple versions that reflected the diverse ethnocultural backgrounds of their particular groups of supporters.[1]

By the mid-1920s this world of cultural and political diversity had narrowed significantly. Most ethnic groups then found it far more difficult to maintain their independence from the cultural mainstream; most radical groups found themselves weak in number and their political ideas excluded from mainstream political discourse. Part of this dramatic change reflected the maturation of long-term centralizing tendencies in economics, communications, and culture, all contributing to the nationalization and homogenization of the American experience. National corporations and their standardized management and marketing techniques increasingly shaped the work and consuming habits of the American people; national newspaper chains and the radio centralized information gathering and processing; movies and national magazines insured that most Americans, especially those in urban areas, would spend a substantial portion of their leisure time in a single transcontinental supermarket of mass cultural products.[2]

---

[1] No single work satisfactorily captures the political and cultural diversity of the pre–World War I world, though the following are suggestive: Herbert Gutman, *Work, Culture and Society in Industrializing America* (New York, 1976); David Montgomery, *The Fall of the House of Labor: The Workplace, the State, and American Labor Activism* (Cambridge, U.K., 1987); John Bodnar, *The Transplanted: A History of Immigrants in Urban America* (Bloomington, Ind., 1985); Nell Irvin Painter, *Standing at Armageddon: The United States, 1877–1919* (New York, 1987); and Robert H. Wiebe, *The Search for Order, 1877–1920* (New York, 1967). John Higham, "Integrating America: The Problem of Assimilation in the Nineteenth Century," *Journal of American Ethnic History* 1 (Fall 1981), 7–25, and William Taylor, "The Launching of a Commercial Culture: New York City, 1860–1930" (unpublished paper), have also influenced my thinking on the subject. The cultural and political diversity of the period can best be grasped by sampling the voluminous literature that now exists on specific political movements, industrial cities, and ethnic groups for the period from 1880 to 1917. See, for example, Nick Salvatore, *Eugene V. Debs: Citizen and Socialist* (Urbana, Ill., 1982); Lawrence Goodwyn, *Democratic Promise: The Populist Movement in America* (New York, 1976); Roy Rosenzweig, *Eight Hours for What We Will: Workers and Leisure in an Industrial City, 1870–1920* (Cambridge, U.K., 1983); Olivier Zunz, *The Changing Face of Inequality: Urbanization, Industrial Development, and Immigrants in Detroit, 1880–1920* (Chicago, 1982); Irving Howe, *World of Our Fathers: The Journey of the East European Jews to America and the World They Found and Made* (New York, 1976).

[2] These various centralizing tendencies are discussed in Alfred D. Chandler, Jr., *Strategy and Structure: Chapters in the History of Industrial Enterprise* (Cambridge, Mass., 1969); Chandler, *The Visible Hand: The Managerial Revolution in American Business* (Cambridge, Mass., 1977); William J. Leiserson, *Adjusting Immigrant and Industry* (New York, 1924); Montgomery, *The Fall of the House of Labor*, 171–256; Michael J. Piore and Charles F.

But the pressures for conformity in the 1920s came not only from such vast, impersonal forces. They resulted also from the deliberate efforts national and state governments (as well as private groups) made to generate a mass citizenry, essentially homogeneous in its cultural and political attitudes. These efforts crystallized in the war, as panicked government officials and private citizens, alarmed at the overwhelming numbers of immigrants with cultural ties to central Europe as well as by the loud, Socialist-led opposition to American war involvement, launched Americanization campaigns, unprecedented in scope and intensity, to strip the masses of their foreign ways and allegedly radical beliefs. These campaigns continued after the war, abating only after the "radical problem" was "solved" by the crushing of the 1919–22 strike wave and the "immigrant problem" was "solved" by closing off America to immigration in 1924.[3] Even after fears of political and cultural subversion subsided, however, the American government, at both the national and state levels, did not fully relinquish its newly gained powers to define the appropriate cultural and political behavior of American citizens. Governmental prohibition of the manufacture and sale of alcohol was

Sabel, *The Second Industrial Divide: Possibilities for Prosperity* (New York, 1984); David F. Noble, *America by Design: Science, Technology, and the Rise of Corporate Capitalism* (New York, 1977); Steve Fraser, "The 'Labor Question,'" in Steve Fraser and Gary Gerstle, eds., *The Rise and Fall of the New Deal Order, 1930–1980* (Princeton, N.J., 1989), 55–84; Stuart Brandes, *American Welfare Capitalism, 1880–1940* (Chicago, 1967); David Brody, "The Rise and Decline of Welfare Capitalism," in his *Workers in Industrial America* (New York, 1980), 48–81; Wiebe, *The Search for Order;* Jerry Israel, ed., *Building the Organizational Society: Essays on Associational Activities in Modern America* (New York, 1972); Robert S. Lynd and Helen Merrell Lynd, *Middletown: A Study in American Culture* (New York, 1929); Rosenzweig, *Eight Hours for What We Will;* Lary May, *Screening Out the Past: The Birth of the Mass Culture and the Motion Picture Industry* (New York, 1980); Stuart Ewen, *Captains of Consciousness: Advertising and the Social Roots of Consumer Culture* (New York, 1976); Carl F. Kaestle, "Pulling Together or Coming Apart? Standardization and Diversity in American Print Culture, 1880–1980," and Susan Watkins, "The Rise of Demographic Nationalism in Western Europe, 1870–1960" (unpublished papers delivered at Shelby Cullom Davis Center Seminar, Princeton University, 1986–87); Taylor, "The Launching of a Commercial Culture."

[3] The best study of the war-inspired Americanization efforts is still John Higham, *Strangers in the Land: Patterns of American Nativism, 1860–1925* (New York, 1975; originally published in 1955); see also Edward George Hartmann, *The Movement to Americanize the Immigrant* (New York, 1948). On the collapse of labor and radical organizations see Montgomery, *The Fall of the House of Labor*, 370–464; David Brody, *Labor in Crisis: The Steel Strike of 1919* (New York, 1965); Stephen Meyer III, *The Five Dollar Day: Labor Management and Social Control in the Ford Motor Company, 1908–1921* (Albany, N.Y., 1981); Robert K. Murray, *Red Scare: A Study in National Hysteria, 1919–1920* (Minneapolis, 1955).

a vivid and daily reminder in ethnic communities throughout the 1920s of the American state's ability and new found willingness to intrude on the personal and cultural habits of individual citizens. Similarly, the citizenship training courses first set up to enforce political loyalty on the foreign-born became a permanent part of public school curricula in every state and thus an obligatory part of every public school student's cultural and political education.[4]

Such state-sponsored campaigns to shape individual behavior by no means created the politically docile or culturally homogeneous citizenry that the Americanization movement's more conservative architects had envisioned. Their effects were far more complex and contradictory; in communities like Woonsocket they would actually generate a greater sense of political opportunity and a higher level of political conflict than had prevailed in the prewar era. But they would do so by forcing ethnic and radical groups through a wrenching period of internal upheaval, forcing their members to struggle with the demands for political and cultural conformity that the external world of government, corporations, the Catholic Church hierarchy, and the mass media ever more insistently thrust upon them. The battles that erupted within ethnic communities and radical groups, and the manner of their resolution, profoundly shaped American working-class politics and culture, and prefigured, in important ways, working-class responses to the Great Depression.

Part I of this book analyzes the cultural and political transformations that Americanization campaigns and economic depression wrought in Woonsocket in the 1920s. In particular it shows how Americanization campaigns and a troubled economy freed the city's two most important working-class groups, traditionalist French Canadians and progressive Franco-Belgians, from the insular ethnic worlds in which they had been confined, how they made political action based on a shared class experience a real possibility, and how they prompted workers to begin fashioning a capitalist critique from the American political traditions that conservative Americanizers had so insistently thrust upon them. These social and political developments form the essential backdrop to the city's Depression experience, and are critical to understanding the 1930s rise of an industrial union with the power to alter fundamentally the working and living conditions of Woonsocket's workers.

[4] Joseph R. Gusfield, *Symbolic Crusade: Status Politics and the American Temperance Movement* (Urbana, Ill., 1963); Robert A. Carlson, *The Quest for Conformity: Americanization Through Education* (New York, 1975); Bessie L. Pierce, *Civic Attitudes in American School Textbooks* (Chicago, 1930), 229–30.

Part II, covering the years from 1929 to 1936, analyzes the process by which Woonsocket's industrial union, the Independent Textile Union (ITU), came into being and secured a foothold in the city. Part III, spanning the years from 1936 to 1941, analyzes the union's successful bid for economic and political power and its elaboration of a working-class Americanism that managed to accommodate both the Franco-Belgians' modernist vision of socialist transformation and the French Canadians' traditionalist vision of corporatist reconstruction. Part IV focuses largely on the years from 1941 to 1946, a period in which the union's French Canadians, aided by a resurgent ethnic middle class, fought and triumphed over the union's radicals, only to relinquish their corporatist vision under pressure from an ideologically powerful wartime state. During these war years the working-class Americanism that through the 1930s had focused so insistently on democratizing relations between capital and labor was transformed into a pluralist creed focused instead on eliminating racial and religious bigotry from American life. This ideological transformation, which was echoed throughout the country, displaced conflict between capital and labor from the central place it had long occupied in the nation's political consciousness and, in the process, severely weakened the labor movement's claim to speak for the down-trodden and oppressed. Ideologically marginalized, Woonsocket's unionists suffered the indignity of presiding over their union's dismantling, which proceeded in lockstep with the city's deindustrialization in the 1950s.

Few words in the 1930s American labor movement resounded as broadly as "Americanism." John L. Lewis, angrily defending his CIO unions against charges that they espoused communism, nazism, or some other "philosophy," declared in 1940: "I yield to no man the right to challenge my Americanism or the Americanism of the organizations which at this moment I represent." Lewis did not attempt to define "his" Americanism; he simply assumed that his audience – in this case a convention hall packed with trade union delegates – knew precisely what he meant.[5] Earl Browder, the chairman of the American Communist Party in the 1930s, also frequently invoked Americanism, as in his well-known, bizarre slogan, "Communism Is Twentieth Century Americanism." In invoking Americanism Browder rarely summoned up the kind of thunderous indignation

---

[5] Quoted in *ITU News*, October 1940, 6. See Melvyn Dubofsky and Warren Van Tine, *John L. Lewis: A Biography* (New York, 1977), 288–90, for an attempt to define Lewis's Americanism.

that was second nature to Lewis; from his perspective, it was important that Americanism imbue the Communist Party with as innocuous and unassailable an aura as mom and apple pie.[6]

Americanism was as popular in the ranks of ordinary American workers as in elite union and radical party circles. In Woonsocket a French-Canadian skilled worker and rank-and-file unionist was fond of yelling at union meetings – again without explication – "Unionism is the spirit of Americanism." And another such rank and filer, speaking to a group of applicants for citizenship in 1938, stressed "the absolute necessity of maintaining unionism as the key factor in Americanism." The radical leaders of this union movement, mostly skilled workers and socialists from northern France and Belgium, also indulged in Americanist talk as when they criticized the "reactionary" Supreme Court justices in 1937 for "blocking" the emergence of "a new, progressive Americanism." And in 1940 they called on their members to insure that Americanism would continue to "mean to the average man the right to 'life, liberty, and the pursuit of happiness.'" Although this last statement is unusual in its explication of the term's referents, even here these remain vague, linked somehow to the Declaration of Independence.[7]

Many scholars have noted that Americanism enjoyed widespread currency in labor and radical circles in the 1930s. But, frustrated by the term's apparent lack of specificity, most have dismissed it as a shallow, rather meaningless political term.[8] The few historians who have seen Americanism as an important political phenomenon have followed the lead of Warren Susman, treating it as the carrier of profoundly conservative political impulses. Susman's argument followed two lines. The first took up a critique of Popular Front culture that Trotskyists and other dissident communists first articulated in the 1940s and 1950s. In this vein, Susman argued that precious little

---

[6] Irving Howe and Lewis Coser, *The American Communist Party: A Critical History (1919–1957)* (Boston, 1957), 175–386. Earl Browder's Americanism, of course, can only be understood as part of the Communist Party's effort – as a result of decisions made by the Communist International in Moscow in 1935 – to present itself as patriotic, democratic, and respectable. Such a rhetorical face-lift was not accompanied by internal changes in the party that might have rendered its radicalism truly nationalist and democratic, and thus its Americanism should not be regarded as a genuine expression of deeply held beliefs. The fact, however, that Browder, in constructing a patriotic veneer for his party, should have chosen Americanism as his keyword amply testifies to its popularity in the ranks of American workers. Leon Samson, in his *Toward a United Front* (New York, 1935), produced the Communist Party's most ambitious treatise on Americanism and its relationship to socialism.

[7] *ITU News*, September 1939, 8; August 1939, 5; May 1937, 7; December 1940, 4.

[8] See, for example, Howe and Coser, *The American Communist Party*, 363–6.

political thought stood behind the symbols of national community that Americans so eagerly embraced in the thirties. Patriotic terms like "Americanism," New Deal icons like the Blue Eagle, and mass cultural images like Frank Capra's nostalgic cinematic rendition of the wholesome, virtuous character of small-town life offered individual Americans security and a sense of belonging to a greater whole in a time of deep distress. These symbols and terms thus encouraged adjustment rather than rebellion, conformity rather than dissent.

In his second line of argument Susman embraced an analysis of Americanism that originated with Gramsci and fellow 1920s European intellectuals of both the left and right. Insofar as Americanism contained any political ideology at all, Susman claimed, it was procapitalist, rooted in the genius of Henry Ford, not of Eugene Debs or of Karl Marx. The exponents of Fordism interpreted democracy in terms of American workers' full participation in the marketplace of American capitalism. They envisioned equality in terms of the mass distribution of consumer goods – cars, clothing, radios – to American families. They promised only the semblance of social equality and participatory democracy, never challenging, in Susman's words, the "essential decision-making power in the shop, industry, the community or the nation." Even the American Communists and Socialists of the 1930s, who deliberately espoused Americanism as a way of introducing radical thought into mainstream political discourse, Susman argued, failed to move beyond this Fordist vision. Their arguments reinforced rather than challenged the fundamental structure of capitalist society.[9]

Susman's analysis is not entirely wrong. Many Americans of the 1930s, especially those of the middle class, drew from Americanism a comforting sense of community and security that saw them through

[9] Warren Susman, "Socialism and Americanism," "The Culture of the 1930s," and "Culture and Commitment," in Susman, *Culture as History: The Transformation of American Society in the Twentieth Century* (New York, 1984), 75–85, 150–210. The Trotskyist roots of Susman's first line of argument can be found in Howe and Coser, *The American Communist Party*; the Gramscian roots can be found in Quintin Hoare and Geoffrey Nowell Smith, eds. and trans., *Selections from the Prison Notebooks of Antonio Gramsci* (New York, 1971), 277–318. For the European conservatives' critique of Americanism see Charles S. Maier, *In Search of Stability: Explorations in Historical Political Economy* (New York, 1987), 22–53, and Victoria de Grazia, "Americanism for Export," *Wedge* 7–8 (Winter–Spring 1985), 74–81. The influence of Trotskyist and Gramscian perspectives on the writing of twentieth-century American cultural history has spread far beyond Susman. See, for example, Richard Pells, *Radical Visions and American Dreams: Culture and Social Thought in the Depression Years* (New York, 1973), and T. J. Jackson Lears and Richard Wightman Fox, eds., *The Culture of Consumption: Critical Essays in American History, 1880–1980* (New York, 1983).

hard times. Likewise, a significant number of reformers, labor leaders, and radicals did construct an essentially procapitalist, consumerist vision out of Americanist materials. But for every individual looking to Americanism for comfort and security, we can counterpose another who found in Americanist rhetoric an inspiration for political revolt, and for every self-professed radical conflating his or her Americanism with Fordism, we can find another using Americanist rhetoric to focus attention directly on the unequal distribution of power between capital and labor that prevailed in the workplace, community, and nation.

The fact that such varied meanings became attached to the term "Americanism" renders impossible efforts to treat it as an ideology. But Americanism was not so amorphous as to resist definition. It can best be understood as a political language, a set of words, phrases, and concepts that individuals used – either by choice or necessity – to articulate their political beliefs and press their political demands. Americanism emerged as a political language in the second and third decades of the twentieth century as a result of a medley of factors noted earlier: first, the Americanization campaigns of World War I and after, through which the government sought to enforce an American identity – "100 percent Americanism" – on the nation's cultural dissenters and political radicals; second, the implementation in the nation's largest firms of a new system of industrial relations – often called Fordism or the American Plan – based on high productivity, high wages, and enlightened schemes of scientific and personnel management; and third, the national diffusion by mass cultural media – movies, radio, and national magazines – of "American" cultural values and, in the process, of the English language. The combined result of these forces, by the twenties, was an unprecedented national emphasis on pledging loyalty to American institutions, on defining what it meant to be an American, and on elaborating an American way of life. Such a preoccupation with "being American" did not in itself procure political or cultural conformity, but it did force virtually every group seriously interested in political power – groups as diverse as capitalists, socialists, ghettoized ethnics, and small-town fundamentalists – to couch their programs in the language of Americanism.[10]

[10] Susman, "Culture and Commitment," in *Culture as History*, 184–210; David O'Brien, *American Catholics and Social Reform: The New Deal Years* (New York, 1968), 212–27; Philip Gleason, "American Identity and Americanization," in Stephan Thernstrom, ed., *The Harvard Encyclopedia of American Ethnic Groups* (Cambridge, Mass., 1980), 31–58; R. W. Dunn, *The Americanization of Labor: The Employers' Offensive Against the Trade Unions* (New York, 1927); Gary Gerstle, "The Politics of Patriotism: Ameri-

In any particular period of time from the 1920s through the 1940s, some groups were invariably more successful than others in appropriating the language and adapting it to their specific political agendas; but success was always tenuous, vulnerable to dramatic economic developments like depression and major political events like war. The substance of American politics, then, changed dramatically over time as different groups gained and then lost control of the language of Americanism. The language of Americanism, in turn, easily accommodated, even camouflaged, such dramatic shifts. This camouflaging, I will argue, has hidden a good part of twentieth-century politics from historiographic view. It has led some historians to see in twentieth-century politics too much mindless patriotism, others to see mostly crass opportunism, still others to see only an obsession with the private – no longer the public – good. Yet, the language of Americanism was a good deal richer, more varied, and more complex than any of these perspectives suggests.

Americanist language can best be understood in terms of four overlapping dimensions that I will call nationalist, democratic, progressive, and traditionalist. The nationalist dimension of Americanism demanded of its adherents fealty to a series of American heroes, foremost among them the Pilgrims, the Founding Fathers, and Abraham Lincoln. Such hero worship entailed admiring the myths collectively woven around these individuals' efforts to secure religious freedom (the Pilgrims), to establish a republic (the Founding Fathers), and to preserve the union and free the slaves at the country's gravest hour (Lincoln). Dwelling on such deeds, of course, led naturally to an emphasis on America's greatness, even uniqueness, among the world's nations. It also, however, allowed political insurgents at home to legitimate their particular goals by linking themselves to the revered causes of the nation's past. As John L. Lewis wrote in 1925, "a return to first principles – a reassertion in practice of the rules laid down by the Fathers of the Republic...has been all that the most ardent champion of popular rights or proponent of public welfare need ask."[11] Such reassertions were often made in plainly opportunistic ways; 1930s labor leaders, for example, unabashedly declared that their pursuit of economic security was but a latter-day version of the Pilgrims' quest for freedom and sustenance. Nationalist language,

canization and the Formation of the CIO," *Dissent* (Winter 1986), 84–92; John J. Bukowczyk, "The Transformation of Working-Class Ethnicity: Corporate Control, Americanization, and the Polish Immigrant Middle Class in Bayonne, N.J., 1915–1925," *Labor History* 25 (Winter 1984), 53–82.

[11] John L. Lewis, *The Miners' Fight for American Standards* (Indianapolis, Ind., 1925), 179–80.

then, frequently imparted a fairly crass tone to political discussions.

The second, democratic dimension of Americanism – linked inextricably to the first – focused less on the identity of American heroes, more on the ideals for which they fought. Such commonly used words and phrases as "democracy," "liberty," "rights," "independence," and "freedom" evoked these ideals. This aspect of Americanism harbored an unacknowledged tension between such competing democratic notions as individual rights and equal rights; free enterprise and industrial democracy stood in similar opposition. The democratic dimension, then, lent itself to justification of goals as disparate as the untrammeled pursuit of individual wealth on the one hand and the democratization of capitalist institutions on the other. Many used it to articulate cultural (rather than economic) visions, such as the pluralist dream that called for the extension of equal rights and equal opportunities to all American citizens irrespective of creed, color, or national origin. The flexibility of this democratic dimension – its nurturing such a range of political and social visions – accounts in large part for the malleability of the language of Americanism as a whole and its appeal to groups as divergent as free enterprisers, political radicals, and cultural pluralists.

The third dimension of Americanism was progressive, entailing a belief in the fundamentally rational, abundant, and ever-improving character of the modern world in general and of American society in particular. This dimension stressed the ability of free and energetic "man" to transform, with the aid of machines, the natural world, to stock the marketplace with a dazzling array of colorful, useful, and pleasing consumer goods, and to put these within reach of virtually every American. An important corollary of this belief was that such consumption made life progressively easier, more satisfying, and more enriching. By eliminating scarcity, the modern world also eliminated sources of social conflict and made enduring social peace possible. The words evoking this progressive view included "progress," "science," "technology," "abundance," "rationality," and "efficiency"; such phrases as "scientific management" and "the American standard of living" also reflected this progressive perspective. Historians recently have tended to associate this view with capitalists and their apologists who sought to divert the masses from seeking economic power, the true source of independence and happiness.[12] But it is well to remember that virtually all socialists, from the late-nineteenth to the late-twentieth century, have shared the

---

[12] See, for example, Ewen, *Captains of Consciousness*.

capitalist faith in the liberating potential of modern society and specifically in the latent ability of modern industry, with its marvelous efficiency and productivity, to deliver all people from the world of scarcity and conflict to the world of abundance and harmony. Lenin was one of Frederick Winslow Taylor's greatest fans,[13] and in 1930s' Woonsocket, working-class radicals would make progressive language a critical component of their Americanist discourse.

The fourth dimension of Americanism was traditionalist, rooted in nostalgia for the mythic, simpler, and more virtuous past when the essence of America was to be found on the farm and in the small town; when family values were paramount; when individuals were hardy, virtuous, and God-fearing; and when all Americans were white, Anglo-Saxon, and Protestant. Family, God, virtue, discipline, manliness, self-reliance, prohibition, and Christianity all evoked this strain of Americanism, which infused movements of religious fundamentalism, anticommunism, racism, nativism, and imperialism with extraordinary patriotic passion. For those who lived in rural areas or small towns, or who belonged to the embattled urban, Protestant middle class, this aspect of Americanism was salient, expressed in national debates on prohibition, immigration restriction, and evolution.[14] In working-class communities composed of new immigrant groups, this strain remained submerged, at least until the end of World War II. Catholics and Jews could not embrace a dimension of Americanism that, in the hands of Protestants, relegated them to a subordinate place in American social life; yet the traditional values associated with it nevertheless powerfully appealed to ethnic Americans, especially Catholics, whose worlds were defined by God, family, and community. It would sneak into the discourse of the 1930s labor movement in odd ways; unionists in Woonsocket sometimes ascribed traditionalist qualities to Abraham Lincoln ("plain, simple, honest, courageous") and portrayed Thanksgiving as a time for "family feasting."[15] But not until World War II thoroughly under-

[13] On Lenin, see E. H. Carr, *The Bolshevik Revolution* (3 vols., London, 1950–53), vol. II, 109–15.

[14] Traditionalist constructions of Americanism were most common in the early 1920s. For glimpses of how this language was used see Gusfield, *Symbolic Crusade*; David M. Chalmers, *Hooded Americanism* (Chicago, 1968); Norman Furniss, *The Fundamentalist Controversy, 1918–1931* (New Haven, Conn., 1954); Ray Ginger, *Six Days or Forever? Tennessee vs. John Thomas Scopes* (New York, 1958); and Lawrence W. Levine, *Defender of the Faith, William Jennings Bryan: The Last Decade, 1915–1925* (Cambridge, Mass., 1965).

[15] *ITU News*, February 1938, 5, and November 1939, cover.

mined nativism did ethnic Americans feel able to embrace the traditionalist perspective of Americanism as their own.[16]

This traditionalist dimension of Americanism stood in sharp con-
tradiction to Americanism's progressive dimension. Many found it
difficult if not impossible to embrace both. Some did, however; Henry
Ford was perhaps the most prominent among them. Ford combined a
faith in the wonders of mass production with a continuing adherence
to a distinctly nineteenth-century set of moral values. This dualism
was imbedded in his most celebrated concept, the five-dollar-a-day
wage, predicated on a new theory of economics that stressed the
economic abundance and profits that would result from putting more
money into workers' hands. Yet Ford insisted on making half of that
daily wage contingent on his workers living a properly moral
domestic life, and he sent sociological inspectors into his employees'
homes to assess their cleanliness, order, and decorum.[17]

The contrary progressive and traditionalist dimensions of Americanism proved complementary, however, when located in different
constituencies of a single social movement. Both the 1930s labor
movement and the New Deal brought radicals and reformers imbued
with a progressive faith together with ethnically minded workers still
committed to their community's moral traditionalism. What cemented
their alliance was their ability to share a common political language
even as they emphasized different dimensions of that language and
imparted to particular words significantly different meanings. Thus,
to reformers and radicals the "American standard of living" often
connoted a plan to use the state to create and distribute economic
abundance to all Americans; to ethnic workers, by contrast, it
sometimes meant the defense of the most essential component of
their community – the patriarchal family. The very contradictoriness
of Americanism, in such instances, served political movements well.

This discussion of Americanism's four dimensions – nationalist,
democratic, progressive, and traditionalist – suggests the multiplicity
of political visions that this political language could and did sustain.
This very multiplicity means that this language cannot be adequately

---

[16] On the place of such traditionalist language in the political consciousness of ethnics
in post–World War II America, see Jonathan Rieder, *Canarsie: The Jews and Italians of
Brooklyn Against Liberalism* (Cambridge, Mass., 1985).

[17] Meyer, *The Five-Dollar Day*; Robert Lacey, *Ford: The Men and the Machine* (Boston,
1986), 87–131. Gramsci mistakenly took Ford to be representative of America's
bourgeoisie and thus attempted to show how Ford's peculiar blend of traditionalist
and progressive views formed the essence of the nation's new bourgeois (and hege-
monic) ideology. His analysis, though often ingenious, is thus flawed in important
ways. See Hoare and Smith, *Prison Notebooks of Antonio Gramsci*, 277–318.

understood from a study of words, symbols, or icons alone. The historian must examine as well the ways in which these ambiguous words and symbols were actually used, looking at how particular groups first selected words and concepts from the language of Americanism and then assembled them into a political world view. This task is particularly urgent in view of the way in which mass production and mass distribution transformed the very nature of political language in the early twentieth century. Mass production eviscerated political language in two ways: First, it encouraged the use of stock images and phrases that could be distributed to an extraordinarily large and diverse population, and, second, it tended to "commodify" words, replacing their intrinsic meanings with ill-defined but appealing congeries of associations. The actual meanings of words and concepts, as a consequence, became harder to discern and more susceptible to change.[18] For this reason, a study of twentieth-century political language profits from being anchored in a local context where the relations between words and their users can be systematically examined.

The relevant groups in this local study are Woonsocket's two working-class factions (radicals and ethnics) that built the ITU, the French-Canadian community's ethnic elite (chiefly, Catholic clergy and Republican Party leaders), Woonsocket's textile employers, and the national bureaucratic elites charged with implementing the government's industrial relations policies. The importance of the working-class factions, whose cultural, class, and political experiences receive the most detailed treatment, lies not only in the critical role they played in building and sustaining Woonsocket's labor movement but also in their representativeness: Virtually every industrial union that arose in the United States in the 1930s depended on the same alliance of radical and ethnic workers that propelled the ITU into being.[19] I have ascertained the influence of elites – ethnic, industrial, and governmental – on local working-class culture and politics, and especially on working-class constructions of Americanism, by focusing on politically tense historical moments that reveal with unusual clarity both the internal political character of elites and their external relationships to the Woonsocket masses. These moments include an

---

[18] On the evisceration of twentieth-century political language see Christopher Lasch, *The Minimal Self: Psychic Survival in Troubled Times* (New York, 1984), 23–59; Lears and Fox, eds., *The Culture of Consumption*. My interpretation of the consequences of such evisceration, however, differs in significant ways from the ones offered in these accounts.

[19] The representativeness of Woonsocket's radical and ethnic worker alliance will be discussed in Chapters 2 and 3.

internecine ethnic elite fight in the 1920s, the divided response of Woonsocket industrialists to New Deal legislation in the early 1930s, a bitterly contested municipal electoral campaign in the late 1930s, and the federal government's attempt to secure working-class political loyalty and shopfloor peace in the 1940s.

My interest in political language springs ultimately from my interest in political power and especially its ebb and flow between elites and masses. Those who control a political language enjoy, in my view, an advantage in their bid for power. The centrality of the language of Americanism to political debate in the 1920s and 1930s may be seen as a victory for elites who saw it as a tool for containing the nation's unruly masses of ethnic workers. Yet, even as that victory foreclosed certain political opportunities, it opened up others for radicals and ethnics who were willing and able to couch their socialist and ethnocommunal ideas in the language of Americanism. I have tried to demonstrate how easily the flexible language of Americanism could accommodate such ideological reformulations, often camouflaging them in ways that have hidden them from historical view. At the same time, I have tried to show how this language's dominance in the interwar years rendered dissident movements of both the right and left vulnerable to containment and sometimes to dissolution.

That this language was both flexible and dominant, that it both accommodated ideas emerging from other political languages and forced them through difficult and risky processes of reformulation, is critical to understanding the relationship of language to power. Language is not all-powerful; it does not, by itself, determine social reality as Gareth Stedman Jones has claimed.[20] Words do not possess such intrinsic meanings that the mere act of speaking or thinking them automatically ties the speaker or thinker to a web of fixed associations, meanings, and values. Words can sometimes have this effect. Equally common, however, are instances where different individuals impart to the same words markedly different meanings and visions.[21] In these latter instances what often determines the primacy of one meaning or vision over the other is the overall balance of power – economic, social, ideological – that prevails between

[20] Gareth Stedman Jones, *Languages of Class: Studies in English Working Class History, 1832–1982* (Cambridge, U.K., 1983); see also the very interesting debate on language and politics sparked by Joan W. Scott's essay, "On Language, Gender, and Working-Class History," *International Labor and Working-Class History* 31 (Spring 1987), 1–36.

[21] For a wide-ranging examination of such instances, see Daniel T. Rodgers, *Contested Truths: Keywords in American Politics Since Independence* (New York, 1987).

contending individuals or groups. The conflict over language, at such moments, is only one of several contests that together comprise a struggle for political power. The battle for control of the language of Americanism, in Woonsocket and elsewhere, can only be understood, I hope to show, as part of a series of political struggles occurring simultaneously on different fronts: in factories, where workers and employers fought for control of the shopfloor; in ethnic communities, where priests, lay elites, and working-class masses vied for political and moral power; in the increasingly important administrative institutions of the American state, where contending social groups tangled with each other and with "public servants" for political and ideological authority. The history of a political language, in other words, can only be understood as part of a broader social and political history. In that spirit, we begin this story not with an examination of political language but with the post–World War I intraethnic struggles in Woonsocket's French-Canadian and Franco-Belgian communities that undermined critically important sets of class relationships in this textile city.

Part I

Ethnictown, 1875–1929

1   The French Canadians

As late as 1930, few could have predicted that Woonsocket, Rhode Island, would soon become the center of textile unionism in New England. A heavily industrialized city of 50,000, Woonsocket's social and cultural life had long been dominated by its 35,000 French-Canadian residents, and everyone "knew" that French-Canadian workers simply did not join unions in large numbers. The French-Canadian elite in Woonsocket and elsewhere thought of their ethnic workers as devout Catholics too preoccupied with their spirituality to concern themselves with such banal, materialist pursuits as unions addressed. Nativists in the labor movement believed that French-Canadian workers lacked the kind of rational intelligence, civic responsibility, and self-improving zeal that American trade unionists "required." Syndicalists and socialists, who had cultivated a great deal of pro-union and radical sentiment in numerous ethnic, working-class enclaves elsewhere in New England, found French-Canadian workers forbiddingly difficult to reach.

This wide-ranging consensus on the unorganizability of French-Canadian workers slipped almost unnoticed and unquestioned into historical scholarship. Today it is difficult to find works that even raise the issue of French-Canadian labor quiescence as a question worthy of study. The relatively few explanations of such quiescence that historians have proposed tend to focus on the inherently conservative, backward-looking nature of French-Canadian culture. But such culturalist explanations cannot account for the rise, in 1930s Woonsocket, of a powerful labor movement with broad, enthusiastic French-Canadian support. French-Canadian working-class quiescence in pre-Depression Woonsocket cannot be ascribed, therefore, to an ethnic culture that inevitably made its adherents meek; it can only be understood in social structural terms – specifically, the subordinate place occupied by French-Canadian workers in an ethnic social order dominated by a clergy steeped in counter-Reformation, antimodernist values. During the years from 1875 to 1914, when that cleric-dominated social order shaped Woonsocket's ethnic life, French-Canadian workers lived up to their quiescent reputation. But once national economic and political pressures plunged that social order

19

into crisis in the years 1914 to 1929, French-Canadian workers began to discover, amidst the shattered state of their elite, the freedom to fashion a vigorous class identity for themselves. They turned increasingly to economic and political institutions like trade unions and the Democratic Party that their ethnic leadership had long frowned upon, and they began reformulating aspects of their "conservative" culture to express better their grievances as wage earners in a capitalist society. To those willing to listen, they had declared by 1930, albeit in halting and confused ways, their desire to fashion an independent life for themselves. Such working-class stirrings, though failing in the short term to alter significantly Woonsocket economic and social life, reveal a great deal about the gathering cultural and political forces that would transform Woonsocket society in the 1930s. To understand these stirrings, and the cultural and political forces underlying them, we must first explore how the ethnic social order that had profoundly shaped French-Canadian working life since the latter years of the nineteenth century first established itself on American soil.

"La ville la plus française aux États Unis," 1875–1914

In the early nineteenth century Woonsocket was one of many rural areas in New England transformed by industrialization. Its access to the water power of the Blackstone River and its location only twenty miles upstream from the textile entrepreneurs of Pawtucket – Samuel Slater, Moses Brown, and David Wilkinson – made it a natural site for cotton manufacture. By 1810 local farmers with choice pieces of land along the Blackstone falls began either selling out to textile entrepreneurs or drawing on Providence capital and Pawtucket artisans to establish their own mills. The first three decades of textile manufacturing witnessed many more failures than successes but, by the 1840s, Woonsocket boasted twenty-one mills and about a thousand operatives. Although cotton textile manufacture predominated, one local entrepreneur, Edward Harris, had introduced woolen manufacture to the city. The success of his economic ventures would eventually make Woonsocket a center of woolen manufacture as well.[1]

Woonsocket's first textile workers came from the ranks of im-

---

[1] Erastus Richardson, *History of Woonsocket* (Woonsocket, R.I., 1876), 121–73; Thomas Steere, *History of the Town of Smithfield, from Its Organization, in 1730–31, to Its Division, in 1871* (Providence, R.I., 1881), 22–160; A. P. Thomas, *Woonsocket, Highlights of History, 1800–1976* (Woonsocket, R.I., 1976), 1–22, 37–43. On the Providence merchants and Pawtucket artisans see Gary Kulik, "The Beginnings of the Industrial Revolution in America: Pawtucket, Rhode Island, 1672–1829" (Ph.D. dissertation, Brown Uni-

poverished Yankee farmers and of Irish immigrants who came to northern Rhode Island in the 1820s to build a canal making the Blackstone River navigable from Worcester to Providence. By the early 1840s, 332 French Canadians had settled in Woonsocket – the first are thought to have arrived as horse dealers in 1815 – and some undoubtedly worked in the textile mills.[2] But the great wave of migration that would transform Woonsocket into a French-Canadian enclave did not begin until the late 1860s.

Agricultural crisis in Quebec and the explosion of textile manufacturing in New England together triggered the mass migration of French Canadians to New England. By the 1860s, the high birth rate of French-Canadian *habitants* (peasants) in conjunction with sharp limits on the amount of arable land created a severe land shortage in the triangular part of southern Quebec, between the northern border of the United States and the St. Lawrence River, where 90 percent of French Canadians lived. American textile manufacturers, meanwhile, were rapidly expanding their enterprises, as the Civil War's end both released a pent-up demand for civilian clothing and made available to the North supplies of the South's raw cotton. Desperate for labor, northern manufacturers sent recruiters to Quebec with promises of economic opportunity in New England's textile mills. The impoverished French Canadian *habitants* did not take long to respond. Between 1861 and 1870, about 200,000 left Quebec for New England. As many as 500,000, representing about a fourth of the entire French-Canadian nation, settled in New England by 1901.[3]

versity, 1980). The best study of the development of the industrial textile villages of the early nineteenth century is Jonathan Prude, *The Coming of Industrial Order: Town and Factory Life in Rural Massachusetts, 1810–1860* (Cambridge, Mass., 1983).

[2] Thomas, *Woonsocket*, 18–22, 37–57; Marie Louise Bonier, *Début de la colonie franco-américaine de Woonsocket, Rhode Island* (Framingham, Mass., 1920), 79–95.

[3] Jean Hamelin, *Le Canada français, son évolution historique, 1497–1967* (Trois Rivières, Quebec, 1967); Hamelin and Yves Roby, *Histoire économique du Québec, 1851–1896* (Montreal, 1971); Marcus Lee Hansen and John Bartlet Brebner, *The Mingling of the Canadian and American Peoples* (New Haven, Conn., 1940), vol. I, 115–81; Ralph Dominic Vicero, "Immigration of French Canadians to New England, 1840–1900: A Geographical Analysis" (Ph.D. dissertation, University of Wisconsin, 1968), Chapter 1; Yolande Lavoie, *L'émigration des Canadiens aux États-Unis avant 1930s: mesure du phénomène* (Montreal, 1972); Gilles Paquet, "L'émigration des Canadiens français vers la Nouvelle-Angleterre, 1870–1910: prises de vue quantitatives," *Recherches sociographiques* 5 (September–December, 1964), 319–70; Albert Faucher, "L'émigration des Canadiens français au XIXe siècle: position du problème et perspectives," *Recherches sociographiques* 5 (September–December, 1964), 277–317. On the growth of the New England textile industry, see Melvin T. Copeland, *The Cotton Manufacturing Industry of the United States* (Cambridge, Mass., 1912), 17–53, and Thomas Russell Smith, *The Cotton Textile Industry of Fall River, Massachusetts: A Study of Industrial Localization* (New York, 1944), 40–79.

A migration of such magnitude made French Canadians one of New England's most important ethnic groups. French-Canadian immigrants and their children comprised 46 percent of the work force in New England's largest industry, cotton textiles, in 1900.[4] They established communities in every major mill town – Fall River, New Bedford, Lowell, Lawrence, Pawtucket, Manchester – and they turned many smaller mill towns like Biddeford and Lewiston, Maine, into virtual colonies of Quebec.[5] The French-Canadian community in Woonsocket increased more than tenfold from 1847 to 1875, from 332 to 3,376, and then quadrupled between 1875 and 1900. In percentage terms, first- and second-generation French Canadians increased their share of the city's population from 7 percent in 1847 to 49 percent in 1900, outstripping the Irish and forming the largest segment of the city's burgeoning textile work force.[6]

The appearance of such large numbers of French Canadians in New England attracted considerable regional attention. Not only were they more "foreign" than other immigrants who predominated in New England – the English and Irish – but they displayed an attachment to their ethnic traditions and homeland that many Americans found threatening. Moreover, they arrived in a period of intense class conflict in American society, when capitalists were still trying to establish firmly their new mode of production in the face of recalcitrant workers, farmers, and shopkeepers. Hostility flared between native-born workers and French-Canadian immigrants. Not only did French Canadians often enter working-class communities as strike-

[4] Herbert Lahne, *The Cotton Mill Worker* (New York, 1944), 71.
[5] Vicero, "Immigration of French Canadians to New England"; Hansen and Brebner, *The Mingling of the Canadian and American Peoples*, 159–81; Leon Edgar Truesdell, *The Canadian Born in the United States* (New Haven, Conn., 1943); Robert Rumilly, *Histoire des Franco-Américains* (Montreal, 1958), passim. For case studies see, for example, Philip T. Silvia, "Spindle City: Labor, Politics and Religion in Fall River, Massachusetts, 1870–1905" (Ph.D. dissertation, Fordham University, 1973); Michael Guignard, "Ethnic Survival in a New England Mill Town: The Franco-Americans of Biddeford, Maine" (Ph.D. dissertation, Syracuse University, 1976); George Theriault, "The Franco-Americans in a New England Community: An Experiment in Survival" (Ph.D. dissertation, Harvard University, 1951); Frances H. Early, "French-Canadian Beginnings in an American Community: Lowell, Massachusetts, 1868–1886" (Ph.D. dissertation, Concordia University, 1980); Peter Haebler, "Habitants in Holyoke: The Development of the French-Canadian Community in a Massachusetts City, 1865–1910" (Ph.D. dissertation, University of New Hampshire, 1976).
[6] Richard S. Sorrell, "The Sentinelle Affair (1924–1929) and Militant *Survivance*: The Franco-American Experience in Woonsocket, Rhode Island" (Ph.D. dissertation, State University of New York at Buffalo, 1975), 103–9; Steven R. Williams, "Language and Social Structure: Bilingualism and Language Shift in Woonsocket, Rhode Island" (honors thesis, Brown University, 1976), 80.

breakers, but they also seemed willing to work for endless hours at miserably low wages and to send their entire families, including women and children, into the mills. They appeared to be the capitalists' dream and organized labor's nightmare. In 1881, Carroll Wright, director of the Massachusetts Bureau of the Statistics of Labor, delivered a verdict that would stigmatize the French Canadians for fifty years. "The Canadian French," Wright wrote, "are the Chinese of the Eastern States. They care nothing for our institutions, civil, political, or educational. . . . They are a horde of industrial invaders."[7]

Similarly dismissive and fearful statements, couched in characterological terms, were penned about many ethnic groups who came to the United States in the same period, testifying to the fear the immigrants could provoke in settled groups of Americans.[8] Like other reformers of his day, Wright resorted to racial rather than environmental factors to explain the unpalatable aspects of French-Canadian behavior. He saw French Canadians as constitutionally fitted to their role as strikebreakers, overlooking the managerial strategies designed to break up unions of the native-born. He blamed the desperately low wages paid to all but the most skilled textile workers and the employment of large numbers of children and women not on the labor market structure of the textile industry but on a French-Canadian propensity to work for any wage and disregard the welfare of their children. "Only so sordid and low a people," Wright claimed, would lie to state officials and millowners about their children's ages in order to put them to work. Widespread French-Canadian fears concerning the Protestant character of American public schools passed Wright by, and he made no allowance for French-Canadian unfamiliarity with the meaning of American citizenship and the practice of American politics. French Canadians simply, in his estimation, "care[d] nothing" for American institutions.[9]

However skewed his interpretation, Wright correctly stressed the singularity of the French-Canadian immigration experience in relation to those of other "old immigrant" groups like the English, Irish, Germans, and Scandinavians. The proximity of New England to

---

[7] Massachusetts Bureau of Statistics of Labor (hereafter Mass. BSL), *Twelfth Annual Report* (Boston, 1881), 469–70.

[8] On late nineteenth-century nativism see John Higham, *Strangers in the Land: Patterns of American Nativism, 1860–1925* (New York, 1975); Alexander Saxton, *The Indispensable Enemy: Labor and the Anti-Chinese Movement in California* (Berkeley, Calif., 1971); Herbert Hill, "Race, Ethnicity and Organized Labor: The Opposition to Affirmative Action," *New Politics* (Winter 1987), 31–82.

[9] Mass. BSL, *Twelfth Annual Report*, 469–70.

Quebec allowed French Canadians an easier and steadier migration of people and ideas than that available to any other immigrant group in New England in the second half of the nineteenth century. And Catholic clergy held an uncommonly powerful position in French-Canadian communities in Canada, which they reproduced in the little Canadas of American mill towns. From their powerful positions they extolled the virtue and godliness of preindustrial French-Canadian society, when their people formed a nation of subsistence farmers devoted to the land, their families, and the Church. They impressed on their parishioners the importance both of preserving the language, faith, and manners of their ancestors and of looking forward to the day when they might escape industrial labor and return to the land. Such views are not necessarily antithetical to the development of a class consciousness: The labor Zionists who settled Palestine merged devotion to an ancestral land and a radical opposition to capitalism in an extremely powerful way.[10] But in the hands of a counter-Reformation clergy, French-Canadian nationalism became a conservative force that made French-Canadian workers suspicious of other groups of workers and inhibited their ability to deal with problems arising from their predicament as wage earners in industrial society.

The character and power of the French-Canadian Church in nineteenth-century New England grew out of its history in seventeenth-and eighteenth-century Quebec.[11] The French-Canadian Church

[10] See Bernard Avishai, *The Tragedy of Zionism: Revolution and Democracy in the Land of Israel* (New York, 1985), 15–132.

[11] The following analysis of French-Canadian culture and the role of the clergy in French-Canadian society is based largely on Sorrell, "The Sentinelle Affair"; Pierre Anctil, "Aspects of a Class Ideology in a New England Ethnic Minority: The Franco-Americans of Woonsocket, Rhode Island (1865–1929)" (Ph.D. dissertation, New School of Social Research, 1980); Mason Wade, *The French Canadians, 1760–1967* (Toronto, 1968), vol. I; *Nive Voisine, Histoire de l'église catholique au Québec (1608–1970)* (Montreal, 1971); Jean-Claude Robert, *Du Canada français au Québec libre: histoire d'un mouvement indépendantiste* (Paris, 1975), 7–169; Fernand Ouellet, *Histoire économique et sociale du Québec, 1760–1850* (Montreal, 1966); Jean Hamelin, *Le Canada français*; Horace Miner, *St. Denis: A French-Canadian Parish* (Chicago, 1963); Marcel Rioux and Yves Martin, eds., *French-Canadian Society* (Toronto, 1964), vol. I, especially articles by Jean-Charles Falardeau, "The Seventeenth-Century Parish in French Canada," 19–32, and "The Role and Importance of the Church in French Canada," 342–58, by Pierre Deffontaines, "The *Rang* – Pattern of Rural Settlement in French Canada," 3–19, by Philippe Garigue, "Change and Continuity in Rural French Canada," 123–36, and by Rioux, "Remarks on the Socio-Cultural Development of French Canada," 162–78. See also Richard C. Harris, *The Seigneurial System in Early Canada: A Geographical Study* (Madison, Wis., 1968) and William F. Ryan, *Clergy and Economic Growth in Quebec (1896–1914)* (Quebec, 1966).

established itself in New France in the seventeenth century at a time when most French Canadians lived on the land in a quasi-feudal society. Although an abundance of land and forests limited the demands which *seigneurs* could place on *habitants* and made the web of ties weaker in practice than in law, a feudal ethos pervaded the society. In addition to notions of reciprocity and mutual obligation, hierarchy, deference, and inequality were stressed as essential aspects of social relations. The Church was the linchpin in this social order. The social reality of New France closely fit the Church's medieval ideal.

The importance of the Church as an institutional and cultural influence increased in the wake of the English conquest of New France in 1763. French Canadians bitterly resented their defeat and swore to resist the conquerors. The last words of the French General Montcalm as he lay dying from wounds received on the Plains of Abraham, *"Je me souviens"* (I remember), became the cry of generations of French Canadians who would forget neither their French heritage nor their mission to resist the conquerors.[12] They not only resisted the conqueror's language, religion, and customs but also the economic, social, and political changes associated with the English industrial revolution. The Catholic Church emerged as a leading advocate of their nascent nationalism. The Church rejected an economy based on industry and material progress and a polity built on the principles of democracy and individual rights. It deliberately cultivated an image of French Canadians as the Catholic remnant in North America, a small group in a sea of Protestantism with a providential obligation to survive. *La survivance* – the perpetuation of French-Canadian faith, language, and manners – became the defining characteristic of French-Canadian nationalism.

Ironically, the Church's ability to preach *la survivance* and attack the British resulted in part from the powers granted it by British rulers. Not only did the British offer the Church full religious autonomy; they also granted it semiofficial status by incorporating its right to collect tithes into civil law. The British further increased the power of the Church by diminishing the power of those groups – traders and *seigneurs* – that in New France had competed with the clergy for power and influence. The British exacted a price for this support. The Church could criticize the values of commerce and industrialism but it could not interfere too much with British plans for trade and economic development. Thus a Church steeped in preindustrial,

---

[12] Montcalm's words today appear on the license plates of every car registered in Quebec.

corporatist values increasingly accepted the inviolability of the laws of laissez-faire and rarely condoned interference with market forces.

This unholy alliance between a counter-Reformation church and Protestant, materialist colonizers also weakened the ideology of republicanism that in the United States and in a number of European countries sustained popular movements against feudal and capitalist domination. Not surprisingly, the republican revolutions that occurred in Quebec's southern neighbor in 1776 and mother country in 1789 generated considerable excitement among intellectual and bourgeois strata in Québecois society in the late eighteenth and early nineteenth centuries. But an 1830s republican revolt against British rule and clerical power led by the lawyer Louis-Joseph Papineau was so decisively beaten by the combined might of British troops and clerical opposition that Quebec's fragile republican tradition withered and all but died. By the time Italians were flocking to Garibaldi's republican banner in the 1860s and the Irish were gathering around Parnell in the 1880s, the French-Canadian middle class was strengthening its ties to a counter-Reformation church. By midcentury French-Canadian *habitants* no longer had easy access to those republican ideas that American and French workers and Irish peasants were using to develop critiques of economic inequality and other aspects of capitalist social relations. Religion suffused their lives and shaped their political and cultural orientation.[13]

The *habitants* did not accept the teachings of their clergy unquestioningly. Subtle but important differences distinguished the two groups' understanding of *la survivance*. Clergy viewed it as a providential mission while workers interpreted it more in terms of family survival and kin loyalty. At certain moments these latent differences flared into open disputes. The most significant of these occurred during the exodus of *habitants* from the Quebec countryside in the second half of the nineteenth century. The hundreds of thousands of *habitants* who trekked to New England did so despite the warnings of the Church that their migration threatened *la survivance*. Few heeded

---

[13] The history of French-Canadian republicanism is explored in Jean-Paul Bernard, *Les Rouges: libéralisme, nationalisme et anticléricalisme au milieu du XIXe siècle* (Montreal, 1971). See also Fernand Ouellet, *Le Bas-Canada, 1791–1840: changements structuraux et crise* (Ottawa, 1976) and Robert, *Du Canada français au Québec libre*, 7–169. On the importance of republicanism to American and French workers, see Sean Wilentz, *Chants Democratic: New York City and the Rise of the American Working Class* (New York, 1984) and William H. Sewell, Jr., *Work and Revolution in France: The Language of Labor from the Old Regime to 1848* (Cambridge, U.K., 1980). On Irish-American workers and republicanism see Eric Foner, "Class, Ethnicity, and Radicalism in the Gilded Age: The Land League and Irish America," *Marxist Perspectives* 2 (Spring 1978), 6–55.

their leaders' pleas to enroll in a repatriation program that would have returned them to Quebec. They viewed their migration pragmatically, as an effort to find work and thereby protect the most essential aspect of their social order, the family, and they cared less for the more abstract formulations of their leadership.[14]

Yet the French Canadians' attachment to their religion and nationality was profound. Father Charles Dauray, a French-Canadian priest who spent the 1870s in Rhode Island on leave from his directorship of a Quebec Catholic college, called for a Mass for French-Canadian families in the lower Blackstone Valley and was stunned by the enthusiastic turnout. No one even knew how many French-Canadian families then resided in the area, or how many yearned for a religious presence in their lives; hence Dauray's surprise when "at the appointed hour [in the words of Dauray's biographer] the church was filled to capacity with an exclusively [French] Canadian congregation."[15]

Such enthusiastic displays of religious and national devotion prompted the Quebec Church to scale back its repatriation efforts and to concentrate instead on perpetuating *la survivance* in New England. Scores of priests soon fanned out through New England's numerous areas of French-Canadian settlement. Drawing on their long experience in ethnic survival and the affection of French-Canadian emigrants for their heritage, these priests helped establish some of the most insular and tenacious ethnic communities in the United States. In cities like Woonsocket, they managed not simply to preserve an ethnic culture but also virtually to reconstitute a social order, like that of Quebec, that granted exceptional power to a conservative, nationalist clergy.

The formal participation of French-Canadian clergy in Woonsocket society began in 1875 when Father Dauray arrived from Central Falls to assume pastoral duties at the city's first French-speaking parish, Church of the Precious Blood. Dauray became the towering figure in Woonsocket French-Canadian life, overseeing the development of a vigorous French-Canadian community from 1875 until his death in 1931. He established the city's first bilingual parochial school in his

---

[14] Jean-Pierre Wallot, "Religion and French-Canadian Mores in the Early Nineteenth Century," *Canadian Historical Review* 52 (1971), 51–94; Nive Voisine, "Les valeurs religieuses de l'émigrant quebecois (1850–1920)" in Claire Quintal, ed., *Deuxième Colloque de l'Institut Français du Collège de l'Assomption* (Worcester, Mass., 1981), 21–37. On the repatriation controversy, see Hansen and Brebner, *The Mingling of the Canadian and American Peoples*, 170–2.

[15] Ambrose Kennedy, *From Quebec to New England: The Life of Monsignor Charles Dauray* (Boston, 1948), 47.

parish in 1885. In 1890 he secured authorization from the Providence bishop for a second French-Canadian parish, St. Anne's; two more were added in 1902 and a fifth in 1909. Dauray established a Catholic high school for boys in 1898 and one for girls in 1911; he opened an orphanage in 1912 and a home for the elderly in 1913. He staffed all these institutions with clergy trained in Quebec. By World War I he had established a network of French-speaking institutions that could encompass the lives of Woonsocket's French-Canadian parishioners from cradle to grave.[16]

Dauray also sought out an alliance with an emerging middle class of shopkeepers, professionals, small businessmen, and newspaper editors. Dauray served as spiritual adviser to the premier mutual benefit society of this middle class, named Société Saint-Jean-Baptiste after the French Canadians' patron saint.[17] In that and similar capacities, he signaled his willingness to sanction the entrepreneurial activities that increasingly attracted middle-class energies. In return, Woonsocket's budding entrepreneurs became some of the city's most fervent proponents of *la survivance*. This middle-class fusion of capitalist and ethnic principles – and its consequences for the city's ethnic community – is best illustrated by the career of Aram Pothier, Woonsocket's most distinguished lay ethnic leader from the 1890s through the 1920s.[18]

Born in southern Quebec in 1854, Pothier migrated to Woonsocket in 1872 to join his family, which had settled there two years earlier. He began his working life as a bank clerk in the Woonsocket Institution of Savings in 1875 and quickly rose to a position of director. He became Woonsocket's first French-Canadian mayor in 1894 and the state's first French-Canadian governor in 1908. He ran as a Republican in these elections, even though the party, during its long stretches of political dominance in the state, had effectively excluded much of Pothier's ethnic group (through restrictions on the franchise and district gerrymandering) from political participation.[19] But Pothier

---

[16] Kennedy, *From Quebec to New England*, 67–148.

[17] Anctil, "Aspects of Class Ideology," 92–115; Kennedy, *From Quebec to New England*, 141.

[18] On Pothier see Bonier, *Début de la colonie franco-américaine*, 296–300; Anctil, "Aspects of a Class Ideology," 132–8; John Robert Veader, "Aram Jules Pothier as Governor of Rhode Island" (M.A. thesis, University of Rhode Island, 1966); Thomas, *Woonsocket*, 97–103; Rosaire Dion-Lévesque, *Silhouettes franco-américaines* (Manchester, N. H. 1957), 743–6.

[19] Duane Lockard, *New England State Politics* (Princeton, N.J., 1959), 172–89; Aaron F. DeMoranville, "Ethnic Voting in Rhode Island," (M.A. thesis, Brown University, 1961), 5–26.

actually saw his involvement with the Republicans as an opportunity to advance the interests of fellow French Canadians. Participation in the Democratic Party would have meant submitting to the dictates of the powerful Irish, who had already demonstrated an eagerness to force French Canadians to Americanize the practice of their Catholicism. The leaders of the Republican Party, on the other hand, anxious to gain French-Canadian support to negate the advantages accruing to the Democrats for corralling the Irish vote, expressed no such Americanizing intentions.[20]

Pothier, moreover, eagerly embraced the procapitalist perspective of the Republican millowners, who dominated the party in the northern half of the state. Not only did he see capitalist development as the path to personal wealth; he also believed that it would enhance the prospects for *la survivance*. During his trips to European industrial expositions of the 1890s, Pothier had established contacts with the textile magnates from the woolen and worsted manufacturing centers of Roubaix and Tourcoing in northern France. The McKinley Tariff, passed in 1890, had all but excluded these manufacturers' high quality worsted goods from the lucrative American market and sparked their interest in acquiring American production facilities. They knew of Woonsocket's reputation for fine woolen goods manufacture, and after learning from Pothier of the city's French-speaking and God-fearing work force, these Catholic manufacturers decided to locate mills there. Between 1899 and 1910, the Desurmont, Tiberghien, and Lepoutre families, all prominent in the textile industry of Roubaix and Tourcoing, established large mills in Woonsocket: the Jules Desurmont Worsted, the French Worsted, and the Lafayette Worsted, respectively. Joseph Guerin, a Belgian immigrant with little capital but years of experience as a worker and foreman in textile mills in Verviers, Belgium, and Schio, Italy, joined them in their American worsted manufacturing venture. Guerin had established a small woolen mill in Woonsocket in 1892; aided substantially by Pothier's ability to attract investors, Guerin's venture had evolved by 1910 into a huge, four-mill complex – the Guerin Mills, Inc. – engaged in the spinning, weaving, and dyeing of woolen and worsted fibers. In the period from 1900 through 1920, the French worsted spinning mills, together with Guerin's enterprises, prospered from their sales in the American market. Their success induced other French manufacturers to establish mills in Woonsocket, and by 1928,

[20] DeMoranville, "Ethnic Voting," 5–26.

European and Guerin capital accounted for 65 percent of the $28 million dollars invested in Woonsocket's textile mills.[21]

Pothier's European salesmanship had two very important consequences for Woonsocket's French-Canadian community. First, the French manufacturers sent their French-speaking superintendents and foremen to America with instructions to conduct business in French.[22] They strengthened further the French character of their mills by recruiting skilled workers from their French mills for their new American production facilities.[23] Increasing numbers of French-Canadian workers in Woonsocket found their ability to speak French prized not only in church and in school but at work as well; this only reinforced the city's ethnic insularity. Second, these manufacturers brought a growth industry to Woonsocket just as the city's cotton industry was entering its long-term decline. Northern cotton manufacturers could not compete with their southern counterparts, who enjoyed the advantage of cheap labor. Northern cities that concentrated in cotton production, like Lowell and Fall River, virtually ceased to grow after 1910 as manufacturers began shifting their operations south or investing their capital in new ventures.[24] The woolen and worsted manufacturers of Woonsocket, however, required a level of skill from their workers that the unskilled labor forces of the South could not match, and the city's woolen and worsted mills prospered in the first twenty years of the century. Their expansion triggered a doubling of Woonsocket's population from

---

[21] Jacques Toulemonde, *Naissance d'une métropole: histoire économique et sociale de Roubaix et Tourcoing au XIXe siècle* (Tourcoing, France, 1966), 61–2; David Landes, "Religion and Enterprise: The Case of the French Textile Industry," in Edward C. Caster II, Robert Forster, and Joseph N. Moody, eds., *Enterprise and Entrepreneurs in Nineteenth and Twentieth Century France* (Baltimore, 1976), 41–86; Thomas, *Woonsocket*, 95–118; Rhode Island Conference of Business Associations, *Book of Rhode Island* (Providence, R.I., 1930), 166, 170, 174, 177; Interview with Robert Guerin, November 3, 1980. The figures on capital invested are from Williams, "Language and Social Structure," 42. Williams, however, omitted the Lafayette Worsted Co. from his calculations and thus underestimated the total capital invested in French-owned textile mills by $2.4 million; the figures in the text have been adjusted accordingly.

[22] See, for example, obituary of Felix DeLathauwer, foreman of the Lafayette, who was brought over by the owners in 1905 to "assist in . . . [the] formation" of the new mills, *Woonsocket Call* (hereafter *WC*), February 20, 1922.

[23] Interview with Ernest Gignac, June 25, 1981; interview with Lawrence Spitz, September 19–20, 1979. The skilled workers who came are discussed in Chapter 2.

[24] J. Herbert Burgy, *The New England Cotton Textile Industry: A Study in Industrial Geography* (Baltimore, 1932), 119–218; Smith, *The Cotton Textile Industry of Fall River*, 80–163; "Fall River: A Dying Industry," *The New Republic*, June 4, 1924, 38–40; Seymour Louis Wolfbein, *The Decline of a Cotton Textile City: A Study of New Bedford* (New York, 1944), 7–90.

nearly 25,000 in 1895 to nearly 50,000 in 1925, and a significant part of this increase came from fresh immigrants drawn from Quebec.[25] Their arrival bolstered the efforts of the French-Canadian leaders in Woonsocket who were dedicated to ethnic survival.

The infusion of French capital that Pothier engineered, then, significantly enhanced the prospects for continued *la survivance* in Woonsocket. The French magnates had not really taken the cause of *la survivance* to heart; they felt their cultural superiority too keenly to immerse themselves in what they regarded as a provincial Québecois venture (a subject to which we shall return in the next chapter). But as long as they managed their mills well, they effectively contributed to the cause of French-Canadian survival. By creating thousands of jobs, they stimulated further migration from Canada; by demanding that French be spoken at their work places, they made the language of *la survivance* an integral part of the city's industrial life; by paying their respects to clerical leaders like Dauray and by making occasional contributions to favored Catholic charities, they helped to create and then to sustain the appearance of a tightly knit ethnic elite devoted wholeheartedly to the maintenance of a French Catholic remnant in North America.[26] Their Woonsocket presence, in sum, helps explain how the city's French Canadians managed to build such a tenacious ethnic community that resisted encroachments of American culture across decades and even generations. In the 1920s, sixty years after migration began, ethnic leaders would still call their city "la ville la plus française aux États-Unis"; and in the 1930s, visitors to the city would still marvel at "the spirit of the Franco-American" that pulsated in city life.[27]

The prewar world of the French-Canadian worker

Two factors, work in textile mills and the culture of a Quebec-style social order, decisively shaped the character of Woonsocket's working class in the years prior to World War I. Some French-Canadian immigrants managed to avoid working in one of the city's numerous textile mills by finding work in the city's small rubber manufacturing or metalworking industries. A few, like Pothier, by dint of unusual ability or fortune, climbed into the ranks of entrepreneurs, merchants, or white-collar workers. But the vast majority of Québecois found

---

[25] Williams, "Language and Social Structure," 80.
[26] Kennedy, *From Quebec to New England*, 235–6.
[27] Sorrell, "The Sentinelle Affair," 108. Federal Writers' Project, Works Progress Administration, *Rhode Island: A Guide to the Smallest State* (Boston, 1937), 101.

their economic condition determined by the realities of textile employment.

The textile industry of the early twentieth century subjected its wage earners to a most precarious economic fate. Textiles never underwent the consolidation process that allowed a few giant, vertically and horizontally integrated, firms to dominate production in the steel, auto, rubber, meatpacking, and electrical industries.[28] By gaining significant control over the national market and sparing themselves from the worst effects of competition, such firms could experiment with higher wages, extensive company welfare plans, and other schemes to ameliorate the lot of their employees: The Ford Motor Company and General Electric, for example, experimented extensively along these lines.[29] The textile industry, however, with its relatively low capital requirements, was never able to resolve efficaciously the chronic overproduction and excess competition that plagued it and caused so much industrial instability.[30] The larger textile corporations never stopped trying to gain oligarchic control over their industry, and a few enjoyed a middling level of success. The Lawrence-based American Woolen Company acquired, over the first four decades of the twentieth century, close to half of the nation's total French worsted spindlage capacity; and the Amoskeag Manufacturing Company in Manchester, whose 15,000 employees easily made it the largest single textile complex in the world in the years prior to World War I, temporarily enjoyed a privileged market position and thus an unusual opportunity to experiment with welfare capitalist schemes.[31] But these firms need only be placed alongside

[28] Alfred D. Chandler, Jr., *Strategy and Structure: Chapters in the History of the Industrial Enterprise* (Cambridge, Mass., 1969).

[29] Stephen Meyer III, *The Five Dollar Day: Labor Management and Social Control in the Ford Motor Company, 1908–1921* (Albany, N.Y., 1981); Ronald W. Schatz, *The Electrical Workers: A History of Labor at General Electric and Westinghouse, 1923–1960* (Urbana, Ill., 1983), 3–27. See also Ronald Edsforth, *Class Conflict and Cultural Consensus: The Making of a Mass Consumer Society in Flint, Michigan* (New Brunswick, N.J., 1987), 1–38.

[30] Copeland, *The Cotton Manufacturing Industry*; Gavin Wright, *Old South, New South: Revolutions in the Southern Economy Since the Civil War* (New York, 1984), 124–55; Louis Galambos, *Competition and Cooperation: The Emergence of a National Trade Association* (Baltimore, 1966). See also Philip B. Scranton, "An Exceedingly Irregular Business: Structure and Process in the Paterson Silk Industry," Scranton, ed., *Silk City* (Newark, 1985), 35–72. Though the silk industry differed from cotton manufacture in important respects, the portrait of deepening industrial instability that Scranton paints illuminates the dilemmas of cotton manufacture as much as those of silk.

[31] ITU, "French Spinning Industry" (typescript, ca. 1936), 4, Woonsocket Woolen Mills file, Record Group 9, Entry 402, National Archives, Washington, D.C.; Tamara K. Hareven, *Family Time and Industrial Time: The Relationship Between the Family and Work*

the likes of U.S. Steel, Ford and General Motors, General Electric and Westinghouse for the relatively modest nature of their successes to be made clear. In a country obsessed with the exploits of its "captains of industry" and "robber barons," not a single textile capitalist ever captured the popular imagination as Rockefeller, Carnegie, Ford, J. P. Morgan, Dupont, and Vanderbilt did so successfully. Apart from those who attended Rhode Island and Massachusetts elementary schools, who knows the story of a Samuel Slater, an Abbott Lawrence, or a William Wood?[32]

The fact that consolidation was limited in the textile industry helped to keep the average textile wage, in relation to the average wage of other industries of its size, at an unusually low level.[33] For much of the nineteenth century, a fraction of textile workers had always escaped the impoverishment that such low wages imposed by rising into the skilled ranks and enjoying the wages that a privileged labor market position conferred. But by 1900, cotton manufacturers had eliminated, through mechanization of existing machines and the introduction of new ones, virtually all skilled labor from the production process itself. Only mill mechanics such as loomfixers and others charged with maintaining textile machinery in good working order could still claim a skilled status and thus a high wage; only such individuals earned sufficient income to support a family.[34]

The presence of large numbers of women and children in textile factories offered manufacturers a convenient rationalization for the low wages they paid, for such workers did not, they argued, need to

in a New England Industrial Community (Cambridge, U.K., 1982), 9–68. Some larger textile millowners in the South experimented with welfare capitalist ("paternalist") schemes but these schemes rarely included the higher wage provisions that were critical to their success in other industries. See Jacquelyn Dowd Hall, James Leloudis, Robert Korstad, Mary Murphy, Lu Ann Jones, and Christopher B. Daly, Like a Family: The Making of a Southern Cotton Mill World (Chapel Hill, N.C., 1987), 114–80; Daniel Nelson, Managers and Workers: Origins of the New Factory System in the United States, 1880–1920 (Madison, Wis., 1975), 3–121.

[32] Samuel Slater founded the nation's first successful textile spinning mill in Pawtucket in 1793; Abbott Lawrence supplied the capital to establish a new center of woolen and worsted production in New England in the 1840s (Lawrence, Massachusetts); and William Wood was an illustrious president of Lawrence's American Woolen Company in the early years of the twentieth century.

[33] Lahne, The Cotton Mill Worker (New York, 1944), 161–74; Donald B. Cole, Immigrant City: Lawrence, Massachusetts, 1845–1921 (Chapel Hill, N.C., 1963), 118–21.

[34] Lahne, The Cotton Mill Worker, 102–36; Hall, et al., Like a Family, 44–113; Wright, Old South, New South, 124–55. Interviews with the following retired textile workers who spent their working lives in Rhode Island cotton mills: William McNeill, weaver, October 7, 1980; John Robinson, mulespinner, October 7, 1980; and Harry Shallis, loomfixer, October 14, 1980.

support entire families. But this reasoning conveniently overlooked how many male heads of households still labored in semiskilled or unskilled positions in the mills, and how dependent these male heads were on the textile wages of their wives, sons, and daughters. Family employment became the *sine qua non* of economic survival in the textile industry.[35] Reformers like Carroll Wright who found textile workers sordid for "forcing" their children to labor in debilitating conditions at a time when these youngsters should have been enjoying school, sunlight, and recreation were blind to this fact.

Very little information on the conditions of work specific to turn-of-the-century Woonsocket mills has survived, though the recollections that a forty-year-old Henry Boucher offered to a WPA interviewer in the late 1930s underscore how poor and precarious was the life of a millworker.[36] His father, Boucher recalled, an immigrant from St. Ours, Quebec, never earned enough money from mill work to support his frail wife and four children. He tried to supplement his textile wages by sawing "wood into stove lengths for anyone who would employ him." But he earned only a dollar for the many hours of labor required to saw and stack each cord. "We were very poor," Boucher remembered, "and my first recollection is of the pot of pea soup that was always simmering on the stove. This pea soup and a few slices of bread, covered with lard, formed our regular diet when work was slack. Why, I was working before I had my first taste of butter."[37]

As a child Boucher, along with his brothers, scavenged woods for firewood and train tracks for stray pieces of coal dropped by passing coal cars. As soon as he turned fourteen, he left school for a job that his brother had found him in a woolen mill; for fifty-five hours every week spent keeping the "automatic feed of four cards full of wool" he received seven dollars – less than thirteen cents an hour.[38] Boucher could not have known at the time that he was fortunate to be earning his thirteen hourly cents in a woolen mill rather than a cotton mill. Since mechanization had proceeded more slowly in woolen and worsted manufacture than in cotton, skilled production workers would remain an integral part of woolen and worsted manufacture

---

[35] Lahne, *The Cotton Mill Worker*, 102–74; Bruno Ramirez, "French-Canadian Immigrants in the New England Cotton Industry: A Socio-Economic Profile," *Labour/Le Travailleur* 11 (Spring 1983), 138–40.

[36] Boucher's recollections have been published in C. Stewart Doty, ed., *The First Franco-Americans: New England Life Histories from the Federal Writers' Project, 1938–1939* (Orono, Maine, 1985), 126–42.

[37] Ibid., 126.

[38] Ibid., 126–7.

thirty to forty years after they had disappeared from cotton manufacture.[39] The young Boucher would thus have considerably more
opportunity for upward occupational mobility than he would have
had in a cotton mill, and the Woonsocket economy as a whole, with
its young, vigorous woolen and worsted sector, would offer its young
workers a greater opportunity to rise into the skilled ranks than the
cotton textile economies of Fall River or New Bedford or Lowell.
But these benefits would not be realized – and to many they would
not even become apparent – until the late 1910s and early 1920s.[40]
In the prewar years, young French Canadians entering the textile
work force could look forward to only the grimmest of workplace
experiences.

Such grimness inclined textile workers in New England to revolt.
The revolts of workers caught in such precarious economic circumstances tended to be spasmodic, erupting with sudden force and
disappearing often without a trace. They nevertheless convulsed
numerous centers of textile manufacture like Fall River and Lawrence
in the late nineteenth and early twentieth centuries, attracting the
nervous attention of political authorities in the region and even the
nation.[41] Throughout this whole period, however, Woonsocket
workers were strangely silent.

That silence reflected the second factor that profoundly shaped the
city's working class and its consciousness of itself: the re-creation in
Woonsocket of a French-Canadian cultural and social order. This
milieu reinforced French-Canadian workers' deep attachment to
their religion and nationality, and impeded the development of an
American class identity. French-Canadian workers were suspicious
of organizations and individuals external to their group. French-
Canadian clergy, the trusted spokesmen of French-Canadian communities who knew well the hardships experienced by those who
toiled in mills ten to twelve hours a day, might have called upon
the corporatist values of their ethnic culture, emphasizing the primacy
of group loyalty over individual advancement and of communal

---

[39] U.S. Department of Labor, Bureau of Labor Statistics, "Productivity of Labor and
Industry: Mechanical Changes in the Woolen and Worsted Industries, 1910–1936,"
Monthly Labor Review 46 (January–June, 1938), 58–93; Arthur H. Cole, *The American
Wool Manufacture* (Cambridge, Mass., 1926), vol. II, 5–38, 79–135, 147–88; Robert
W. Dunn and Jack Hardy, *Labor and Textiles: A Study of Cotton and Wool Manufacturing*
(New York, 1931), 11–83; interview with James Cullen, retired Woonsocket woolen
and worsted weaver and cotton knitter, September 9, 1980.

[40] Doty, *The First Franco-Americans*, 131–35.

[41] David Montgomery, *The Fall of the House of Labor: The Workplace, the State, and American
Labor Activism, 1865–1925* (Cambridge, U.K., 1987), 154–70.

welfare over pecuniary gain, to develop a critique of industrial capitalism. But they chose not to. Even the papal encyclical letter of 1891, *Rerum Novarum*, which called on the representatives of the Church to recognize the concerns of industrial workers and to offer Catholic solutions to the problems of industrialism, such as Catholic trade unions, did nothing to diminish their reluctance. Local clergy encouraged French-Canadian textile workers to find comfort in spirituality and suffering rather than through the assertion of their communal values in the sphere of industry.[42]

French-Canadian *habitants* had demonstrated in their exodus from Quebec their ability to think independently of their religious leaders and to act on their own economic interests. In New England intraregional migration continued to serve as a way of escaping the worst effects of economic hardship and exploitation. Networks of kin and friends in various Little Canadas spread news of work, found jobs for recent arrivals, and helped them adjust to new surroundings. Many long-time residents of New England continued to return periodically to Quebec to visit friends and relatives. Many clung to a dream of eventual escape from the working class in New England to small family farms in Quebec. In such ways did French Canadians register protests against the economic circumstances that made their lives so difficult.[43]

French-Canadian workers used their kin networks to exert some control over conditions of work. Tamara Hareven has shown how kinship groups clustered in various workrooms of the Amoskeag Manufacturing Company in Manchester, New Hampshire. Drawing

[42] Joseph M. Corrigan, ed., *Two Basic Social Encyclicals: On the Condition of Workers (Rerum Novarum), Pope Leo XIII; Forty Years After, On Reconstructing the Social Order (Quadragesimo Anno), Pope Pius XI* (Washington, D.C., 1943), 2–81. I disagree with Pierre Anctil's assertion that the leadership of the French-Canadian community in Woonsocket was heavily influenced by *Rerum Novarum*. They may have paid lip service to it, but no evidence suggests that they tried to implement its instructions through the formation of Catholic trade unions or other such associations. See Anctil's "Aspects of Class Ideology," 154–65.

[43] Young Henry Boucher dreamed of escaping Woonsocket even before he entered the mills. His childhood hero was a free-spirited uncle who spent his autumns and winters chopping wood in the forests of Maine and his springs and summers carousing with friends in Woonsocket saloons. Boucher, in a bittersweet recollection, called this uncle's arrival every spring "the one bright spot" of his childhood years. Doty, *The First Franco-Americans*, 126–7. On migration see Hareven, *Family Time and Industrial Time*, 101–19. On the dream of returning to Quebec see Anctil, "Aspects of Class Ideology," 44–66. See also Jean Hamelin, ed., *Les travailleurs québecois, 1851–1896* (Montreal, 1973); Jacques Rouillard, *Ah Les États!: Les travailleurs canadiens-français dans l'industrie textile de la Nouvelle-Angleterre d'après le témoignage des derniers migrants* (Montreal, 1985), 75–82, 87–155 passim.

on their traditions of cooperation and mutual care, they established informal organizations on the shopfloor and gained for themselves some voice in matters of hiring, firing, training, work-load assignments, and grievance resolution.[44] Although the sorts of detailed company records necessary to reconstruct such kin networks do not exist for Woonsocket mills, it is likely that French-Canadian workers in them, like those in the mills of Manchester, used familial ties to find work and to ameliorate somewhat the difficult circumstances of textile labor. Henry Boucher's older brother, as we have already noted, found him his first job. Within a few hours of starting work, moreover, the all-male card-room employees had put Henry through their gang's initiation rites, dispatching him on a mad, futile search for a nonexistent left-handed wrench. There is no indication of a kin relationship binding Boucher to any members of the card-room gang other than his brother, but these men clearly belonged to a closely knit, informal work group that quickly hazed the newly employed Boucher and then welcomed him into their ranks. This group was probably composed largely, if not entirely, of French-Canadian workers; their quick acceptance of Boucher, an individual fluent only in French, suggests that they shared a linguistic and cultural background with him.[45] Boucher's narrative, moreover, suggests that this group was engaged in some sly forms of workplace control. When Boucher returned to his work station, after discovering that a left-handed wrench did not exist, his foreman pulled him aside and said: "You don't want to believe anything that these fellows tell you. They are like a bunch of monkeys, always thinking up fool stunts. The only thing that they never think about is their work."[46] This foreman's frustration hints at the ongoing efforts of his workers to limit their production, enhance their workplace autonomy, and enliven their daily routines.

Such oblique confrontations with foremen, however, rarely escalated into direct confrontations with employers or clergy. New England's French-Canadian workers rarely challenged their clergy's advocacy of laissez-faire or of other doctrines antithetical to unionism. Protests through strikes or through trade-union organization – actions that directly challenged the prerogatives of employers and interfered with the laws of the market — were difficult and risky ventures. French-Canadian workers were noticeably less involved than other ethnic groups in labor protests throughout New England.

[44] Hareven, *Family Time and Industrial Time*, 90–101.
[45] Doty, *The First Franco-Americans*, 127–8.
[46] Ibid.

Few French Canadians played important leadership roles in strikes. A labor recruiter in Fall River told Carroll Wright that his client manufacturers always wanted to hire French-Canadian laborers because "they are not so apt to rebel as...the people from Lancashire."[47] Similar reports poured in from other mill towns in New England, including Woonsocket. Joseph Bouvier, a Woonsocket grocer, told Wright in 1882 that the "citizens" of Woonsocket – meaning the manufacturers – "always tell me that they had rather have the French help than any other nation."[48] As French Canadians began to emerge as a majority of the population in cities like Woonsocket, the frequency of labor protests dropped. Between 1886 and 1894, only five strikes occurred in Woonsocket; only two broke out in its textile industry. In 1894, a year of massive labor protest throughout America, the Rhode Island Bureau of Labor recorded no strikes in Woonsocket; only 170 workers belonged to unions.[49] At the same time, the English and Irish textile workers in Fall River attracted the attention of an anxious state and nation because of their persistence in challenging the power and domination of capital in their city.[50]

The low rate of French-Canadian participation in labor protests, one might argue, was due less to the peculiar character of French-Canadian society than to the prejudices of native-born and English and Irish workers who predominated in the leadership of municipal and state labor organizations. Indeed, hostility to foreign labor spread throughout the ranks of Rhode Island's native-born workers. One laborer complained to Rhode Island state officials in 1888 that "Canadians, Italians, Germans, or imported English...will live on any kind of food, wear the shabbiest clothes and have the worst houses and beds."[51] A weaver, convinced that "a great deal of disease" originated in French-Canadian privies, called on the state to "stop immigration from Canada."[52] A carpenter condemned all immigrants as "immoral men and women...who come here not to work, but to be supported and stir up strife."[53] Not all native-born

---

[47] Mass. BSL, *Thirteenth Annual Report* (Boston, 1882), 64. On the militance of the Lancashire English and Irish see John T. Cumbler, *Working-Class Community in Industrial America: Work, Leisure, and Struggle in Two Industrial Cities* (Westport, Conn., 1979), 144–94, and "Transatlantic Working-Class Institutions," *Journal of Historical Geography* 6 (1980), 275–90.

[48] Mass. BSL, *Thirteenth Annual Report*, 73.

[49] Rhode Island Commissioner of Industrial Statistics (hereafter R.I. CIS), *Ninth Annual Report* (Providence, R.I., 1896), 84–93.

[50] Silvia, "Spindle City," 491–545.

[51] R.I. CIS, *Third Annual Report* (1890), 65.

[52] Ibid., 67

[53] Ibid., 79.

workers subscribed to such views; many struggled to combat the tendency to blame the chronic problems of working-class life – the poverty, the disease, the personal and class strife – on the inborn traits of particular ethnic groups. Still, a working class living in an age when a belief in a hierarchy of races dominated both popular and intellectual thought could never free itself entirely from racist tendencies. Such tendencies, even when present only in latent form, engendered suspicion between native-born trade union leaders and immigrant workers like the French Canadians, and made cooperation between the two groups problematic.[54]

But while ethnic hostility might explain why French-Canadian participation in Anglo-American trade unions was low, it cannot explain why French Canadians formed so few unions of their own. In Lawrence, Massachusetts, in the early twentieth century, many groups of workers – Lithuanians, Italians, Poles, Jews, and Franco-Belgians – made their ethnic lodges into centers of labor activity, but French Canadians did not.[55] In Rhode Island, Italian laborers, subject to the same nativist prejudice as French Canadians, gained a reputation for labor militancy. Striking Italian workers figure prominently in the late nineteenth- and early twentieth-century annual reports of the commissioner of labor; by contrast, French-Canadian workers are conspicuously absent.[56] Woonsocket's Italian Workingmen's Club became a center of labor discussion and organizing, and the city's Franco-Belgians would, in the 1920s and 1930s, put their ethnic lodge, the Franco-Belge Club, to similar use.[57] No ethnic lodge served such a purpose for French-Canadian workers. Among all the French-Canadian workers in Woonsocket in the early twentieth century, only one small group formed their own French-speaking union, Local 801 of the Carpenters and Joiners Union.[58]

French-Canadian culture contained the seeds of a powerful critique of capitalism, making the absence of labor protest and organization all the more striking. The culture's emphasis on solidarity and mutuality

[54] On nativist and racist attitudes of American workers in this time see Saxton, *The Indispensable Enemy*, and Hill, "Race, Ethnicity, and Organized Labor."
[55] Cole, *Immigrant City: Lawrence, Massachusetts, 1845–1921* (Chapel Hill, N.C. 1963), 177–205; Melvyn Dubofsky, *We Shall Be All: A History of the Industrial Workers of the World* (New York, 1969), 227–62; David J. Goldberg, "The Lawrence Strike of 1919" (seminar paper, University of Pittsburgh, 1978).
[56] See, for example, R.I. CIS, *Sixteenth Annual Report* (1903), 144, 183, 187; *Nineteenth Annual Report* (1906) 168, 170; *Twentieth Annual Report* (1907), 16–17.
[57] Interview with Lawrence Spitz, September 12, 1984, and Angelo Turbesi, October 9, 1980.
[58] R.I. CIS, *Nineteenth Annual Report* (1906), 159.

might have served as the basis for a labor movement seeking to put the collective interests of workers and the welfare of the community ahead of the interests of individual employers. French-Canadian ethnicity had long nurtured a spirit of defiance toward all powers and influences deemed harmful to the health and survival of the French-Canadian community. In Quebec this spirit was directed at English political rule and cultural influence. In America it was directed at a host of organizations associated with Anglo-American politics and culture, ranging from public schools to Irish-dominated labor organizations. It also appeared in a particularly militant form in religious affairs. In Fall River in 1888, for example, the French-Canadian parishioners of Notre Dame de Lourdes refused to accept the bishop of Providence's appointment of an Irish priest to their church. When their appeal to the Providence diocese failed to secure them a French Canadian, they began disrupting services at Notre Dame to the point of shouting obscenities and threatening the Irish priest with bodily harm. Relations between the parishioners and their pastor grew so tense that the bishop ordered the church closed. The parishioners carried their demand for a French-Canadian priest to Rome and were ultimately vindicated by a papal decree recognizing the right of ethnic minorities to form national parishes.[59]

A similar drama unfolded in Woonsocket in 1914 when the parishioners of St. Anne's Church refused to accept the bishop's appointment of a Marist priest of Belgian nativity. Hundreds of French Canadians picketed the church day and night in March of that year, and virtually all of the parishioners joined a seat-rent strike and refused to pay the ten-cent pew offertory during Mass. Such a display of solidarity induced the bishop to change his mind and appoint to St. Anne a priest born in French Canada.[60]

Picketing, striking, displays of solidarity: These were the stock-in-trade of labor militants, and Woonsocket's French Canadians were clearly well-versed in their ways. But they rarely directed their anger or protest at an economic authority such as an English or Yankee millowner. The clergy's opposition to labor movements and its pervasive power in the community made such confrontations unimaginable. Few French-Canadian workers were willing to undertake a protest that would lead them into confrontation with their French-Canadian Church. Those who were so inclined lacked allies and ideological resources. Among the lay middle-class leadership, few if any individuals were willing to challenge the Church's authority on

[59] Philip T. Silvia, Jr., "The Flint Affair," *Catholic Historical Review* 65 (July 1979), 414–35.
[60] Sorrell, "The Sentinelle Affair," 146–7.

community matters. Workers continued to lack access to ideologies other than the Church's teachings, such as republicanism, that might have legitimated their grievances, and they were thus unable to establish a distinctive voice for themselves. While Lawrence, Massachusetts, the other major center of woolen and worsted manufacture in New England, erupted in protest in the years before World War I, French-Canadian workers in Woonsocket dealt quietly with their shopfloor difficulties through networks of kin, through migration, and through the solace offered by their faith.

The crisis of an ethnic order, 1914–1929

As successful as French-Canadian religious leaders were in re-creating the social relations of the Quebec countryside in American mill towns, ultimately they would not succeed in realizing their dream: the maintenance of an ethnic community in New England impervious to American cultural, social, and political influence. French-Canadian clergy never received from the American government the semiofficial status they enjoyed in Quebec, and the thoroughly industrialized character of Woonsocket precluded the kind of economic isolation and self-sufficiency that helped the Church sustain a pristine ethno-religious culture in Quebec's rural parishes. On the contrary, Woonsocket's urban, capitalist economy forced its French-Canadian residents into commercial relationships with individuals from other ethnic groups involved in the distribution of raw materials and the marketing of finished goods. Even the many textile workers who had little contact outside the city found their lives shaped increasingly by the imperatives of an international economy of capital and labor. Thus, for example, as the pace of industrial development quickened in Quebec in the early decades of the twentieth century, the rate of outmigration of French Canadians to New England declined. In 1920 the census showed that for the first time American-born French Canadians in Woonsocket exceeded the numbers of those born in Quebec.[61] At the same time, the migration of other ethnic groups to Woonsocket increased. The Irish retained their position as the second largest ethnic group in the city, approaching 10 percent of the city's total population. Significant groups of Poles, Italians, Belgians, and

[61] U.S. Department of Commerce, Bureau of the Census, *Fourteenth Census of the United States, 1920, Population* (Washington, D.C.), vol. I, 85, vol. II, 766–7, 954–5. On textile development in Quebec, see Jacques Rouillard, *Les travailleurs du coton au Québec, 1900–1915* (Montreal, 1979); Yves Roby, *Les Québecois et les investissements Américains (1918–1929)* (Quebec, 1976); Ryan, *The Clergy and Economic Growth in Quebec*.

European French comprised the majority of Woonsocket's "new immigrants," and they, along with small populations of twenty other immigrant groups, swelled the non–French-Canadian proportion of the city's population to one third.[62] Moreover, members of these other ethnic groups tended to wield power and influence beyond their numbers. The Irish had gained control of the local Democratic Party in the late nineteenth century and had gerrymandered the city's wards to insure a perpetuation of their power into the twentieth. The Yankees in the Republican Party, while successfully courting the French-Canadian vote and using it to establish a secure majority on the Board of Aldermen and City Council from 1900 through the early 1920s, effectively limited French-Canadian officeholders to only two of the city's four Republican wards. Only in Ward Five, the city's most densely populated French-Canadian district, did ward politics take on the colorful and intensely partisan character associated with local politics in Quebec.[63] In other wards and even more in citywide and statewide politics, French-Canadian politicians found it necessary to interact with other ethnic groups and adjust themselves to alternative values and beliefs. By the time Aram Pothier became governor in 1908, he represented an emerging group of moderates within the French-Canadian elite that increasingly viewed its ethnic identity as Franco-American rather than French-Canadian and that called for a degree of accommodation to the American way of life.[64]

In labor protest as well, other ethnics gained an importance out of proportion to their numbers and began to influence the French-Canadian majority. Italians, as previously noted, increasingly protested workplace grievances through immediate strikes. Irish and English workers predominated among the leaders of the many small craft unions belonging to the American Federation of Labor (AFL). As French-Canadian workers rose into the ranks of skilled labor in the early twentieth century and mixed with English and Irish trade unionists, they began to develop a craft identity to complement their

[62] U.S. Department of Commerce, Bureau of the Census, *Fourteenth Census of the United States*, vol. I, 85, vol. II, 766–7, 954–5.

[63] *Providence Journal Almanac: A Reference Book for the State of Rhode Island* (Providence, R.I.), 1900, 60; 1902, 70; 1904, 24; 1906, 29; 1908, 78; 1910, 55; 1912, 45; 1915, 41; 1918, 91; 1920, 141; 1922, 108. On local politics in Quebec, see Miner, *St. Denis*, Chapter 3 and Everett C. Hughs, *French Canada in Transition* (Chicago, 1963), Chapter 9.

[64] Sorrell, "The Sentinelle Affair," 204–13. The term "Franco-American" first became popular among elements of the French-Canadian elite in the last years of the nineteenth century. See Gerard J. Brault, *The French-Canadian Heritage in New England* (Hanover, N. H., 1986), 2; Robert A. Beaudoin, "Le nom 'Franco-Américain,'" *Bulletin de la Société Historique Franco-Américaine* (1967), 151–4.

firmly established ethnic one. In 1905 a member of the Carpenters and Joiners Union became the first French Canadian to hold a union presidency. In the next five years French-Canadian workers achieved similar positions in the local mulespinner, loomfixer, teamster, bricklayer, and painter unions.[65]

These craft unions largely ignored the thousands of semiskilled and unskilled French-Canadian workers who labored in textile mills, but the several hundred French and Belgian trade unionists who appeared in the worsted mills after 1905 made the organization of Woonsocket's textile masses their primary goal. These unionists were radicals who had been blacklisted for their participation in the European worker insurgencies of 1905 and who came to America in search of economic sustenance and political liberty. They tended to settle in woolen and worsted centers like Lawrence and Woonsocket, where they could ply their skills as mulespinners and weavers. They had little patience for the conservative trade unionism of the AFL, and gravitated to the radical Industrial Workers of the World (IWW). They enjoyed little success with the French-Canadian masses in the prewar years, as their organizing desire far exceeded their organizing acumen (a subject we will take up in Chapter 2). But their mere presence in the worsted mills offered French-Canadian workers an alternative model for working-class behavior than that they had learned of from their parish priests. Occasionally the Franco-Belgians and French Canadians would link up, and their alliance would yield startling results. A Franco-Belgian – led strike at the French Worsted in 1913, for example, forced Governor Pothier to intervene to insure the reputation of his city for industrial peace. The strike did little to alter labor relations in the city, but it suggested to some the enduring benefits that might result from a more permanent alliance of the two groups.[66]

The political and economic impact of war dramatically accelerated the encroachment of the outside world on this ethnic enclave. Prior to 1917, the American state exerted virtually no influence on the cultural life of Woonsocket's French Canadians; Congress and the executive branch, worried since the early years of the new century about the immigrant presence in American society, had commissioned numerous studies of the effects of immigrants on industry, on the family, on politics, and on many other aspects of American life. But by 1916

---

[65] R.I. CIS, *Nineteenth Annual Report* (1906), 159; *Twentieth Annual Report* (1907), 41–2; *Twenty-First Annual Report* (1908), 1130–1; *Twenty-Second Annual Report* (1909), 622–3; *Twenty-Third Annual Report* (1910); 453–4; *Twenty-Fourth Annual Report* (1911), 300.

[66] Ibid., *Twenty-Seventh Annual Report* (1914), 117–18; *WC*, July 24 and 29, August 23, 1913; *La Tribune* (hereafter *LT*), July 24, 1913.

these investigations had as yet yielded few national policies, such as immigration restriction, Americanization, or prohibition, that significantly impinged on the autonomy of ethnic cultural life. All that changed, however, with the coming of war in 1917. The loyalty of the country's millions of immigrants, especially those with ties to European nations aligned with the enemy camp, became an urgent political issue in ways that it had not been before. George Creel's Committee on Public Information saturated the country with demands for patriotism – 100 percent Americanism.[67] Moreover, the prerequisites of war mobilization – military conscription, the production of war matériel, and the amassing of a financial war chest – swept away the popular and elite opposition to a strong state that had long been so prominent a feature of American politics. Quite suddenly millions of Americans were thrust into encounters with federal authority. French Canadians in Woonsocket felt pressured to subscribe to liberty bond drives, to send their young men to war, and to teach their own children in parochial schools less about the achievements of early modern French explorers and more about the glories of American democracy. By and large they complied, purchasing large numbers of war bonds, sending 800 of their youth to fight, and attending Americanization classes.[68]

How such external compliance with the demands of a government-sponsored war machine affected the consciousness of Woonsocket's French Canadians is, given the sketchy data available, a difficult matter to ascertain. A tight labor market, combined with the Wilson Administration's recognition of collective bargaining rights, prompted Woonsocket workers to press their demands for better wages and better working conditions. Between 1916 and 1919 in Woonsocket, the average number of strikes per year more than doubled over the previous four-year period while the average number of striking workers increased more than sixfold, from 227 to 1,416.[69] Given the

---

[67] Higham, *Strangers in the Land*, 194–263; David M. Kennedy, *Over Here: The First World War and American Society* (New York, 1980), 45–92.

[68] In the process, they sharply distinguished themselves from their countrymen and countrywomen in Quebec who met the calls to fight an "Anglo" war with cynicism and conscription into an "Anglo" army with resistance. Albert Bélanger, *Guide Franco-Américaine: Les Franco-Américains et la Guerre Mondiale* (Fall River, Mass., 1921), 314–15; Rumilly, *Histoire des Franco-Américains*; John Daniels, *America via the Neighborhood* (New York, 1920), 143–4. On the conscription crisis in Quebec, see Wade, *The French Canadians, 1760–1967*, vol. II, 708–80; Miner, *St. Denis*, 18–19.

[69] R.I. CIS, *Twenty-Sixth Annual Report* (1913), 63–4, 88–102; *Twenty-Seventh Annual Report* (1914), 67–8, 87–121; *Twenty-Eighth Annual Report* (1915), 41–51; *Twenty-Ninth Annual Report* (1916), 32–3, 57–69; *Thirtieth to Thirty-Third Annual Reports* (1920), 49–51, 125–206. See also Daniel Nelson, *American Rubber Workers and Organized Labor* (Princeton, N.J., 1988), 65–6.

correspondence between this local rise in militancy and the rises occurring in most other centers of industrial production during the war years, it seems likely that French-Canadian workers were engaged in the same reformulations of wartime propaganda characteristic of workers' thinking elsewhere.[70] Some undoubtedly gained a greater familiarity with the discourse on Americanism and began inserting their notions of "rights," "citizenship," and "democracy" into local political debate. The fact that the number of Woonsocket residents voting in national elections rocketed up from less than 2,500 in 1912 to almost 10,000 in 1920 dramatically reveals the magnitude of the political mobilization triggered by wartime economics and ideology.[71]

A portion of the French-Canadian elite, meanwhile, seems to have seized on the wartime notion of "self-determination" for all peoples to legitimate their desire to preserve the cultural autonomy of their ethnic group in American society. They did not hesitate to proclaim their political loyalty to America, and increasingly referred to their group as Franco-American rather than French Canadian. A group of Woonsocket lawyers formed the Independent Club to encourage French-Canadian immigrants to naturalize and to exercise their right to vote, and even gained the endorsement of several local priests. But the whole point of taking on this political identity was not to encourage assimilation but rather to gain the political power necessary to preserve their ethnic community's cultural integrity. After the war, some elite members boasted that they had successfully demonstrated their American patriotism without weakening their ethnic identity, and they pointed to the still-vigorous French character of the schools, fraternal organizations, lodges, and other such institutions as evidence of the thriving nature of their ethnic culture.[72]

The architects of Woonsocket's French-Canadian community were entitled to a few rounds of self-congratulation in 1919. Had Horace Kallen visited Woonsocket at that time, he might well have deemed it a stunning example of the kind of autonomous and vibrant ethnic community that his theory of cultural pluralism, if widely implemented as a social policy, could nurture throughout American society. But, in truth, the superficially American but essentially French-Canadian

---

[70] See, for example, David Brody, *Labor in Crisis: The Steel Strike of 1919* (Urbana, Ill., 1987), 71–5; David A. Corbin, *Life, Work, and Rebellion in the Coal Fields: The Southern West Virginia Miners, 1880–1922* (Urbana, Ill., 1981), 176–252; David Montgomery, "Nationalism, American Patriotism, and Class Consciousness among Immigrant Workers in the United States in the Epoch of World War I," in Dirk Hoerder, ed., *"Struggle a Hard Battle": Essays on Working-Class Immigrants* (DeKalb, Ill., 1986), 327–51.

[71] *Providence Journal Almanac*, 1913, 45–6; 1921, 134.

[72] Bélanger, *Guide*, passim; Daniels, *America via the Neighborhood*, 143–4.

character of Woonsocket was a most fragile construct whose survival depended on a virtual historical impossibility – namely, that the political and economic processes accelerated by the war would be reversed or simply eliminated as factors affecting Woonsocket life. Two of these processes, however, showed no signs of reversal or disintegration: One was the inclination of the American government, at both the national and state levels, to use its power to shape the political and cultural identities of its citizens; the other was the internationalization of textile production. The political and economic pressures unleashed by these historical processes would soon fracture the city's ethnic leadership and doom their efforts to control the cultural destiny of their community. Ironically, these same forces would simultaneously offer Woonsocket's workers, and especially the French-Canadian majority among them, an unprecedented opportunity to fashion a class identity for themselves and to bid for political power.

The Americanization pressures generated by war patriotism did not abate after the war. Nativists and conservatives seized on patriotic symbols as ways of subduing and even ridding the country of radical and foreign elements. A Senate committee investigating the frightening 1919 steel strike ascribed the unruly and radical sentiments of so many workers to their foreign character and called for renewed emphasis on Americanization campaigns. Such calls from the nation's premier legislative body prompted numerous patriotic groups, ranging from the well-established DAR to the newly established American Legion, to concentrate their efforts on Americanization. Employers gathered in Massachusetts in 1919 to devise new strategies to Americanize their employees and thereby increase their productivity and corporate loyalty. Cities stepped up their Americanization programs, attempting to enroll ever greater numbers of immigrants in their adult-education classes. Boy Scouts went door-to-door in many immigrant communities distributing invitations to Americanization classes. Teacher colleges throughout the country stressed training in Americanization work. By 1922 the U.S. Bureau of Education was distributing the *Federal Textbook on Citizenship Training* to more than 3,500 communities to aid local efforts in Americanization.[73]

---

[73] Higham, *Strangers in the Land*, 234–63; Bessie Louise Pierce, *Citizens' Organizations and the Civic Training of Youth* (New York, 1933); John F. McClymer, "The Americanization Movement and the Education of the Foreign-Born Adult, 1914–1925," in Bernard J. Weiss, ed., *American Education and the European Immigrant, 1840–1940* (DeKalb, Ill., 1982), 96–116; Robert A. Carlson, *The Quest for Conformity: Americanization Through Education* (New York, 1975); John J. Mahoney, "Americanization in

Americanizers in Rhode Island carried on a multifaceted campaign. The state's commissioner of public schools began issuing "Americanization circulars" to teachers. The state legislature authorized the establishment of an Americanization division in the department of education to promote Americanization training among prospective teachers. Civics and American history classes occupied more and more space in school curricula. Since the Fourth of July lay beyond the reach of the school year, schools staged extravagant patriotic celebrations on Rhode Island Independence Day (May 4) and Grand Army Flag Day. And since the state's parochial school population lay beyond the reach of public school authority, the State Assembly, in 1922, passed the Peck Law mandating that the required subjects of public school – American history, civics, math, and English – be taught in English at all parochial schools in the state.[74] To ethnic groups like the French Canadians, for whom parochial school autonomy was the key to cultural survival, the Peck Law was anathema. French Canadians feared, moreover, that the Irish-controlled diocese, though worried about this (and every other) governmental intervention in Church affairs, sympathized with the Peck Law's Americanizing intentions and thus would facilitate the law's implementation.

For the amount of energy and ideology expended on public and private Americanization campaigns in the five years after the end of World War I, the results, at the level of individual assimilation, were not especially impressive. The vital signs of Woonsocket's French-Canadian community life looked healthy throughout the 1920s. In 1924 French-Canadian voters in Woonsocket along with ethnic allies throughout the state ousted from office so many legislators who had voted for the Peck Law that the State Assembly substantially weakened the statute's enforcement mechanism the next year. Parochial elementary schools, which throughout the 1920s continued to educate three quarters of Woonsocket's schoolchildren, thus maintained *la survivance* – education in the language, religion, and

the United States," U.S. Department of the Interior, Bureau of Education, *Bulletin* (Washington, D.C., 1923); U.S. Department of Labor, Bureau of Naturalization, *Annual Report* (Washington, D.C., 1922), 17–23.

[74] Bessie Louise Pierce, *Civic Attitudes in American School Textbooks* (Chicago, 1930), 240–1; Mahoney, "Americanization in the United States," 14, Charles Carroll, *Rhode Island: Three Centuries of Democracy* (New York, 1932), vol. II, 946–53; Rhode Island, *Acts and Resolves Passed by the General Assembly* (Providence, R.I., 1922), 162–5; Rhode Island Office of Commissioner of Education, *Annual Program for Patriotic Exercises in Schools, 1909–1933, in Commemoration of the 133rd to 157th Anniversary of Rhode Island Independence Day* (Providence, R.I., 1909–1933); Sorrell, "The Sentinelle Affair," 160–2. See also Charles Carroll, "Americanization," address delivered at Rhode Island College, May 14, 1923 (John Hay Library Archives, Brown University).

mores of the French-Canadian people – at the very heart of their curricula.[75] The continued immersion of so many Woonsocket youngsters in the essentials of French-Canadian culture suggests this ethnic enclave was weathering the assimilation storm remarkably well.

Bessie Bloom Wessel, a Connecticut College sociologist who came to Woonsocket in 1926 to study the city's ethnic groups, was certain, however, that she had found indisputable evidence of French-Canadian assimilation. She surveyed the linguistic and marriage habits of the families of 5,000 Woonsocket schoolchildren, and reported a dramatic decrease in the rate of monolingualism among French Canadians, from 85 percent in households headed by immigrant parents to 46 percent in households headed by native-born parents.[76] She also reported a dramatic increase in rates of intermarriage among French Canadians, from 8 and 9 percent among the first two generations to 35 percent among the third. Wessel concluded that in time "even the most tenacious of cultures gives way to the culture pressures of the immediate environment"; "with the lapse of three generations . . . the hold loosens."[77]

Yet the fact that the city's Catholic authorities had refused Wessel access to the three quarters of Woonsocket's French-Canadian schoolchildren who attended the city's parochial schools skewed her statistics, compromised her analysis, and testified to the community's continued distrust of outsiders. Wessel's analysis, so heartening to Americanizers, rested on the small number of French-Canadian families who had already taken the fateful "Americanizing" step of sending their children to public elementary schools. And even this public school "vanguard" was assimilating at an unusually slow rate. More than 80 percent of the French-Canadian families in her sample spoke either only French or a combination of French and English in the home, and almost 50 percent of her third-generation French-Canadian youngsters – the grandchildren of immigrants who came in the late nineteenth century – grew up in homes where only French was spoken. One can only assume that the figures were much higher for the vast majority of French-Canadian families who continued to make instruction in *la survivance* the centerpiece of their youngsters' education.[78] Such figures help make sense of a remarkable charac-

[75] Sorrell, "The Sentinelle Affair," 118–19, 163–9.

[76] Bessie Bloom Wessel, *An Ethnic Survey of Woonsocket, Rhode Island* (Chicago, 1931), 204–5.

[77] Ibid., 115, 205.

[78] Wessel knew, of course, that the French-Canadian children to whom she did gain access, the minority attending public school, undoubtedly belonged to the most

teristic of Woonsocket in the 1970s: the large numbers of elderly French Canadians who, though born in Woonsocket, spoke English in a halting, heavily accented, and ungrammatical way. In the 1910s and 1920s, these individuals, like most French-Canadian youngsters of the time, had spoken only French at home and had attended French-language parochial schools.

Mass culture, thought to be a great Americanizer, penetrated Woonsocket's French-Canadian community during the postwar years much as it did virtually every American city and town large enough to support a movie theater and car dealership. In 1919, hysterical reaction among the clergy to the opening of movie theaters in the heart of Woonsocket's French-Canadian commercial district suggests that this new cultural medium enjoyed as widespread a popularity among the city's French Canadians as it did among every other group of ethnic Americans at this time.[79] The city's French press began selling considerable amounts of advertising space to car and radio dealers in the 1920s, and the yearning to acquire such goods, judging from such evidence as Henry Boucher's razor-sharp recollection of the day he purchased his first Ford, reached down at least to the stable, well-paid strata of the working class.[80] Such developments may have generated a sense of unease and foreboding among the community's more traditional proponents of *la survivance*, yet there was no immediate indication that mass culture or mass consumption diminished the community's commitment to ancestral values. French-Canadian leaders in Woonsocket and elsewhere in the state had no difficulty in mobilizing the masses in 1924 to defeat legislators who failed to pledge themselves to repeal the Peck Law.[81] Ethnic leaders, moreover, had demonstrated a capacity to turn some forms of mass culture to their own advantage. By the 1920s, for example, Church leaders had organized a parish baseball league to help satisfy their parishioners' long-standing passion for the sport. Even the most militant advocates of *la survivance* either participated in or encouraged

Americanized portion of this ethnic population. She simply assumed that the intergenerational trends she established among this minority would be at work, albeit at a slower pace, among the parochial school majority. But how much slower was the pace among the families of parochial-school children? Would they reach a 35 percent rate of third generation intermarriage in five years, ten years, or twenty-five? Wessel never concerned herself with such questions. Ibid., 9–12.

[79] *WC*, January 27, 1919.

[80] Boucher, by this time, had climbed into the skilled worker ranks. Richard S. Sorrell, "Sports and Franco-Americans in Woonsocket, 1870–1930," *Rhode Island History* 31 (November 1972), 126; Doty, *The First Franco-Americans*, 131–5.

[81] Henry Lawrence, "Historical Sketch," in Wessel, *Ethnic Survey*, 233.

the league, sure that it posed no threat to the cultural integrity of their community.[82]

As long as the educational, religious, and at least part of the leisure life of the French-Canadian masses remained within their control, Woonsocket's ethnic leaders apparently felt that the dangers of mass culture and mass consumption could be contained. Thus what worried them most was not the increasing preoccupation of Woonsocket residents with cars and movies but the efforts of outside authorities to undermine their educational and religious autonomy. And what triggered a devastating internecine fight within this leadership was not the opening of a movie theater in the Social District but the Providence bishop's opening of a panethnic diocesan high school for boys in the center of Woonsocket.

The impetus for building such a school, ironically, had come from Monsignor Dauray, an aged but still prominent figure in Woonsocket's French-Canadian community. The sheer expense of such a project had forced Dauray to turn to the Irish-controlled diocese in Providence for aid. The diocese took charge of the project and envisioned the school as an institution open to all Catholics, regardless of ethnic origins. Such a pan-Catholic plan alarmed Elphège Daignault, a Woonsocket lawyer and leader of a small band of ethnic militants who had concluded, by the early 1920s, that French Canadians had to resist all external efforts at Americanization. Daignault and his supporters viewed the diocesan desire to open the high school to all Catholic youth, expressed in the midst of the state's attempt to Americanize Woonsocket's parochial education system through the Peck Law, as a devious plot to integrate French-Canadian boys with the boys of other ethnic groups and thus accelerate their assimilation. When their opposition failed to halt the construction of the school, Daignault's group, increasingly called Sentinelles after the name of their newspaper, began a campaign to exclude the diocese from all local parish affairs. Only local control, they argued, would allow French-Canadian clergy and parishioners in Woonsocket to practice their religion and express their ethnicity as they pleased.[83]

The Sentinelles' position outraged a much larger group of self-styled moderate ethnic leaders. As central as *la survivance* was to French-Canadian life, these moderates felt, it could never justify the sort of radical attack on the structure of the Catholic Church that the Sentinelles, determined to free Woonsocket's parishes from diocesan control, were mounting. In the moderates' view, it was better to risk

[82] Sorrell, "Sports and Franco-Americans," 122–3.
[83] This summary draws heavily on Sorrell, "The Sentinelle Affair."

exposing French-Canadian boys to American culture in a multiethnic high school than to challenge a divinely ordained religious structure. The moderates probably had the better argument, if only from a pragmatic point of view; when the high school finally opened, French-Canadian youth drawn from the Woonsocket area comprised the bulk of the student body.[84] Moreover, the moderates, led by such prominent political figures as Aram Pothier, formed a much larger and more powerful faction in the city's French-Canadian elite, and their predominance seemed to augur well for a quick moderate victory and for their ability to reestablish a single, authoritative, elite voice in community affairs. The actual development and resolution of the conflict, however, could hardly have followed a more different and more debilitating course.

The Sentinelles were in no mood to listen to the moderates' call for compromise – not when they felt their ethnic community's very identity imperiled. Nor were they willing to bow to the authority that numbers and prestige conferred on the moderate faction; the behavior of some moderates in the fight over the Peck Law, in Sentinelle eyes, had fatally compromised this faction's claim on the leadership of Woonsocket's French Canadians. A member of the French-Canadian moderate faction, Rhode Island Governor Emery San Souci, had allowed the Peck bill to become law, not because he supported it but because he felt powerless to oppose it. A veto, he felt, would render the state's French-Canadian population even more vulnerable to nativist attacks than it was already and perhaps cost individuals like himself the prominent places they had achieved in the state Republican Party.[85] This conciliatory course outraged ethnic militants, who felt that San Souci, by failing to veto the bill, was complicit in the destruction of his own people's cultural integrity. Given the depth of feeling in both camps of Woonsocket's ethnic elite, a quick and bloodless resolution of their fight was simply not possible. The sparring between the militants and moderates triggered by the high school issue in 1924 was but the opening round in an ugly, demeaning slugfest that would last five years. By the time the flailing had stopped in 1929 and the Pope had intervened to declare the moderates the nominal winners, the whole ethnic elite and their dream of a French-Canadian oasis in New England had been battered beyond recovery.

---

[84] Sorrell, "Sports and Franco-Americans," 123.

[85] DeMoranville, "Ethnic Voting in Rhode Island," 51–77. San Souci tried to go on record as opposing the bill by "vetoing" it after his veto authority had expired. Rhode Island courts quickly invalidated this late veto and upheld the constitutionality of the Peck Law. See Sorrell, "The Sentinelle Affair," 163.

The brawl, which came to be known throughout New England and Quebec as the Sentinelle Affair, not only engulfed the entire ethnic elite and forced each member to choose between two hostile and uncompromising camps; it also spilled beyond the ranks of the elite and aroused the partisan loyalties of the French-Canadian masses. Daignault spoke to mass meetings of thousands. In some parishes, like St. Anne's and St. Louis, majorities of parishioners heeded Daignault's call to boycott diocesan fund drives and to refuse to pay pew rent.[86] Moderates responded with aggressive tactics of their own. On one Sunday in 1927, the staunchly moderate priests of the Holy Family Church stood at the church doors and actually refused entrance to any parishioner who declined to pay pew rent. Later that year, Bishop Hickey removed Father Prince, an alleged Sentinellist sympathizer, from his pastoral duties at St. Louis. Thousands of his angry supporters retaliated by refusing to enter their parish churches for two weeks, choosing instead to attend a "rump" Mass in a tent parish set up in nearby Bellingham. Sunday afternoons they held massive rallies involving thousands of supporters on the grounds of St. Louis parish.[87] The debacle – with its boycotts, rallies, and vitriolic debate – continued until 1929 when the Pope issued excommunication bans for prominent Sentinelles. Daignault and his followers, for all their opposition to the Church hierarchy, could not imagine an existence outside the Church of Rome.[88] They abandoned their cause, repented, and appealed for readmission to the Church. Their appeal marked their acceptance of Rome's authority and thus ended the Sentinelle Affair.

Any satisfaction that the moderates may have felt in victory was tempered by the realization that the length and fury of the battle had done extensive damage to their standing in the community. The years of fighting consumed their energies and prevented necessary parish works and the extension of social services.[89] Even more damaging, perhaps, was the sheer ugliness of the conflict – the name calling, the removal of popular priests, the physical church-door confrontations between priests loyal to the diocese and Sentinellist parishioners – that tore apart an elite that had long prided itself on its gentility, its communalist spirit, and above all its godliness. It is easy to assign

[86] Sorrell, "The Sentinelle Affair," 273–93.

[87] Ibid., 225–31.

[88] In this respect they differed from religious militants in the Polish and Lithuanian communities who did secede from the Church of Rome. See Victor Greene, *For God and Country: The Rise of Polish and Lithuanian Ethnic Consciousness in America, 1860–1910* (Madison, Wis., 1975).

[89] Sorrell, "The Sentinelle Affair," 344–64.

blame for the crisis – the French-Canadian governor who "betrayed" his people, the band of Sentinelles who violated the structure of a Church ordained by God – as contemporaries were apt to do. But the whole affair had a sad inevitability about it. In 1920s America it had simply become impossible to maintain the kind of cultural autonomy that the French-Canadian ethnic leadership so desperately wanted for its community. The growing influence of mass culture and mass consumption made it imperative that this leadership strengthen its control over local educational and cultural institutions; but the experience of war had made both public and private authorities beyond Woonsocket eager to use their political power to extend their control over those very local institutions in the interest of creating a more culturally and politically homogeneous citizenry. Perhaps if local Woonsocket leaders could have been more patient, more restrained in their responses, realizing that they had the votes in the state to force the Peck Law's repeal as well as enough community power to exercise de facto if not de jure control over the new diocesan high school, they could have parried the thrusts of these state and diocesan policies and maintained the cultural integrity of their community. But it was almost impossible in the nativist climate of the 1920s, amidst unprecedented state and mass cultural intrusions into local cultural life, to think in such calm and shrewd ways. It was much easier, even more natural, to feel under siege, to feel as though Armageddon was at hand. The resultant rush into combat, not surprisingly, hastened the decline of cultural authority that the French-Canadian elite was so desperate to protect.

Working-class stirrings, 1922–1929

The world of Woonsocket's French-Canadian masses in the 1920s was, in many ways, an inversion of the one inhabited by their elite. Elite French Canadians in the 1920s lived in economic comfort while consumed with anxiety about the impending collapse of their cultural autonomy. The French-Canadian masses, on the other hand, lived their cultural life much as they had always done but were consumed with worry about their precarious economic predicament. The source of their economic anxiety was the city's failing cotton textile industry.

Just as the war had unleashed the Americanization pressures that had fragmented the French-Canadian elite, it triggered the economic forces that hastened the collapse of Woonsocket's and the rest of New England's cotton textile industry. The war stimulated demand for cotton yarn and cloth and thus induced many northern manufacturers to increase their productive capacity. At the war's end, when government orders ceased, these manufacturers began fighting each other for shares of a shrinking market. Export opportunities vanished since, during the war years, countries like India and Japan, once large importers of textile products, had developed indigenous textile industries capable of supplying their domestic needs. With so much excess capacity, the industry had to shrink. The greatest contraction occurred in New England, where manufacturers simply could not produce as cheaply as their southern competitors. While much of the nation was enjoying an economic boom in the 1920s, New England's cotton mill towns sank into a deep economic depression.[90]

The industry did not collapse all at once. Manufacturers first tried to compete with the South by reducing their own labor costs: lengthening the hours and reducing the wages of their employees. Textile workers, emboldened by the economic gains they had made during the war, resisted these attacks on their living standards. Between 1919 and 1928, bitter strikes broke out in nearly every major center of cotton production in New England, from Manchester, New Hampshire, to New Bedford, Massachusetts.[91] The largest strike occurred in Rhode Island in 1922. When employers imposed a 10 percent wage cut in January 1922, tens of thousands of textile workers from across the state (though not from Woonsocket) walked off their jobs. Capitalists desperate to reduce costs confronted workers determined to retain the improvements in wages and hours they had won in the aftermath of the war. Strikers, attracting deep-seated support in the communities where they lived, held out for nine months until manufacturers, in September, agreed to negotiate a compromise solution. Workers actually won some important concessions on wage levels, but such victories brought them only a temporary reprieve. The sheer intensity of class conflict in 1922 – numerous casualties had resulted from the periodic confrontations of angry strikers with local police and National Guardsmen assigned to protect millowner property – accelerated the flight of capital out of the region.[92]

The Woonsocket economy, with its concentration in woolen and worsted textiles, was spared the absolute devastation other textile centers suffered, but it was not spared economic hardship. In 1920,

[90] Burgy, *The New England Cotton Textile Industry*, 119–218; Dunn and Hardy, *Labor and Textiles*, 11–83.
[91] Lahne, *The Cotton Mill Worker*, 203–15; Robert R. R. Brooks, "The United Textile Workers" (Ph.D. dissertation, Yale University, 1935); Dunn and Hardy, *Labor and Textiles*, 212–33; Hareven, *Family Time and Industrial Time*, 287–354.
[92] Susan E. Jaffee, "Ethnic Working Class Protest: The Textile Strike of 1922 in Rhode Island" (honors thesis, Brown University, 1974).

one third of the city's manufacturing work force – approximately 5,500 persons – worked in cotton mills or in plants that produced cotton textile machinery. This total had declined to fewer than 3,500 workers (a fourth of the work force) ten years later.[93] The loss of jobs increased the labor surplus in the city and enticed manufacturers in other industries to lower wages and lengthen hours. Any cut in family earnings, through a reduction in wages or unemployment of one wage earner, resulted in hardship. As employers cut wages and as the numbers of unemployed swelled, more and more families found themselves slipping into poverty.[94]

Ethnic leaders might have reacted to this brewing economic crisis by seizing on the corporatist messages imbedded in *Rerum Novarum* and mounting a communitywide attack on the evils of unfettered capital. Taking a cue from the developing course of industrial relations in Quebec, they might even have encouraged the formation of Catholic unions.[95] With priests as supervisors, these unions could have pressed their case against employers without violating Christian doctrine or unduly interfering with employer prerogatives. A few Woonsocket employers, in the wake of the statewide textile strike of 1922, indicated a willingness to move in this direction.[96] But most members of the elite did not. A corporatist campaign would have entailed a major reorientation of prevailing ethnic doctrines. An elite preoccupied with its own internal squabbles could not muster the necessary resolve. A sizable portion of this elite, moreover, still believing in the inherently docile character of French-Canadian workers, did not appreciate the threat that the economic crisis posed to elite power. Noting that the furious statewide textile strike of 1922 involved few Woonsocket workers, the editors of the Woonsocket French weekly, *La Tribune*, confidently declared that "the current malaise...will dissipate fast if all the [striking] workers were to become Catholics and...follow humbly and piously the holy refuge [their religion] as do our Franco-American workers."[97] Woonsocket's

[93] Figures compiled from employment statistics given for individual firms in the *Providence Journal Almanac*, 1920, 47–54; 1925, 37–50; 1930, 66–82.
[94] Lahne, *Cotton Mill Worker*, 104–5; George L. Collins, "54 or 48? The Issue in Rhode Island," *Labor Age* 16 (July 1927), 4–5.
[95] Jacques Rouillard, *Les syndicats nationaux au Québec de 1900 à 1930* (Quebec, 1979), 157–305.
[96] See, for example, ads taken out by the French Worsted Company and American Paper Tube in *Album souvenir: fête Saint-Jean-Baptiste, 24 juin 1922, Woonsocket, R.I.* (Woonsocket, R.I., 1922).
[97] *LT*, March 18, 1922; quoted and translated in Jaffee, "Ethnic Working Class Protest," Chapter 3, p. 51.

ethnic leadership did not need to worry about the city's worsening economic predicament because the humble and pious French-Canadian workers would never rebel. But a shrewder, more circumspect chronicler of the local scene might have cast a wary eye on the unusually high degree of strike involvement among French-Canadian workers in other parts of the state, and such an observer might have worried that such worker restlessness would make its way to Woonsocket, as the economic crisis continued to worsen and as Americanization pressures cost the French-Canadian elite first its cohesion and then its authority in local working-class life.

One French Canadian did assess the statewide situation in these terms, though it caused him little worry. Horace Riviere, a Providence-based organizer for the United Textile Workers (UTW) who had organized French-Canadian workers during the 1922 strike, noticed considerable dissatisfaction among Woonsocket's apparently quiescent textile workers during that strike and envisioned parleying that discontent into a significant union movement.[98] He arrived in Woonsocket sometime in 1924 and stimulated, in the next three years, organizing drives that netted the UTW eleven textile locals involving several thousand textile workers.[99] We know little about how he pitched his union appeal to Woonsocket workers, though given his close ties to Thomas McMahon, Francis Gorman, and other national textile union leaders in Providence, it seems likely that he communicated at least some of that leadership's emphasis on the intrinsically American character of UTW unionism and on the fundamental right of all American workers to join unions and bargain collectively with employers.[100] He also, no doubt, used his French-Canadian identity to good advantage with his predominately French-Canadian audiences. Whatever he said, however he cajoled, he succeeded in inspiring significant numbers of the area's workers with the union gospel. When Manville Jenckes, the city's largest textile employer, announced in February 1927 its need to increase the work week at its Social and Nourse mills from forty-eight to fifty-four hours, employees refused to work the extra six hours. These workers, largely French-Canadian, had fought hard to gain the forty-eight hour week and refused to accept Manville Jenckes' claim that the move was an unavoidable response to financial difficulties. When management announced it would shut the mills if workers persisted in their refusal, the work forces of the Social and Nourse mills walked off their jobs.[101]

[98] Jaffee, "Ethnic Working Class Protest," Chapter 3, pp. 56–9.
[99] *The Textile Worker*, 1924–1927, passim.
[100] This emphasis will be discussed in Chapter 2.
[101] *The Textile Worker*, February 1927, 649–52; April 1927, 16; July 1927, 234–6.

The city's ethnic and political leadership, belatedly recognizing the threat the conflict posed to the city's economy, tried to arrange a settlement. But their initiative was too late, too ineffectual. A committee of fifteen prominent citizens organized to resolve the crisis asked the workers, as their employers had done, to agree to work fifty-four hours rather than forty-eight.[102] The clergy, likewise, had little to offer. A priest of Notre Dame, whose parish was one of the hardest hit by the strike, advised his parishioners to "accept whatever sacrifice was necessary and to have recourse to prayer," but his appeals to sacrifice failed to move the strikers.[103] Their six-month-long resistance cost them dearly. Manville Jenckes announced that the two mills shut down by the strikers would never reopen. More than 1,000 workers lost their jobs.[104]

The strike of 1927 thus ended as a staggering defeat for Woonsocket workers. In the wake of the closings, the solidarity and militance they had demonstrated as union members and strikers dissipated. Many fell into the ranks of the despairing unemployed. Riviere gave up the Woonsocket fight and sought new organizing opportunities in New Bedford (Massachusetts), Manchester (New Hampshire), and Lewiston (Maine).[105] But the conflict nevertheless remained full of significance for the French-Canadian community: It revealed that French-Canadian workers had found the capacity to act in direct opposition to their ethnic leaders.

The growing independence of Woonsocket's French-Canadian workers was apparent in electoral politics as well. French-Canadian workers began turning against the French-Canadian leadership in the state's Republican Party because of its failure to protect its working-class constituency. San Souci, the governor who in 1922 ordered out the National Guard to protect millowner property against the striking textile workers, was the last Republican gubernatorial candidate to carry Woonsocket for almost twenty years. In 1924 and 1926, Aram Pothier easily won the governor's race in the state but failed both times to carry his native Woonsocket. His failure resulted in part from the success of Daignault and other Sentinelles in stirring up the French-Canadian voters against the moderate, accommodationist faction represented by Pothier. But just as important was the increasing conviction of working class voters in Woonsocket – whose numbers climbed sharply throughout the 1920s – that the state Republican Party, with its close ties to the state's millowners, would

[102] Ibid., February 1927, 656; *Providence Evening Bulletin*, February 28, 1927.
[103] *Providence Evening Bulletin*, February 28, 1927.
[104] *The Textile Worker*, July 1927, 234–6.
[105] Ibid., December 1928, 526–7.

not defend workers' economic interests. In the mid to late 1920s, Woonsocket's French-Canadian working-class voters established a loyalty to the Democratic Party in state and national elections that overrode ethnic ties and would prevail, with one or two exceptions, for the next half century.[106]

The growing support among French-Canadian workers for unions and the Democratic Party did not entail a repudiation of their ethnic culture. French-Canadian workers did not suddenly discard the Québecois heritage that had been integral to their lives for so long. By almost any measure – high rates of parochial school and church attendance and French language usage, low rates of intermarriage – ethnic traditions were central to French-Canadian working-class life throughout the 1920s.[107] Even as they turned outward toward political institutions in American society, French-Canadian workers reshaped the doctrines of their ethnic culture to express their aspirations and grievances as industrial workers in American society.

This process of reformulation is most clearly manifest in the militant ethnic and nationalist Sentinelle movement that spanned the years 1924 to 1929. By 1927 and 1928, in the wake of their defeat at Manville Jenckes, many working-class French Canadians were finding the movement a vehicle through which to express their economic grievances. The Sentinellist spokesman Daignault attracted thousands to his rallies in the parishes of St. Anne's and St. Louis that were located in the Social District, the center of French-Canadian working-class life in the city.[108] Both churches were but a quarter mile from the Social and Nourse Mills that Manville Jenckes shut down in February 1927 and a stone's throw from the company tenements that housed so many Manville Jenckes workers. Although it is impossible to identify the thousands who attended the Sentinelle rallies, it is likely that many were former Manville Jenckes workers who found a special meaning in Daignault's warnings about hostile forces working to destroy the French-Canadian community. Manville Jenckes offered a convenient target for their rage; as a large, Yankee-owned corporation with no special interest in Woonsocket, it appeared the embodiment of hostile Anglo-American forces threatening the community.[109] Daignault's insistence that any compromise or accommodation to American life threatened French-Canadian existence may have rung

[106] DeMoranville, "Ethnic Voting in Rhode Island," 78–123; *Providence Journal Almanac*, 1925, 165; 1926, 155–6; 1928, 149, 1929, 160–1; Jaffee, "Ethnic Working Class Protest," Chapter 3, pp. 56–9.
[107] Wessel, *Ethnic Survey*, 115, 204–5, 239. Sorrell, "The Sentinelle Affair," passim.
[108] Sorrell, "The Sentinelle Affair," 386.
[109] *The Book of Rhode Island*, 181.

true to workers who had refused to bow to the wage and hour demands made by their American employer. His calls for defiance and for assertion of ethnic pride and values may have emboldened a working-class community sinking into poverty. Sentinellism did not become a self-conscious class movement directed at the city's manufacturers, and there is no evidence of an overlap in the leadership of the union and religious movements. But for many workers, Sentinellism may have expressed some deeply felt economic resentments. For French-Canadian workers who had internalized the principles of *la survivance*, Sentinellism made sense of their predicament and offered an opportunity to express their fears that their community and way of life were being destroyed.

The political behavior of the voters of the Fifth Ward, the ward that encompassed the Social and Nourse mills and St. Anne and St. Louis parishes, supports such an interpretation. In 1926 and 1928, the voters in this ward elected to the Board of Aldermen a young, ambitious politician, Ernest Dupré, who ran as a Republican and as a Sentinelle. Dupré's Sentinellist sentiments did not run deep. He was a colorful, roguish, and unabashedly opportunistic politician who would not hesitate to change his political line to insure his place at the center of Woonsocket politics. When Sentinellism declined and Daignault was ostracized in 1928, Dupré simply transformed himself from a Sentinellist into a "good-government" Republican and won reelection.[110] But if opportunism was one hallmark of his career, the other was an uncanny ability to articulate the most pressing concerns of the Fifth Ward voters. His espousal of Sentinellism in the mid-1920s was a sure sign that this political message resonated deeply among Woonsocket workers.

In French-Canadian workers' support of Sentinellism, like their support of trade unionism, we can see the efforts of an ethnic working class to find an independent voice to express their concerns and organizations that would defend their interests. As their trade union involvement suggested a break with their past, their Sentinellist enthusiasm showed the persistent relevance of traditional ethnic symbols and values. If they were attracted to an American working-class identity, they were also searching for ways to refashion their ethnic culture to express better their class concerns. The events of the 1920s in Woonsocket revealed a deep ambivalence among French-Canadian workers about their ethnic heritage that would profoundly influence politics and society in the city for the next twenty years.

---

[110] *Providence Journal Almanac*, 1928, 169, 1930, 121; *Providence Journal*, December 7, 1949; Sorrell, "The Sentinelle Affair," 250–1, 340–1.

Ambivalence may seem a frail reed on which to build a labor movement. But the mere fact that French-Canadian workers could simultaneously express a class identity and an ethnic loyalty in a community whose ethnic leadership had always insisted on the fundamental incompatibility of the two was a measure of how much autonomy these workers had gained. Their demonstrations of ethnic loyalty, moreover, took a form that Aram Pothier and other prestigious members of their ethnic leadership denounced harshly. Publicly confronting their ethnic leaders in such ways, even repudiating them as Woonsocket workers did in voting against Pothier in the gubernatorial elections of 1924 and 1926, were inconceivable acts in the elite-controlled ethnic society of prewar Woonsocket.

The ambivalence that revealed the growing independence of French Canadians from their ethnic order would also help them negotiate the terms of their entry into American society. In the 1930s, French-Canadian workers, while showing an increasing eagerness to be American, would nervously insist that becoming American did not preclude retaining a Catholic, French-speaking, or working-class identity. They would thus be less susceptible than workers already part of an American cultural mainstream – like the Lynds' Middle-towners perhaps – to governmental, mass cultural, or corporate notions of what being an American entailed, and they would be correspondingly more inclined to insist that their new American identity serve their economic and cultural needs. They would soon experience a much more conflictual and varied political life, one that offered them a much higher level of political opportunity, than had existed in Woonsocket at any time since the first days of French-Canadian settlement.

2   The Franco-Belgians

Though Woonsocket was home to twenty-eight ethnic groups in the 1920s, only one, other than the French Canadians, would significantly shape the city's economy, culture, and politics: the Franco-Belgians. The Franco-Belgians barely qualify as an ethnic group. Their numbers small, first and second generation totals never topping 2,000, they comprised a mere 4 percent of the city's population.[1] No common immiseration, no shared steerage experience, and no widely shared commitment to ethnic survival bound them. Nor did a single religion unite them (some were Catholic, others Protestant), and they could not point to a single nation (some came from France, others from Belgium) as their ancestral home.[2] Only language – all spoke French in America – and an adherence to congeries of secular, cosmopolitan values stressing education, individuality, and the liberating possibilities of modern, industrial society gave Franco-Belgians a common ethnic identity. In a city other than Woonsocket, the espousal of such values would probably not have been singular enough to sustain an ethnic identity. But in this traditionalist city, it was. Woonsocket's French Canadians saw the Franco-Belgians as different from themselves and underscored that difference by referring to the Franco-Belgians as "the France French."[3] The predominance of prestigious millowners, powerful mill superintendents, and contentious labor radicals in the ranks of the France French lent them a marked presence and a degree of influence entirely out of proportion to their numerical representation in Woonsocket society. The Franco-Belgians, in other words, provided Woonsocket with a disproportionate amount of textile capital, controlled the hiring, firing, and promotions of a goodly portion of the city's work force, and provoked a large share of the strikes and organizing efforts that disrupted textile production. The part of their experience that concerns us here

[1] U.S. Department of Commerce, Bureau of the Census, *Fourteenth Census of the United States, 1920, Population* (Washington, D.C.), vol. I, 85, vol. II, 766–7, 954–5; *Fifteenth Census of the United States, 1930, Population*, vol. III, part II, 769.
[2] The Belgians themselves, of course, were divided into the Flemish and the Walloons.
[3] This was the term used to describe the Franco-Belgians in every interview I conducted with Woonsocket residents.

is the process by which the labor radicals in their ranks devised a union ideology and organization that would appeal to the masses of French-Canadian millworkers. But the radicals' story must be preceded by that of the Franco-Belgian millowners and superintendents who not only were responsible for the presence of European radicals in Woonsocket, but whose own fall from grace in the turbulent 1920s created a new political opportunity for the radicals.

"The aristocrats"

In the vision of French-Canadian lay ethnic leaders like Aram Pothier, the arrival of French and Belgian capital in Woonsocket in the years from 1890 to 1910 was bound to enhance the prospects for *la survivance*. Not only would French be spoken at many new workplaces but a crucial portion of the city's elite, the millowners, would be committed to perpetuating French culture and religion in this American city. Until the 1920s, Pothier could plausibly have thought that his vision was becoming reality. The Belgian capitalist who ran the largest of the new textile complexes, Joseph Guerin, had settled in Woonsocket, set up numerous partnerships with Aram Pothier, married a son into the Pothier family, and taken an active role in civic and religious affairs.[4] The fact that the other capitalists, those based in Roubaix and Tourcoing, France, spent little time in Woonsocket and knew little of the city and its people, did not seem to matter too much, for these capitalists made their contributions to local Catholic charities and paid their respects to prominent French Canadians like Pothier in annual or semiannual tours of their American production facilities.

Such courteous behavior flattered Pothier and other members of his elite French-Canadian circles and blinded them to the resentment toward these foreign capitalists building up among French-Canadian workers. The hardships of textile labor, which contrasted so sharply with the luxury that the industry conferred on the men who owned it, nurtured a good part of this resentment; workers' perceptions that their French employers – the owners, superintendents, and foremen – treated them with disdain added to it. The origins of this resentment are obscure, but in the 1920s, when the Sentinelle Affair prompted many working-class French Canadians to sort out the friends and enemies of their ethnic community, it crystallized into a widely shared and deeply felt belief that the French employers were a threat to French-Canadian survival. Woonsocket workers began

[4] A.P. Thomas, *Woonsocket: Highlights of History, 1800–1976* (Woonsocket, R.I., 1976), 104–7.

uttering two epithets, first in whispers to each other and then more loudly and in public, that would stigmatize these employers for the next thirty years: They were "absentee owners" with little concern for the welfare of individuals in the community; worse yet, they were "aristocrats" who treated their help like the serfs of the Middle Ages. Workers reflecting on their experience fifty years later would still use these evocative sobriquets to set the stage for the common tale they had to tell: The French millowner arrives for his annual visit, struts through his mill in expensive clothes, never comes close enough to any worker even to exchange nods (let alone words) and then disappears, not to be seen again for a year. The story had crystallized into a piece of popular lore expressing working-class anger at snobbery, pretension, and class inequality.[5] The resentment it codified suggests that the presence of French capital in Woonsocket, far from securing the power and legitimacy of Pothier's ethnic elite, may well have hastened its decline.

In what relation do these stories stand to the actual facts of French absentee ownership? It is virtually impossible to penetrate the world of these French textile magnates directly, for they have disappeared from Woonsocket without leaving even a trace of paper behind. The literature on their values and industrial relations practices in France is contradictory and, in any case, no sure measure of the values that informed their practices in Woonsocket.[6] But oral history from two individuals, one a grandson of Joseph Guerin and the other a

[5] Interviews with the following: Lawrence Spitz, September 19–20, 1979; Angelo Turbesi, October 9, 1980; Leona, Leonel, and Normand Galipeau, all on October 22–23, 1980; Leo Cloutier, June 26, 1981; George Butsika, Arthur Moretti, Livio Gramolini, and Angelo Turbesi, all on September 14, 1984.

[6] David Landes has suggested that these magnates, steeped in Catholicism, established religiously inspired paternalist regimes at their Roubaix-Tourcoing factories. Bonnie Smith has argued, on the other hand, that their application of religion to enterprise was strictly utilitarian and should not distract us from the strict bourgeois code that, in truth, governed their approach to production and industrial relations. See Landes, "Religion and Enterprise: The Case of the French Textile Industry," in Edward C. Caster II, Robert Forster, and Joseph N. Moody, eds., *Enterprise and Entrepreneurs in Nineteenth and Twentieth Century France* (Baltimore, 1976), 41–86; and Smith, *Ladies of the Leisure Class: The Bourgeoises of Northern France in the Nineteenth Century* (Princeton, N.J., 1981), 18–33. I tend to agree with Smith, but even if one agrees with Landes, one would still know very little about the French magnates' practice of industrial relations in faraway Woonsocket. Industrial history abounds with examples of corporations pursuing one set of labor policies at their base facilities and quite another at their distant, frequently foreign, satellites. On the bourgeoisie in this region see also Louise A. Tilly, "Rich and Poor in a French Textile City," in Leslie Page Moch and Gary Stark, eds., *Essays on Family and Historical Change* (College Station, Tex., 1984) 65–90.

granddaughter of a superintendent of the French Worsted, lends weight to the image of these magnates that dominates working-class lore.

Robert Guerin stressed the respect that characterized his grandfather Joseph's and father Edmond's relations with their several hundred employees. His knowledge of his grandfather, the Belgian skilled worker who established Woonsocket's first Guerin mill in 1892, is secondhand, but the recollections of his father, Edmond, who ran Woonsocket's American Paper Tube Company (which manufactured cardboard tubes for mule spindles) from 1923 to 1935, were quite vivid.[7] His father's love of machinery and his desire to be involved personally in the nitty-gritty problems of production stood out most clearly in Robert's mind. "If he were walking through the mill," Robert recalled, "and saw something [wrong] with the machine, [say]...he didn't like the sound of it running, he'd be in a work jacket very soon, and he'd be talking Italian with the set-up man and the worker, and they'd be arguing like crazy."[8] Such relations made for excellent rapport with his workers and contrasted sharply with prevailing practices at the French-owned mills. The French owners, Robert Guerin recalls, would "walk through a mill, nose[s] up in the air, not talking to the labor" but rather grumbling to their assistants and instructing them to tell the workers what to correct.[9]

Edmond Guerin's involvement with his workers on the shopfloor translated into a paternalist concern for their individual and communal welfare. He gave substantial sums toward the construction of a new church and to the improvement of Woonsocket's medical facilities. He distinguished himself in 1927 by volunteering to meet with a committee representing the striking workers of Manville Jenckes in an effort to stave off management's theatened shutdown. During the Depression he was one of the few employers to set up a soup kitchen, and he quietly subsidized his workers' clothing expenses by arranging private deals with Woonsocket retailers.[10] Robert Guerin recalls the extraordinary outpouring of workers'

---

[7] Joseph died in 1923, only a year after Robert was born.

[8] Interview with Robert Guerin, November 3, 1980. Edmond followed his father's habit of hiring Italians for a disproportionate number of foremen and supervisory positions. The habit was rooted in Joseph Guerin's efforts, soon after arriving in Woonsocket in the 1890s, to bring over skilled workers and foremen known to him from his years as a textile worker and superintendent in northern Italian mills.

[9] Ibid.; all other Guerin quotes are from this one interview.

[10] Ibid.; *Providence Evening Bulletin*, January 29, 1927; *Providence Journal*, November 22, 1935.

sympathy for his family on the occasion of his father's sudden death in 1935. The many workers who came to the Guerin mansion to pay their last respects began telling Robert and his mother stories of his father's charitable deeds that they had never heard before: of his father making it financially feasible for a working-class boy to attend Assumption College in Worcester, of his purchasing a wheelchair for a disabled worker who could not afford to buy his own, and other similar acts of generosity.[11]

Away from work Edmond always maintained a stiff, formal distance from his workers. His sense of class superiority, manifested by his living in a mansion and riding to work in a chauffeur-driven limousine, not only underscored how vast was the divide between him and his workers but also made possible the paternalist concern he showed for them: His wealth and his stature conferred on him the duty to look after those lower on the social scale.[12] His adherence to such a premodern, almost Tory ethos tied him to the hierarchical, deferential, and communal aspects of French-Canadian culture and may well account for Guerin's popularity among those who worked for him. Had there been more capitalists like Guerin in Woonsocket, the city might have become known for its welfare capitalism, for the paternalist attitudes governing the city's industrial relations. But Guerin was a singular figure in Woonsocket's bourgeoisie. Guerin's decision to concentrate his capital and time in the manufacture of paper tubes for textile spindles freed him from the ruthless competitive pressures afflicting textile manufacture itself.[13] Most Woonsocket employers, their capital invested in a volatile industry constantly in danger of depression, literally could not afford Guerin's largesse. Some of Guerin's paternalism eventually would influence local textile employers tied to Guerin by blood, friendship, or business partnership. But such benevolence was entirely absent from the managerial style practiced in the large spinning mills owned by the French textile magnates.

Because French owners spent so little time in Woonsocket, local management of their mills fell to their superintendents and foremen. The superintendents were trusted men from the base facilities in Roubaix and Tourcoing. These superintendents, in turn, hired foremen from the base facilities who had, like themselves, unimpeachable records of loyalty. This emphasis on hiring familiar and

[11] Interview with Guerin, November 3, 1980.
[12] Ibid.
[13] The Guerin family relinquished majority control of the Guerin Mills complex to Providence bankers in the 1920s; the reasons for this will be discussed in Chapter 3.

loyal faces to run the American facilities resulted in part from the intensely personal character of these family-held French firms and in part from a determination to avoid hiring nettlesome employees like the socialists who incited so much rebellion in Roubaix and Tourcoing. French superintendents and foremen shuttled back and forth across the Atlantic to do their tours of duty. With time, not surprisingly, more and more stayed in Woonsocket.[14]

These men rarely, however, felt comfortable in the provincial French-Canadian world they found there. Charles Goval, for example, a manager of the French Worsted during the first two decades of the twentieth century, came with Virginie, his wife, to Woonsocket from Roubaix in 1901 to work in the French Worsted.[15] Goval was an ardent French nationalist throughout his life, convinced of French superiority over not only the French Canadians who worked for him at the French Worsted but the "provincial" Americans as well. He and his family lived comfortably in the years prior to World War I, possessing enough wealth to hire two Belgian servants – a maid and a laundress – and to travel in the exclusive circles of the French managerial elite. War put an end to this life, however, as Goval returned to France to defend his country against the Kaiser's armies. When he returned to Woonsocket – and to Virginie and his daughter Fernande – in 1918, he decided to invest his money in another textile company, only to lose it all in the depressed years of 1919 to 1922. He abandoned his family after that, never to return to Woonsocket until he died in 1932.

Fernande Goval idolized her father and continued to do so even after he disappeared. She kept her memory of him alive by trying to emulate in her life the values that had governed his. This was no easy task; her father's brush with bankruptcy meant that Fernande could no longer travel in exclusive French circles and certainly not marry into their ranks. She married instead a French Canadian, Bordes, a man acceptable to her father only because *his* father had come from an island off Newfoundland which was still a French possession. The

---

[14] Landes, "Religion and Enterprise"; interviews with Robert Guerin, November 3, 1980, Leo Cloutier, June 26, 1981, and Ernest Gignac, June 25, 1981. See also obituaries on Felix DeLathauwer, Palemon Glorieux, and Gaston H. Warlop, French-born managers at the Lafayette, French Worsted, and Branch River Combing Mill, respectively, in *Woonsocket Call* (hereafter *WC*), February 20, 1922, July 29, 1922, and December 26, 1973.

[15] Interview with Charlotte LeBlanc, July 16, 1981. LeBlanc did not know her grandfather personally, since he died in 1932, the year she was born. She came to know him, though, through the stories told her by her mother and even more so by the life her mother tried to live. She was named after him.

fact that Bordes was a clerical worker employed in the front office of the French Worsted and thus did not dirty his hands on machines further eased his entry into this bourgeois family.

But Bordes's marks of white-collar status were superficial. He came from a French-Canadian working-class background and would never really leave that world. His white-collar position would prove temporary, as he spent most of his working life as a weaver in the Montrose Worsted. Fernande could never accept that reality or her fall in status thus implied. She refused to live in the Social District, where most working-class French Canadians resided, or to attend St. Anne's Church, where they worshipped. She insisted instead on living in the Bernon district, a petit-bourgeois section of Woonsocket perched high on the Blackstone River's south side, where she could attend Mass with the city's "better sort" at Precious Blood parish and "look down" upon the Social District's tenements. The Bordes family, however, could not really afford Bernon. The first seven children were born in different houses; the fourth child, Charlotte Bordes, remembered the family being evicted for nonpayment of rent. Their housing problems only stopped when her father's brother bought them a small, one-family house – in petit-bourgeois Bernon, of course.

Denied the affluence that Charles Goval had once given his family, Fernande poured her energies into cultivating those values that were within her grasp. None was more important than education and upward mobility. She insisted that her children learn French as the French spoke it and not stoop to the patois common among French Canadians. She refused to let her children leave school at age fourteen or fifteen to work in the mills as was French-Canadian custom. She drilled into all ten of her children, even the four oldest who were daughters, that they must go to college. She taught them to believe that education was the most important activity in a young person's life. Not only did it allow an individual to cultivate his or her mind and sensibilities – she liked to recall her father's fondness for the opera and his involvement with a Rhode Island opera group – but it also held the key to social mobility.

This emphasis on education and mobility made life difficult for the Bordes children. One of them, Charlotte, recalled "even in little social group circles, [French-Canadian] kids laughing at [her] French because it wasn't their French"; and she remembered that people would taunt her father because he bowed to his French wife's insistence that his daughters be rendered "useless" by being kept in school and out of the mills. When she was young, Charlotte became very angry at the taunts and somewhat disdainful – as her mother certainly was – of the dismissive attitude toward education charac-teristic of so many of Woonsocket's French-Canadians. As she grew older, though, she began to appreciate the positive qualities in these French Canadians. As a group they were remarkably free of "social climbers." They were not pretentious; they were little interested in such superficial personal characteristics as fashionable clothes or stately homes. They were simple, hardworking people, with an unusually deep commitment to their families, their religion, and their heritage.

What Charlotte Bordes had encountered in her personal life was the vast cultural abyss separating her mother and her French past from French-Canadian life in Woonsocket. Fernande's emphasis on education, self-improvement, and social mobility marked her as thoroughly bourgeois. Charles Goval, involved as a textile mill manager in the capitalist transformation of northern French society, had instilled in his daughter a fervent belief in the opportunities modern industrial society offered. He had also defined opportunity and success in personal, educational, and monetary terms. Only if individuals worked with their minds, attended college, appreciated the opera and other arts, earned substantial incomes, and owned the houses in which they lived, could they be deemed successes in life.

By this measure, most of Woonsocket's French Canadians had to be judged failures. To many French-Canadian workers, of course, the measure itself was absurd. The premodern values that still structured their lives ran counter to those associated with the industrial and bourgeois revolutions: Family and communal welfare was to them more important than individual success; spiritual well-being counted for more than material well-being; relevant knowledge came from religious instruction or practical, task-oriented training, not from an open-ended, secular process of intellectual or aesthetic inquiry; the modern world was to be escaped or endured, but not embraced.

The only time that Fernande acknowledged the validity of this French-Canadian world view was during childbirth, when she called upon her French-Canadian relatives. Her embrace of the bourgeois world of rationality, mobility, and order did not help her much in the realm of family planning. She gave birth to ten children, all at home, with her Québecois mother-in-law and aunt invariably in attendance. Although she did not much like her French-Canadian in-laws, she called on their skill and looked to them for comfort in childbirth. They were the ones who understood a woman's birthing predicament best, they were the ones to handle these precarious moments of a woman's life when she was most vulnerable. Her own mother, Virginie, ever the Frenchwoman, would never, to her granddaughter Charlotte's recollection, "get her hands dirty doing that kind of thing"; she would come later, accompanied by a doctor.[16] Though Fernande suspended her harsh feelings toward her French-Canadian in-laws during her birthing episodes, she never reconsidered her hostility toward the Québecois as a whole.

Like the Govals, many Franco-Belgians looked on their linguistic cousins with a contempt that was all too apparent to the French Canadians who worked in the French mills. The French textile magnates, through their Woonsocket representatives, might have tried to impart their bourgeois values to their workers as many American employers like Henry Ford were attempting to do through scientific management techniques and crash Americanization programs.[17] The French magnates did experiment with programs in welfare capitalism at their base facilities in Roubaix and Tourcoing.[18] But in Woonsocket they chose not to, perhaps because they regarded Woonsocket as a distant, Third World outpost where workers were to be driven, yarn was to be spun, and profit was to be made – nothing more, nothing less. Such attitudes made relations between French-Canadian workers and their French employers tense, and rendered any sustained participation by the French magnates in *la survivance* impossible. Such attitudes also opened up opportunities for another group of Franco-Belgians, the labor radicals, intent on toppling the textile magnates and the whole capitalist system along with them.

"Brave ouvrier et vaillant prolétaire"[19]

The prospect of spinning yarn without having to worry about the radical workers who formed such a formidable presence in their French mills sparked French textile magnates' initial enthusiasm for Woonsocket. But these magnates quickly ran into an unexpected skilled-worker shortage in Rhode Island that forced them to extend their recruitment of French workers beyond the ranks of those workers they knew and trusted. It did not take long for blacklisted radical workers in northern France to hear about job opportunities in Rhode Island and for them to cross the Atlantic in search of Woonsocket. The French millowners soon discovered that the labor militants who had repeatedly interrupted production in the Roubaix-Tourcoing

---

[16] Ibid.
[17] See Stephen Meyer III, *The Five Dollar Day: Labor Management and Social Control in the Ford Motor Company, 1908–1921* (Albany, N.Y., 1981).
[18] Landes, "Religion and Enterprise."
[19] Lyrics from song sung by Franco-Belgians in Woonsocket in the 1930s; sung to author by Lawrence Spitz, October 22, 1976.

mills had reappeared, like the plague, in their new transatlantic production facilities.

These radicals were, in many respects, the mirror image of the French textile magnates. They shared the textile magnates' belief in the liberating possibilities of modern, industrial society. They believed in the capitalist system's ability to generate wealth and abundance and that great social benefits would result from the application of reason and science to ever greater areas of human life. And, like the magnates, they saw in the modern era unprecedented opportunities for cultivation of individuals' intelligence and sensibilities.

They differed from the textile magnates in one crucial ideological respect, however. To their minds, it was clear that none of the advantages of modern times would be available to the masses until the capitalist system was toppled and replaced by socialism. The radicals were not entirely of a piece. Some of them adhered to a gradualist political strategy like that favored by the social democratic Belgian Workers Party. Others, however, were fascinated with the syndicalist theories gripping many younger European socialists and looked forward to a general strike of all workers that would bring the capitalist system crashing down; these sentiments were reinforced in America through encounters with members of the syndicalist Industrial Workers of the World.[20]

The Franco-Belgian radicals differed from the textile magnates, too, in their rejection of certain aspects of the bourgeois life-style. Many were mulespinners, the most highly skilled and highly paid production position in the French spinning mills both in Europe and America. Their status and income – in prosperous times reaching a

[20] On labor and radicalism in Belgium and northern France see Emil Vandevelde, *Le Parti Ouvrier Belge, 1885–1925* (Brussels, 1925); Michelle Perrot, *Les ouvriers en grève, France, 1871–1890* (Paris, 1974), 727–34; Alexandre Zévaès, *Jules Guesde, 1845–1922* (Paris, 1929), 109–27, 167; C. Willard, *Les Guesdistes: le mouvement socialiste en France, 1893–1905* (Paris, 1965); Maurice Petitcollot, *Les syndicats ouvriers de l'industrie textile dans l'arrondissement de Lille* (Lille, France, 1907), 80–145; Laurent Marty, *Chanter pour survivre: culture ouvrière, travail et techniques dans le textile Roubaix, 1850–1914* (Lille, France, 1982); Joan Scott, "Social History and the History of Socialism: French Socialist Municipalities in the 1890s," *Le mouvement social* 111 (April–June, 1980), 145–53; Judy A. Reardon, "Belgian Workers in Roubaix, France, in the Nineteenth Century" (Ph.D. dissertation, University of Maryland, 1977); William Reddy, *The Rise of Market Culture: The Textile Trade and French Society, 1750–1900* (Cambridge, U.K., 1984), 289–325. See also Leslie Page Moch, "Urban Structure, Migration and Worker Militancy: A Comparative Study of French Urbanization," in Michael Hanagan and Charles Stephenson, eds., *Proletarians and Protest: The Roots of Class Formation in an Industrializing World* (Westport, Conn., 1986), 107–26.

hefty sixty dollars a week – would have enabled them to settle in the petit-bourgeois sections of Woonsocket like Bernon. They repudiated such a life-style and everything that it implied, however, and chose to live somewhat shabbily in the working-class tenements of the Social District. They deliberately cultivated a masculinist, plebeian style that rejected the refinement, delicacy, and restraint of bourgeois life. They swore, drank, gambled at cards, and caroused.

Secular, anticlerical, and rough, these men were prone to settle disputes through fistfights rather than through calm, reasoned deliberations. The roughness of one Joseph Schmetz so disturbed Robert Guerin (son of Edmond) that he considered him a gangster.[21] Few Woonsocket employers understood that these radicals deliberately cultivated their "toughness" to mark out a way of living that stood in clear opposition to their "class enemies." Schmetz liked to tell his Woonsocket comrades about the time his fellow unionists in Verviers, Belgium, erected a huge statue of a martyred socialist, arm upraised in defiance, staring at the cathedral whose clergy had been, they believed, complicit in the socialist's murder. A worker had to show defiance and anger, Schmetz believed, in order to keep his class enemies off balance and far away from friends and family. But Schmetz also knew that defiance and anger hardly made for a solid radical political program. Underneath Schmetz's gruff exterior, as we shall see, resided one of the shrewdest and most thoughtful minds in Woonsocket.[22]

The Franco-Belgian radicals adjusted slowly and fitfully to their Woonsocket environment. The presence of French superintendents and foremen lulled them into conceiving of the New World as very much like the Old, and they were thus easily enticed into fighting, or continuing, Old World battles. None of these battles was more important than the struggle against their French foremen for control of the shopfloor.

Skirmishing between Franco-Belgian radicals and French foremen

---

[21] Interview with Robert Guerin, November 3, 1980.
[22] This collective portrait is based largely on the recollections of Woonsocket residents who once knew the Franco-Belgian radicals quite well. None of the radicals themselves, unfortunately, was still alive when I began interviewing in the 1970s. The closest relative I found was Joseph D. Schmetz, son of the most important Franco-Belgian radical in the 1930s and 1940s. Interviews with the following: Arthur Rock and Lionel Harnois, both on October 8, 1976; Joseph D. Schmetz, October 15, 1976; Lawrence Spitz, October 22, 1976, September 19–20, 1979, and August 27, 1980; Angelo Turbesi, October 9, 1980; Apostole Moussas, October 20, 1980; Leona, Leonel, and Normand Galipeau, all on October 22–23, 1980; Herve Duhamel, October 27, 1980; Robert Guerin, November 3, 1980; Ernest Gignac and Arthur Riendeau, both on June 25, 1981.

began as early as 1904 in the French mills. Between that year and 1911, at least nine strikes broke out among small groups of skilled workers at the French mills as the radicals attempted to establish their shopfloor authority over such issues as wages, working conditions, and hiring and firing. The Lafayette Worsted wool sorters walked off their jobs in 1906, refusing to work under newly installed electric lights. Alsace Worsted mulespinners struck in 1907 when management failed to keep them properly supplied with bands for their machines; they walked out again that year when one of their fellow workers was unfairly discharged. The Desurmont mulespinners told their foremen in 1909 they would not work until the piece-rate system was replaced by a fixed scale of weekly wages. The Montrose Worsted weavers demanded in 1911 that "certain windows be taken out of the mill in order to admit more air"; they struck when "the manager was unable to grant the request owing to the way the windows were constructed."[23] These thumbnail sketches of strike activity, which appeared in the annual reports of the Rhode Island Department of Labor, testify to the wide-ranging nature of the radicals' struggle for control. They also suggest that the workers and their foremen were engaged in something of a grudge match to see which side could most intimidate the other. That workers were willing to walk out over such issues as the quality of lighting, the availability of production supplies, and the number of open windows suggests that a pervasive climate of hostility and mistrust, probably carried over from Europe, dominated relations between managers and workers in Woonsocket's French mills.

The efforts of mulespinners at the French Worsted to force the firing of an unpopular foreman (in the early 1920s) testify to the highly charged state of labor relations in the French mills. Charles Tiberghien of Roubaix, the owner of the French Worsted, angrily told *Woonsocket Call* reporters in May 1922 that in the previous six months, his employees had "overstepped all bounds of the relationship between wage earner and wage payer. They have treated the mill as if it were a baseball ground: They have played ball inside the mill with bobbins, broken windows, and have really acted worse in the factory than they would in their own homes."[24] When the foreman ordered them to stop, the workers demanded that upper management replace

---

[23] Rhode Island Commissioner of Industrial Statistics (hereafter R.I. CIS), *Eighteenth Annual Report* (Providence, R.I., 1905), 273, 277; *Nineteenth Annual Report* (1906), 168; *Twentieth Annual Report* (1907), 19–24; *Twenty-First Annual Report* (1908), 1097, 1112; *Twenty-Third Annual Report* (1910), 431, 436; *Twenty-Fifth Annual Report* (1912), 182.
[24] WC, May 12, 1922.

him with someone else. Tiberghien refused, and 200 French Worsted workers walked off their jobs. The strike outraged Tiberghien, who saw it on the one hand as a fundamental challenge to his own authority and on the other as a violation of bourgeois norms of acceptable behavior. He warned the strikers that he would remove his capital from Woonsocket unless they withdrew their demands. Two months later, the strikers capitulated and voted to return to work under conditions set by Tiberghien. By that time, however, Tiberghien had filled many of their positions with mulespinners from other mills.[25]

That workers would risk their jobs by engaging in sabotage and walkouts to force the dismissal of a foreman testifies to the depth of their anger toward those who owned and controlled their industry. But it testifies also to the economic security they enjoyed because their skills were in such demand. They could afford reckless militancy; if fired from one French mill, they could easily find work at another. The world of Franco-Belgian industrial relations, though punctuated by furious fights between radicals and their employers, was strangely stable, its participants protected from the consequences of some of their more outlandish actions. In such circumstances some Franco-Belgian radicals may well have concluded that familiar, Old World patterns of capital–labor antagonism, having survived transplantation to a new continent, would last forever.[26]

Such dogged adherence to Old World ways delayed the Franco-Belgians' adaptation of their radical ideas to the social and political realities of Woonsocket. In particular, it impeded their ability to reach out to French-Canadian workers who were barely comfortable with the idea of trade unionism, let alone with displays of reckless militancy. But two developments, first Franco-Belgian involvement with American radical unions in Lawrence, Massachusetts, in the 1910s, and second the political awakening of Woonsocket's French Canadians in the 1920s, combined to pierce the balloon in which Woonsocket's Franco-Belgian radicals had been drifting and force them down to New World earth.

A Franco-Belgian community developed in Lawrence simultaneously with that in Woonsocket. Though no French capital migrated to Lawrence, some of the city's capitalists began implementing

---

[25] Ibid., May 12, June 9, and July 20, 1922.

[26] A similar kind of conflictual yet stable framework of industrial relations seems to have existed in Paterson's silk industry. See Philip Scranton, "An Exceedingly Irregular Business: Structure and Process in the Paterson Silk Industry," in Scranton, ed., *Silk City* (Newark, N.J., 1985), 35–72.

French mulespinning technology in their mills around 1900 and thus came to depend on the skilled labor of European mulespinners and worsted weavers. There, as in Woonsocket, these workers quickly developed a radical reputation. As early as 1910, the U.S. Immigration Commission noted there was "no church among them and there is not likely to be one . . . Unlike the French Canadians, but true to the traditions of their own land, they are quick to espouse the cause of trade unionism in their new home."[27]

The trade unionism that Lawrence's Franco-Belgians espoused was as American as Woonsocket's was European. No familiar European capitalists resided in Lawrence, so these workers were not tempted to replay Old World battles. On the other hand, the presence of significant numbers of other radically minded workers, most notably the syndicalist-leaning Italians, encouraged Lawrence's Franco-Belgians to fashion an American working-class identity. Their militant spirit led them away from the conservative and craft-oriented American Federation of Labor (AFL) and toward the young, radical star of the American labor movement, the Industrial Workers of the World (IWW).

A syndicalist organization founded by "Big Bill" Haywood in 1905, the IWW sought to unite all workers, irrespective of skill or ethnic origins, into "one big union" and to topple the capitalist system through an escalating series of ever larger and fiercer strikes. Over the next ten years, the IWW would inspire America's most unskilled and marginal workers – and its Bohemian intellectuals – with a vision of a world transformed by the collective struggle of the laboring poor.[28] Its most dramatic moment came in Lawrence in 1912 when thousands of previously unorganized workers, drawn from numerous skill levels and ethnic backgrounds, walked off their jobs. Few other strikes of that era so dramatized the disturbing class realities of American industrial society, and no single group of workers played a more important role in sustaining that strike through weeks of bitterly cold weather than the Franco-Belgian lodge of the Lawrence IWW. Drawing on their firsthand knowledge of the Belgian Workers Party's cooperative experiments in production and distribution, they organized kitchens that sustained 23,000 strikers and their 30,000 dependents for two months. Lawrence millowners, unnerved by

[27] U.S. Congress, Senate, Immigration Commission, *Immigrants in Industries*, Sen. Doc. 633, 61st Cong., 2nd Sess. (Washington, D.C., 1911), vol. 10, part 4, 784.
[28] Melvyn Dubofsky, *We Shall Be All: A History of the Industrial Workers of the World* (New York, 1969); Paul Brissenden, *The IWW: A History of American Syndicalism* (New York, 1919).

such resistance, capitulated to the strikers and handed the IWW its greatest victory.[29]

The IWW, however, failed to build on its victory. To the contrary, it found itself worn down by a determined employer counterattack and a vigorous Americanization campaign, designed by conservative elements in Lawrence's established ethnic communities to strip the city's immigrants of their foreign habits, thought to be the mainspring of their radical inclinations. The federal government, as it geared up for war in 1916, began aiding such local efforts, first with its demands for "100 percent Americanism" and then with its campaign to eliminate radical organizations like the IWW from American life. In 1917 and 1918, the Wobblies saw their offices raided and wrecked by government officials, their leaders rounded up and jailed, and their political philosophy declared treasonous. By 1919, the IWW had ceased to function as a viable economic or political organization. That year, a government raid shut down the IWW's only surviving Lawrence branch.[30]

The Franco-Belgians survived this period of repression by shifting their political activity underground to their ethnic lodges. They played a crucial role in another Lawrence strike that broke out in 1919 over the issue of the millowners' determination to cut workers' wages. Fifteen thousand Lawrence workers struck for more than 100 days, attracting the attention of radicals and reformers throughout the Northeast. Out of this strike came not only a 15 percent wage increase for Lawrence workers but a new radical union, the Amalgamated Textile Workers of America, ready to assume the organizing

---

[29] Dubofsky, *We Shall Be All*, 146–70; Donald B. Cole, *Immigrant City: Lawrence, Massachusetts, 1845–1921* (Chapel Hill, N.C., 1964), 188, 193; U.S. Congress, Senate, *Report on the Strike of Textile Workers in Lawrence, Massachusetts in 1912*, Sen. Doc. 870, 62nd Cong., 2nd Sess. (Washington, D.C., 1912), 11, 63, 68; Studs Terkel, *American Dreams: Lost and Found* (New York, 1980), 106–13; James Ford, *Co-operation in New England* (New York, 1913), 37–9. I am indebted to David Goldberg for this last reference.

[30] The Espionage Act (1917) and Sedition Act (1918) permitted the government to prosecute individuals or organizations whose language, in any written or oral form of communication, profaned or abused the Constitution, the flag, or the military. David M. Kennedy, *Over Here: The First World War and American Society* (New York, 1980), 76–88; John Higham, *Strangers in the Land: Patterns of American Nativism, 1860–1925* (New York, 1975), 194–263; Cole, *Immigrant City*, 195–206; Dubofsky, *We Shall Be All*, 349–468; David J. Goldberg, "The Lawrence Strike of 1919" (seminar paper, University of Pittsburgh, 1979), part I, 12; Ernest Ray Closser, "Some Day a Silent Guard: Political Prisoners and the Amnesty Issue in Post-World War I America" (senior thesis, Princeton University, 1984), 4–35; Robert K. Murray, *Red Scare: A Study in National Hysteria, 1919–1920* (Minneapolis, 1955).

work that the shattered IWW could no longer undertake. The Franco-Belgians of Lawrence sent delegates to the founding convention of the Amalgamated in New York City in April 1919 to emphasize their enthusiastic support.[31]

Once again, however, the radicals failed to consolidate their gains. Another wave of conservative patriotism, promoted by the city's merchants and conservative ethnic leaders, swept over the city and weakened support for the Amalgamated in ethnic neighborhoods. During a downturn in textile production in the early twenties, the new radical union's Lawrence branch collapsed.[32] A. J. Muste, the radical Dutch Reformed minister who had been elected leader of the Amalgamated in 1919, dejectedly withdrew from political action and sought refuge in the newly established Brookwood Labor College in bucolic Katonah, New York.[33]

The Amalgamated's collapse shortly after its 1919 victory revealed how vulnerable radicals were to the powerful, conservative currents of American society. In the 1920s, the government maintained its pressure on radicals in New England through the conviction and execution of Sacco and Vanzetti, two Italian anarchists accused of murder. At the same time many manufacturers embarked on a campaign, euphemistically called the American Plan, to eliminate independent unions from the shopfloor. Union activity in Lawrence declined to its lowest levels since the nineteenth century. Radicals found themselves persistently harassed and progressively losing influence on the shopfloor and in city politics; many lost their jobs as well.[34]

Woonsocket's Franco-Belgians closely watched the struggles of their ethnic counterparts in Lawrence. In 1913, when they initiated a

---

[31] Goldberg, "The Lawrence Strike of 1919," passim.

[32] Ibid., part 5.

[33] Jo Ann Ooiman Robinson, *Abraham Went Out: A Biography of A.J. Muste* (Philadelphia, 1981), 19–31; Nat Hentoff, *Peace Agitator: The Story of A.J. Muste* (New York, 1963), 47–72.

[34] Roberta Strauss Feuerlicht, *Justice Crucified: The Story of Sacco and Vanzetti* (New York, 1977); R.W. Dunn, *The Americanization of Labor: The Employers' Offensive Against Trade Unions* (New York, 1927); Irving Bernstein, *The Lean Years: A History of the American Worker, 1920–1933* (Boston, 1960), 45–263; James Green, *The World of the Worker: Labor in Twentieth-Century America* (New York, 1980), 100–32; Robert H. Zieger, *Republicans and Labor, 1919–1929* (Lexington, Ky., 1969), 1–26; David Montgomery, *The Fall of the House of Labor: The Workplace, the State, and American Labor Activism, 1865–1925* (Cambridge, U.K., 1987), 370–464. On the decline of Lawrence radicalism see David J. Goldberg, "Immigrants, Intellectuals and Industrial Unions: The 1919 Textile Strikes and the Experience of the Amalgamated Textile Workers of America in Passaic and Paterson, New Jersey and Lawrence, Massachusetts" (Ph.D. dissertation, Columbia University, 1983), 259–69.

mulespinner strike that shut down the French Worsted, and again in 1919, when they led out 2,300 workers – skilled and unskilled – from the city's French spinning mills, they patterned confrontations with their employers on the models Lawrence radicals had set.[35] The Woonsocket confrontations were, in both cases, but faint echoes of the Lawrence battles; neither the IWW nor the Amalgamated ever established an organization with any clout in Woonsocket. Precisely because their conflicts were relatively minor and the institutional presence of radical unions so weak, however, the Woonsocket radicals were spared the crushing counterattack employers and Americanizers visited upon the Lawrence radicals. They benefited, too, from the unwillingness of Woonsocket's French-Canadian elite to use an Americanization campaign to root out the radical dissenters in its community. Woonsocket's radicals thus entered the 1920s with morale higher than their Lawrence counterparts, and they would eventually demonstrate a far greater capacity than that of Lawrence's IWW and Amalgamated veterans to absorb lessons from the 1910s struggles and to fashion a new, more enduring kind of radical politics.

First, however, they had to envision an alternative to the powerful legacy of the relentlessly confrontational Old World style of labor conflict they still espoused. That they tried to establish a recklessly radical union, the Worsted Spinners Organization of Woonsocket, in the wake of the bitter demise of the IWW and Amalgamated in Lawrence is testimony to the resilience of their belief in the impregnable character of their insular Franco-Belgian world.[36]

The apparently sudden militancy French-Canadian workers displayed in the Manville Jenckes strike of 1927 shattered that belief. From the French-Canadian perspective, of course, there was nothing sudden about this strike. The previous ten years had witnessed the fragmentation of their community's ethnic elite, economic hardship for the thousands working in the city's cotton textile industry, and the slow but unmistakable cohering of an ethnic working-class presence. But the Franco-Belgians, living in their own ethnic bubble, had been slow to comprehend these developments. The strike of 1927 caught them unaware and unprepared: It seemed suddenly that the climactic struggle between capital and labor in Woonsocket they had been anticipating for twenty years was about to unfold without them.

---

[35] R.I. CIS, *Twenty-Seventh Annual Report* (1914), 117–18, and *Thirty-Third Annual Report* (1921), 191–6; WC, July 24, 29, and August 23, 1913, January 27 through March 11, 1919, passim, and March 18, 1919.

[36] On the obscure Worsted Spinners Organization see WC, August 7, 1922; interviews with Apostole Moussas, October 20, 1980, and Ernest Gignac, June 25, 1981.

Many hastily shed their remaining affection for bold, reckless confrontation and joined local 1580 of the United Textile Workers, a craft local of worsted mulespinners. Although this move was a minor event in the course of the losing struggle against Manville Jenckes, drawing no press attention, its consequences for organized labor and industrial relations in Woonsocket would soon prove momentous. This can best be grasped through the personal odyssey and writings of one Belgian radical, Joseph Schmetz.

The Americanization of Joseph Schmetz

Joseph Schmetz, the most important labor leader in Woonsocket from the late 1920s through the early 1940s, was born in 1893 in Verviers, a center of woolen and worsted manufacture in eastern Belgium. A mulespinner, trade-union militant, and Belgian Workers Party sympathizer from the time he was a young man, he fled war-ravaged Belgium in 1919 along with his wife and two children. Toronto was his first stop – a local manufacturer had advanced the funds for Schmetz's overseas travel against future earnings – Buffalo his second, and Lawrence his third.[37] Settling into Lawrence's community of French and Belgian textile workers in the early 1920s, Schmetz learned as much as he could about the triumphs and defeats of the IWW and the Amalgamated. The industrial unionism and rank-and-file sovereignty that so characterized these two radical organizations deeply impressed him – neither had been particularly important in his labor experience in Verviers – and he would soon make them guiding principles of his own experiments in textile unionism.

Schmetz seems to have absorbed the lessons of the Lawrence radicals' defeats more slowly. He arrived in Lawrence eager to throw himself into radical activity and convinced that the New World, with its much-vaunted tradition of political freedom, would allow him to say whatever he pleased and to join any kind of organization without penalty. His starry-eyed vision of America lost a good deal of its luster in 1925, when strike activity cost him his job and earned him a place on the city's notorious blacklist. Political liberty in America, he learned, did not extend to the workplace. The only liberty now available to him, if he wished to continue working as a mulespinner,

---

[37] Interviews with Joseph D. Schmetz, October 15, 1976, and Lawrence Spitz, October 22, 1976; WC, August 30, 1941; U.S. Department of Justice, "Petitions for Naturalization," vol. 28, no. 5728, Providence Superior Court (hereafter PSC), Providence, R.I. On labor and socialism in Verviers, see Laurent Dechesne, *L'avènement du régime syndical à Verviers* (Paris, 1908); Léon Delsinne, *Le mouvement syndical en Belgique* (Paris, 1936), 99–112.

was the freedom to move to another city where manufacturers would not know or care about his political beliefs. Some of Lawrence's blacklisted radicals had traditionally sought work in Woonsocket, an eighty-mile train ride to the southwest. Schmetz followed suit, up-rooting his family for the fifth time in six years and settling into a Franco-Belgian community, situated along the Social District's northern rim. Schmetz immediately got himself hired at the French Worsted and joined the cadre who had managed to keep alive the radical Worsted Spinners Organization, but he had barely started work when this union suffered its final defeat in a strike against Tiberghien. Schmetz moved on to the Jules Desurmont spinning mill where, in 1927, as part of the tardy Franco-Belgian effort to play a role in the UTW-led protests at Manville Jenckes, he joined the UTW's mulespinning local 1580.[38]

At first glance, the retreat of Schmetz and others to the UTW appears to mark an abandonment of their radical project. UTW leaders, after all, preached accommodation to capitalism, not resistance to it. Professing to be a union for workers "of all crafts and degrees of skills," it allowed craft locals to dominate its affairs and repeatedly failed in its efforts to organize the unskilled.[39] Moreover, it had embarked on a campaign to increase the already substantial distance separating it in public eyes from the radical industrial unions. In an age of Americanization campaigns designed to strip immigrants of their foreign habits and of American plans intended to eliminate independent unions from the shopfloor, the UTW portrayed itself as the union of "God and Country." It pledged its allegiance to American institutions and condemned the efforts of "outlaw" unions, such as the IWW and the Amalgamated, to overthrow the American government or tear up the Constitution.[40] The UTW had always opposed the aims and tactics of radical unions but never had it

---

[38] Interviews with Joseph D. Schmetz, October 15, 1976, Lawrence Spitz, October 22, 1976, and Ernest Gignac, June 25, 1981; *The Textile Worker* November 1925, 8; Robert Maurice Mooney, "The Origins, Nature, Internal and External Operations of the Industrial Trades Union of America" (M.A. thesis, Catholic University of America, 1947), 7–11.

[39] Thomas McMahon, "United Textile Workers of America," Workers Education Organization Series, no. 2 (New York, 1926), 53; Herbert Lahne, *The Cotton Mill Worker* (New York, 1944), 189–215; Robert R.R. Brooks, "The United Textile Workers of America" (Ph.D. dissertation, Yale University, 1935); Richard Kelly, *Nine Lives for Labor* (New York, 1956).

[40] *The Textile Worker*, 1920–1925 passim. The Amalgamated found itself pegged by bosses and conservative unions alike as "un-American" despite its efforts to emphasize its own American character. See Goldberg, "Immigrants, Intellectuals and Industrial Unions," 230–3.

made its opposition so public and so vicious.[41] Its fear of being tagged with a radical label led the UTW, by 1925, to eschew all political involvement and to stress the very limited and American nature of its one aim: to make working and living conditions "wholesome and comfortable for American workers and their families."[42]

If the timidity and antiradicalism of the UTW had meant acquiescence to any employer demand for the sake of survival, radical unionists like Schmetz could not have remained members for long. In fact, however, northern textile employers were so hostile to working-class demands in the depressed economic climate of the 1920s that even moderate bread-and-butter UTW demands for shorter hours and higher wages generated bitter class conflict.[43] As previously noted, the UTW played a major role in a nine-month general strike of textile workers that swept through Rhode Island in 1922. Its ability to organize eleven Woonsocket locals between 1924 and 1927, and to provide financial and organizational support to the Manville Jenckes strikers in 1927, further demonstrated its growing prowess.[44]

The Franco-Belgian radicals drew inspiration from UTW successes. They thought that this AFL union, for all its flaws, could offer them a sanctuary while they regrouped and determined how to sustain a more ambitious union movement in American society. As they settled into their new union – Schmetz spent four years in Local 1580 – they began to appreciate the UTW's stability. From the secure, high ground of historical perspective, mere survival is easily judged a modest accomplishment. But the radicals of the 1920s, who had seen the IWW and the Amalgamated rise and fall and who had lost their own jobs for political activity, learned to value survival. Even as Schmetz and others grew frustrated by the UTW's bureaucratic inefficiency, its failure to supply promised organizers and benefits, and its inability to realize its professed commitment to industrial unionism, the radicals gained some respect for the union's moderate tone, its limited aims, and its insistence on its essentially American character. Thus when Schmetz and a small group of mulespinners

---

[41] See, for example, *The Textile Worker*, March 1920, 550–1.

[42] Ibid., October 1925, 395–6.

[43] The same circumstances forced the United Mine Workers into battle, undermining the leadership's conservative, accommodationist strategy. See Melvyn Dubofsky and Warren Van Tine, *John L. Lewis: A Biography* (New York, 1977), 69–178.

[44] Susan E. Jaffee, "Ethnic Working Class Protest: The Textile Strike of 1922 in Rhode Island" (honors thesis, Brown University, 1974); *The Textile Worker*, 1924–1927, passim, and July 1927, 234–6; Edmund J. Brock, *The Background and Recent Status of Collective Bargaining in the Cotton Industry in Rhode Island* (Washington, D.C., 1942), 88–105.

seceded from Local 1580 in 1931 to form the Independent Textile Union (ITU), denouncing the UTW for its craft domination and financial sloppiness, they issued a constitution drawing heavily on the political orientation of the UTW.[45] Unlike the constitution of the radical Amalgamated, the ITU constitution scrupulously avoided references to "class struggle," the "means of production," and a "workers party."[46] The union justified its existence in more moderate terms, declaring simply the need for an organization capable of saving the country from economic ruin and securing social peace. The union would not promote revolution; in fact, it would steer clear of all political involvements. It would simply "attempt to secure wages and good working conditions for all its members," and hopefully promote "the well-being of all conscientious people."[47]

A fierce commitment to industrial unionism and to rank-and-file sovereignty was the only clue in this constitution to the radical heritage of the union founders.[48] "One union for all workers," declared the founders in their declaration of principles.[49] In their constitution they made clear that all workers in a single place of work, regardless of occupation, were to be members of the same local. Craft workers would not be allowed to form separate locals, as they did in the UTW, nor would they be granted other privileges.[50] The governing structure established by the constitution reveals a concern for financial solvency and for efficiency in day-to-day operations that drew heavily on the business orientation of conservative craft unions.[51] This structure was meant, however, to insure that effective power in the ITU would reside in the rank and file, not in the detached, bureaucratic leadership that so burdened the UTW. Each local reserved the right to strike if its grievances were not satisfactorily addressed by the employer. No union money could be expended without the approval of the entire membership. None of the four union members elected to Executive Board positions and charged

---

[45] ITU, *Constitution and By-Laws* (Woonsocket, R.I., 1933).
[46] "Constitution of the Amalgamated Textile Workers of America" (mimeo, Baker Library, Harvard University, n.d.).
[47] ITU, *Constitution*, 1.
[48] Robert Mooney was not aware of the radical origins of the ITU though he wrote his masters' thesis on the union. See Mooney, "The Origin . . . of the Industrial Trades Union," 11–14.
[49] ITU, *Labor Review, 1931–1942* (Woonsocket, R.I., 1942), 7–9
[50] ITU, *Constitution*, 5–8. For comparison with the UTW, see UTW, *Constitution and By-Laws, Revised September, 1928* (New York, 1928), passim.
[51] See Brooks, "The United Textile Workers of America," for history of conservative craft unions in the textile industry.

with the administration of union affairs between union meetings drew a salary; all, in a striking departure from UTW practice, continued to labor full-time in the mills.[52] Such a commitment to rank-and-file sovereignty reveals how much the spirit of Lawrence's radical textile unions lived on in the ITU.

The attempt of Schmetz and other radical trade unionists to clothe the radical spirit of the IWW and Amalgamated in the plain, conservative garb of the UTW was a tacit admission that an explicitly radical labor organization could not survive in American society. Twenty years of defeat had led Schmetz and his radical colleagues to jettison their socialist rhetoric and focus their efforts on establishing an industrial union that would endure. But it would be a misreading to cast these radical Europeans as AFL bread-and-butter unionists. Schmetz remained a socialist at heart. He developed close ties with prominent Rhode Island socialists in the 1920s that he maintained into the 1930s.[53] Moreover, in 1936, after the ITU was firmly established in Woonsocket, Schmetz began to reveal his radicalism in union publications with talk of "a new economic order which would substitute planning for chaos, service for profit, and abundance for poverty."[54]

The program he would outline in the 1930s far surpassed the ideas for reform entertained by conservative AFL unionists. "Any action," he wrote, "must be based upon a fundamental program striking at the roots of the profits system."[55] Workers, of course, had to develop powerful unions to defend their economic interests and to gain the self-respect and confidence necessary to strive for "peace, security and domestic happiness."[56] But, he argued, they also had to bring "a measure of justice and humanitarianism into the administration of all institutions, economic and political, which affect the lives of countless people."[57] Schmetz wanted workers to establish a political party to promote welfare legislation for the unemployed and unorganized, the weak and disabled. He stressed the need for cooperatives that would enable workers to buy their goods more cheaply and initiate the replacement of "a profit economy with one based on service." And he wanted unions to sponsor a variety of educational and recreational activities, ranging from schools to newspapers to drama

[52] ITU, *Constitution*, 6–8.
[53] Interview with Lawrence Spitz, October 22, 1976.
[54] *ITU News*, July 1936, 7.
[55] Ibid.
[56] Ibid., August 1936, 1, 17.
[57] Ibid.

groups to sports leagues, in which workers would learn about themselves and each other and begin to envision the possibility of establishing a radically different system of social relations.[58]

Schmetz's emphasis on social-welfare legislation, cooperation, and education marks him as a social democrat, a radical who believed in a reformist road to socialism. "We are not yet strong enough, the world is not yet ready enough for a drastic revision of customs," he wrote.[59] He disagreed with those radicals, including the Wobblies and some among the Franco-Belgians, who believed that the working class might suddenly rise up, throw off its chains, and abolish capitalism. He was of the opinion that "the working class is ordinarily conservative and decisions to strike are usually taken after long deliberations."[60] Moreover, many workers, especially those who suffered most from capitalist exploitation, did not always act in their best interests. The "bitterness which eats away at the heart of a man who feels himself the victim of circumstances," he noted, "renders him easy prey to Fascism and Nazism."[61] Schmetz's assessment of the worker's vulnerability in capitalist society might have induced him to gravitate toward the communists, who offered the omniscient vanguard party as a corrective to the myopia of the working class. But he was too much a democrat at heart to embrace communism. He insisted that his program for a comprehensive and gradual social movement was the only acceptable road to socialism. Unions, cooperatives, recreational leagues, social services, and educational programs were all schools in which workers would discover the true potential of human society, gain experience in the practice of cooperation and democracy, and prepare themselves for "the drastic revision in customs" demanded by socialism.[62]

Schmetz's vision of socialism was close to that offered by the Socialist Party of America. Norman Thomas, the party's leader from 1928, called for a gradual, democratic approach to radical change. But Schmetz's program for a comprehensive social movement could not have derived its chief inspiration from a socialist party that poured so much of its energy into a single arena of struggle, electoral politics.[63]

---

[58] Ibid., March 1937, 2.
[59] Ibid., September 1936, 1.
[60] Ibid., November 1936, 2.
[61] Ibid., July 1936, 3.
[62] Ibid.
[63] On 1920s Socialist Party, see David Shannon, *The Socialist Party of America: A History* (New York, 1955), 150–203; Bernard K. Johnpoll, *Pacifist's Progress: Norman Thomas and the Decline of American Socialism* (Chicago, 1970), 32–86; James Weinstein, *The Decline of Socialism in America* (New York, 1967), 234–339.

Rather, his program drew heavily on the dreams and accomplishments of the socialist party of Schmetz's native land, Le Parti Ouvrier Belge or Belgian Workers Party (BWP).

The BWP, by the late 1920s, had compiled a record of electoral triumphs that made Belgium look like the promised land to America's band of wandering socialists. Even more impressively, it had established a comprehensive network of unions, cooperatives, fraternal societies, and schools involving 700,000 Belgian working men and women. A Belgian socialist noted in 1929 that the BWP "grasps or tries to grasp man entirely at every age, and in all manifestations of his existence. Belgian workmen practice socialism at every moment. . . in their cooperative, their trade union, their mutuelle, when they eat bread, when they buy shoes, when they make sport, take on an insurance against fire or try to make their savings fructify." The party, he concluded, formed virtually "a state within a state."[64] The Belgian socialists' record was so impressive that the New York state legislators who authored the antiradical Lusk report of 1920 could not help praising the "wonderfully strong organization of the Belgian party" and the "wonderful success" of its cooperative experiments.[65] Schmetz hoped to follow the BWP plan of involving workers in a comprehensive network of institutions that would encourage them to practice a radically different set of social relations.[66]

Thus Schmetz, while accommodating his union to the realities of American politics, clung to the radical vision that had motivated his labor organizing and militance since his first exposure to trade unionism and politics in Belgium. But what would he call this radical vision? If explicitly socialist language and politics were beyond the bounds of American political discourse, how would he convey to union members the fact that the ITU was more than just a bread-and-butter organization? Once again, Schmetz's writings in union publications in 1936 and 1937 are revealing. As frequent as his evocations of a Belgian socialist vision were his references to the political institutions and heritage of the American people. He referred constantly to the Declaration of Independence, the Constitution, the Revolution, and quoted freely from Jefferson, Franklin, Lincoln, and Daniel Webster.[67] Despite his anger at the prevailing judicial practice

---

[64] Louis Pierard, *Belgian Problems Since the War* (New Haven, Conn., 1929), 41–2.

[65] State of New York, Senate, Joint Legislative Committee Investigating Seditious Activities, *Revolutionary Radicalism: Its History, Purpose, and Tactics with an Exposition and Discussion of the Steps Being Taken and Required to Curb It* (Albany, N.Y., 1920), vol I., 114.

[66] On the BWP, see Emil Vandevelde, *Le Parti Ouvrier Belge*.

[67] *ITU News*, 1936–1937, passim.

that had deprived him repeatedly of his civil liberties, Schmetz never lost his admiration for American political traditions. He still marveled at the American republican system that had bestowed the vote on American workingmen almost one hundred years before the Belgian workers secured universal manhood suffrage. And he was "much impressed with the character of a people" who had saved thousands of Belgians from starvation through food relief programs during and after World War I.[68]

But Schmetz expressed more than a greenhorn's pride in his new country of residence. Following the example of UTW unionists, he was identifying unionism with the American political heritage to legitimate the existence of a working-class organization. He stressed how deeply rooted the concept of union was in American history. "E Pluribus Unum," he wrote, was the basis of "the greatest union that ever was, or ever will be."[69] Just as the American Revolutionists, through the union of thirteen colonies, withstood European attack, so too American workers, through their union, would "be as American men and women should be, possessors of self-respect in an industrial democracy."[70] Though it is impossible to determine exactly when Schmetz began writing in this language of Americanism, it seems plausible that he gained his first sustained exposure to it during the years of his UTW affiliation. Schmetz clearly hoped to use such language to push beyond the minimalist trade union goals of the UTW and establish the legitimacy of his social democratic agenda. Would the language of Americanism prove supple enough to allow such a radical effort to succeed? Schmetz understood the difficulty of the task. But he believed that by applying the concepts of independence, rights, and democracy to the realm of the economy he might indeed develop an Americanized radicalism.

Schmetz's ideological odyssey, from the time he left Belgium in 1919 until he founded the ITU in 1931, was as wide-ranging as the peregrinations that took him from Belgium to Toronto, Buffalo, Lawrence, and Woonsocket. His odyssey may be understood as an attempt to find a style of organization and a style of politics that would allow him to realize in his new home the socialist vision of the BWP. His contact with veterans of the IWW and the Amalgamated instilled in him a passionate commitment to industrial unionism and rank-and-file sovereignty. At the same time the defeats these radical organizations suffered led him to emulate the moderate tone and political nonpartisanship of the UTW. He also found in the UTW's

---

[68] Interview with Lawrence Spitz, October 22, 1976; WC, August 30, 1942.
[69] ITU News, October 1936, 1.
[70] Ibid., August 1936, 9.

language of Americanism the ingredients of a new radical language that would, unlike Marxism, fit within the parameters of American political debate. His ITU, then, was a bold venture to redefine working-class radicalism in a language that all Americans would understand and accept.

The leap from Belgian socialist to American radical, while great, was not so difficult that we should regard it as an act of desperation. Socialism and the language of Americanism, in fact, shared a great deal. The concept of citizenship stood at the very heart of Belgian socialism, and the struggle for universal manhood suffrage was an issue around which BWP leaders had long mobilized a good deal of their support. Notions of liberty, democracy, and individual rights were intrinsic to a discourse on citizenship, and any Belgian socialist who took those concepts seriously was bound to be intrigued by both their ubiquitous usage and their particular meanings in the United States. The ease with which an immigrant like Schmetz, whose formal schooling barely extended beyond elementary school, identified with American forefathers and quoted from the writings of figures like Thomas Jefferson and Daniel Webster suggests how familiar the core ideas in American politics must have seemed to him.

The language of Americanism resembled socialist doctrines in another way as well: The progressive dimension of Americanism, like a key socialist perspective, embraced modernity. Both stressed the value of science and rationality and the ability of "man" to master his environment. With such mastery would come economic abundance and an unprecedented opportunity for each individual to develop fully his or her natural abilities and cultivate fully his or her senses. The language of Americanism often lent itself, of course, to non-socialist, even antisocialist, plans for achieving such mastery, but such divergences should not be allowed to obscure the deeply progressive streak present in both Americanist and socialist discourse.

Schmetz's facility with the language of Americanism suggests that it may have sounded strange to those Woonsocket French Canadians who were still adhering to the prescriptions of their premodern culture. But few French Canadians would have been unfamiliar with that discourse in the 1920s, sixty years after French-Canadian settlement in Woonsocket began. More and more were showing interest in it as the tumultuous events of the 1920s – ongoing Americanization campaigns and economic decline – made it clear to French-Canadian workers how imperative it was that they acquire and then exercise their citizenship rights. We cannot know whether Schmetz already perceived in the late 1920s that the upswing in French-Canadian participation in unions and their movement into the Democratic Party signified a growing, if ambivalent, desire on their part to "be American." But by the mid-1930s, he had premised his entire strategy for building a successful working-class movement on that crucial fact. He would try to accomplish what the French textile magnates had declined to attempt: yank Woonsocket's French-Canadian working class into the modern world. And he would try to do it in a way that contributed to the triumph of his radical Americanist message over more conservative varieties.

Joseph Schmetz's efforts to Americanize his radicalism may be understood as an assimilative or acculturative process, though of a distinctly limited sort. Schmetz did not intend his Americanization campaign to encompass all sorts of private behavior: what language a family used in the home, what social values parents taught their children, the ethnic origins of the spouses that children, once grown, married, and so on. For Schmetz, Americanization was a process meant for the public sphere: He wanted to acquire the language of Americanism because he saw it as an instrument of working-class power. During his period of "language acquisition" he demonstrated no parallel effort to acquire American patterns of private life. He lived among French Canadians and Franco-Belgians on Diamond Hill Road, the northern border of the Social District. He spent a good deal of his leisure activities with friends from Belgium, speaking French and engaging in activities – drinking, card-playing, and the telling of tall tales – long characteristic of a Belgian working-class world. In the lighter moments of political work, he and fellow Franco-Belgians delighted in introducing French Canadians and other Woonsocket workers to the revolutionary songs of their European youth. These remained such a vital part of Woonsocket union culture through the late 1930s and early 1940s that a Providence-born Jewish radical who joined the ITU in 1937 could still sing them from memory forty years later. In his home, Schmetz and his Belgian wife, Marie, did not insist that their two children escape their ethnic pasts or their working-class presents: Their daughter would marry a Woonsocket Belgian and their son would remain part of working-class Woonsocket for his entire life.[71]

Such a balance between a public American life and a private Franco-Belgian life would not, in the long term, be easy to maintain. Efforts to appropriate the language of Americanism and to gain power in the real world of politics would step up the pressure to Americanize private life as well. If Schmetz wanted his union

[71] Interviews with Joseph D. Schmetz, October 15, 1976, and Lawrence Spitz, October 22, 1976, and September 19–20, 1979.

members to regard seriously his reverence for the Pilgrims – and accept his argument that ITU unionists were simply fulfilling the ideals that the Pilgrims had held dear – then Thanksgiving had to become an important day of celebration in Woonsocket working-class homes. If he wanted his union's power to endure beyond the 1930s, he would have to participate in the administrative-bureaucratic machinery set up by the American state in the 1930s to protect working-class rights, and adhere to the kinds of bourgeois values like the impartiality of the law, the superiority of legal reasoning over other forms of thinking, and deference to bureaucratic expertise that he had long ago rejected. And if he wanted French-Canadian workers to subscribe to his radical American dreams, he might need to carry his public Americanization efforts into their private worlds in order to break their vestigial ties to conservative elements of French-Canadian culture. In the 1920s, however, a radical like Schmetz did not worry much about such dilemmas. He likely drew comfort from the knowledge that he could enjoy in his private Franco-Belgian world a respite from the difficult public task – transforming his socialism into the language of Americanism – he had undertaken; and he no doubt drew strength from the knowledge that he could define an American identity for himself and his fellow unionists without letting that American identity thoroughly define him.

Schmetz did not embark on this ambitious political venture alone. More than twenty other French and Belgian radicals became leaders of the ITU. Eight worked alongside Schmetz in the mule room of the Jules Desurmont, and another thirteen were scattered throughout the spinning and weaving rooms of the city's worsted mills.[72] A majority of these trade unionists came from Verviers or from the Roubaix-Tourcoing region in France.[73] Like Schmetz, they were radical, skilled workers who had left their European homes between 1905 and 1919 in search of economic opportunity and political liberty. Like Schmetz, they traveled widely before settling in Woonsocket. One ITU leader spent time in Brussels, one in Leeds, and a number in Lawrence.[74]

[72] The identification of these individuals involved two steps: first, compilation of lists of ITU leaders from oral histories and in-house accounts of ITU history: second, the search for the petitions of naturalization (in PSC) and the 1935 Rhode Island Manuscript Census cards (in Rhode Island State Archives, Providence, R.I.) for individual leaders. Both the petitions and census cards indicate the occupation and country of birth of the individual.

[73] Of the seventeen Frenchmen and Belgians whose petitions for naturalization I have found, ten were born or lived in either Verviers or Roubaix.

[74] See the naturalization papers of Leopold Herpels, Jean Schneiders, and Lucien Dumalin in U.S. Department of Justice, "Petitions for Naturalization," vol. 29, 5862, vol. 11, 2534, vol. 21, 7680, PSC.

The most seasoned traveler in the group, Anatole Goethals, was born in Roubaix in 1897, left Paris for Lawrence in 1919, returned to Paris sometime before 1926, and then returned to Lawrence in 1928 before settling in Woonsocket in 1929.[75] These itinerant radicals may well have played a crucial role in helping Woonsocket's more settled Franco-Belgian radicals break out of their hermetic European enclave and adapt their political strategies to the economic and cultural realities of an American textile city. Those who had spent time in Lawrence and had lived among IWW and Amalgamated veterans there were especially important in this regard.

Not every Franco-Belgian radical followed Schmetz's lead in seeking ways to Americanize their radicalism. Some became conservative unionists, and some dropped out of the labor movement altogether to join the petit-bourgeois stratum in Woonsocket's Franco-Belgian community, which owned shops or filled the supervisory posts in the mills. Still others frowned on Schmetz's course as too moderate and would later seek a return to the more radical unionism of the 1910s and early 1920s. But many in the late 1920s and early 1930s accepted Schmetz's leadership and wholeheartedly supported his efforts to develop a union whose structure and ideology might serve as a vehicle for mass organization and socialist transformation.

The Franco-Belgian founders of the ITU, skilled at work and radical in politics, closely resemble the pioneers of industrial union initiatives in other industries in the 1930s. The founders of local unions in the heavy manufacturing plants of General Electric and Westinghouse, for example, also belonged to an elite stratum of their industry's work force. They, too, had either emigrated from areas of northwestern Europe or were the children of parents who had. They had worked at their jobs for years and had long been involved in union activities. Many had also been members of the Socialist and Communist parties. These characteristics sharply distinguished the union founders from the rest of the electrical industry's work force, which was heavily southern and eastern European in origin and overwhelmingly semi-skilled and unskilled with almost no history of union involvement or support for radicalism.[76]

In attempting to account for the centrality of skilled, radical unionists to the 1930s organizing efforts in the electrical industry, Ronald Schatz has pointed to the confidence that skilled workers

[75] Ibid., vol. 81, 11563.
[76] Ronald W. Schatz, *The Electrical Workers: A History of Labor at General Electric and Westinghouse, 1923–1960* (Urbana, Ill., 1983), 80–104.

gained from their power in the production process, their experience in union and political organizing, and their ideological commitment to industrial unionism. All these factors help explain the prominence of the French and Belgians in leadership positions in Woonsocket, but there is an additional factor as well. The Franco-Belgians, trying to build a successful working-class movement in America, were willing to adjust their politics to the circumstances of American life. When their radical unions collapsed in the twenties and the moderate UTW demonstrated surprising success, the French and Belgian militants revised their organizing strategies. They dropped their radical rhetoric, restrained their reckless militancy, and poured their energy into establishing a nonpartisan industrial union. Their industrial union would hopefully accomplish what no other labor organization in America had done before: the involvement of the masses of textile workers in a labor movement with the power to alter, in fundamental ways, the conditions of work and life. Although the socialist goals of these union founders were clearly subordinated to trade union aims, they were not discarded. Schmetz clung to his vision of a society based on service, not profit, and began reformulating it in the Americanist language that most Americans would understand and accept. The democratic and progressive strains imbedded in the language of Americanism, so familiar to a radical steeped in Belgian socialism, facilitated this reformulation. Through such efforts on the part of Woonsocket radicals, a new kind of union, the Independent Textile Union, appeared in 1931. This industrial union, militant but nonpartisan, ambitious but pragmatic, radical but deeply American, would appeal to French-Canadian textile workers struggling to regain some sense of control over their labor and their community, and serve as the vehicle for the greatest organizing drive in the city's history.

The success of that organizing drive in the 1930s would mark the end of the ethnictown era of Woonsocket history. The label "ethnictown" connotes not simply a town full of ethnics. It connotes as well a town in which ethnic relationships, ethnic values and ideas, and ethnic societies structured social life. In the first three decades of the twentieth century, a Woonsocket individual's ethnic identity shaped, to a large extent, his or her world of friends and acquaintances, his or her personal dreams, and his or her political ambitions. This reality applied as much to the Franco-Belgians as it did to the French Canadians even though the two groups lived in remarkably different ethnic worlds. This ethnic reality came to an end in the 1920s, as external political and cultural forces shattered Woonsocket's cultural insularity and as external economic pressures (and the consequent decline of the city's cotton textile industry) pushed issues of class to the fore with ever greater urgency. The consequent collapse of Woonsocket's two ethnic orders, one controlled by a middle-class French-Canadian elite and the other by an upper-class French elite, would prove as vital a precondition to the working-class successes of the 1930s as would the 1929 collapse of the nation's economic order. Even before the Great Depression struck, class divisions began superseding ethnic divisions as the political fault lines in Woonsocket society.[77] The events of the 1930s would hasten that restructuring process to completion.

[77] For a similar argument made in connection with a very different kind of city (and relying on very different kinds of historical material), see Olivier Zunz, *The Changing Face of Inequality: Urbanization, Industrial Development, and Immigrants in Detroit, 1880–1920* (Chicago, 1982).

Part II

The emergence of an industrial union, 1929–1936

3   *Beginnings, 1929–1934*

The Great Depression remains, in popular consciousness, a cataclysmic event that very nearly destroyed the country's social fabric. The most popular visual images of those years portray a society of unrelieved poverty and gloom: endless lines of stooped men waiting for a handout of old bread and thin soup; sprawling acres of dilapidated wooden boxes and scrap metal sheds on abandoned city lots that offered the unemployed their only shelter; and chronically undernourished children in tattered rags standing barefoot on parched earth. Many statistics seem to ground these impressions in "objective facts": From 1929 to 1932, for example, private investment plunged from $1 billion to barely one-third of $1 billion, while unemployment shot up from 5 to 25 percent. New York, boasting one of the highest relief rates in the country, offered its thousands of indigent families only $2.39 a week.[1]

Recent scholarship has suggested, however, that such portraits of national devastation obscure a much more complicated picture of diverging economic fortunes. Some industries showed surprising vigor after the initial financial crash while others seemed incapable of recovery. Such uneven impact often provoked within the industrialist community bitter disagreements over political strategies: Industrialists split on whether or not to support the New Deal in general, whether or not to accept particular pieces of legislation such as the National Industrial Recovery Act of 1933 or the National Labor Relations Act of 1935.[2] Understanding political responses to the Great Depression, not just among industrialists but among workers as well, requires therefore that we set the popular image of national calamity to one side and inquire into the particular experiences of individual industries and groups of workers. Executing such an analysis for

---

[1] William E. Leuchtenberg, *Franklin D. Roosevelt and the New Deal, 1932–1940* (New York, 1963), 1–40; Robert S. McElvaine, *The Great Depression: America, 1929–1941* (New York, 1984), 72–94; Malcolm Cowley, *The Dream of the Golden Mountains: Remembering the 1930s* (Harmondsworth, U.K., 1964), 21–30, 94–105.
[2] See Thomas Ferguson, "From Normalcy to New Deal: Industrial Structure, Party Competition, and American Public Policy in the Great Depression," *International Organization* 38 (Winter 1984), 41–94; Michael A. Bernstein, *The Great Depression: Delayed Recovery and Economic Change in America, 1929–1939* (Cambridge, U.K., 1987).

Woonsocket is crucial to understanding why this city, and not Lawrence or Fall River or New Bedford, became during these years the
bastion of textile unionism in New England.

The peculiarities of an industry

At first glance, the Depression seems to have devastated Woonsocket
industry. The value of the city's manufactures fell by almost half from
1929 to 1936, from $81 million to $43 million.[3] The number of jobs
available in manufacturing shrank from 15,000 in early 1930 to 11,000
in 1935, a loss of almost 30 percent. As late as 1935, less than half the
city's wage earners had full-time employment: 30 percent worked
only part-time – nine months of the year or less – and 20 percent had
no work at all.[4] No worker, not even the most highly skilled, could
depend any longer on steady employment. The family strategy of
relying on three to four wage earners to minimize the risks of economic adversity was viable no longer. The thousands in need of relief
had few places to turn, and the small amounts of charitable funds
parishes made available were quickly exhausted. Only one employer
in the city, Edmond Guerin of American Paper Tube, attempted to
relieve distress by distributing clothes, coal, and food to his employees.[5] The inauguration of the Federal Emergency Relief Administration in 1933 eased conditions for some workers; by 1935, 1,101
or about one-fourth of the unemployed were being paid for relief
work. But this program still left most unemployed workers without
assistance.[6]

[3] U.S. Department of Commerce, Bureau of the Census, *Fifteenth Census of the United
States, 1930, Manufactures* (Washington, D.C.) vol. III, 473, and *Biennial Census of
Manufactures, 1937* (Washington, D.C.), part I, 1573.
[4] Rhode Island (hereafter R.I.), *Population Census of 1935* (Providence, R.I., 1936), 61–8.
The census defined the labor force as the number of "gainfully occupied" workers –
those who were accustomed to regular employment at a particular job. I revised this
definition, adding to the gainfully occupied those workers who were seeking work
but who had never held regular jobs (mostly young people). This revision increased
the size of the labor force in 1935 from 20,524 to 21,765. The unemployed figure
includes only those out of work for lack of employment, not due to physical in-
capacity or industrial disputes. The part-time figure has been computed by adding
those workers who described themselves as part-time to those who identified themselves as full-time but who worked nine months of the year or less in 1935.
[5] Interview with Robert Guerin, November 3, 1980; *Providence Journal*, November 22,
1935.
[6] R.I., *Population Census of 1935*, 62. The state set up a Free Employment Bureau to help
the unemployed find jobs, but its efforts, at least in Woonsocket, were rather inconsequential. See R.I. Department of Labor (hereafter DOL), *Annual Report* (Providence,
R.I.) 1935, 135, 190.

Table 3.1. *Number of workers employed by Woonsocket industries,*
1920–1940

Industry	1920		1925		1930		1935		1940	
	No.	%	No.	%	No.	%	No.	%	No.	%
Woolen and worsted	5709	36.8	6764	44.2	9022	60.6	7871	72.1	8790	78.2
Cotton	3750	24.2	3894	25.4	2875	19.3	1425	13.1	770	6.9
Rubber	2800	18.1	2350	15.4	1540	10.3	400	3.7	400	3.6
Machinery and tools	1900	12.3	1729	11.3	1130	7.6	695	6.4	780	6.9
Other	1341	8.7	576	3.8	330	2.2	525	4.8	500	4.5
Total[a]	15,500		15,313		14,897		10,916		11,240	

[a] Totals may exceed 100% due to rounding error.

Source: *Providence Journal Almanac: A Reference Book for the State of Rhode Island* (Providence, R.I.), 1920, 1925, 1930, 1935, 1940. The *Almanac* listed each manufacturing establishment in the state by industry. In this table, the woolen and worsted labor force includes those employed in woolen spinning, French worsted spinning, Bradford worsted spinning, woolen and worsted weaving, and wool dyeing establishments; the cotton labor force includes those employed in cotton spinning, cotton weaving, cotton plush, and cotton knitting establishments. The numbers employed in the industries must be treated as approximate; some manufacturers reported the precise number of workers employed in their establishments, while others estimated the number customarily employed. Establishments with fewer than fifty employees have not been included in these calculations.

What these aggregate statistics hide, however, is the differential impact of the Great Depression on Woonsocket's workers. The Depression struck hardest at workers employed in the three Woonsocket industries – cotton, machinery, and rubber – already ailing in the 1920s. The cotton industry had long been losing its battle to manufacture yarns and cloth as cheaply as mills in the South. The local textile machinery industry, having risen in tandem with the region's cotton industry, declined along with it. The troubles of the local rubber industry resulted from retrenchment decisions made at U.S. Rubber's corporate headquarters. Only the woolen and worsted industry, still protected from southern competition by its dependence on highly skilled labor, prospered in the 1920s. It would be the sole Woonsocket industry to survive the Depression intact.

The diverging fortunes of the various sectors of Woonsocket's economy appear in Table 3.1, which shows the numbers of persons employed in each of the city's four major industries at five-year intervals from 1920 to 1940. In 1930, the woolen and worsted industry was Woonsocket's largest, employing three of every five manufac-turing wage earners. But cotton, textile machinery, and rubber manu-facture were still important to the city's economy, providing almost 40 percent of Woonsocket's employment base. In the next ten years, this 40 percent shrank to less than 20 percent: four cotton mills, one textile machine shop, and one rubber mill shut down, costing the city 3,315 jobs. In contrast, the woolen and worsted sector rebounded from the depressed years of the early 1930s, and, by 1940, approached pre-Depression levels of employment. It thereby increased its share of Woonsocket industrial employment until it employed almost four of every five manufacturing wage earners working in the city.

The recovery of the woolen and worsted industry to which trends in employment levels point is supported by the movements in the industry's production values and wage rates charted in Figure 3.1a and b. From 1929 to 1933, the value of production and level of wages in the state's woolen and worsted industry (no local figures are available) fell sharply; in real terms, the former fell by one-third and the latter by about one-sixth. But the years 1933 to 1935 appear as years of recovery, as the real value of production and real wages reached, by 1935, their pre-Depression levels. In contrast, the data on production and wages in the state's cotton industry contained in Figure 3.2a and b, show steep, uninterrupted declines.

The divergence in the economic fortunes of the two sectors of Woonsocket's textile industry is confirmed, finally, by the rates of un-employment in each sector. Although the city's general rate of un-employment in 1935 was 20 percent, the rate among woolen and worsted workers was a relatively low 12 percent – 1,016 of 8,277. The cotton industry, on the other hand, suffered from an unemployment rate of 38 percent, a figure that may significantly understate the magnitude of the problem.[7] The many former Woonsocket cotton workers who had found a new occupation or who had lost all hope of returning to their old jobs were not counted in the unemployed cotton worker totals.

The relative vigor of the woolen and worsted industry in Woon-socket, and, as a result, its increasing dominance of the area's economy, suggests that Woonsocket's Depression experience may have been less severe than those of textile cities like Fall River, New Bedford, and Lowell, so dependent on cotton manufacture. This did not, however, make Woonsocket's woolen and worsted manufac-turers bullish on the future of their city's economy or expectant of a quick return to pre-Depression manufacturing levels. Even after

[7] Computed from R.I., *Population Census of 1935*, 64.

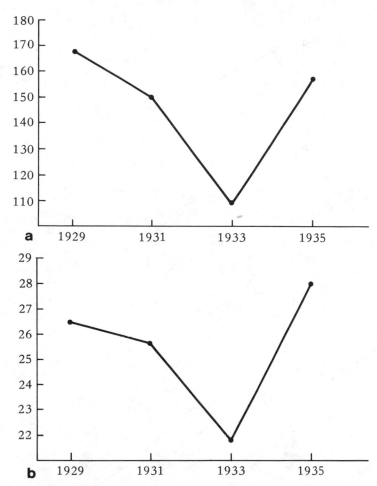

Figure 3.1. The Rhode Island woolen and worsted industry, 1929–1935.
(a) Value of production (in millions of dollars, real terms; base year = 1926).
(b) Wages (in millions of dollars, real terms; base year = 1926). *Source*: U.S.
Department of Commerce, Bureau of the Census, *Fifteenth Census of the United
States, 1930, Manufactures* (Washington, D.C.) vol. II, 412–19, and vol. III,
477, and *Biennial Census of Manufactures, 1931* (Washington, D.C.), 362–5,
1933, 212–16, *1935*, 406–10. The 1935 figures were not, according to the
census, "exactly comparable" to the 1933 figures, since some manufacturers
of woolen blends had been reclassified. The affected manufacturers,
however, formed a minuscule percentage of the total. The 1935 figures
introduced a greater distortion by including woolen and worsted dyeing and
finishing in the industry's total. I have determined from earlier years' figures
that this sector accounted for about 3 percent of the industry's total and have
reduced the 1935 figures accordingly. I calculated real value of production
and real wages using a U.S. Department of Labor Wholesale Price Index and
a Cost of Living Index, respectively. See U.S. Department of Labor, Bureau of
Labor Statistics, *Handbook of Labor Statistics, 1936* (Washington, D.C.), 81,
1941, 85–6, 715–20.

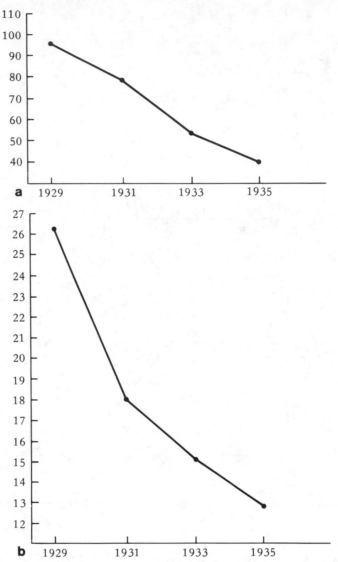

Figure 3.2. The Rhode Island cotton industry, 1929–1935. (a) Value of production (in millions of dollars, real terms; base year = 1926). (b) Wages (in millions of dollars, real terms; base year = 1926). *Source*: U.S. Department of Commerce, Bureau of the Census, *Fifteenth Census of the United States, 1930, Manufactures* (Washington, D.C.), vol. III, 247, 265–9, and *Biennial Census of Manufactures* (Washington, D.C.), *1931*, 226, *1933*, 152, 160 and 162–3, *1935*, 259–60, 262–3. These figures include both the census categories of "cotton goods" and "cotton small wares." In 1935, the dyeing and finishing departments of cotton mills were excluded from these categories. This loss was offset by the addition of some manufacturers of mixed fabric. The census concluded that the 1935 figures were "roughly, but not exactly comparable." For the calculation of real value of production and real wages, see caption of Figure 3.1.

unemployment patterns between cotton and woolens and worsteds diverged markedly in 1934 and 1935, woolen and worsted manufacturers were less encouraged by signs of recovery than worried about the depressed conditions of 1932 and 1933 when the value of their production, in real terms, was one-third less than it had been in 1929.

Fearing a renewed depression, woolen and worsted manufacturers were reluctant to expand production. Rather than produce in anticipation of future orders, they tended to produce only in response to orders in hand. This cautious course led to wide fluctuations in production during the course of the year and exaggerated the industry's already large seasonal swings.[8] Wide fluctuations in production led to wide fluctuations in employment. Workers were hired for a month or two to work on a job and then let go. Manufacturers could easily rely on the Woonsocket labor force to comply with this production strategy, for the failure of the cotton, textile machinery, and rubber industries had left a great surplus of labor in need of employment. Thus the rate of part-time employment in the woolen and worsted industry increased dramatically from 11 percent in 1929 to 21 percent in 1931 to 40 percent in 1933. By 1935, the percentage had declined to 19 as the industry pulled itself into a recovery. Significantly, however, part-time employment remained almost two-thirds higher than its pre-Depression level.[9]

The actual level of part-time employment was even higher in Woonsocket than these percentages suggest.[10] In a city where the woolen and worsted industry was by far the largest source of employ-

---

[8] U.S. Employment Service, Providence Community Research Center, "Labor Market Study, Section V: The Demand for Labor, Preliminary Report of the Woolen and Worsted Industry in Rhode Island," typescript (Providence, 1939), 20–21; and *Occupational Monograph: The Woolen and Worsted Industry* (Providence, R.I., 1940), 22.

[9] I have constructed this measure of part-time employment by subtracting the year's minimum monthly employment figure in the state's woolen and worsted industry from the maximum monthly figure and then dividing the difference by the maximum monthly figure (and multiplying by 100). Thus, in 1929, the maximum monthly employment was 25,665 and the minimum was 22,741; the difference, 2,924, divided by the maximum figure, 25,655, and multiplied by 100, yields a percentage of 11.4. The maximum/minimum figures for 1935 were 27,417/22,292. U.S. Department of Commerce, Bureau of the Census, *Fifteenth Census, Manufactures*, vol. III, 477; *Biennial Census of Manufactures*, 1931, 362–5; 1933, 212–16; 1935; 406–10. The maximum/minimum figures for 1933 were quarterly, not monthly, figures.

[10] My measure of part-time employment tends to underestimate the number of part-time workers because it relies for its labor force figure on the maximum number employed during a single month, not the total number employed during the year. Using the former figure, invariably smaller than the latter, reduces the difference between the maximum and minimum numbers employed and thus the percentage of part-time employment. No total employment figures for the year are available.

ment in 1935, more than 30 percent of the labor force of 21,765 worked less than ten months of the year – a figure 50 percent greater than the 1935 rate of unemployment.[11] Part-time employment, or under-employment (since most of those working part-time were doing so out of necessity rather than choice), was thus a far more per-vasive Depression-era scourge in Woonsocket than hard-core un-employment.

The pervasiveness of underemployment would have immense consequences for union building in the city. The underemployed, despite a chronic insufficiency of work, remained active as wage earners; the unemployed did not. It is a truism to say that a labor union can only be built where people are actually laboring, but it is one worth contemplating. A job and a workplace give an individual a class identity. The unemployed of the 1930s were wage earners in theory of course, and thus abstractly shared an identity with those who were employed. But as the months and sometimes years of idleness accumulated, the unemployed's class identity lost its con-creteness. Refused entry to the world of production, they no longer experienced the social relations of production, the divisions between managers and workers, between "them" and "us," that are so crucial to the spread of unionism. The unemployed increasingly confronted instead the extreme psychological perils of long-term joblessness. Excluded from critical production and consumption activities, many found no satisfactory outlet for their frustration. Some turned their anger inward and then suffered through that emotion's metamorphosis into a debilitating kind of self-blame.[12] The *under*employed of the 1930s, on the other hand, more easily understood that their fate as workers was intimately linked to business decisions made by their firms and hiring decisions made by their foremen. They recognized or

[11] Computed from R.I., *Population Census of 1935*, 63.
[12] Philip Eisenberg and Paul Lazarsfeld, "The Psychological Effects of Unemploy-ment," *Psychological Bulletin* 35 (1938), 358–90; E. Wight Bakke, *The Unemployed Worker: A Social Study* (New Haven, Conn., 1934) and *Citizens Without Work: A Study of the Effects of Unemployment upon the Workers' Social Relations and Practices* (New Haven, Conn., 1940); Mirra Komarovsky, *The Unemployed Man and His Family* (New York, 1940); J. A. Garraty, "Unemployment During the Great Depression," *Labor History* 17 (Spring 1976), 133–59; Alexander Keyssar, *Out of Work: The First Century of Unemployment in Massachusetts* (Cambridge, U.K., 1986), 143–76. The unemployed occasionally have managed to escape such self-blame – often as a result of the educa-tional efforts of political radicals coming from outside their ranks – and to turn their anger into political protest; such protests, however, have been notoriously hard to sustain. See Roy Rosenzweig, "Organizing the Unemployed: The Early Years of the Great Depression, 1929–1933," *Radical America* 10 (July–August 1976), 37–60, and Keyssar, *Out of Work*, 222–49.

at least intuited that unemployment was a complex, social phenomenon and not simply an indication of individual inadequacies. And
they encountered, on a daily or almost daily basis, an individual – a
foreman, a personnel director – with the power to decide their fate.
Such an authority figure offered them a focus for their anger and
frustration.

We will encounter later in this chapter and in the next as well the
raw anger that long-retired Woonsocket workers felt toward the
"bosses" who, fifty years earlier, made decisions about hiring and
firing, work loads and promotions that effectively determined who
would be able to feed the family one week and who would not. Such
anger, one of the deepest and most ubiquitous working-class sentiments in Woonsocket in the 1930s, propelled countless workers into
the city's emerging labor movement. These workers, subjected for
years to the authority of capricious foremen, did not consider themselves fortunate to be associated with an industry, like woolen and
worsted manufacture, beset by chronic underemployment. But in
comparison to the workers in cotton manufacturing cities like Fall
River, Woonsocket workers were privileged indeed. The daily confrontations between Woonsocket workers and their foremen gave
the former an outlet for their frustration and anger that unemployed
cotton workers simply did not have. Such sentiments did not themselves produce a labor movement in Woonsocket, but they did create
a political environment in which a group of working-class radicals
could launch a bold experiment in industrial unionism.

The birth of a union

In October 1931, Joseph Schmetz and his fellow radicals at the Jules
Desurmont mill were following carefully the progress of a UTW-led
strike in Lawrence, in which thousands of workers had taken to
the streets to protest a 10.5 percent wage cut.[13] The small band of
Woonsocket militants had already made a strategic decision: If the
UTW lost the strike and demonstrated once again its inefficacy as a
labor organization, they would secede from the UTW and launch
their own experiment in textile unionism. The heart of the radical
nucleus was the mule room of the Desurmont, but Schmetz and other
cadre had nurtured links with most departments and occupational
groups in the mill. When the Lawrence strike sputtered and then
failed in late fall, Woonsocket's Independent Textile Union came into

---

[13] Edmund Wilson offers a riveting account of this strike in his *The American Earthquake: A Documentary of the Twenties and Thirties* (New York, 1979), 421–31.

being.[14] Within months these insurgents had brought most of the workers in the Desurmont into their union. French-Canadian workers belonged to this union as did Poles; skilled mulespinners joined hands with unskilled machine tenders, as did men with women. When management cut employee wages by 17.5 percent in early 1932, union members walked off their jobs *en masse*. A stunned management not only rescinded the wage cut but granted workers a 7.5 percent wage increase.[15]

The element of surprise made the ITU's first victory seem deceptively easy and allowed the Desurmont radicals to believe that their dream of organizing all the city's textile workers into "one big union" was indeed realizable. Any dispassionate analysis of the prospects of organizing a significant portion of the city's working class, however, would have yielded a far gloomier forecast. The Desurmont was but one of forty-eight textile mills in Woonsocket, and its 500 workers amounted to less than 5 percent of the city's textile work force. Woonsocket's forty-eight mills belonged to nine different sectors of the textile industry, each with a distinctive technology, scale, and labor force structure.[16] The relative ethnic homogeneity of the city's working class reduced the divisive effects of the industrial diversity, and French-Canadian workers had demonstrated in the 1920s that, contrary to the stereotypical image of them as inherently conservative and antiunion, they could be organized. But no union in the entire country had yet been able to overcome the debilitating economic and psychological effects of the Depression. The ITU militants were wrong to blame the defeat of the Lawrence strikers on the ineptitude of the UTW. Edmund Wilson, concluding a year-long trek across America in Lawrence in late 1931, believed that no union could have saved the Lawrence strikers from defeat: The forces arrayed against them were simply too powerful.[17] It seemed equally unlikely that a

---

[14] ITU, *Labor Review, 1931–1942* (Woonsocket, R.I., 1942), 7; *The Textile Worker* (October–November 1931), passim.

[15] ITU, *Labor Review*, 7, 9; interviews with Joseph D. Schmetz, October 15, 1976, and Eva Proroczok, June 22, 1981; Robert Maurice Mooney, "The Origins, Nature, Internal and External Operations of the Industrial Trades Union of America" (M.A. thesis, Catholic University of America, 1947), 14.

[16] The nine sectors and the number of mills involved in each are as follows: French worsted spinning — six; Bradford worsted spinning – eight; woolen spinning – five; worsted and woolen weaving – seven; wool top dyeing – nine; cotton spinning and weaving – five; cotton plush weaving – three; cotton knitting – four; and rayon spinning – one. Calculated from *Providence Journal Almanac: A Reference Book for the State of Rhode Island* (Providence, R.I., 1930), 66–82; R.I. DOL, *Annual Report, 1935*, 203–4; R.I. Office of the Commissioner of Labor, *Classified Index of Rhode Island Industries Employing More Than Five Persons* (Providence, R.I., 1928), 13, 53–5.

[17] Wilson, *The American Earthquake*, 425.

small, inexperienced Woonsocket union would succeed or even survive.

The ITU enjoyed another organizing success at Lawton Spinning, a cotton mill, but then saw its vigor and its resources consumed in a losing strike at the Branch River Wool Combing Company in nearby North Smithfield.[18] In early 1933, it found itself under attack at its home base. Confident that a winter strike would debilitate the ITU, Jules Desurmont's management reimposed the 17.5 percent wage cut that it had rescinded a year earlier. The workers struck for two months in cold winter weather but still could not force management to retreat from its position or even to agree to negotiations. The strikers finally exhausted their relief funds and, without money for food or coal, returned to work under conditions set by management. One of those conditions was that Schmetz and other union leaders sign "yellow dog" contracts stating that they would not join or support unions for the duration of their employment.[19]

Only government action in June 1933, in the form of Roosevelt's National Industrial Recovery Act (NIRA), saved the ITU from oblivion. Intended to promote business recovery by encouraging capitalists in each industry to establish production quotas and uniform prices and wage levels, the NIRA instead accentuated latent divisions in Woonsocket's capitalist class. ITU unionists, already emboldened by the NIRA's clause 7(a) guaranteeing labor's right to organize and bargain collectively, seized on this moment of employer weakness as an opportunity to launch a score of organizing drives. By the end of 1934, the ITU had organized seventeen mills and stood more than 3,000 members strong.[20]

Divided employers

The business provisions of the NIRA, those calling on employers to subscribe to codes governing production, wages, and working conditions in their particular industries, seem to have provoked little disagreement among Woonsocket employers. Woonsocket workers filed few complaints about illegal business practices with the National Recovery Administration (NRA), the agency set up by the NIRA to supervise the design and implementation of the industrial codes.[21]

[18] Mooney, "ITU," 14.

[19] ITU, *Labor Review*, 9.

[20] Information on these early organizing drives has been assembled from the following: histories of ITU locals appearing in the *ITU News*, 1936–42, passim; letter from Lawrence Spitz to author, May 11, 1977; interviews with ITU members; R.I. DOL, *Annual Report*, 1935, 203–4.

[21] The few complaints can be found in the NRA Records Relating to Employee Com-

The millowner disunity that allowed the ITU its critical opening was rooted instead in disagreements over whether to comply with the NIRA's labor provisions; these called on employers to recognize employees' rights to join a union and bargain collectively and, in the case of all outstanding labor disputes, to abide by the decisions of joint labor-management boards. Woonsocket's capitalist class split along the familiar and well-established line that divided local from absentee owners. The Guerin Mills led the industrial faction subscribing to the NIRA labor provisions, while the French textile magnates led the faction determined to resist.

The willingness of the Guerin Mills to abide by the NIRA labor provisions was probably the single most important factor contributing to the early success of the ITU. Four of the first seventeen locals organized by the ITU were in mills owned by the Guerin Mills; these four – the Alsace, Montrose, Rosemont, and Philmont – gave the ITU 40 percent of its first 3,285 members.[22] The ITU also benefited from participation of the Guerin Mills in four different sectors of the city's woolen and worsted industry. Some manufacturers in each of these sectors, especially those in wool top dyeing, showed an inclination to follow the example set by the giant Guerin Mills.[23]

The Guerin Mills's acceptance of the NIRA's labor provisions cannot be understood simply as a reflection of the goodwill of the Guerin family. Control of the mill complex had passed, in the early 1920s, to a group of Providence bankers.[24] This shift in control was meant to be temporary, with the bankers acting as receivers supervising the reorganization of the enterprise's finances. But, for reasons that remain unclear, the arrangement persisted. Some Woonsocket workers believed that the bankers deliberately weakened the Guerin Mills's financial situation in order to perpetuate the receivership. The Guerin Mills's willingness to abide by the NIRA and negotiate with the ITU, in this view, reflected the bankers' desire to impair the corporation's

Footnote 21 (cont.)

plaints in the Textile Industry. See, in particular, these files: Rayon and Synthetic Yarn Excerpts, Wool Excerpts (1933), and Wool Excerpts (1934), Record Group 9, Entry 398, National Archives, Washington, D.C. (hereafter RG 9, Entry 398, NA).

[22] ITU News, 1936–42, passim; letter from Lawrence Spitz to author, May 11, 1977; R.I. DOL, Annual Report, 1935, 203–4.

[23] The four different sectors were French worsted spinning, Bradford worsted spinning, woolen and worsted weaving, and wool top dyeing.

[24] A.P. Thomas, Woonsocket: Highlights of History, 1800–1976 (Woonsocket, R.I., 1976), 106. The Guerin family still owned stock in the Guerin Mills and occupied several posts on the corporation's board of directors. Interview with Robert Guerin, November 3, 1980.

competitiveness and deepen its dependence on bank credit.[25] This scenario seems farfetched. The Providence bankers were hardly exceptional in their acceptance of the wage, hour, and production quota provisions of the woolen and worsted NRA code; numerous northern textile industrialists, including Woonsocket's own recalcitrant French magnates, accepted those provisions in the hope that such self-regulation would bring some stability and profitability to their troubled industry.[26]

More exceptional was the willingness of the Providence bankers to allow the Guerin Mills's management to negotiate with an independent union. Many textile employers simply refused to comply with the NIRA's union provisions altogether or else offered to negotiate only with "company unions" – labor organizations sponsored and supervised by management itself.[27] The explanation for the Providence bankers' unusual prolabor policy may lie in their affinity for a new pro-union philosophy taking root among a network of entrepreneurs located in such consumer-oriented sectors of the American economy as garment manufacture and retail trade. This entrepreneurial network sought to give organized labor a boost, not on account of benevolence but as a result of some enlightened though hardheaded thinking about what the American economy needed to get back on track. The economy, these businessmen believed, needed industrial peace to permit uninterrupted production, and high wages to sustain high levels of consumption. Unions, if properly domesticated, could critically assist efforts to procure both by insuring harmony at the workplace and by giving workers the economic muscle necessary to wrest wage increases from their employers.[28] We have no direct evidence that Providence bankers held these views, though their proximity to Boston, where the Filene brothers and Felix Frankfurter formed a crucial band of prestigious publicists for these

---

[25] Interview with Ernest Gignac, June 25, 1981.

[26] On employer attitudes toward the business provisions of the NRA codes, see Ellis Hawley, *The New Deal and the Problem of Monopoly: A Study in Economic Ambivalence* (Princeton, N.J., 1966), 19–146; George B. Galloway et al., *Industrial Planning Under the Codes* (New York, 1935), 117–43; Louis Galambos, *Competition and Cooperation: The Emergence of a National Trade Association* (Baltimore, Md., 1966), 173–279.

[27] Irving Bernstein, *The Turbulent Years. A History of the American Worker, 1933–1941* (Boston, 1969), 172–216. Manville Jenckes opted for this second option in their nearby Manville mill. See Manville Jenckes Co. file, RG 9, Entry 398, NA.

[28] See Steve Fraser, "From the 'New Unionism' to the New Deal," *Labor History* 25 (Summer 1984), 405–30, and "The 'Labor Question,'" in Steve Fraser and Gary Gerstle, *The Rise and Fall of the New Deal Order, 1930–1980* (Princeton, N.J., 1989), 55–84.

new industrial relations attitudes, lends plausibility to this inter-pretation.[29] Such an interpretation would also account for the Providence bankers' appointment of John Lacouture, a manager with remarkably explicit prolabor sympathies, to the Guerin Mills's corporate presidency.

John Lacouture was a French-Canadian success story, having risen quickly from his humble beginnings as an unskilled laborer in the Guerin Mills coal yards to the head of the whole corporate opera-tion. Lacouture's employees simply adored the fact that he never sought to complement his dramatic occupational rise with a trans-formation in social status. Away from work, Lacouture continued to drink with his working-class pals and to gamble with them in card games. We cannot know whether Lacouture's determination to re-main part of a working-class world of leisure simply reflected unshak-able convictions rooted deep within him, or whether it also reflected an angry reaction to shabby treatment that he may well have suffered at the hands of Woonsocket's genteel French-Canadian elite. In either case, he bonded himself to his workers in ways that corporation presidents rarely do.[30]

Such bonding helps explain his quick, barely contested capitulation to union organizing efforts in his mills in 1932. One of his closest friends was Maurice Pierre, a radical Frenchman who spearheaded the ITU's drive in the Alsace mill. Pierre and fellow radicals seem to have parked themselves in Lacouture's office in 1933, arguing with him about the merits of unionism, demanding that he recognize and bargain with the ITU local in the Alsace. Lacouture put up some verbal resistance, but he hastened to meet their demands when the organizing committee threatened to strike. Lacouture not only recognized the ITU in the Alsace but soon extended the same recognition to union activists in the other manufacturing operations in the Guerin complex: the Montrose weave mill, the Rosemont dye house, and the Philmont spinning mill. In less than one year, the ITU gained more than 1,000 members in four different branches of Woonsocket industry without having to resort to a single strike.[31]

Lacouture's behavior toward the union stood in dramatic contrast to the attitudes displayed by the French textile magnates who controlled four of the city's six French spinning mills. Lacouture

---

[29] We know, moreover, that some northern textile industrialists held such views; see Ferguson, "From Normalcy to New Deal," 69.

[30] Interviews with Angelo Turbesi, October 9, 1980, Herve Duhamel, October 27, 1980, and Lawrence Spitz, September 19–20, 1979.

[31] Interviews with Angelo Turbesi, October 9, and Herve Duhamel, October 27, 1980.

could hardly wait to shed his corporate role so that he could carouse with the people who worked for him. French textile magnates like Charles Tiberghien of the French Worsted, by contrast, could not bear the thought of such social leveling. Even after he had capitulated to ITU power in the late 1930s, Tiberghien still refused to lower the social barriers that he believed necessarily divided capitalist from worker. Thus when a union negotiating committee arrived at his office in the French Worsted in 1937 to begin contract bargaining, he refused to provide committee members with chairs. Bourgeois etiquette required that a worker stand in the presence of his employer.[32]

The point of stressing this contrast between Lacouture and Tiberghien is not to applaud the former and condemn the latter, but rather to point out that the industrial relations approach espoused by each reflected fundamentally divergent personal values. Lacouture believed in social equality, Tiberghien in social hierarchy. Such fundamental differences in world views made industrialist unity in Woonsocket difficult to achieve. Such personal differences, of course, were not the only source of industrialist disagreement. The Guerin Mills, party to a complicated legal agreement with Providence bankers that might someday be scrutinized in court, felt obligated to obey the letter of such American laws as the NIRA and the National Labor Relations Act. Tiberghien and other French owners felt no such obligation. One unionist recalled Tiberghien once saying that he (Tiberghien) "did not feel a responsibility to live up to the laws of the United States; they did not apply to him. He was a citizen of France, and that he would take his direction from [Prime Minister] Pierre Laval."[33] Moreover, if the Providence bankers who controlled the Guerin Mills did indeed take their ideological direction from the group of progressive capitalists gathered around the Filenes and Frankfurter in Boston, their industrial relations approach would have been worlds apart from that favored by the French magnates.

For these reasons, Woonsocket's employers, though civil toward each other and associating in such groups as the Woonsocket Chamber of Commerce and Taxpayers' Association, found it impossible to iron out a common approach to industrial relations. While the Guerin Mills and its allies accepted the union on their premises, the French magnates resisted tooth and nail. The Jules Desurmont mill, owned by Jules Desurmont et Fils of Tourcoing, almost broke the union in early 1933 by forcing it to strike and then refusing to negotiate on any of the outstanding issues. This strategy had been first used against

---

[32] Lawrence Spitz, speech delivered at Woonsocket High School, September 12, 1984.
[33] Ibid.

the ITU in 1932 by the management of another French-owned mill, the Branch River Wool Combing Company.[34] The French Worsted was forced in 1933 to make some concessions to an ITU local on its premises but seized every opportunity to undermine the unionists' base of support. Its strategies kept the local weak and internally divided until the late 1930s. The Lafayette mill, owned by the Lepoutre family in Roubaix, blacklisted union activists to stall union organizing in their mill. Fewer French and Belgian mulespinners worked there than in any other mill.[35]

Neither the Guerin Mills nor the French owners controlled a sufficiently large fraction of local industry to impose their industrial relations approach on the smaller, "unaffiliated" mills in Woonsocket. The Guerin Mills employed, on average, 15 percent of the city's textile workers, while the French magnates employed about 18 percent. The Guerin Mills's percentage of textile employment rises to 19 percent if we add those plants tied by kinship or friendship to the Guerin family, while the French mills's percentage, adding in several American absentee firms, rises to about 33 percent.[36] Even with allies, then, the two antagonistic blocs remain relatively balanced. The other 50 percent of the city's textile labor force worked in thirty small mills (averaging fewer than 150 workers apiece) owned by more than a score of small, local industrialists who were themselves often divided on matters of labor policy.[37]

Such millowner disunity had profound implications for labor organizing in the city. It allowed the ITU a range of opportunities it otherwise might not have enjoyed. The union, in its early years, decided to organize the Woonsocket mills one at a time rather than through the tactic of a general strike. To undermine this strategy, the millowners might have brought the full power of their class to bear on the union by provoking a strike or initiating a lockout of all workers in the area; alternatively they might have agreed among themselves not to negotiate with the union. The counterparts of Woonsocket's industrialists in Fall River, New Bedford, and Lawrence had used both tactics with great success in the past.[38] Either tactic in the years

[34] The Prouvost-Lefebvre families of Roubaix owned this outfit. Thomas, *Woonsocket*, 109–10.

[35] Interview with Lawrence Spitz, September 19–20, 1979.

[36] Computed from R.I. DOL, *Annual Report*, 1935, 203–4.

[37] Computed from R.I. DOL, *Annual Report*, 1935, 203–4, and from *Providence Journal Almanac*, 1930, 66–82, and 1935, 91–102. Too little is known about these owners to offer a persuasive explanation of their splits, though fragments of evidence suggest that one split ran along ethnic lines: French-Canadian owners resisted union organization much more determinedly than Yankee owners.

[38] See John T. Cumbler, *Working-Class Community in Industrial America: Work, Leisure,*

1933 to 1935 probably would have worn down the workers' resources, weakened their resolve, and broken the union. But neither kind of effort was forthcoming from Woonsocket owners. They developed no common policy for dealing with the union. No mill could hope to mobilize more than a fraction of the total financial and political resources of Woonsocket's capitalist class. The recognition accorded the union by some owners diminished the ability of others determined to resist. Such displays of disunity repeatedly opened the door to union victories.

A network of mulespinners

A relatively healthy woolen and worsted industry, favorable national legislation, and a divided employer class created an environment in which a union could effectively operate. But those circumstances alone would have amounted to little had there not been in Woonsocket a group of experienced union activists able to capitalize on opportunities handed to them. Such a cadre group had indeed cohered, in the form not simply of Franco-Belgian radical nuclei but of a network of mulespinners that extended well beyond the ranks of the European radicals. In no other 1930s textile city did mulespinners and their assistants form as large a part of the textile work force as they did in Woonsocket: They labored in eleven of the city's forty-eight mills, and in each of those mills they formed one-third to one-half of the work force.[39] Eight of these eleven mills had become ITU locals by

and *Struggle in Two Industrial Cities, 1880–1930* (Westport, Conn., 1979), 165–217; Donald B. Cole, *Immigrant City: Lawrence, Massachusetts, 1845–1921* (Chapel Hill, N.C., 1964), 177–205. The domination of Lawrence's textile industry by a few giant companies like the American Woolen Company permitted a single labor policy to be ironed out there. The capitalist classes in Fall River and New Bedford, by contrast, were composed of large numbers of owners; these owners, unlike their counterparts in Woonsocket, were bound together tightly by ties of kinship or friendship which permitted them to develop common labor policies. See Robert K. Lamb, "The Development of Entrepreneurship in Fall River, 1813–1859" (Ph.D. dissertation, Harvard University, 1935); Sylvia Chace Lintner, "A Social History of Fall River, 1859–1879" (Ph.D. dissertation, Radcliffe College, 1945); Seymour Wolfbein, *The Decline of a Cotton Textile City: A Study of New Bedford* (New York, 1944).

[39] Each pair of ordinary mules required four full-time workers and one half-time floor boy, and a typical worsted mill housed twenty to thirty mules. In the Desurmont, mule-room workers comprised 46 percent of the work force on each shift, in the French Worsted 37 percent, in the Lafayette 32 percent, in the Alsace and Masurel 30 percent. These percentages are based on full employment figures, but there is no reason to think that the proportion of mule-room workers to the total would have changed during depressed times. Rhode Island Conference of Business Associations, *The Book of Rhode Island* (Providence, R.I., 1930), 166, 174, 188; *Providence Journal Almanac*, 1930, 66–82; interview with Ernest Gignac, June 25, 1981.

1934, and in all eight, mulespinners emerged as local presidents.[40] Mulespinners had led an organizing drive in one of the Guerin Mills plants, the Alsace.[41] Even more importantly, their leadership and organizing skills made possible the expansion of the union into six mills beyond the Guerin Mills orbit. Mulespinner networking in combination with the pro-union stance of Guerin Mills's management brought the ITU eleven of its first seventeen locals and 2,830 of its first 3,285 members (see Table 3.2).

The central role of mulespinners in the organizing process reflects the ties that existed between members of this craft and their long history of trade-union experience. At a time when the ITU was reeling from defeat in 1932, Schmetz could turn to this network, confident that they would organize with skill, dedication, and the necessary circumspection. He could reach out beyond the ranks of his fellow Franco-Belgians to French Canadians who had risen into the mulespinner ranks over the years and who had come to share with the Europeans pride in their craft and commitment to trade unionism. These bonds were not limited to Franco-Belgian and French-Canadian mulespinners. In one mill, the Falls Yarn, the mulespinning ranks included a significant number of Italians, and they were as prominent as the French Canadians in union organizing.[42] This network of cadre made possible the growth of the union in 1933 and 1934 throughout the city. And the representation of French-Canadian mulespinners in this network facilitated union efforts to reach out beyond the mulespinning craft to all grades of textile workers. French-Canadian trade unionists could persuade the majority of French-Canadian workers, in ways that Schmetz could not, of the value of union membership.[43]

---

[40] Franco-Belgians led the Desurmont, Alsace, and French Worsted locals, and French Canadians led the Falls Yarn, Bonin Spinning, Woonsocket Spinning, River Mill, and Belmont Woolen locals. Interviews with Joseph D. Schmetz, October 15, 1976, Lawrence Spitz, September 19–20, 1979, Angelo Turbesi, October 9, 1980, Ernest Gignac, June 25, 1981, Leona Galipeau, October 22–23, 1980, and Arthur Riendeau, June 25, 1981.

[41] Within the Guerin Mills itself union agitation emerged from a cadre of Alsace mulespinners, led by Maurice Pierre.

[42] Interviews with Lawrence Spitz, September 19–20, 1979, and Leona Galipeau, October 22–23, 1980. The most prominent Italian in the Falls Yarn was Victor Canzano, later to become vice president of the ITU.

[43] Kinship networks strengthened union locals where they existed but could not, at least at this stage of union development, substitute for them. Specifically, kinship ties aided the mulespinners in their efforts to reach out beyond the mule room to other mill departments. In the Desurmont, the original ITU local, the wife and daughter of Joseph Schmetz worked on the second floor in the Preparation De-

Table 3.2. *Woonsocket mills organized by ITU (Fall 1932–Summer 1934)*

Mill	Textile sector	No. of employees
I. Owned by Guerin Mills		
Alsace	French spinning	524
Philmont	Bradford spinning	285
Montrose	Woolen and worsted weaving	303
Rosemont	Wool top dyeing	184
Subtotal: 4		1296
II. Mulespinners employed		
Alsace	French spinning	—
Desurmont	French spinning	329
French Worsted	French spinning	450
River Mill	Woolen spinning	177
Belmont	Woolen spinning	78
Bonin	Woolen spinning	246
Falls Yarn	Woolen spinning	141
Woonsocket Spinning	Woolen spinning	113
Subtotal[a]: 7		1534
III. Miscellaneous		
Blackstone Dye	Wool top dyeing	95
Enterprise Dye	Wool top dyeing	143
Fairmount Dye	Wool top dyeing	75
Florence Dye	Wool top dyeing	81
Star Carbonizing	Wool carbonizing	50
Lawton Spinning	Cotton spinning	11
Subtotal: 6		455
Total: 17		3285

[a] Alsace mill not counted in this subtotal.
Source: List of organized mills reconstructed from *ITU News*, 1936–1942; Lawrence Spitz to author, May 11, 1977; interviews with ITU members. Employment figures from Rhode Island Department of Labor, *Annual Report* (Providence, R.I.), 1935, 203–4.

partment. The names of four other founders of the Desurmont local – Garceau, Herpels, Houle, and Bell – reappear among the names of women working in the Preparation Department. Eva Proroczok, a Polish unionist in the Desurmont, worked in the mill along with her mother and father. These ties assumed particular importance in mills like the Desurmont where a combination of company policies and the need to tend continuously running machines prevented union activists from traveling from department to department and from floor to floor. Kinship networks seem to have made little difference, however, in spreading the union from one mill

As the mulespinners spread Schmetz's union throughout the city, however, they also introduced a view of unionism significantly different from that entertained by Schmetz and his Franco-Belgian comrades. French-Canadian mulespinners grew up in a profoundly conservative ethnic milieu where the rights of labor were not generally recognized or supported and where any form of radicalism was roundly condemned as godless collectivism. The fact that these mulespinners, upon reaching the skilled ranks, joined trade unions indicates that they had achieved some distance from their ethnic background. They were enthusiastic about Schmetz's commitment to industrial unionism and even to his vision of one big union. But they did not share his desire for social transformation. Their enthusiasm for the ITU was tied much more to a desire to defend themselves and their families from further economic calamity, and to find a way of adapting their rich but burdensome ethnic identity to the realities of American society.

These French-Canadian mulespinners were generally men in their thirties who had grown up in Woonsocket and reached the skilled ranks in the 1920s.[44] Ernest Gignac, for example, starting as a backboy in the French Worsted in 1924, rose to the position of mulespinner in the course of three years.[45] In the relatively prosperous 1920s, mulespinning brought substantial material returns. Gignac remembers

Footnote 43 (*cont.*)

to another, even in instances where a union member transmitted his or her enthusiasm for the ITU to family members working in nonunion mills. The mulespinners formed the essential nuclei. Norman T. Allen, "Drawing Room Day Set Books," 1924–1926, MS 15.3–5, Museum of American Textile History. Allen was a foreman in the Preparation Department of the Desurmont in the 1920s and kept a daily record of the wages earned by each employee. Interview with Proroczok, June 22, 1981.

[44] This analysis is based on twenty-one French-Canadian mulespinners who emerged as leaders of their locals in the years 1931 to 1934. The eighteen whose age is known averaged thirty-six years in 1935. Of the seventeen whose place of birth is known, nine were born in the United States, mostly in Rhode Island. Of the eight born in Quebec, a number had come to Woonsocket when they were very young.

The names and union positions of the twenty-one were compiled from references to their pre-1935 involvement appearing in the *ITU News*, 1936 to 1942. Information on their age, residence in Woonsocket, marital status, number and age of their children, etc., has been compiled from oral histories, the 1935 Rhode Island Manuscript Census, Rhode Island State Archives (hereafter RISA), Providence, R.I., and the U.S. Department of Justice, "Petitions for Naturalization," Providence Superior Court, Providence, R.I. Linking ITU leaders to census manuscripts and naturalization records is a relatively straightforward process. The 1935 census takers put each individual on a separate punch card and arranged the cards alphabetically by city. The naturalization records of the immigrants to Providence County are indexed by name of petitioner.

[45] Interview with Ernest Gignac, June 25, 1981.

that his wages as a mulespinner reached fifty to sixty dollars a week, four times the average earnings of most textile workers.[46]

These workers saw their high pay as a just reward for their central role in the production process. The mule was one of the most complex and certainly the most awkward machine in a textile mill. Invented by Samuel Crompton in the late eighteenth century and automated by Robert Roberts in the 1830s, the machine produced such a superior yarn that it remained an integral part of cotton production through 1900 and of woolen and worsted production through the 1940s. The automation of the machine in the early nineteenth century was supposed to eliminate the need for skilled operators, but the spinning process remained such a delicate affair, susceptible to the slightest changes in temperature and all sorts of band and gear breakage, that unskilled workers simply could not maintain production at peak quality or peak efficiency. Highly skilled mulespinners continued to operate the machines.[47]

The operation of a worsted mule involved supervising the outward and return movement of a metal carriage that held a row of spindles. Carriages could reach eighty feet in length and hold up to a thousand spindles (Figure 3.3). Slivers – partially spun yarn – of wool ran from bobbins positioned on the back rack of a mule to each one of the carriage's spindles. The spindles revolved as the carriage moved outward, twisting the sliver at the same time as they thinned it by "drawing out" the sliver's countless cotton fibers. The simultaneity of twisting and drawing was the key to the mule's spinning superiority. It permitted slivers to be spun into much finer and more consistent yarn than was possible on the mule's chief rival, the spinning

---

[46] Ibid.

[47] A number of historians have contended that the self-acting mule eliminated the skill of the mulespinner, making the job suitable for unskilled women and children. They have then explained the persistence of the highly paid adult male mulespinners in terms of their utility to employers as supervisors of unskilled and unruly assistants. This argument, made in reference to English mulespinners, fails to explain the persistence of adult male, highly paid mulespinners in American mills where supervision was in the hands of overseers and second hands. The accurate explanation for the persistence of mulespinners after the invention of the self-acting mule lies in the persistent need for their skill. Self-acting mules may have changed the nature of the mulespinning skill, but they did not eliminate it. Interviews with John Robinson, October 7, 1980, and Angelo Turbesi, October 9, 1980. Andrew Ure, *The Philosophy of Manufactures, or an Exposition of the Scientific, Moral, and Commercial Economy of the Factory System of Great Britain* (London, 1835 and 1967), 366–73; John Foster, *Class Struggle and the Industrial Revolution: Early Industrial Capitalism in Three English Towns* (London , 1974), 229–34; William Lazonick, "Industrial Relations and Technical Change: The Case of the Self-Acting Mule," *Cambridge Journal of Economics* 3 (1979), 231–62.

Figure 3.3 Worsted mule of the sort used in Woonsocket's French spinning mills. Société Alsacienne de Constructions Mécaniques, Mulhouse, France. (Reproduced by permission of the Museum of American Textile History.

frame, which performed the drawing-out process before imparting a twist.

When the carriage reached its outermost point, the spindles briefly reversed their motion, thus releasing the spun yarn that had gathered at the spindle's tip. The spindles then resumed their original motion as the carriage began to "back up" or return to the bobbin rack, and thus wind the newly spun yarn onto cops, narrow cardboard cylinders sitting on the lower parts of the spindles. All this work was automatic. The mulespinner, however, had to adjust the quadrant, a mechanical device that controlled the speed of the turning spindles and of the outward and return journey of the carriage, to maintain just the proper amount of tension on the spinning slivers. He also had to understand the entire mechanical system of the mule and to monitor all the gears and bands to identify trouble spots before they caused inferior spinning or a complete breakdown in the machine. Finally, the spinner patrolled the length of the carriage, searching for broken ends – slivers no longer connected to the spindles – and piecing them back together (Figure 3.4). One or two semiskilled piecers assisted him in this last operation. But the other operations required years of training and experience. Most mulespinners, like Ernest Gignac, began working in the mule room as backboys and doffers – the unskilled workers who kept the back rack supplied with full bobbins and who removed full cops from the carriage spindles –

Figure 3.4. Mulespinner, Woonsocket, 1944. U.S. Office of War Information, Ruth Ames, photographer. (Courtesy Library of Congress.)

and slowly progressed through the job of piecer before reaching the rank of spinner.[48]

Individuals who acquired mastery of the mule also gained an appreciation for their indispensability to the production process. This appreciation was in part a natural reaction to the complexities of the job and in part a result of socialization into the proud and defiant company of mulespinners. From early-nineteenth-century Oldham, England, to late-nineteenth-century Fall River to early-twentieth-century Woonsocket, mulespinners prompted organizing campaigns and sparked working-class challenges to managerial authority. Only the elimination of mules from production (or the threat of such an action) succeeded in taming mulespinner pride and militancy.[49]

[48] This description is based on Harold Catling, *The Spinning Mule* (Newton Abbot, U.K., 1970), and on my interviews with mulespinners and mulepiecers, especially John Robinson, October 7, 1980, Ernest Gignac, June 25, 1981, and Angelo Turbesi, October 9, 1980.

[49] Foster, *Class Struggle and the Industrial Revolution;* Cumbler, *Working-Class Community in Industrial America*, 50–72, 100–2, 107–18, 125–60; Philip T. Silvia, "Spindle City: Labor, Politics, and Religion in Fall River, Massachusetts, 1870–1905" (Ph.D. dis-

Arthur Riendeau, like other retired mulespinners in Woonsocket, vividly recalled the pride and power he once enjoyed on the shop-floor: "When they had the mules in there [Bonin Spinning] we were more powerful than the rest of the mill together. What the mule-spinner used to say, used to go by."[50] Leona Galipeau, a mulespinner most of his life in the Falls Yarn, revealed a tremendous pride in his manual skill. Mulespinners like him, he claimed, could run any machine in a woolen mill. Sitting next to his son, a highly skilled card stripper, and describing the all-around mechanical knowledge re-quired by his former occupation, he boasted: "Mule...I work on anything. I work on cards, I work on picker room, I work on finishing room...I can go right in there today, give me two hours I can run the cards just as good as him [referring to his son]."[51]

Leona Galipeau, reminiscing about his mulespinning days, asso-ciated his skill as a worker with his ethic of hard work and providing for his family: "If you talk about work let me say this to you. I never pull out of work. If I had to work extra, if I had to do that [I did it]. I had a big heart and a small body. And the only thing I did care was to feed them [his family members], dress them decently, send them to school."[52] In 1935, Leona Galipeau had three children ranging in age from ten to fifteen years. Most other French-Canadian mulespinners active in union affairs in the early 1930s had at least two children, nearly all of them younger than fifteen years of age.[53]

These skilled workers occupied positions of status in their com-munities and responsibility in their families. Years of hard work had brought them high-paying, high-prestige positions. Their power in the production process and their high wages entitled them to respect both on the shopfloor and in the community. They took pride in their work – both their skill and their diligence – and they expected commensurate rewards. In the early years of the Depression their family responsibilities were great: They provided the family's sole source of income, as their children were too young to work and needed too much care to allow the mothers to work. These men ex-

Footnote 49 (*cont.*)
  sertation, Fordham University, 1973), 491–545; Joseph L. White, *The Limits of Trade Union Militancy: The Lancashire Textile Workers, 1900–1914* (Westport, Conn., 1978).
[50] Interview with Arthur Riendeau, June 25, 1981.
[51] Interview with Leona Galipeau, October 22–23, 1980.
[52] Ibid.
[53] Fifteen of eighteen mulespinners were married; all but one of these couples had children in 1935, averaging more than two apiece. In ten of the thirteen families for which I have information, all the children were fifteen years of age or less in 1935. Information drawn from Rhode Island Manuscript Census of 1935, RISA.

pected their jobs to generate the income necessary to care for their children in a respectable manner; in Leona Galipeau's words, "to feed them, dress them decently, send them to school."

The Depression was a shattering experience for these workers. Their incomes plunged to poverty levels. Ernest Gignac remembers three consecutive years when he earned only $600 a year, or an average of less than twelve dollars a week. Leona Galipeau's wages plummeted from an average of forty-five dollars in the 1920s to less than fifteen dollars in the early Depression years. Such sharp drops in income undermined these mulespinners' ability to provide for their families – Galipeau had three children all too young to work, and Gignac married in 1932 – and robbed them of the satisfactions that these patresfamilias had come to expect.[54]

The mulespinner's power at the workplace likewise fell victim to the Depression. During the depressed years of 1929 to 1933, manufacturers operated at such a low level of capacity that there was a constant surplus of mulespinners. Foremen kept the number of mulespinners employed on a regular basis to an absolute minimum, and often favored assistant foremen and kin for those precious positions. Most mulespinners trudged to the mills every day without any certainty of getting hired. Even if they knew work was available, they could never count on it. Foremen bound themselves to no plan for sharing work; many took delight in humiliating proud mulespinners by making them plead for work and then rejecting them. French-Canadian mulespinners suffered additionally because they often came up against the ethnic prejudices of Italian and Franco-Belgian foremen. Leonel Galipeau, Leona's eldest son, vividly remembers the pain of seeing his father constantly failing to get work. Every morning he would walk from the house to the mill, a distance exceeding a mile, and wait at the gate to hear about the possibility of work.

> Depression time...The man was sitting out there in the cold... for hours, waiting to be told there's no work today. He'd walk all the way back home. I'd see him walk in, he'd take the shot gun, take one lousy...five-cent shell, and we'd walk all the way into the woods. I'd jump on piles of brush, so he could shoot a rabbit, so that we could have something to eat.[55]

The predicament of Leona Galipeau and other mulespinners was by no means unique. All kinds of workers could tell a similar story. But to the mulespinner who had been so secure and so well-paid, the

---

[54] Interviews with Ernest Gignac, June 25, 1981, and Leona Galipeau, October 22–23, 1980.
[55] Interview with Leonel Galipeau, October 22–23, 1980.

experience of powerlessness and penury was especially painful.[56]

These memories of skilled workers arose in response to queries about their motivations for joining the ITU. Their emphasis on personal and familial injury suggests that their involvement was primarily defensive in nature. These workers looked to the ITU as a way of protecting themselves from further abuse and perhaps of ultimately restoring the way of life to which they had become accustomed. But it would be wrong to attribute their involvement simply to their despair about lost income and status. For the vehicle they chose to restore a familiar way of life challenged the ethnic milieu that shaped Woonsocket working-class life. They lived in a community which had traditionally valued the practice of Catholicism and the preservation of French-Canadian culture above all else and had regarded trade unionism as materialist and atheist and thus as a threat to that way of life. If French-Canadian skilled workers had organized a Catholic and French-speaking trade union, unionization might not have represented a challenge to their traditional community. But they committed themselves to a union leader, Joseph Schmetz, whose antireligious sentiments were far more pronounced than his religious affections, a man who displayed no interest in preserving French-Canadian customs and traditions. And they endorsed a union constitution that stipulated that union leaders had to gain proficiency in English, a provision that deliberately challenged the traditional prescription for living a French-Canadian life.[57]

The reasons for the attraction of these French Canadians to a secular American union are difficult to unearth through oral history alone. Those interviewed did not want to admit that the goals of their union conflicted in any way with the goals of their ethnic community. But we can begin to understand their attraction to this union by situating the life histories of the French-Canadian mulespinners in the broader social history of their community.

The lives of French-Canadian skilled workers active in the ITU encompassed both the years of security and the years of crisis in Woonsocket's French-Canadian community. Born around 1900, they had lived their early years either in Quebec or in Woonsocket when it was a Québecois enclave in New England. They spoke French before learning English, practiced Catholicism, attended parochial school,

---

[56] On similar reactions of skilled workers elsewhere in Rhode Island, see the letter from Martha Gellhorn to Harry Hopkins, December 1934, reprinted in James Patterson, ed., "Life on Relief in Rhode Island, 1934: A Contemporary View from the Field," *Rhode Island History* 39 (August 1980), 90.

[57] ITU, *Constitution and By-Laws* (Woonsocket, R.I., 1934), 8.

and embraced the values of their ancestors from the North. But they began to experience a different world in their late teens and twenties. The intense nationalism of World War I made them feel their foreignness in ways they never had before. Their rise into the ranks of skilled labor brought them into craft unions and thus into close contact with workers outside their enclave. The high incomes they earned put the new products of mass technology and culture – radios, autos, and movies – within their grasp.[58] They became increasingly conscious of their individual and group limitations – their spotty knowledge of English, their lack of leadership positions in unions, and their lack of clout in local and state politics – and they grew resentful of the second-class treatment that a French-Canadian identity seemed to impose on them. At the same time they began to doubt the ability of their traditional ethnic leadership to secure the first-class treatment they felt they deserved. They noted the inability of this leadership to do anything about the 1,000 Woonsocket cotton textile workers who lost their jobs in the 1920s.

In the 1930s the Depression dramatically deepened the economic crisis engulfing the city; unemployment shot past 20 percent and overwhelmed local sources of relief. The French-Canadian mulespinners were no longer simply observers of economic calamity but its victims. Months of hardship arising from unemployment and poverty convinced them that their ethnic leadership did not possess the resources to restore their community's well-being. They began to associate their poverty with their cultural isolation. Recovery to them meant more than access to decent jobs. They wanted to learn English, participate in American cultural life, and gain for themselves the rights and entitlements of American citizens. They began to turn to an American union in their midst as a way of overcoming an acute sense of economic and cultural deprivation.

The life of Ernest Gignac illustrates the experience of those French-Canadian skilled workers who committed themselves to the ITU.[59] Gignac immigrated with his family to Woonsocket from Embrun, Ontario, in 1916 when he was eleven years old. He attended school at St. Anne's, the largest French-Canadian parish in the city, where all instruction was in French, even the classes that were supposed to be in English. He left school to work at the age of fourteen or fifteen, and held a number of unskilled positions before landing a job as a backboy in the mule room of the French Worsted. Most people at work, like

[58] C. Stewart Doty, *The First Franco-Americans: New England Life Histories from the Federal Writers' Project, 1938–1939* (Orono, Maine, 1985), 131–5.
[59] Based on interview with Ernest Gignac, June 25, 1981.

those at school and at home, spoke French. His limited ability to speak English began to gnaw at him. His rise to the rank of mule-spinner in 1927 only intensified his feeling of inferiority. When he joined the ITU in 1932 or 1933, he received encouragement to master English for the first time. Gradually he achieved fluency, and his crowning personal triumph came in 1938 when he won, with union support, a seat in the Rhode Island General Assembly. The union had given him the tools and the confidence to venture outside his local, ethnic society.

Gignac's journey outward from his ethnic enclave was neither quick nor easy. He and others like him cannot be characterized as rebellious youth eager to repudiate the ghettoized heritage of their parents. Their early years in a more stable and secure ethnic society had left a mark in the form of old cultural habits to which they still adhered. They believed in the values of family, religion, and community, which they had internalized while growing up in Woonsocket, and they wanted to pass these values along to their children. Those with school-age children chose to send them to local parish rather than local public schools, to be educated in the essentials of French-Canadian culture as they themselves had been. Through such practices French-Canadian mulespinners made clear that their willingness to venture outside their ethnic community depended on the assurance that they would not be cut off.

This ambivalence expressed itself most clearly in religious matters. The religious leaders in Woonsocket – still vested in the 1930s with enormous moral authority – did not encourage or even sanction French-Canadian involvement in the ITU. They reacted with fear once the dimensions of French-Canadian support for this union became clear in the mid-1930s. Realizing it was too late to attack the union as irreligious or antithetical to French-Canadian values, they embarked on a campaign to smear the union's radical leadership as foreign, atheist, and communist.[60] Yet, in interviews, French-Canadian union veterans repeatedly denied the existence of any conflict between the clergy and the union. Ernest Gignac pulled out the rosary beads he had carried every day of his life to demonstrate his lifelong religious devotion. Arthur Riendeau insisted that the union and the Church "never had no trouble getting along."[61]

These memories are not entirely faulty. In the 1940s, a group of ITU trade unionists, led by the same French-Canadian skilled workers who had breathed life into the ITU in the early 1930s, ousted the

[60] This campaign will be discussed in Chapter 7.
[61] Interviews with Ernest Gignac and Arthur Riendeau, both June 25, 1981.

radical leadership and effected a rapproachement with local clergy. From 1945, until the collapse of the union in the mid-1950s, relations between the two institutions were quite harmonious. But why the inability or refusal to recall an earlier period of conflict? It is likely that the conflicts caused French Canadians considerable pain. They genuinely believed that there need not have been any conflict between unionism, Catholicism, and French-Canadian identity, and they proceeded to expunge the knowledge of conflict from their own historical memories. They viewed their own union involvement not as a way of repudiating their heritage but rather as a way of adapting it to life as industrial workers in American society.

These French-Canadian workers, then, were a quite different group from the radical Franco-Belgians. They were less interested in transforming the world than in negotiating between the worlds they inhabited. They showed an increasing enthusiasm for a new class and American identity, but they remained committed to their ethnic traditions. This duality is strikingly exemplified by the union and religious involvement of the family of François Gagne, an early French-Canadian leader in a dye-house local. In 1935, four of his daughters worked in Woonsocket mills and were active members of the ITU. At the same time, three other daughters resided in convents in Massachusetts and Quebec, preparing to become nuns. The family prided itself on its equal commitment to both a religious and union life.[62]

This duality posed some obvious problems for Schmetz and his fellow radicals. Devotion to ethnic traditions meant a continuing suspicion of radical ideas; it could also temper French-Canadian enthusiasm for a new class identity. Indeed, by the late 1930s and early 1940s, skilled workers began to oppose their radical leaders, counterposing a Catholic, corporatist vision to Schmetz's radicalism. But the duality of the French Canadians also brought the union great strength, especially in the early 1930s. Their attachment to ethnic traditions gave them a credibility in the eyes of the masses of semi-skilled and unskilled French-Canadian textile workers that Schmetz and his fellow radicals could never have gained for themselves. These semiskilled and unskilled workers shared many of the experiences of the skilled workers – poverty, unemployment, a gnawing feeling about the inadequacy of their own ethnic culture. They too tended to conflate their economic plight with their cultural isolation. Lawrence Spitz, a future leader of the ITU brought to Woonsocket by Schmetz in 1937, recalled that these workers "felt they had been looked down upon, underpaid, underprivileged in a remote corner of the state."

[62] *ITU News*, August 1937, 11.

They, like the skilled workers, wanted to overcome their deprivation and, as Spitz remarked, "be part of the mainstream."[63] But they lacked the confidence that years of high wages and production power had instilled in the mulespinners. They were less familiar, on the whole, with the world of unions. Thus they feared venturing in a new direction and participating in unfamiliar organizations. They would be much more inclined to act, however, if they heard fellow French Canadians advocating the cause of industrial unionism and if they saw them active in the ITU.[64]

In communicating with the masses of French-Canadian textile workers, then, the French-Canadian skilled workers were the crucial publicists for Schmetz's vision of industrial unionism. They played a critical role in reaching out beyond the mulespinning ranks to establish genuine industrial union locals. Their contribution went beyond networking. They brought to the union a rich ethnic heritage that put the welfare of the community over individual well-being. They would engineer a remarkable blending of the communal values of French-Canadian workers with the collective aims of the radical unionists. Throughout the 1930s their ethnic communalism would infuse the union with exceptional solidarity and generate an unusually vibrant union life. The ITU's rise to power rested to no small degree on its ability to solidify the ranks of labor organization with a deep ethnic communalism.

[63] Interview with Lawrence Spitz, September 19–20, 1979.

[64] A few groups of lesser-skilled workers did figure prominently in ITU organizing. Dye-house workers, for example, who counted in their ranks no equivalent stratum of skilled workers, were remarkably successful in organizing their places of work. By 1934 they had organized two-thirds of the city's dye houses, a level of unionization second only to what mulespinners had achieved in the city's French spinning and woolen spinning mills (see Table 3.2 and Appendix A). Two sets of workplace conditions seem to have forged dye-house workers into a tightly knit and militant group. First, the unusually hot, damp, dirty, and health-threatening dye-house working conditions – nasty even by textile industry standards – gave dye-house workers a special status; second, dye-house workers, not tied to particular machines like so many textile workers, could roam the workplace, easily converse with their workmates, and develop a cohesive workplace culture. Dye-house workers may also have been emboldened by the knowledge of their importance to the city's woolen and worsted industry. Since most of the wool used in the city's spinning mills had to pass through a local dye house first, a strike by dye-house workers could quickly bring the entire city's industry to a standstill. Interview with Stanley Rypsyc, October 30, 1980. See also David J. Goldberg, "Immigrants, Intellectuals and Industrial Unions: The 1919 Textile Strikes and the Experience of the Amalgamated Textile Workers of America in Passaic and Paterson, New Jersey and Lawrence, Massachusetts" (Ph.D. dissertation, Columbia University, 1983), 32–3.

The important role of French-Canadian skilled workers in the ITU challenges a school of historical interpretation, popular in the early 1970s, that saw in the establishment of the new industrial unions the work of a uniformly radical rank and file.[65] Early union initiatives depended on an alliance between different groups of rank and filers – some radical, some conservative, some skilled, some unskilled, some steeped in union traditions, and some in ethnic traditions. The question to pose about these early unions, then, is not "Were they radical or conservative?" but rather, "What made an alliance of different working-class constituencies possible?" No single-factor explanation of this phenomenon will suffice. The leveling effect of impoverishment, the willingness of radicals to give the building of nonpartisan industrial unions a greater priority than their political aims, the desire of second and third generation ethnic workers to participate more fully in American culture and politics are all critical elements of the story. But as important a factor as any other was the existence of a stratum of workers with the ability and desire to forge links between constituencies that had little in common. The French-Canadian skilled workers comprised this stratum in Woonsocket. Their duality – their commitment to unionism and to their ethnic heritage – allowed them to link the world of the European radicals with the world of the French-Canadian worker.

The role these workers played was not unique to Woonsocket. Peter Friedlander, in his work on a UAW local in the predominantly Polish city of Hamtramck, Michigan, uncovered a group of second-generation Polish union activists remarkably similar in occupational, demographic, and political characteristics to the French-Canadian cadre in Woonsocket. Joshua Freeman's work on transport workers in New York City has revealed the critical intermediary role played by Irish republicans in bringing together communist leaders and masses of devoutly Catholic and anticommunist Irish workers in the Transport Workers Union. John Bodnar's work points to a similar development among ethnic workers in the coal fields and steel mills of Pennsylvania.[66]

---

[65] See, for example, James Green, "Working-Class Militancy in the Great Depression," *Radical America* VI (November–December, 197?), 1 36; Staughton Lynd, "The Possibility of Radicalism In the Early 1930s: The Case of Steel," *Radical America* VI (November–December, 1972), 37–64; Alice and Staughton Lynd, eds., *Rank and File: Personal Histories by Working-Class Organizers* (Princeton, N.J., 1981); and Jeremy Brecher, *Strike!* (San Francisco, 1972), 144–263.

[66] Peter Friedlander, *The Emergence of a UAW Local, 1936–1939: A Study in Class and Culture* (Pittsburgh, Pa., 1976), 22–37, 93–110; Joshua B. Freeman, "Catholics, Com-

Seeing the rank and file as a collection of diverse groups of workers, and the new industrial unions as alliances among them, results in an approach to union politics somewhat different from the one that labor historians have customarily employed. It is not sufficient to interpret labor union development, as some have done, as a struggle between a militant rank and file and an accommodationist and bureaucratic leadership;[67] nor is it particularly helpful to draw conclusions about the development of unions from ethnocultural characteristics that inevitably predispose workers to conservative and acquiescent behavior.[68] Rather, union development should be analyzed in terms of the struggle of competing rank-and-file groups for power and influence. In Woonsocket, the major contestants for union leadership would be Schmetz's group of European radicals and Galipeau's group of French-Canadian mulespinners. Their struggle did not emerge immediately. There was still so much organizing work to be done, such a large agreed-upon agenda to accomplish, that the struggle would not become acute for years. And the course of the struggle and its outcome would be determined not simply by the actions and beliefs of each group, but also by the responses of employers, clergy, and politicians to union initiatives, and by the dramatic economic and political upheaval caused by mobilization for world war.

Footnote 66 (cont.)
   munists, and Republicans: Irish Workers and the Organization of the Transport Workers Union," in Michael H. Frisch and Daniel J. Walkowitz, Working Class America: Essays on Labor, Community, and American Society (Urbana, Ill., 1983), 256–83; John Bodnar, Workers' World: Kinship, Community and Protest in an Industrial Society, 1900–1940 (Baltimore, Md., 1982).
[67] See, for example, Frances Fox Piven and Richard Cloward, Poor People's Movements: When They Succeed and How They Fail (New York, 1977), 96–180.
[68] This is the approach followed in Friedlander, The Emergence of a UAW Local.

4   *Citywide mobilization, 1934–1936*

The building of the Independent Textile Union in Woonsocket occurred so quietly that few outside the mills in which it was organizing
took notice. No newspapers covered the union's activities before the
summer of 1934. The situation changed dramatically when, in August,
the United Textile Workers of America (UTW) called a national textile
strike for September 1 to protest employer infractions of the NRA
codes. On September 8, members of the ITU joined the nationwide
walkout and set out to shut down every textile mill in the city. Woonsocket burst into the national headlines on September 12 and 13 when
thousands of workers in the city furiously attacked the only mill in
the city that had refused to comply with ITU demands. Workers
fought National Guardsmen in pitched battles and then rioted through
the city's mercantile district. These battles brought to the surface deep
class resentments and introduced to the city a consciousness of class
division that would shape its politics for the rest of the decade.

The strike of 1934

The textile strike of 1934, involving 400,000 textile workers from
Maine to Alabama, was the single largest industrial action in the history of American labor. Its origins can be traced to a series of political
and social developments set in motion by the 1933 NIRA. Clause 7(a)
of this act, which entitled workers to organize into unions of their
own choosing and bargain collectively with their employers, stimulated a nationwide surge of unionization. In one year, the UTW grew
from a moribund organization of 20,000 to an enthusiastic movement
of 400,000 textile workers. As workers' interest in unionism soared,
however, the willingness of their employers to abide by the NRA's
textile industrial codes, which included collective bargaining provisions, declined. This growing recalcitrance reflected, in part, a
deep-seated antipathy among textile employers to unions – especially
to those that their very own employees had dared to organize. It also
reflected the economic failure of the NIRA. The NRA codes in various
industries, including textiles, initially attracted the support of large
numbers of industrialists. The textile industry's cotton sector even

enjoyed a few months of economic recovery as the willingness of numerous employers to restrict production and the hours of work diminished the glut of textile goods on the market and stimulated a modest demand. But such economic arrangements, dependent on the voluntary compliance of individual employers, were of the most precarious sort. The moment that the mild recovery stalled, employers, especially those in cotton manufacture who feared the imminent collapse of their own enterprises, lost confidence in the codes and reverted to the autarchic behavior that had characterized their industry in the years before 1933. Employers increasingly disregarded the NRA codes governing wages, hours, and work loads, and the government lacked the statutory power to punish their noncompliance.[1]

Employer violations of the codes produced a quick deterioration in working conditions. Workers watched their hourly wages decline and their weekly hours rise. Even worse, from their perspective, were the dreaded speedups in their machinery's rate of operation and the stretch-outs in the number of machines that each worker had to operate.[2] Workers subjected to such terms of employment might have angrily turned on the federal government for failing to establish an administrative mechanism of legal force sufficient to compel employer compliance with the terms of the NIRA. But such sentiments of betrayal are almost impossible to find. The passage of the NIRA and the coming of the New Deal had aroused such widespread faith in Roosevelt's genuine concern for ordinary Americans and his desire to use the federal government to improve their lot – "The President Wants You to Join a Union" John L. Lewis reminded millions of workers in his radio addresses – that most workers were not prepared, in 1933 or 1934, to believe that Roosevelt had failed them. Instead, their anger increasingly focused on employers for violating both the spirit of Roosevelt's Administration and the law that the Congress had passed.[3]

---

[1] Ellis Hawley, *The New Deal and the Problem of Monopoly: A Study in Economic Ambivalence* (Princeton, N.J., 1966), 19–146; Louis Galambos, *Competition and Cooperation: The Emergence of a National Trade Association* (Baltimore, 1966), 173–279; George B. Galloway, et al., *Industrial Planning Under the Codes* (New York, 1935), 117–43; James A. Hodges, *New Deal Labor Policy and the Southern Cotton Textile Industry, 1933–1941* (Knoxville, Tenn., 1986), 3–78.

[2] Irving Bernstein, *The Turbulent Years: A History of the American Worker, 1933–1941* (Boston, 1969), 298–303.

[3] See Robert McElvaine, *Down and Out in the Great Depression: Letters from the "Forgotten Man"* (Chapel Hill, N.C., 1983), passim; Gerald Markowitz and David Rosner, *"Slaves of the Depression": Workers' Letters About Life on the Job* (Ithaca, N.Y., 1987), passim; Gary Gerstle, "The Politics of Patriotism: Americanization and the Formation of the CIO," *Dissent* (Winter 1986), 84–92.

During the summer of 1934 wildcat strikes broke out among groups of Alabama cotton workers angry at their employers' refusal to abide by the NRA cotton industry code. The strikers notified their employers that they would not return to work until employers recognized the United Textile Workers as a bargaining agent, reinstated employees fired for union organizing, halted all stretch-outs, and observed the minimum wage (twelve dollars per week) and maximum hour (thirty hours per week) provisions of the NRA code. The leadership of the UTW, pressured by the government to maintain peace in their ranks and fearing the surge of militancy from below, initially counseled patience and tried to restrain the strikers. But the militancy would not be contained. It spread quickly to other parts of the South and then to the North, until the clamor for a general strike reached national proportions. UTW leaders reluctantly called a general nationwide strike for September 1. They publicly announced that all textile workers in the country would refuse to work until employers agreed to abide by the NRA codes.[4]

With a national strike pending, authorities in Woonsocket worried about the quiet union in their midst. Many Woonsocket residents must have been surprised to read that a union called the ITU was "in control of the labor situation in the city." The *Woonsocket Call* sought out Joseph Schmetz for information on the strike plans of his union. Schmetz tried to assuage fears by stressing his union's commitment to industrial peace. ITU members did not share the grievances of textile workers elsewhere. In seventeen mills they had worked out collective bargaining agreements with employers which enforced and often bettered the terms stipulated in the NRA woolen and worsted code. Employers had abided by the terms of this agreement, and the union intended to do the same. Schmetz warned, however, that the ITU also had obligations to its fellow textile workers elsewhere. If the UTW strike developed force, ITU members might stage a sympathy walkout. Its purpose would not be to wrest further concessions from Woonsocket employers but to increase the pressure on the government to intervene in the industry to standardize conditions throughout the country. On the eve of the strike, he described the attitude of his union as one of "watchful waiting."[5]

---

[4] For accounts of the strike, see Bernstein, *The Turbulent Years*, 298–315; Herbert J. Lahne, *The Cotton Mill Worker* (New York, 1944), 216–31; Robert R.R. Brooks, "The United Textile Workers of America" (Ph.D. dissertation, Yale University, 1935), 349–397; Jacquelyn Dowd Hall, James Leloudis, Robert Korstad, Mary Murphy, Lu Ann Jones, and Christopher B. Daly, *Like A Family: The Making of a Southern Cotton Mill World* (Chapel Hill, N.C., 1987), 289–357; Hodges, *New Deal Labor Policy*, 86–118.

[5] *Woonsocket Call* (hereafter *WC*), August 28, 1934.

When the national strike began on September 1, Woonsocket workers remained at their jobs. But as hundreds of thousands of textile workers across the country went on strike, pressure began to mount in the ranks of the ITU for a supportive action. On September 8, 1934, ITU members voted overwhelmingly, 1,756 to 84, to walk off their jobs.[6] That Woonsocket's Catholic, ethnic unionists would so quickly and eagerly join a national working-class protest, especially one that required them to identify their interests with workers as foreign to them as Alabama's Protestant and native-born strikers, reveals in part the influence of radical and cosmopolitan Franco-Belgian ITU leaders on their thinking. But this near-unanimous strike vote must also be interpreted as a dramatic demonstration of the national dimensions of the working-class movement inspired by the New Deal. As the New Deal reached down with its economic programs and patriotic gusto into every industrial city in America, it induced workers as different as Woonsocket's French Canadians and Alabama's old-stock Americans to feel the commonality of their predicament and to make common cause.[7]

Woonsocket manufacturers met the strike movement with little resistance. By September 10, local newspapers reported that the union had shut down all but two of Woonsocket's textile mills. Schmetz reiterated his earlier claim that the ITU was striking not against Woonsocket manufacturers but in solidarity with textile workers elsewhere. He emphasized the importance of united action on the part of the nation's 1 million textile workers to secure the necessary improvements in working conditions.[8]

The strike might have run a peaceful and orderly course in Woonsocket had it not been for the defiant actions of one manufacturer, Woonsocket Rayon. On September 11, this firm was the only textile mill still operating in the city. The union realized that an immediate shutdown would allow chemicals in the machines to solidify and cause substantial damage. Accordingly, it gave mill management five

[6] Ibid., September 9, 1934.
[7] One sure sign of the New Deal's ability to inspire individual Americans and shape their political thinking was the incorporation of the NRA's famous emblem, the Blue Eagle, into local political discourse. In Woonsocket, the ITU placed a blue eagle on the letterhead of its stationery, and individual textile workers often mentioned the hopes inspired by the Blue Eagle [or, in the words of one French Canadian, 'bleu Aegle' (sic)] in letters they wrote to Roosevelt and other New Dealers. See Frank D. Roy to Mr. Johnson, November 13, 1933, Manchester Co. file, Record Group 9 (hereafter RG 9), Entry 398, National Archives, Washington, D.C. (hereafter NA); Joseph Schmetz to NRA, May 6, 1935, Woonsocket Falls Mills file, RG 9, Entry 402, NA.
[8] La Tribune (hereafter LT), September 10, 1934.

days to drain the chemicals out of the machines and close the mill. Management spurned the union's terms, claiming that the plant was not properly part of the textile industry because it produced only rayon thread. It would stay open unless forced to close.[9]

That evening, a crowd of about 2,000 gathered in front of Woonsocket Rayon and began hurling a barrage of stones and other "missiles" at the mill. The attack continued for two hours. When a Woonsocket policeman grabbed a fleeing protestor, the mob roared its protest, surrounded the policeman, and freed the prisoner from his grasp. At midnight, National Guardsmen arrived from nearby Saylesville where riots had already erupted, and dispersed the crowd with tear gas.[10] The next morning the city reacted with shock to the previous night's attack. Both the ITU and the UTW denied responsibility for the rioting, claiming they were withholding their pickets from the mill until Saturday, September 15. A spokesman for the ITU hinted that outside agitators may have incited the crowds. Schmetz issued a plea for nonviolence.[11]

His plea fell on deaf ears. Toward evening, 8,000 to 10,000 restless, angry people gathered at the gates of Woonsocket Rayon and confronted the state militia men guarding mill property. At that moment Schmetz and other leaders of the ITU were meeting, in another part of town, with workers of the Rayon interested in forming a union local. In the middle of the meeting, Schmetz later recalled, a foreman from the Rayon "sneaked in and got six men out of the hall and hustled them into a waiting taxi." ITU members quickly discovered this infiltration and surrounded the taxi before it could get away. They began rocking the car, preparing to overturn it; cooler heads prevailed, however, and the car was permitted to leave. The car headed for Woonsocket Rayon to deliver the foreman and his six strikebreakers to work. Schmetz later speculated that the arrival of a taxi full of scabs at the gates of Woonsocket Rayon set off the crowd.[12] Protestors began throwing stones and rushing the mill gates. The guardsmen defending the Rayon tried to disperse the crowd with tear gas. When this failed to deter the crowd, the soldiers fired their guns. A *New York Times* journalist reported that they "fired two volleys of 22.5 shots into the mass." This too failed to restore order. Soon the tumult

---

[9] *New York Times* (hereafter *NYT*), September 11, 1934.

[10] *WC*, September 12, 1934, and *NYT*, September 13, 1934. For the textile strike in Saylesville and the rest of Rhode Island, see James Findlay, "The Great Textile Strike of 1934: Illuminating Rhode Island History in the Thirties," *Rhode Island History* 42 (February 1983), 17–29.

[11] *WC*, September 12, 1934.

[12] *ITU News*, September 1936, 3.

spilled over from the Woonsocket Rayon plant to the nearby Social
District. Rioters began smashing store windows and stealing merchandise. With the bulk of the local police force deployed at the
Rayon, the "mobs of looters and window smashers in the business
quarter of town had complete sway almost without molestation."
They broke street lights, overturned automobiles, and set fire to
wagons. Stones were flying in every direction. Woonsocket's police
commissioner pleaded with the governor of Rhode Island for National
Guard reinforcements, warning "it is absolutely necessary that we
have more troops or we shall perish."[13] Schmetz, writing two years
later, vividly recalled the bedlam. "The streets became pitch dark,
the populace was electrified by the apprehension of some imminent
disaster," he wrote. "Thousands of people were in the danger zone,
groups of the younger element held conversations in the back alleys,
stones were flying and so were tear gas bombs. Any stone that found
its target brought an exclamation of delight from the crowd. Police
tried to disperse the mob, but to no avail for more people went about
looking for ammunition in the form of stones."[14] More troops finally
did arrive and managed to retake the Social District from the rioters.

A stunned city awoke the next morning to scenes of human and
physical devastation. One person lay dead and fifteen, including four
policemen, required hospitalization for their wounds. The retail area
of the Social District – the heart of French-Canadian working-class life
in the city – lay in shambles. Thirty-seven stores had their windows
smashed and their merchandise looted. Damages and losses exceeded
$100,000.[15] Woonsocket Rayon had been physically damaged, forcing
its management to shut down production. The National Guard placed
Woonsocket under martial law and imposed a 9:00 p.m. curfew on
the population. Guardsmen cordoned off the Social District and prevented all traffic from entering the area. No more rioting occurred,
but city life did not easily return to normal. The ITU kept all the city
mills shut for another two weeks until the national strike was called
off. Woonsocket residents gradually overcame their shock and tried
to make sense of the riots that had engulfed their city.[16]

What happened? Newspaper reporters from the Anglophone press
entertained two theories concerning the riots. One simply treated the
rioters as "hoodlums" who went on a rampage when they realized

[13] NYT, September 13, 1934.
[14] ITU News, September 1936, 3.
[15] WC, September 13, 1934; Alton P. Thomas, Woonsocket: Highlights of History,
1800–1976 (Woonsocket, R.I., 1976), 136–8; one of the wounded subsequently died.
[16] For the aftermath of the riot, see WC, September 14–28, 1934.

that the forces of law and order had been stretched thin. The other attributed the riotous behavior to the inflammatory and manipulative speeches of communists or other outside agitators.[17] Both the ITU and the UTW publicly supported the second view in an effort to absolve their own organizations of any possible blame.[18] Neither view, however, satisfactorily explains the participation of thousands of people in the riots. "Hoodlums," when they sensed an opportunity for property destruction and personal gain at little risk to themselves, may have carried the riot to the business part of the Social District. But the thousands who attacked a mill defended by National Guardsmen armed with tear gas and rifles had more than excitement or personal gain in mind. If outside agitators played a critical role in inflaming the crowd, it seems surprising that none has ever been identified. Police did arrest ten alleged communists in Providence the day after the riot and accused them of inciting riot and disorder. But none could be placed in Woonsocket the night of the riot. If these alleged agitators somehow sneaked into town, ignited a 10,000 person attack on a mill, and slipped away before the debris settled, they must have tapped a deep vein of resentment or anger in the local population.[19]

The city's local French daily, *La Tribune*, recognized that the riotous behavior reflected serious social problems in their community. The editors maintained an official view that French-Canadian workers in Woonsocket were not responsible for the violence.[20] But they knew better. The rioters came from the ranks of their own people. The individual killed, and most of the eleven hospitalized for their wounds were Woonsocket French Canadians. Of the twenty-eight arrested for drunken and disorderly behavior and for looting, at least twenty had French-Canadian names. Twenty-two lived in Woonsocket and the other six in nearby mill towns like Uxbridge, Manville, and Slatersville.[21] Rather than dismiss these people as "looters," "rioters," and "hoodlums" as the Anglophone press had done, the editors of *La Tribune* sought explanations for their behavior. They found one in the conditions shaping French-Canadian working-class life. Many workers simply could not earn enough to support themselves and

---

[17] WC, September 13–14, 1934, and NYT, September 13–14, 1934.

[18] WC, September 14, 1934; ITU, Labor Review, 1931 1942 (Woonsocket, R.I., 1942), 11.

[19] See NYT and WC, September 14, 1934, for a list of alleged communists arrested in Providence.

[20] LT, September 14–21, 1934, passim.

[21] Providence Journal (hereafter PJ), September 14, 1934. By September 17, the number arrested had climbed to fifty, with the percentage of local French Canadians climbing to more than three-quarters of the total. PJ, September 17, 1934.

their families. Without some assurance of jobs and minimum income levels for these people, the editors admitted that "no peace is possible, no social life is possible."[22]

La Tribune accurately identified the devastating effect of the Depression on a significant part of Woonsocket's working class. All the rioting occurred in a relatively small area of the Social District, which had once been the center of Woonsocket's thriving cotton industry. By 1934, most cotton manufacturing companies had shut down their Woonsocket mills, costing the city thousands of jobs. Economic hardship alone, however, cannot explain the rioting. Conditions in cities like Fall River and Lowell were at least as difficult as those in Woonsocket's dying cotton district, but they produced no rioting. An explanation for the events in Woonsocket must look not only to the fact of economic hardship but also to the community's perception of that hardship.

Elements of ethnic culture heavily influenced the rioters' understanding of their economic predicament. French Canadians had long shaped their culture around *la survivance* – a determination to survive foreign domination. Their ethnic leaders instructed them to defy external forces deemed harmful to the community. Traditionally, this effort found expression in ethnic or nationalist channels as French-Canadian communities fought English influence in Canada and American influence in the United States. But in Woonsocket in the 1920s and 1930s, significant portions of the French-Canadian community began to express their determination for cultural survival in class terms. The Americanization pressures in the 1920s had freed French-Canadian culture from the grasp of an archconservative, middle-class leadership, and years of economic hardship caused by a declining cotton textile industry prompted some French-Canadian workers to locate a threat to their survival not in external political authority but in external economic powers. Such a reformulation of ethnic doctrines had surfaced first in the Sentinelle Affair; it surfaced again in the growing conviction of Woonsocket workers that the French textile magnates who ran mills in their community were "aristocrats" who despised the French-Canadian workers they employed; and it surfaced a third time in the riot that began at the mill gates of Woonsocket Rayon in September 1934.

Woonsocket Rayon was owned by the Manville Jenckes Corporation. Though headquartered in nearby Providence, Manville Jenckes was perceived in Woonsocket as a distant, national corporation with no interest in the welfare of the city beyond the profitability of its

---

[22] *LT*, September 21, 1934.

mills. Since 1927, it had shut down three large cotton mills in the city, depriving 1,500 to 2,000 workers of their jobs. While Manville Jenckes was not the only corporation curtailing operations in Woonsocket, its policies affected a larger number of Woonsocket workers than those of any other firm. Formed in a 1923 merger that vastly inflated the true value of its stock, Manville Jenckes had suffered from financial instability almost from the start. Such instability periodically impelled its managers, as part of an ongoing search for cost reductions and productivity enhancement, to reduce employee wages and lengthen their weekly hours. When such efforts generated employee resistance, management usually refused to compromise. In 1926 it called on state law enforcement agencies to break a strike in a cotton mill it operated in nearby Manville, and in 1927 it closed two of its large productive enterprises in Woonsocket rather than negotiate an agreement with worker representatives.[23] In 1933 it closed the last of its Woonsocket cotton production facilities, the Globe Mill.[24] In October of that same year, it violated the NIRA by firing all the workers who had joined a UTW organizing drive at its Woonsocket Rayon plant; and then in September 1934 it rubbed salt in the wounds of its former workers by refusing to shut Woonsocket Rayon for the duration of the textile strike.[25]

[23] For 1926 Manville strike see *The Textile Worker*, 1926, passim. On chronic financial instability of Manville Jenckes, see Liston Pope, *Millhands and Preachers: A Study of Gastonia* (New Haven, Conn., 1942), 223–30; *The Textile Worker* (February 1929), 650–2; Henry F. Lippitt II, "The Financial History of the Manville Jenckes Company, Manville, Rhode Island, A New England Cotton Textile Concern" (unpublished paper, MIT, 1936), 5–86. Lippitt's paper is located in the archives of the Rhode Island Historical Society. From its formation in 1928, Woonsocket Rayon was one of the corporation's most profitable operations; it even turned a hefty profit during the years 1931–1933, when the corporation was in receivership. See Lippitt, "Financial History," 182.

[24] Findlay, "The Great Textile Strike of 1934," 14.

[25] *WC*, September 14, 1934. On firing of union activists in 1933, see complaint from Woonsocket Rayon employee filed with the Cotton Textile National Industrial Relations Board, n.d., Rayon and Synthetic Yarn: Excerpts file, RG 9, Entry 398, NA; Woonsocket Rayon Co. file, RG 9, Entry 398, NA; Woonsocket Rayon Co. file, RG 9, Entry 402, NA. In this last folder are five letters addressed to Roosevelt and NRA administrators from Albert Pelchat, one of the Woonsocket Rayon unionists who lost his job in October 1933. Their contents will be discussed in the next chapter. About seventy-five workers, half of Woonsocket Rayon's 1933 work force, seem to have been fired for union activities. I have found no information in the NRA records or in the Manville Jenckes business records (at the Rhode Island Historical Society) that would illuminate the process by which Woonsocket Rayon's management settled on its hard-line, antiunion stance.

Manville Jenckes's reputation for antilabor policies extended well beyond Woonsocket. It owned the Loray Mill in Gastonia, North Carolina, site of a bitter conflict in

We do not know the identities of the thousands of people milling around Woonsocket Rayon's gates on the evening of September 12. But the fact that the riot there was touched off by the arrival of a carload of strikebreakers suggests a close connection between the violent protest that ensued and a decade of corporate actions that had deprived so many Woonsocket residents of their livelihood. By September 1934, the victims of the corporation's policies, including those individuals who had lost their jobs because of mill shutdowns and strike activity, numbered in the thousands. If we measure victimization in terms of family members affected by lost jobs, then the number of victims could have exceeded 10,000. It would have been easy for Woonsocket's French-Canadian workers, long taught by ethnic leaders to see themselves as a social remnant constantly besieged by evil external powers, to have believed that Manville Jenckes had embarked on a deliberate plan to destroy their community. Only such a belief can satisfactorily explain the frightful scene at Woonsocket Rayon's mill gates on the night of September 12, chillingly recorded by the *New York Times* reporter: the thousands of "howling men and women who had surrounded the [Rayon] plant...kept on charging despite the fact that the guardsmen had spent their tear gas bombs on them and had fired two volleys of 22.5 shots into the mass."[26] Years of smoldering anger at the corporate policies of Manville Jenckes had exploded into a violent rage.

The rage expressed throughout the night of September 12 had its irrational side, vented especially in the wanton destruction carried out by youth gangs in the Social District as well as in the special fury that some rioters reserved for their attack on two Social District shops owned by Jewish merchants.[27] But there was also a rational dimension to this rage, expressing a bitter resentment at class inequality: On the one side of the great class divide stood Manville Jenckes, so powerful that it seemingly suffered none of the consequences of its harmful corporate policies. On the other side knelt the workers, so powerless that they could do nothing to resist their victimization other than to throw themselves screaming at phalanxes of National Guardsmen. Woonsocket society, of course, was far more complex, its social structure much more stratified, than this vision of class

Footnote 25 (*cont.*)
   1929 that left several strikers and police dead. See Irving Bernstein, *The Lean Years: A History of the American Worker, 1920–1933* (Boston, 1960), 20–8, and Pope, *Millhands and Preachers*, 207–84.
[26] *NYT*, September 13, 1934.
[27] Thomas, *Woonsocket*, 137–8.

relations implied. But in the days following the riot, only one social division mattered: that dividing capital from labor.

Never before had such a consciousness of class division pervaded city life. Members of the ITU, though deploring the violence of the riot, felt a need to identify with those who had rioted. On the morning of September 14, 550 union members appeared at the funeral of Jude Courtemanche, the nineteen-year-old shot and killed during the riot. As the union's official history put it, "Thousands of Woonsocket workers marched behind the hearse, jammed the church and overflowed into the streets. The silent emotion of the tense crowd filled the air. They were paying their last respects to Jude Courtemanche, first casualty in the union struggle for a better life."[28] Courtemanche had not been a member of the union, nor is it clear that he even supported the strike. The union history portrayed him as an "innocent bystander" who, on his way home from "visiting his girlfriend," stopped at the liquor store to find out why it had attracted such a crowd. He was shot dead while standing in the shop's doorway.[29]

The portrayal of Courtemanche as an "innocent bystander" may have been true, but Courtemanche could easily have been one of the roaming youths who vandalized the liquor store. In the wake of the riot, however, what he actually did on the night of the riot did not seem to matter. What mattered was that Courtemanche was a working man killed, ITU members believed, by a police force that had placed a higher priority on protecting bourgeois property than on preserving working-class lives.[30] Against such an affront, unionists felt that all working people, regardless of their attitudes toward the union or their actual behavior during the strike, had to demonstrate their solidarity.

Manufacturers likewise interpreted the riot as the outbreak of class warfare. Robert Guerin, then a youth of eleven, remembers being hustled out of a movie house to his home where he sharpened his saber and awaited the proletarian attack. The suspicion between manufacturers and workers ran so deep that his mother would not

---

[28] ITU, *Labor Review*, 11.

[29] Ibid.

[30] ITU veterans claimed that if more police had been dispatched to the Social District rather than to the banks and residences of the city's manufacturing and financial elite, the riot never would have gained momentum. ITU members were further angered by the fact that no one was ever charged with and placed on trial for Courtemanche's death. Normand Galipeau's bitter comment, "Courtemanche got killed by a gun that came out of a police station display case," reflects the widespread union belief that the guilty man was a police officer whose role in the killing was covered up by fellow officers. Interviews: Normand Galipeau, October 22–23, 1980; Arthur Riendeau, June 25, 1981; Lawrence Spitz, September 19–20, 1979.

wear her fur coat to church for months after the strike.[31] The children of working-class militants were also powerfully affected. George Butsika, then a sixteen-year-old who took little interest in the union before the events of September, recalls that the ITU's huge funeral procession for Courtemanche awakened in him feelings of class solidarity that propelled him into a lifelong career as a trade unionist.[32]

The ethnic leaders of the French-Canadian community were stunned by the events of September. They did not support or sanction the strike or riot, but felt powerless to oppose either. They recognized that the riot had unleashed a rage at class inequality in their community but could not understand its roots. They saw class consciousness in essentialist terms, as the product of radical and socialist doctrines foreign to French-Canadian culture. French-Canadian workers, insisted La Tribune, were not revolutionary.[33] In one sense, this perception was correct: The Depression experience had not measurably increased support among French-Canadian workers for the Socialist and Communist parties. But the conviction of ethnic leaders that class consciousness was a doctrine foreign to their culture blinded them to the ways in which their own ethnic doctrines fueled class resentment.

The ITU was the chief beneficiary of this class resentment. The ITU demonstrated to this community in September 1934 that it could provide the leadership and organization necessary to alter significantly the conditions of working-class life. It kept the mills shut for two weeks after the riots ended and a week after the national strike had been called off.[34] It dispatched "flying squadrons" – autos full of union members – to aid fellow strikers throughout Rhode Island and Massachusetts. In one particularly dramatic action, it organized a parade of 100 automobiles to circle a huge wool processing plant until it agreed to shut down.[35] In none of these actions did the union overextend its financial resources or overreach its membership. Virtually alone among textile unions in the country, it emerged from the strike of 1934 with a solid organization and enhanced visibility in the community.[36]

French-Canadian workers joined the ITU in large numbers after the strike. From late 1934 through 1936, the union increased in size by

---

[31] Interview with Robert Guerin, November 3, 1980.
[32] Interview with George Butsika, September 14, 1984.
[33] LT, September 14, 1934.
[34] WC, September 28, 1934.
[35] ITU, Labor Review, 11.
[36] On the collapse of the UTW in the aftermath of the strike see Lahne, The Cotton Mill Worker, 232–9.

50 percent, from approximately 3,000 to 4,500 members. In early 1937, it added another 1,500 members, making the ITU one of the most powerful labor organizations in the state.[37] It expanded beyond the woolen and worsted sector and beyond the textile industry to include more than a thousand workers drawn from rubber mills, retail stores, offices, bakeries, barber shops, shoe repair shops, and such construction trades as electrical and sheet metal work.[38] Schmetz, with his vision of one big union, provided the initial impetus for the expansion by approaching bakery workers and persuading them of the virtues of his union.[39] But the rapidity of the expansion across trade-union and occupational barriers resulted from the interest of the French-Canadian working class in the union. Word of the union and its accomplishments spread quickly in the densely populated working-class areas of Woonsocket. Many in the community thought that, if union membership benefited French-Canadian workers in the textile industry, it would benefit those in other industries as well. Entire districts of pro-union sentiment appeared. Lawrence Spitz, a leading ITU official in the second half of the 1930s, recalls the widespread nature of union membership in the Social District. The members, Spitz

[37] *ITU News*, 1936–1937, passim; ITU, *Labor Review*, 9; Robert Maurice Mooney, "The Origins, Nature, Internal and External Operations of the Industrial Trades Union of America" (M.A. thesis, Catholic University of America, 1947), 21. Appendix A to the present book lists all ITU locals, their memberships and their date of entry into the ITU. Membership figures for other unions are difficult to establish but, beginning in early 1937, reporters, government investigators, and the officers of rival textile unions repeatedly noted and marveled at the size and power of the ITU. See, for example, *Christian Science Monitor*, November 16, 1936, and *WC*, November 5, 1937. See also James L. Bernard to Samuel L. McClurd, (labor mediator and executive assistant, respectively, of the Textile Division Conciliation Service, U.S. Department of Labor), November 15, 1936, and January 23, 1937, Woonsocket Woolen Mills file, RG 9, Entry 402, NA; Richard Rohman, "Report to Emil Rieve on Rhode Island," Textile Workers Union of America papers, Mss 396, Box 54, Independent Textile Union of America file, Wisconsin State Historical Society, Madison, Wis.; Federal Writers' Project, Works Progress Administration, *Rhode Island: A Guide to the Smallest State* (Boston, 1937), 311–18; and Robert Harry Ferguson, "Textile Unions in Rhode Island" (M.A. thesis, Brown University, 1940), 254.

[38] *ITU News*, 1936–1937, passim; letter from Lawrence Spitz to author, May 11, 1977; Rhode Island Department of Labor (hereafter R.I. DOL), *Annual Report* (Providence, R.I.) 1935, 200–4. The approximate number of workers in each of these sectors organized by the ITU was as follows: 507 rubber workers (American Wringer), seventy-five bakery employees (seven of nine city bakeries), seventy barbers (about 75 percent of the city's total), 235 store clerks (forty-nine stores), 110 electricians, and ninety sheet metal workers. The number of office clerks and shoe repairers in the union is unclear; I have guessed a hundred of the former and fifty of the latter. See Appendix A for more information on these locals.

[39] Interview with Heliodore Comeau, June 24, 1981.

commented, "lived one next to another. You went down Clinton Street, three decker houses, and...they were all ITU members. It was very difficult to go through the Social Area of Woonsocket and find a house that didn't have ITU members in it...almost impossible."[40] The ethnic solidarity of the French-Canadian community enlarged, diversified, and solidified the ranks of a class-conscious organization.

The infusion of ethnic solidarity into the union presented a new challenge for Schmetz and his fellow radicals. Although French-Canadian ethnic ties and consciousness unquestionably strengthened the union, they also increased support in the union for a more moderate trade-union program. The September 1934 strike vote indicated how much union radicals, with their desire to incorporate Woonsocket workers into a national labor movement, enjoyed the upper hand in ITU affairs. But the riot had brought into the union legions of enthusiastic French-Canadian workers more interested in restoring their ethnic community to an earlier period of vitality than in promoting socialism or even a national union for all textile workers. These new recruits might well encourage the ITU's cadre of French-Canadian skilled workers to peddle a more ethnic-oriented union ideology and to vie with Schmetz for union power. If Schmetz wanted to foreclose this possibility, the ITU had to widen the gap that had emerged between French-Canadian workers and their traditional ethnic leaders. It also had to encourage French-Canadian workers to venture out further from the conservative world in which they had grown up and contemplate alternative, more radical ways of organizing society. In the years 1934 to 1936, union radicals hoped that the experience of work in union shops and of participation in union affairs would arouse French-Canadian enthusiasm for a widespread transformation of social relations.

The union experience

ITU members gained significant power on the shopfloor between 1934 and 1936. The earliest written document pertaining to shopfloor relations is a 1934 agreement that defined, in eight factory rules, relations between the foremen and workers of a French spinning mill or woolen mill.[41] Cumulatively the rules amounted to a concerted effort on the union's part to wrest control of the duration, distribution, and

---

[40] Interview with Lawrence Spitz, September 19–20, 1979.
[41] Mooney included this agreement in his master's thesis. The seventeen agreements which the union reached with employers before 1934 were verbal in nature and never recorded. See Mooney, "ITU," 69, and his Appendix B.

intensity of work away from the employer. Two rules stipulated that management could not run its machines more than sixteen hours a day or hire an individual to labor more than eight. A third rule eliminated the foreman from the work distribution process by establishing a share-the-work system that insisted that "each employee [have] an equal amount of work in his respective department." Other rules established mulespinner work loads and obligated management to consult union members before implementing any personnel changes and "innovations affecting working conditions."[42] Workers did not gain control over their enterprises through such infringements on customary managerial prerogatives, but they certainly gained control over their jobs. One worker succinctly conveyed the essential meaning of the agreement: "The union took over and did the job of foreman."[43]

Significant improvements in working conditions flowed from such control. Textile workers in the ITU were among the only ones in New England in the 1930s to implement a plan for the equitable distribution of work.[44] Their work loads were considerably lighter than those of similar workers elsewhere. Each worsted mulespinner in Woonsocket, for example, had two piecers (assistants) per pair of mules while Lawrence mulespinners had only one.[45] The restrictions on work loads, in combination with the right of union members to consultation before "innovations affecting working conditions," protected ITU members against the sudden stretch-outs and speedups that were so common in the textile industry. Samuel Angoff, an attorney for the ITU and many other New England unions in the 1930s, recalls that workers in Woonsocket were "way ahead of anyone else" in the region in limiting the number of machines assigned to individual spinners and weavers. Unlike most of the unions he represented, they managed to hold out against the "terrific drive [among the employers] to increase the work load."[46]

---

[42] Ibid.
[43] Interview with Leonel Galipeau, October 22–23, 1980.
[44] Interview with Lawrence Spitz, September 19–20, 1979.
[45] ITU, "French Spinning Industry," (typescript, ca. 1936), 4. The ITU sent this memo in late 1936 to Representative Ellenbogen of Pennsylvania to argue the case for federal wage legislation. Copies survive in the Lawrence N. Spitz Collection, Rhode Island Historical Society, Providence, R.I., and in the Woonsocket Woolen Mills file, RG 9, Entry 402, NA.
[46] Interview with Samuel Angoff, October 29, 1976. Other evidence of ITU restrictions on work loads can be gleaned from the failure of a European manufacturer of textile machinery, *Société Alsacienne de Constructions Mécaniques*, to sell the Jules Desurmont a differential motion to improve the productivity of mules. The management of the Desurmont would not buy the attachments: "To speed up the mules to a point

ITU members were also "way ahead of anyone else" in hourly earnings. In early 1937, the *Christian Science Monitor* reported, almost in passing, that Woonsocket was "acknowledged to be the highest paying textile center in the nation."[47] Indeed, when Woonsocket unionists demanded 10 to 12 percent wage increases in late 1936 and 1937, Woonsocket manufacturers marshaled evidence to show that any further rise in local wage rates would put them at a severe competitive disadvantage. Woonsocket woolen manufacturers complained to James Bernard, a federal labor mediator, that they were already paying wages 10 to 60 percent higher than those prevailing in other Rhode Island and Massachusetts woolen mills. The city's French spinning manufacturers simultaneously informed Bernard that 1933 to 1935 wage rates in their mills had exceeded by 20 percent those mandated by the NRA woolen and worsted codes.[48] A 1936 wage survey conducted by the National Association of Wool Manufacturers buttressed these claims. The survey showed that mulespinners in eight French spinning mills in Rhode Island (six of which were in Woonsocket) averaged ninety-eight cents an hour, 13 percent more than their counterparts in Massachusetts and 31 percent more than Pennsylvania and New Jersey mulespinners. The Rhode Island wages for mulepiecers and backboys were also significantly higher than those of their counterparts in other eastern states.[49]

Bernard gave Schmetz the opportunity to refute these manufacturer claims and, in the process, defend his unionists' demands for wage increases. Rather than dispute the manufacturers' evidence, however, Schmetz merely argued that circumstances peculiar to Woonsocket textiles – especially the particularly harsh nature of working conditions and the unusually high skill and performance levels required of local woolen and worsted workers – entitled his members to the

Footnote 46 (*cont.*)

where this increase [in productivity] could be obtained," they wrote, "would simply necessitate putting more help in the alleys and nullify the benefits to be derived." It seems quite plausible that union regulations governing the pace of work were responsible for the attitude expressed by the Desurmont managers. A.H. and Co., "Outward Foreign Letters," December 15, 1933–April 16, 1935, Museum of American Textile History (hereafter MATH), North Andover, Mass., 323.

[47] *Christian Science Monitor*, January 27, 1937.

[48] Bernard to McClurd, November 25, 1936, and January 23, 1937, Woonsocket Woolen Mills file, RG 9, Entry 402, NA; WC, November 19, 1936. On one occasion Schmetz even claimed that the hourly wages of his mulespinners exceeded those of mulespinners in Lawrence by 50 percent; see ITU, "French Spinning Industry," 4, Woonsocket Woolen Mills file, RG 9, Entry 402, NA.

[49] "Code of Fair Competition Data, 1935," Box 60, and "Labor: Wage Survey and Hourly Earnings in Selected Occupations, 1936," Box 100, National Association of Woolen Manufacturers Collection, MATH.

industry's highest wages.[50] But Schmetz offered no proof for either of these counterclaims. In truth, the high level of Woonsocket wages had far more to do, as Bernard gradually discovered, with the exceptional power of the ITU – both in individual shops and in the city economy as a whole – than with the harsh or specialized character of Woonsocket mill work.[51]

Mulespinners in the city's woolen and worsted spinning mills formed the most powerful shop committees and enjoyed the highest wage rates in the city. But their success in gaining wage increases, not just for themselves but for the semiskilled and unskilled in their mills, inspired an unprecedented wave of militancy among workers in other textile sectors and in the city's service industries as well. Thus the city's dye-house workers won a 10 percent wage increase in the autumn of 1936 soon after the city's woolen-mill workers had done so.[52] Even more significantly, retail clerks won a contract that same autumn in which forty-nine Woonsocket merchants agreed to pay employees a minimum of thirty-one to thirty-two cents an hour. These hourly wage rates – along with other contract provisions that limited weekly hours to forty-four or forty-eight and restricted the use of part-time employees – portended significant improvements in this low-wage, irregular-shift industry.[53] The minimum retail wage still amounted to only a third of the mulespinner's wage, but Schmetz told his retail clerks and other unskilled members that the ITU was committed to raising their wages at a rate double that achieved by skilled workers.[54] This coupling of actual wage increases with the promise of significantly narrowed skilled–unskilled wage differentials helps explain why enthusiasm for the ITU spread so quickly throughout Woonsocket's working-class neighborhoods.

High hourly wage rates only yielded decent and reliable incomes, of course, when employees regularly worked a sufficient number of hours. And in the depressed economic climate of the 1930s, hours were in chronically short supply. Worse, the imbalance between wage earners and wage positions gave foremen great latitude in dis-

---

[50] Bernard to McClurd, November 25, 1936, Woonsocket Woolen Mills file, RG 9, Entry 402, NA; *WC*, November 19, 1936.

[51] Bernard to McClurd, November 15, 1936 and February 6, 1937, Woonsocket Woolen Mills file, RG 9, Entry 402, NA.

[52] *WC*, November 22, 1936.

[53] *ITU News*, October 1936, 11. Merchants also agreed to refrain from using junior or apprentice employees in a manner which diminished the work available to any regular employee, and to submit all controversial matters relating to the contract to binding arbitration by a board chosen by both sides.

[54] Bernard to McClurd, November 15, 1936, Woonsocket Woolen Mills file, RG 9, Entry 402, NA.

tributing available work. Few foremen followed a seniority plan, meritocratic system, or other form of job distribution that could claim to be just or reasonable. Bosses earned reputations for favoring male workers "willing to bring the boss a bottle of wine" and female workers who offered the boss candy or sexual favors.[55] In a number of mills, foremen always offered the few available jobs – regardless of their nature – to their assistants, the second hands.

Foreman abuses respected no boundaries of skill, age, or ethnicity. Foremen delighted in humbling proud workers, whose skill had once made them indispensable and autonomous participants in production. But young, unskilled laborers looking for their first job were subjected to some of the worst abuses. A new worker often had to offer the boss his or her first two weeks of pay. Sometimes bosses took on new workers as "learners," who were not paid until they mastered the job. And, as one former worker recounted, "We would have to work six weeks learning the job, and then the seventh, we'd get fired and another would get the job."[56]

French-Canadian workers felt themselves singled out for abuse. They formed a majority of the work force in most mills but only a minority of the foremen, and frequently had to contend with prejudiced Italian and Franco-Belgian bosses. Leona Galipeau remembered his pain and humiliation at being constantly passed over during slack times at the Falls Yarn mill because the Italian foremen gave preference to their fellow countrymen. He recounted one occasion when he complained to his boss: "'Your honor, when there's a lot of work, I'm perfectly good to work for you, right?'" But when work was short, he never seemed to be as good as an Italian:

> Because they have an Italian name, they gonna eat a full bread every day, and me, I don't eat nothing. So I got to wait at your door, just to get a crumb of bread whereas they eat a whole bread because [of] their name. . . . I say that's not fair. If I'm employed by you I want to have the same weight of blood that your Italian people have.[57]

Galipeau's resentment might have led him to demand that French Canadians be appointed foremen with the power to favor other French Canadians. But Galipeau found himself at meetings not only with other French-Canadian workers but with Italian, Franco-Belgian, and Polish workers as outraged at foremen abuses as himself. Victor

---

[55] Interview with Joseph D. Schmetz, October 15, 1976, and Eva Proroczok, June 22, 1981.
[56] Interview with Joseph D. Schmetz, October 15, 1976.
[57] Interview with Leona Galipeau, October 22–23, 1980.

Canzano, an Italian and fellow worker from the Falls Yarn, took a leading role in opposing foreman power there. And Angelo Turbesi, an Italian piecer at the Alsace spinning mill, made it clear that ethnic ties would not dilute his conviction that the prevailing system of job distribution constituted a violation of justice. Turbesi recounted an argument with his Italian foreman at the Alsace in the following manner:

> Many times he told me: "Angelo, you're a good boy, you don't smoke, you don't drink, and you do what I tell you; but don't get interested in the union." I used to say, "Mr. Cigala, I believe in that [the union]. I believe that together we can get somewhere.... I don't want to blame you too much because you of course have to take orders from the higher-ups. But the injustice of this thing, Mr. Cigala, is it fair for all the bosses to work and we who are your people, what would you do without us? Suppose tomorrow there was a lot of work and suppose we wouldn't work – who would man the machines? You couldn't get the bosses to run the machines. So you need us as much as you need the bosses. So if you want to be sincere, if there's [only] one shift running, make the bosses share their work and give us our own work." [Mr. Cigala would respond:] "Oh no, no, you can't talk like that, you talk like a radical, we must take care of our people first." [To which Angelo would say:] "Not fair, Mr. Cigala...it is not justice like that."[58]

Members of different nationalities and skill levels agreed on the need to develop a new system of work distribution that was genuinely "just" and "fair." It was not enough to remove abusive foremen from their positions; nor was it enough to deny foremen the power of job distribution. It was also necessary to institute a system that recognized the fundamental equality of all workers and did not discriminate on the basis of ethnicity, sex, or age. The share-the-work scheme that began appearing in ITU contracts as early as 1934 was such a system. It stipulated that each regular worker in a department, regardless of seniority, sex, or age, had to receive the same amount of work during the course of the year. If a mill department operated only six months, each worker was entitled to half-time employment or a total of three months a year. The union committee in the mill posted a chart with everyone's name, and on it they recorded everyone's cumulative work hours. Periodically, work assignments were adjusted to even out unequal time distribution. At the end of a contract year, all the workers in a department had to be within forty hours of each other in amount of time worked. One union veteran remarked that "for

---

[58] Interview with Angelo Turbesi, October 9, 1980.

people who were not union-minded to begin with, the control the union was able to exercise over the distribution of work was what attracted them to the union."[59] Such control, more than wage increases, constituted the most intensely felt achievement of ITU members during the 1930s.

In addition to the egalitarian principle expressed in work-sharing systems, ITU members increasingly embraced democratic principles as well. The impulse for this commitment arose in part from union efforts to "democratize" industry. But in the early to mid-1930s, this impulse arose even more strongly from the union's internal affairs. The union encouraged high levels of participation on the part of members and distributed decision-making powers to a large number of elected officials.[60] Each local met once a month to discuss its own business. Once a year the members of each local elected three general officers and two stewards from each department to administer local affairs between monthly meetings. The general-officer positions – president, vice president, and secretary – were dominated by male, skilled workers, but the representation of each department in local governance insured that the interests of lesser skilled female and male workers would be represented as well. Women like Josephine Proulx of the Alsace emerged as key union cadre in the large, female-dominated preparation departments of French worsted spinning mills, and played central roles in their locals' affairs. Proulx, like many of the early women activists, was drawn from the ranks of Franco-Belgian immigrants. Few of the early female activists came from the ranks of the French-Canadian women workers.[61] The radical culture of the Franco-Belgian community allowed women a greater role in public affairs than the more traditional and patriarchal culture of the French Canadians.

The voices of unskilled women in the unionized work force were heard much less beyond the local level. All union members could participate in General Meetings, the sovereign governing body of the union. But as the union grew to include thousands of members, the General Meeting became an unwieldy form of governance. The Executive Council, originally designed to meet only when a General Meeting could not be convened, increasingly assumed legislative

---

[59] Interviews with Angelo Turbesi, October 9, 1980, Leonel Galipeau, October 22–23, 1980, and Lawrence Spitz, September 19–20, 1979; *ITU News*, July 1936, 17.

[60] ITU, *Constitution and By-Laws* (Woonsocket, R.I., 1933), 5–8.

[61] Interviews with Angelo Turbesi, October 9, 1980, and Lawrence Spitz, September 19–20, 1979. A number of Franco-Belgian activists, like Marie Schmetz and Marthe Goethals, were married to Franco-Belgian mulespinners.

authority.[62] Composed of the three general officers from each local, the council was dominated by male, skilled workers. Of thirty-three Executive Council delegates in the years 1931 to 1936 whose occupations I have identified, 58 percent were skilled workers. Only 9 percent were drawn from the unskilled ranks, and only one of the thirty-three came from female ranks.[63] The union, then, did little in its early years to open its legislative assembly to female workers.[64]

Although the union hardly touched male dominance, it did trigger important advances in interethnic cooperation. French Canadians predominated in the Executive Council: Of thirty-six delegates in the years 1931 to 1936 whose ethnicity I have identified, twenty-eight, or more than three-quarters, were French Canadian. This percentage at least equaled and perhaps exceeded the proportion of French Canadians in Woonsocket's total labor force. But more than 20 percent were drawn from the ranks of other ethnic groups, led by the Franco-Belgians with 14 percent and Italians with 6 percent. Not every ethnic group active in the union was adequately represented on the Executive Council: Greeks and Poles who had played leading roles in organizing various locals were barely represented. But the participation of French Canadians and non–French Canadians in numbers approximately proportional to their numbers in Woonsocket's total population represented a substantial achievement in democratic participation for the ITU.[65] Such an ethnic mix diminished the possibility that the union would become simply an extension of the French-Canadian ethnic community, and it seemed to augur well for Schmetz's aspirations to make the union a vehicle not for ethnic revival but for class solidarity.

Democratic practice, of course, arises only in part from the character of representation of an institution's governing bodies; it depends as well on the quality of participation. The evidence on this matter is un-

[62] This de facto change was made de jure in a new constitution which the ITU approved in 1939. See ITU, *Constitution and By-Laws* (Woonsocket, R.I., 1939), 10–18.

[63] Names of the thirty-three leaders were compiled from references to their pre-1937 involvement appearing in the *ITU News*, 1936–1942. Occupational information drawn from 1935 Rhode Island Manuscript Census, Rhode Island State Archives (hereafter RISA), Providence, R.I.; U.S. Department of Justice, "Petitions for Naturalization," Providence Superior Court (hereafter PSC), Providence, R.I., and oral history.

[64] Women comprised approximately one-third of the union membership in 1936. R.I. DOL, *Annual Report*, 1935, 200–4; Spitz to author, May 11, 1977.

[65] Names of the thirty-six leaders were compiled from references to their pre-1937 involvement appearing in the *ITU News*, 1936–1942. Ethnic information drawn from 1935 Rhode Island Manuscript Census, RISA, U.S. Department of Justice, "Petitions for Naturalization," PSC, and oral history.

ambiguous. All those interviewed spoke enthusiastically about the democratic nature of their union. Meetings were well attended and exciting. All kinds of union members, even those limited by a faulty knowledge of English or fear of public debate, spoke their minds on issues that mattered to them.[66] The most eloquent statement of the importance of democracy in the union consisted not of words, however, but of one unionist's mementoes. Leona Galipeau, interviewed when he was in his eighties, insisted that he had saved no materials from his thirty-plus years of union activism – not newspapers, contracts, minutes of local meetings, or mementoes. At a certain point late in the interview, however, he excused himself for a few moments and returned with a highly polished gavel and a dog-eared paperback copy of *Robert's Rules of Order*. He had used these tools to run the meetings of his Falls Yarn local in the 1930s. These, the only materials he had saved from his lengthy union career, spoke volumes about the centrality of democratic rules and procedures to his union experience. They conveyed, far more effectively than words, what democratic participation must have meant to individuals long subjected to autocratic foremen at work and long excluded from the democratic promise of American political life.[67] Workers like Galipeau responded eagerly to the opportunity to build democratic institutions, and their experience with democratic practice in union affairs would have significant implications for their relations with employers and other authorities in the city.

The struggles on the shopfloor and participation in union affairs emboldened French Canadians to venture further out from their ethnic culture. The union experience began to change the motivations of some for belonging to the union: Instead of merely hoping to restore a customary way of life, they began to envision reconstructing society on a more just and democratic basis. This forward-looking vision should not be exaggerated. French Canadians did not easily apply the principle of equality to the distribution of wealth and power in American society, nor did they yet endorse a plan to democratize the nation's major economic and political institutions. But they did challenge the inequality and autocracy so prevalent in their world. And they demonstrated loyalty to Schmetz, a socialist who believed that, gradually and incrementally, workers might transform the world.

[66] Interview with Normand Galipeau, October 22–23, 1980. See also Pierre Anctil, "Aspects of Class Ideology in a New England Ethnic Minority: The Franco-Americans of Woonsocket, Rhode Island (1865–1929)" (Ph.D. dissertation, New School for Social Research, 1980), 87.

[67] Interview with Leona Galipeau, October 22–23, 1980.

Schmetz had good reason in 1936 to regard the progress of the ITU in Woonsocket with satisfaction. The ITU had organized thousands of workers in an industry long considered incapable of sustaining an industrial union movement. It had mobilized an ethnic group long known for its antilabor bias. It had accomplished this task largely on its own, without the help of a national union. The UTW had collapsed in the wake of the 1934 defeat. Though its leaders were more eager than ever to make the UTW a vehicle for industrial union mobilization, they had signed up, by 1936, fewer members in the entire state of Rhode Island than the ITU had organized in Woonsocket.[68]

Yet the achievements of the ITU were still partial and vulnerable to reversal. The ITU encountered obstacles in its efforts to organize a number of textile mills in the city, especially those in the Bradford worsted spinning sector. The union had little influence in electoral politics and had not developed a political agenda to complement its efforts on the shopfloor. Most immediately, the inexorable forces of economic competition threatened to undermine all that the ITU had painstakingly established. Schmetz and fellow leaders wrote to prolabor congressmen in 1936 that "we have taken care of ourselves in a manner which may become a business handicap."[69] The wage gains and work-load restrictions achieved by the ITU made labor costs in Woonsocket significantly higher than Lawrence. Lawrence already claimed 45 percent of the French spindles in the country, and its cheap labor costs were increasing its dominance. The ITU admitted that "on account of price competition," the mills in Woonsocket were unable "to run at more than a small percentage of capacity." Restricted production hours made the "actual earnings of [Woonsocket] employees much less favorable" than they appeared. In 1934 when mulespinners would have earned $38.88 to $41.40 a week working full-time, they actually earned only $6.56 to $20.85.[70]

The reality of high wage rates and low weekly wages pointed to the limits of unionism in one city. Capitalist enterprise would always tend to concentrate in industrial areas with the lowest wage scales. Labor costs had to be equalized throughout the country – brought up to the wage scales prevailing in Woonsocket – for ITU members to gain durable security of employment and continuing income gains. Standardization could be achieved either through a "[n]ational hourly minimum for operators" or a "[n]ational piece-work scale, based on

---

[68] See Ferguson, "Textile Unions in Rhode Island," 254.

[69] ITU, "French Spinning Industry," 1, Woonsocket Woolen Mills file, RG 9, Entry 402, NA.

[70] Ibid., 5.

the production turned out by the spindles."[71] Both proposals required a textile union able to bargain nationally on questions of wages and work loads, or a prolabor federal government willing to legislate minimum wage and work-load standards for every mill in the country. The time had come, Schmetz concluded, for the ITU to cast its lot, organizationally and politically, with industrial unionists elsewhere; the time had come, as well, to pursue the ambitious program of social reconstruction that he had nurtured since his Belgian youth.

[71] Ibid., 2.

Part III

Working-class heyday, 1936–1941

5   "A new, progressive Americanism"

Twice in the twentieth century American labor seemed to be on the march, ready to play the historic, socially transformative role that numerous radicals and reformers since the days of Karl Marx had assigned it. The first such moment occurred in the years following World War I when millions of workers went on strike, invested the cautious American Federation of Labor (AFL) with the energy and political ambition it had rarely demonstrated, and stirred up the body politic with bold, confident talk of social reconstruction, nationalization, industrial democracy, and independent political action. The second such moment occurred in the middle years of the 1930s when American workers, again striking in large numbers, forced AFL labor leaders to create a new labor federation, the Congress of Industrial Organizations (CIO), and made their political grievances – debilitating economic insecurity, the lack of workplace rights, pervasive class inequality – the central issues of national debate and New Deal reform. In both instances, the most radical and ambitious within labor's ranks were carried away with the notion that labor's march would sweep all before it and leave in its wake an utterly new society. Such elation, of course, could not last long; formidable foes gathered on labor's flanks, and internal feuds over fundamental goals weakened labor from within. But before that elation had passed, radicals and other activists managed, in many instances, to set in motion plans for gaining working-class power that would significantly shape their society's culture, economy, and politics for years to come. This was particularly true of the 1930s.

Woonsocket's working class, barely touched by the labor insurgency of the post–World War I years (the Franco-Belgian workers excepted, of course), was swept up in the 1930s insurgency. Joseph Schmetz, sensing a moment of unprecedented working-class opportunity in 1936, as heady talk of industrial unionism and independent political action swept through the ranks of American labor, chose to plunge his union into an ambitious effort to remake Woonsocket society in the image of Belgian social democracy. That effort, a complex five-year affair involving the elaboration of a radical Americanism, an economic campaign for industrial democracy, and a political campaign for municipal electoral power (which will be taken up, in turn, in this and the following two chapters), though ultimately falling short of its goal, would fundamentally alter the experience of class and ethnicity in Woonsocket society. And as long as this social democratic initiative lasted – even as it was being vigorously challenged both from within the ITU and by its opponents outside – Woonsocket workers enjoyed a degree of ideological and economic independence unprecedented in their city's history. This brief historical moment, then, was their heyday.

Unveiling a radical dream

Joseph Schmetz embarked on his ambitious political program in the spring of 1936. He established a Woonsocket Labor Club as a forum for union members to discuss political issues and build support for progressive local and national government agendas. He started a monthly magazine, the *ITU News*, and filled it with news of national political significance. "It is high time," he declared in the first issue, "for the ITU to discontinue playing the role of the ostrich and realize the absolute necessity of merging union with political activities."[1] The union enthusiastically endorsed Roosevelt's bid for a second term and worked hard for his reelection. It also encouraged Woonsocket workers to develop an interest in a national American labor movement by reporting in depth on the activities of John L. Lewis's newly formed CIO.[2]

The *ITU News* editors underscored their advocacy of a national political and labor orientation by filling their newspaper with information on American history and culture. They wrote every article in English – in the first issue only the union song appeared in French – and they encouraged French-Canadian workers to acquire American citizenship. Topics of French-Canadian cultural or religious interest were excluded from the newsmagazine. Schmetz could hardly have been more emphatic that involvement in the ITU necessitated an increasing commitment to an American labor and political identity.[3]

There were good, pragmatic reasons for such an orientation. Schmetz wanted to make the ITU a vehicle for all Woonsocket workers and not just the French-Canadian majority among them. He also wanted to seize the opportunity available in 1936 to involve the ITU in a national labor movement and in an emerging coalition of pro-

[1] *ITU News*, July 1936, 5.
[2] Ibid., July 1936–April 1937, passim.
[3] Ibid.

gressive labor leaders and left-wing New Dealers.[4] But Schmetz's insistence on such a thoroughgoing Americanization campaign seems, in retrospect, curious and unnecessarily risky. If French-Canadian workers felt that a labor alliance or political activity threatened their ethnic identity, they might have rejected both as dangerous incursions into their customary way of life. Union leaders might have tried to strike a balance in their newspaper between union and ethnic concerns, and between the use of English and French, but they did not.

Schmetz never accounted for this. He merely claimed that the ITU's new course upheld the union's established role as the defender of Woonsocket's workers. "Through this trade union," he stated, "we hope to maintain ourselves and our dependents in a proper civilized state of existence; we mean to safeguard our liberties and our only means of obtaining the necessities of life and to consolidate our defensive positions by using the ballot box and by supporting those law-makers sympathetic and cognizant of our needs." As soon as Schmetz began discussing the details of his "defensive" campaign, however, he revealed some larger ambitions. The union, he noted, was "growing in power daily." Soon it would be able to serve its members in all respects. "We plan," Schmetz wrote, "to institute an employment bureau, a loan agency to protect workers from usury and financial exploitation by banks and money lenders and we hope to institute a social service system to alleviate the suffering of those who are unemployed or unable to work, due to illness or circumstances beyond their control."[5]

Schmetz's new policy was far more than a pragmatic or defensive strategy for survival. Employment bureaus, worker loan agencies, and a social service system had never been part of the French-Canadian worker's world, but these, in Schmetz's vision, were "the tangible benefits which the union bestows upon its members rendering them better citizens, and consequently making the community a better place in which to live."[6] In announcing his desire for the union to serve its membership in all respects, Schmetz was

---

[4] Schmetz was being courted, at this time, by officials of the CIO's Textile Workers Organizing Committee who regarded him as "the most competent [labor] man in the state" of Rhode Island. See Richard Rohman, "Report to Emil Rieve on Rhode Island" (no date); Joseph Schmetz to Sidney Hillman, March 15, 1937; Hillman to Schmetz, February 3, 1939; all in Textile Workers Union of America papers, Mss 396, Box 54, Independent Textile Union of America file, Wisconsin State Historical Society (hereafter WSHS), Madison, Wis.

[5] *ITU News*, July 1936, 3.

[6] Ibid.

drawing on his Belgian trade-union vision of socialist transformation. In this vision, workers would gradually assume control of the various aspects of their lives through cooperatives, fraternal societies, educational agencies, and recreational activities, until they had the skill, the strength, and the will to transform the world.[7]

Although Schmetz did not attach the word "socialist" to his analysis, it bore the mark of his socialist orientation. He envisioned "a new economic order which will substitute planning for chaos, service for profit, and abundance for poverty." He called attention to the "titanic struggle [emerging] between CAPITAL AND LABOR" for control of American society. He heralded the working class's intention to "gain...the highest amount of wealth which our labor creates." As he saw it, struggles were proceeding not only on the shopfloor but in politics as well. "Labor will demand a voice in industry, people will demand law control [sic] of important necessities such as money, oil, electric power which are too important to be left in private hands." Schmetz proclaimed the ITU's support for the Workers' Rights Amendment to the Constitution, which called for the regulation of all aspects of working conditions and the nationalization of essential resources and manufacturing concerns.[8]

Schmetz evidently saw an opportunity in 1936 to inaugurate a far-reaching social and political program. His articles and editorials contained both an anticapitalist critique of society and a coherent plan for transforming America into a social democracy. But instead of calling this program socialism or social democracy, he portrayed it simply as the natural fulfillment of American political traditions. He peppered his articles with reverential references to the Founding Fathers and the goals of the American Revolution. He encouraged union members to identify with the ideals, struggles, and aspirations of the American revolutionists of 1776. He linked the principles of justice, rights, and democracy that lay at the heart of their union experience to the principles on which the country was founded.[9]

This attempt to construct an Americanized radicalism grew quite naturally out of Schmetz's personal and political experience. During the 1920s, he had witnessed the death of two radical unions, the IWW and the Amalgamated, as government repression intensified and a stigma was attached to their "un-American" aims. Only the United Textile Workers (UTW) survived, in part because of its moderate demands and in part because of its insistence on its essential American

[7] Ibid., March 1937, 3.
[8] Ibid., July 1936, 7, 16–17; April 1937, 5–7; March 1937, 3, 6; December 1936, 3.
[9] Ibid., July 1936–April 1937, passim.

character. It declared its patriotism, endorsed American democratic ideals, and emphasized its role as the guardian of the American standard of living. Schmetz did not share the UTW's sense of the limits of trade unionism, but he was impressed by its ability to gain legitimacy and to survive in American society. Moreover, he still harbored an admiration for the American political heritage that had given American workers the vote one hundred years earlier than their Belgian counterparts. Schmetz, in the 1920s, began to express his socialist beliefs in the language of Americanism. If he could present socialism as "a new, progressive Americanism,"[10] as the application of the central political concepts of the revolutionary heritage – democracy, rights, and independence – to twentieth-century industry and society, then perhaps, he reasoned, America's aversion to socialism could be circumvented and a social democracy effectively promoted. This reformulation process quickened in the 1930s as the economic crisis made workers more open to alternative political programs.

Yet why did Schmetz opt for a radical vision that so rigidly excluded all aspects of French-Canadian culture? Why did he not incorporate French-Canadian traditions, especially those rich in communal values, into his radicalism? Part of the answer, no doubt, lies in the simple fact that Schmetz, in constructing his Americanized radicalism, drew on ideological material readily available to him, material produced by radicals, industrial unionists, and left-wing New Dealers who lived outside Woonsocket and were indifferent to the survival of French-Canadian culture. But another part is more complex, intriguing, and speculative. Schmetz seems to have felt that French Canadians in his union would only support his radical political agenda if they broke decisively with the Quebec-oriented, conservative leadership of their ethnic community. By encouraging French-Canadian unionists to Americanize, he hoped to strain relations between the two groups until they ruptured. Cultural liberation, in other words, would speed along his program for class liberation. Schmetz constructed his political program to promote both.

Schmetz, of course, never considered – as Henry Ford and other Americanizers once had – monitoring compliance with the cultural aspects of his program, determining, for example, whether French-Canadian unionists were celebrating Thanksgiving or using English among themselves. His own reluctance to Americanize his private life would have made such an overt effort to enforce codes of private behavior on others unthinkable. Still, his strategy of denying the culture or heritage of French-Canadian workers – a strategy that contrasted

[10] Ibid., May 1937, 7.

markedly with his eagerness to include in the *ITU News* relevant material from his European past – unmistakably conveyed to French-Canadian union members his low opinion of their culture.

The arrival of Lawrence Spitz, Popular Front radical

When it came to implementing this strategy of class and cultural liberation in French-Canadian Woonsocket, Schmetz quickly realized that he could not carry it out alone or with the resources available to him locally. He had already effected a major change in the leadership structure of the union by getting the Executive Council to approve a large enough salary to permit him to leave his job at the Desurmont and devote himself full-time to the presidency.[11] But his radical Americanization campaign required more than time. He needed a sophisticated knowledge of American political culture to Americanize his socialist ideals. In order to make and sustain contacts with the wider world of organized labor and to promote political campaigns, he would need fluency in English and a thorough knowledge of the mechanics of American electoral politics. The Wagner Act, for example, demanded an understanding of the intricacies of the law and the procedures of the National Labor Relations Board. Schmetz was a talented, energetic individual, who probably could have handled any of these tasks with ease. But he could not tackle them all without help.

Schmetz also found himself frustrated by the opposition to his presidency that was coalescing around French-Canadian skilled workers. When General Secretary Raoul Vandal – the union's second highest ranking officer – resigned in 1936, Schmetz feared that his opponents would elect one of their followers to the post and gain control of the Executive Board. To forestall such a development, and to bring more leadership talent into the ITU, Schmetz took the unprecedented step of nominating an outsider – Lawrence Spitz – who did not belong to the ITU and who had never worked in a Woonsocket mill.

Despite his youth, Spitz, a twenty-five-year-old UTW organizer based in Providence, was no labor movement novice. A protégé of UTW leaders Thomas McMahon and Horace Riviere, he had attended the first conference in Washington, D.C., in 1935 of the eight secessionist AFL unions that had formed the CIO. In 1936, John L. Lewis

---

[11] A special General Meeting of the ITU on May 9, 1936, approved a salary of forty dollars a week; "Report of Executive Committee to Study Question of President's Salary," April 25, 1936, Lawrence N. Spitz Collection, Mss 31 (hereafter Spitz Collection), Box 8, Rhode Island Historical Society (hereafter RIHS), Providence, R.I.

had appointed him to the three-member committee directing CIO activities in Rhode Island. By 1937 he was recognized as a leading figure in Rhode Island's industrial union movement. Moreover, Spitz had established working relationships with a broad spectrum of ITU leaders during the course of his organizing activities for the UTW. Both the pro-Schmetz and anti-Schmetz factions believed that adding Spitz to the union's Executive Board would enhance the overall strength of the union without undermining their own power base within it.[12] Although Spitz seemed like the ideal compromise candidate, Schmetz saw him as an ally, not as a peacemaker. The two had already agreed, in private conversations, on the desirability of reaffiliating the ITU with a national union. Spitz, with his knowledge of industrial unionism and his contacts with CIO cadre throughout New England, would catalyze that process. Moreover, Schmetz hoped that Spitz, a radical, would help transform the ITU into a European-style social democratic movement.[13]

Spitz's radicalism grew out of circumstances dramatically different from those that had shaped Schmetz's political beliefs. Spitz was American-born; his family aspired to middle-class, not working-class, respectability; he was radicalized by the sudden collapse of the American economic machine (and with it of his own dreams of social mobility), not by the kind of immutable class divisions that had drawn the young Schmetz to Belgian socialism. Angry, impatient, ambitious, Spitz found himself attracted, like many of his age, class, and ethnic background, to the Communist Party.

Born on Long Island, Spitz grew up in Providence. The grandson of Jewish immigrants from a German-speaking region of the Austro-Hungarian empire, he learned to speak German in his home before English. But he was not religious and had only a vague ethnic identity. He had attended Commercial High School, a public institution in Providence where educational emphasis had been on American and secular, not ethnic and religious, concerns. If some element of his Jewish past – its messianism or generations-old tradition of social justice – fueled his budding radicalism, it played a far smaller role than it did in the politics of the Yiddish-speaking, needle-trades socialists of New York, Philadelphia, Chicago, and Boston. In fact what made him so striking a figure in Woonsocket was his apparent detachment from any sort of ethnic or plebeian past. He spoke English

---

[12] "Interview with John Strohmeyer" (typescript, 1954), 3–4, 13–14, Spitz Collection, Box 2, RIHS. This document is a seventeen page, single-spaced transcript of Spitz's three interviews with John Strohmeyer, a reporter for the *Providence Journal*.

[13] Interview with Lawrence Spitz, October 22, 1976.

without an accent and without pause. He excelled at the tasks that most Woonsocket workers found forbiddingly technocratic and cosmopolitan: managing complicated union finances, lobbying state legislators, broadcasting Labor Day radio addresses, organizing political campaigns, and interpreting the obfuscatory language of state and federal statutes. Had the prosperity of the 1920s continued, this talented and academically successful lower-middle-class youth – his father was a foreman in a Providence watch factory – might well have completed the college education he had started at Boston University and gone into the world of corporations, finance, or civil service. But the Depression dashed that life course – as it did for Walter Reuther and many other talented working-class and lower-middle-class youths of the period – and propelled Spitz into a life of opposition to the dominant corporate structures that he held responsible for causing so much human misery and personal distress.[14]

The Depression not only threw Spitz off the social mobility ladder; it also plunged his family into poverty. Spitz found himself in 1930 and 1931 scrounging for jobs – any job – for sustenance. He labored in textile mills, jewelry plants, and the merchant marine but never worked long in any one place; he was fired from several jobs for insubordination.[15] At some point in the early 1930s, probably while working at his several textile jobs, he met Horace Riviere, still a UTW organizer.[16] Riviere took an interest in Spitz, then barely twenty years old, and found him part-time work as a staffer and organizer for his union. He also introduced Spitz to the world of Providence radicalism. Radicals of many persuasions – socialists, communists, syndicalists, and anarchists – were meeting nightly during these years at the Waldorf Cafeteria on Weybosset Street in downtown Providence to debate the problems of unemployment, war, and fascism, to argue politics, and to discuss ways of attracting American workers to the labor movement. The young Spitz was entranced by these radicals, their world-historical ideas, and the political debates that stretched far into the night.[17]

---

[14] Interview with Lawrence Spitz, October 22, 1976, and August 27, 1980, and with Angelo Turbesi, October 9, 1980; "Interview with Strohmeyer," 1, and "Biographical Data of Lawrence N. Spitz" (prepared for Brown University Commencement Exercises, 1976), 1, Spitz Collection, Box 2, RIHS.

[15] Interview with Spitz, October 22, 1976.

[16] For a sketch of Riviere, see Richard Kelly, *Nine Lives for Labor* (New York, 1956), 89–107.

[17] "Interview with Strohmeyer," 1–2, Spitz Collection, Box 2, RIHS; interview with Spitz, October 22, 1976, and July 15, 1983.

The radical who exerted the greatest influence on Spitz was Joseph Coldwell, a forty-year veteran of the Socialist Party whose experiences had ranged from municipal socialist campaigns in 1890s Brockton to antiwar agitation in the 1910s (an activity which landed him in the Atlanta Federal Penitentiary alongside Debs).[18] When Spitz met him in the late 1920s, Coldwell was a poor, aging but still-dedicated Socialist who lived in the small photography shop he operated out of Olneyville Square in Providence. Unlike many Socialists of his generation, he had neither been disillusioned by the futile attempts to organize workers in the lean 1920s nor consumed by his hatred of the Communists. He identified more with the young Militants in the Socialist Party than the tired Old Guard of social democratic AFL labor officials, and supported the former's efforts to instill the party with a revolutionary combativeness.[19]

What initially drew Spitz to Coldwell, in addition to his radical world view, was precisely his militant style. Spitz fondly recalled how Coldwell, even in his infirm old age, was alway available for picket duty, for leaflet distribution, and for strike relief. Nothing – not the time of day, the weather, or the threat of physical danger – would deter him from answering a call to action. Spitz knew no one else so dedicated to the working class.[20] But as much as Spitz admired Coldwell, he could not follow him into the Socialist Party. He saw Norman Thomas, the party's leader, as a middle-class reformer preoccupied with electoral politics, evincing little real fellow feeling for American workers. He regarded the Old Guard Socialists, ensconced in AFL bureaucratic jobs, as too complacent and almost fearful of vigorous labor organizing campaigns. Spitz might have made common cause with the young, direct-action faction of Militants in the party; instead, he turned to the political organization that the Militants were trying to emulate – the Communist Party.[21]

By the early 1930s, Communist organizers around the country had established a reputation as the leading critics of the moribund AFL and the most active leaders of the new industrial unions. Their con-

---

[18] For glimpses of Coldwell's largely unknown history, see typescript, n.d., Socialist Party Papers, NN, Reel 111, microfilm, U.S. Department of Labor Library, Washington, D.C.; interview with Spitz, October 22, 1976; Nick Salvatore, *Eugene V. Debs: Citizen and Socialist* (Urbana, Ill., 1982), 321, David Shannon, *The Socialist Party of America: A History* (New York, 1955), 126–49.

[19] Interview with Spitz, October 22, 1976; Irving Howe, *Socialism and America* (New York, 1985), 71–2.

[20] Interview with Spitz, October 22, 1976; letter from Spitz to Richard Padden Clark, September 17, 1973, Box 14, Spitz Collection, RIHS.

[21] Interview with Spitz, August 27, 1980. On Socialists in the 1930s, see Howe, *Socialism and America*, 49–86.

fidence, their organizing abilities, and their willingness to throw themselves into battle made them appear more glamorous than the Socialists, who seemed hampered by endless ideological squabbles and a pervasive *Weltschmerz*. Only later did it become clear to many of these young radicals how much the vigor and militance of the Communists derived not from a genuine commitment to the masses but from an excessive faith in the precision of Marxist analysis and the omnipotence of their party.[22]

Spitz joined the National Maritime Union, a Communist-led organization, when he shipped out on the merchant marine in 1934. In the textile strike of that same year, the Providence police, acting on a tip from Joseph Sylvia, a UTW official, arrested Spitz in a roundup of area Communists. In 1935 and 1936, he served as secretary of a local chapter of a Popular Front organization, the American League Against War and Fascism. And while managing a UTW tour of the labor play, *Let Freedom Ring*, he wrote for a Communist-influenced journal, *New Theatre*. He would maintain some contact with Popular Front organizations through the mid-1940s, though the intensity of his involvement declined sharply after 1936.[23] Spitz repeatedly denied that he ever joined the party, and no conclusive evidence to the contrary has ever surfaced. His name does not appear in the volumes of HUAC investigations dealing with Rhode Island or textile unionism. Intensive research in the 1950s by John Strohmeyer, a *Providence Journal* reporter, failed both to establish his party membership and to prove that he followed the party line. Schmetz, who asked fellow Rhode Island Socialists for their opinions of Spitz before inviting him into the ITU, concluded that Spitz was free of Stalinist taint. A number of individ-

---

[22] The best history of the Communist Party during the 1930s is still Irving Howe and Lewis Coser, *The American Communist Party: A Critical History (1919–1957)* (Boston, 1957), 175–386. See also Harvey Klehr, *The Heyday of American Communism: The Depression Decade* (New York, 1984). On the CP in the 1920s, see Theodore Draper, *The Roots of American Communism* (New York, 1957) and *American Communism and Soviet Russia: The Formative Period* (New York, 1960).

[23] "Interview with Strohmeyer," 2–3, 5, Spitz Collection, Box 2, RIHS; interview with Lawrence Spitz, September 19–20, 1979; *Providence Journal*, September 13, 1934 (the issue ran a picture of Spitz along with other alleged Communists arrested, but mistakenly identified him as Morris Spitz); *Blackstone Valley Youth Conference* (pamphlet, March 29, 1936), in author's possession; Lawrence Spitz, "'Let Freedom Ring' on Tour," *New Theatre* (November 1936), 24–5. The play *Let Freedom Ring* was written by Albert Bein who based it on Grace Lumpkin's proletarian novel, *To Make My Bread* (New York, 1932). Spitz took the play to twenty-four cities in Rhode Island, Connecticut, New York, and New Jersey in the summer of 1936, and claimed that about 25,000 textile workers had seen it performed (Brookwood Labor College supplied the bus for the actors and their props). "Petition for a National Workers' Theatre," September 18, 1936, and undated press clipping, in author's possession.

uals who, in the late 1940s and 1950s, attacked Spitz for being a Communist later admitted that their accusations were unfounded.[24]

This evidence notwithstanding, it is clear from his organizational associations that the Communist Party, for a time, influenced Spitz's politics. It is impossible to determine the precise nature of that influence: Repeated efforts over the years by conservative trade unionists to discredit his politics and his leadership by labeling both communist have made Spitz unwilling to acknowledge any influence at all.[25] Two theories of Spitz's relationship to American communism are, nevertheless, worth pondering. One is that his involvement with communism was a brief romance that ended when Spitz encountered the party's Leninist core and unwavering subservience to Moscow. The other is that Spitz remained a clandestine member of the party (or secretly close to it) until the mid-1940s.

Lending plausibility to the first theory is the fact that the period of Spitz's intense involvement with party organizations lasted less than two years. He had gravitated to the Communist Party in 1934–1935 as it shifted from the revolutionary politics of its so-called Third Period to the more patient, populist-style politics of its Popular Front. Many party members and sympathizers, especially those long committed to Leninist doctrine, found this change wrenching. Some, however, genuinely embraced the Popular Front precisely because it seemed to be drawing the party away from Leninism; they also saw it as an opportunity to overcome their isolation from American workers and their marginality in American politics. They enthusiastically set about constructing a new radical language, one that was respectful of American political traditions and consonant with cherished American notions of freedom, independence, justice, and equality. Spitz, who deepened his involvement in party organizations in 1935 and 1936, may have belonged to this latter group.[26] Popular Front ideology may

---

[24] "Interview with Strohmeyer," 11, Spitz Collection, Box 2, RIHS. Interviews with Lawrence Spitz, October 22, 1976, September 19–20, 1979, August 27, 1980; Mons. Edmund Brock, July 7, 1983; Phileas Valois, July 5, 1983.

[25] As late as 1964 Spitz's conservative opponents in the United Steel Workers of America were still using this tactic against him; the communist stigma may have cost him a victory in his 1964 bid for directorship of District 1 of the United Steel Workers of America. See John Herling, *Right to Challenge: People and Power in the Steelworkers Union* (New York, 1972), 189–97.

[26] Coldwell may have pushed Spitz in this ideological direction: He was one of the sponsors (and the only one from Rhode Island) of the Socialist Party's Continental Congress of Workers and Farmers for Economic Reconstruction held in Washington, D.C., May 6–7, 1933. See Emil Rieve's call for a continental congress in David J. Saposs papers, Mss 113, Box 22, Folder 20, WSHS; see also Shannon, *The Socialist Party*, 227–8.

have tapped a deep yearning in him for an Americanized radicalism; and when he discovered that the party's Americanization was nothing more than what Irving Howe has called "a brilliant masquerade," disguising rather than transforming the organization's authoritarian core, his enthusiasm for communism may have declined precipitously and prompted his break with the party.[27]

The other possible interpretation of Spitz's political history is that he remained a clandestine member of the Communist Party when he joined the ITU, and that he had been instructed by party superiors to prepare the way for an eventual Communist takeover of the ITU. Some evidence supports this view, most notably the fact that Spitz hired onto the ITU staff in the early 1940s two individuals with party connections; also, Spitz would, in 1943, successfully maneuver Schmetz's ouster from the ITU presidency and install a loyalist of his own in his place.[28] But other evidence argues against this conspiracy theory. First, Spitz, in interviews, readily acknowledged the communist sym-

---

[27] Thousands of radicals who became party members left as soon as they encountered its Leninist core; the annual turnover rate among Communist Party members rarely dipped below 50 percent. See Klehr, *Heyday of American Communism*, 365–78, for a systematic analysis of turnover rates. On the shift from the Third Period to the Popular Front, see Howe and Coser, *The American Communist Party*, 319–86, and Klehr, *Heyday of American Communism*, 167–85. The success of the Popular Front in tapping a yearning for an Americanized radicalism is still an inadequately understood historical phenomenon. For an evaluation of the existing literature see my "Mission from Moscow: American Communism in the 1930s," *Reviews in American History* 12 (December 1984), 559–66. See also Maurice Isserman, "Three Generations: Historians View American Communism," *Labor History* 26 (Fall 1985), 517–45, and Howe, *Socialism and America*, 87–104. Memoirs offer the best introduction to the range of experiences among radicals who became party members or fellow travelers. See, for example, the following: George Charney, *A Long Journey* (Chicago, 1968); Louis Budenz, *This is My Story* (New York, 1947); Jessica Mitford, *A Fine Old Conflict* (London, 1977); Theodore Draper, "Preface," to republication of *American Communism and Soviet Russia* (New York, 1986), ix–xx; Al Richmond, *A Long View from the Left: Memoirs of an American Revolutionary* (New York, 1972); Nell Irvin Painter, *The Narrative of Hosea Hudson: His Life as a Negro Communist in the South* (Cambridge, Mass., 1979); Steve Nelson, James R. Barrett, and Rob Ruck, *Steve Nelson, American Radical* (Pittsburgh, Pa., 1981); Peggy Dennis, *The Autobiography of an American Communist: A Personal View of a Political Life, 1925–1975* (Westport, Conn., 1977); Malcolm Cowley, *The Dream of the Golden Mountains: Remembering the Thirties* (Harmondsworth, U.K., 1964); Joseph Freeman, *An American Testament: A Narrative of Rebels and Romantics* (New York, 1936); and J.B. Matthews, *Odyssey of a Fellow-Traveler* (New York, 1938).

[28] Gus LeBlanc was a Boston-based CP member or fellow traveler whom Spitz hired as an organizer; Henry Anderson was brought in from the Rhode Island WPA to serve as the ITU educational director. Interview with Lawrence Spitz, July 15, 1983. During the war years Spitz also directed the Rhode Island chapter of the Russian War Relief Society, presumably a Popular Front organization.

pathies of the two staffers in question and criticized them as foolish and misguided, and second, his battle with Schmetz turned far more on matters of ego than on matters of ideology (a subject that Chapter 8 will address).[29]

But suppose that the conspiracy theory, contrary to the weight of evidence, is true? Spitz would then have been striving in Woonsocket to carry out the party line, which meant, in the late 1930s, developing an Americanized radicalism, generating enthusiasm for the CIO, and maintaining support for Roosevelt's New Deal. These were precisely the policies favored by Schmetz. Spitz would have been acting out of different motives from Schmetz – especially a desire to carry out the Communist International's policies and to enroll more workers in the Communist Party; but these hidden motives would have counted for little as long as Spitz remained subordinate to Schmetz in union politics. And Schmetz intended to keep Spitz subordinate. The very fact that Schmetz chose a cosmopolitan, Jewish outsider to serve as his trusted lieutenant in a parochial Catholic city suggests that he was determined to prevent that individual from ever developing a rival power base in the ITU. Spitz would eventually develop far more of a following than Schmetz or anyone might have expected. The rank and file of the ITU would come to respect the intelligence, dedication, and élan he brought to union affairs. He enthralled working-class audiences with knowledgeable lectures on American history, deft explanations of the Wagner Act's legal intricacies, and eloquent flights into class-conscious oratory. Still, he had to watch his step. French Canadians did not react to his technocratic skills, unabashed nationalism, and militant speeches without ambivalence. He periodically received anonymous letters from Woonsocket residents attacking his Jewishness and radicalism.[30] And if someone in this Catholic, anticommunist city found the "smoking gun" proving his Communist Party membership, his tenure as an ITU leader would immediately end.

Spitz's vulnerable position in the world of Woonsocket trade-union politics, then, renders the question of his Communist Party membership rather immaterial. He could not have promoted Marxist-Leninism, the Communist Party, or socialist revolution even if he (or the Comintern) were so inclined. The only realistic, programmatic option

---

[29] Also, there is no indication that Spitz attempted to make ITU attitudes toward war and fascism mirror the sudden ideological reversals forced on Communists by the Nazi–Soviet pact of 1939 and then the Nazi invasion of the Soviet Union in 1941. See the *ITU News*, September 1939 to June 1941, passim.

[30] Interview with Lawrence Spitz, September 19–20, 1979; some of the anti-Semitic letters (invariably unsigned and undated) can be found in the Spitz Collection, RIHS.

for a radical – communist, socialist, or otherwise – in 1930s Woon-socket involved promoting an Americanized radicalism, building the CIO, and extending the New Deal. These were Schmetz's goals; they would become the goals to which Spitz wholeheartedly committed himself as well.[31]

The following reconstruction of the ITU's "progressive American-ism" is based on the political analysis, editorials, and illustrations that appeared in the union's newsmagazine, the *ITU News*. Although as many as a dozen union members worked on producing the magazine at any one time, Schmetz and Spitz decisively shaped its ideological voice through both their writing and their editing. The content of their Americanized radicalism can best be understood from an exam-ination of each of three dimensions of Americanism – nationalist, progressive, and democratic – they employed in its construction, as well as of their refusal to use the fourth, traditionalist dimension. The radicals, who were merely trying to express deeply felt ideas in the familiar terms of American political discourse, did not self-consciously employ three distinct dimensions. The following analysis, in fact, will demonstrate the difficulty of isolating each dimension and analyzing it independently of the others: The nationalist and democratic dimen-sions, and the nationalist and progressive dimensions, in particular, were thoroughly intertwined. Nevertheless, a recognition of the several linguistic streams flowing into political discourse is essential to understand the possibilities and the vulnerabilities of 1930s radicalism.

The nationalist dimension

The nationalist dimension of Americanism was prominent in ITU discourse throughout the years of Schmetz and Spitz's joint leader-ship. Union radicals regularly, solemnly, and reverentially invoked the traditional heroes of American history – the Pilgrims, Washington, and Lincoln – hoping to nurture not a complacent patriotism but, rather, an unassailable association between these traditional American heroes and modern-day trade unionists. Such a linkage, they believed, would confer the respectability of history on the labor movement's

---

[31] Some scholars, of course, have discerned a potential for a more "purely" radical movement in the 1930s and have usually blamed the New Deal, the bureaucratic leadership of the CIO, or the Communist Party for obstructing it. But such argu-ments tend to exaggerate the "truly" radical potential of the 1930s and to ignore the political conservatism that still characterized much of the polity and labor move-ment. Those groups, like the Socialists and Trotskyists, that hewed to what might be called a purer radical line, had sunk, by the late 1930s, into political oblivion.

aims. American workers, ITU radicals repeatedly told their members, were simply carrying on the nation's three-hundred-year-old quest for freedom, independence, democracy, and economic security.[32]

Such invocations appeared in various forms. Illustrations of Lincoln or Washington (or both) graced the covers of the *ITU News* every February while those of the Pilgrims appeared every November (Figures 5.1, 5.2, and 5.3).[33] The editors delighted in printing for their members such well-known Lincoln aphorisms as "labor is prior to, and independent of, capital" and "there is no America without labor, and to fleece the one is to rob the other." They affixed such patriotic slogans as "We Want a Declaration of Independence" and "We the

[32] See *ITU News*, July 1936, 3, 5; October 1936, 3; March 1937, 5; February 1938, 5; February–March 1941, 15.

[33] These pictures were generally supplied by the Federated Press (FP), a left-leaning and possibly Communist-controlled news service that sent its news reports, illustrations, and cartoons to sixty labor papers of widely divergent political orientations. The combined 1939 circulation of these papers was about 1.5 million. By 1944, 139 papers with an estimated circulation of 6 million used FP releases. "Federated Press Release," February 9 and March 8, 1942, and September 8, 1944, Federated Press, 1940–42, and Federated Press, 1943–44 files, Box 79, Federated Press Collection, Columbia University (hereafter FPC, CU). For a brief, in-house history of the news service, see Carl Haessler, "FP: Initials of Progress," *Labor Today* (May 1942), 1–5.

HUAC placed the Federated Press on its list of Communist-front organizations in the early 1950s. Harry Fleischman, a long-time Socialist and manager of several Norman Thomas presidential campaigns, also alleged (in a November 9, 1984, interview) that the Federated Press was Communist-controlled. Harvey O'Connor, in a June 17, 1985, interview, denied Fleischman's claim. Material in the Federated Press's manuscript collection at Columbia University confirms that many Communists were employed by the news service without, however, proving that the news service was a Communist-front organization. Unfortunately the FPC contains almost no information on the identities and politics of the artists who drew these pictures.

The government's rather vague case against the Federated Press can be reconstructed from the following reports: U.S. Congress, House of Representatives, Committee on Un-American Activities, *Guide to Subversive Organizations and Publications (and Appendixes)*, H. Doc. 398, 87th Cong., 2d. sess. (Washington, D.C., 1961) (this updated the first guide put out under the same title in 1951); U.S. Congress, House of Representatives, *Investigation of Un-American Propaganda Activities in the United States: Report of the Special Committee on Un-American Activities*, House Report 1311, 78th Cong., 2d sess. (Washington, D.C., 1944), 75–6, 143, 147; U.S. Congress, House of Representatives, *Investigation of Communist Influence in the Field of Publications (March of Labor): Hearings Before the Committee on Un-American Activities*, 83rd Cong., 2d sess., July 8 and 15, 1954, 5855–6, 5880; U.S. Congress, Senate, *Institute of Pacific Relations: Report on the Committee on the Judiciary*, Sen. Doc. 2050, 82d Cong., 2d sess. (Washington, D.C., 1952), 95, 146, 150; and U.S. Congress, Senate, *The Communist Party of the United States of America: What It Is, How It Works: A Handbook for Americans*, Sen. Doc. 117, 84th Cong., 2d sess. (Washington, D.C., 1956), 91.

Figure 5.1. Abraham Lincoln. *ITU News*, February–March, 1941 (cover). (Reproduced by permission of The Rhode Island Historical Society.)

Figure 5.2. "In memory of a surveyor and a rail-splitter." *ITU News*, February 1939 (cover). (Reproduced by permission of The Rhode Island Historical Society.)

Figure 5.3. Pilgrims' Thanksgiving. *ITU News*, November 1938 (cover). (Reproduced by permission of The Rhode Island Historical Society.)

Workers" atop numerous editorials.[34] The editors also praised the archetypical American folk hero – the pioneering farmer of the West – and argued that American trade unionists were the wise, hardy, and staunch pioneers of modern industrial society. Just as the nineteenth-century farmers "laid the basis for a rich, vast Republic," the editors wrote under one illustration (Figure 5.4), so too were twentieth-century workers "determined to build a powerful trade union movement that will make democracy in the United States an everlasting reality."[35]

The tone of this nationalist discourse was usually mild, even banal, as though the central role of labor in the life of the republic were a commonly acknowledged and agreed-upon fact. But occasionally this rhetoric took on a harsher, more confrontational tone. For example,

[34] *ITU News*, July 1936, 3, 5; March 1937, 5; February–March 1941, 15.
[35] Ibid., July 1937, cover; see also April 1940, cover.

Figure 5.4. "Pioneering." *ITU News*, July 1937 (cover). (Reproduced by permission of The Rhode Island Historical Society.)

ITU leaders once described their struggle with employers as an irrepressible conflict between "the *common right* of all humanity" and "the *divine rights* of kings." Quoting Lincoln, ITU leaders defined slavery "as the spirit that says, 'You work and toil and earn bread, and I'll eat it.' No matter in what shape it comes, whether from a mouth of a king, or from one race of men as an apology for enslaving another race, it is the *same tyrannical principle*." Following Franklin D. Roosevelt's lead, ITU radicals also depicted capitalists as "economic royalists" who treated the nation as their private domain, breaking democratic laws with impunity, stripping loyal workers of their jobs, and seizing – without right – the fruits of their workers' labor.[36] "Is this," ITU radicals wondered in 1936, "what Washington, Jefferson, Adams, and the other American revolutionists fought for?"[37]

This language, replete with talk of divine rights, tyranny, and royalists, resonated deeply, 150 years after American revolutionists had uprooted monarchical rule and substituted republican government in its place, among the ethnic workers of Woonsocket. To them it was

[36] Ibid., February 1938, 5; May 1937, 5; October 1937, 9.
[37] Ibid., September 1936, 3, 4.

"Boy, what a day for speedup!"

Figure 5.5. Arthur Redfield cartoon, "The Upper Crust," *ITU News*, June 1938. (Reproduced by permission of The Rhode Island Historical Society.)

plausible that monarchical sympathies still flourished among the rich, that fundamental principles of the republic – such as "one man, one vote," "equality before the law" – had yet to be secured. To them it appeared that certain groups of employers – like the French textile magnates – belonged to a social world utterly inaccessible to ordinary people. This vast gulf was not a social circumstance peculiar to Woonsocket. In many areas the rich marked out a life-style of conspicuous and lavish consumption that most Americans simply could neither aspire to nor attain. One of the most popular artists in labor and radical circles in the 1930s was Arthur Redfield, whose syndicated cartoon series, "The Upper Crust," lampooned the life-style of the very rich.[38] The central figures in these cartoons, which appeared regularly in the *ITU News*, were the portly, piggish, and small-minded rich; formally attired, they lived in huge mansions and were chauffeured around town in limousines (see Figures 5.5, 5.6, and

[38] Redfield was the favorite cartoonist of Federated Press subscribers. See "Federated Press Release," March 9, 1942, Federated Press, 1940–42 file, Box 79, FPC, CU.

"Junior just ran over someone."
"I hope the papers will spell our name right this time."

Figure 5.6. Arthur Redfield cartoon, "The Upper Crust," *ITU News*, August 1938. (Reproduced by permission of The Rhode Island Historical Society.)

5.7). This was not the world of the rich depicted in such modern TV shows as *Dallas* in which the dress, homes, bedrooms, and cars of the wealthy look thoroughly familiar. The 1930s world of the rich was seen as utterly different. Their society was closed; it was, in the eyes of Woonsocket workers, aristocratic.

Increasingly it seemed to workers that these "Tories" – as *ITU News* editors sometimes called them – were turning their social privileges into political privileges, exempting themselves from the law of the land.[39] This view crystallized in the mid-1930s as a result of the widespread refusal of employers to abide by the labor provisions of the National Industrial Recovery Act of 1933 and the National Labor Relations Act of 1935. A mixture of motives stood behind such employer refusals – a fear of economic failure, a confidence that the courts would overturn the legislation, an arrogance that refused to admit the government's right to regulate mighty corporations. To workers,

[39] *ITU News*, October 1937, 9.

"Psst . . . Are we alone?"

Figure 5.7. Arthur Redfield cartoon, "The Upper Crust," *ITU News*, June 1940. (Reproduced by permission of The Rhode Island Historical Society.)

however, it simply appeared as though employers were breaking the republic's most fundamental principle – equality before the law.

The most egregious example of such behavior in Woonsocket was Woonsocket Rayon's firing of all its workers who had joined a union in 1933. One of those fired, Albert Pelchat, had been forced to leave Woonsocket in search of work and shelter. Writing to Roosevelt from Baltimore in 1935, where he and his wife were trying to survive on the $1.00 a week paid them by the city's Federal Transient Relief Bureau, Pelchat wondered why his complaint of illegal firing had never been addressed by the NRA. "Is it because this company [Manville Jenckes] has shareholders that are important official[s] of the state of Rhode Island? If I, myself, break certain laws, we are liable to punishment; and any concern that breaks laws should not be an exception." Mr. President, Pelchat wrote on another occasion, "if people can be arrested for violating certain laws and pay the penalty, why can't this company?'' Why, Pelchat was asking, are employers allowed to live beyond the reach of the law?[40]

Such questioning might have led individuals like Pelchat to pronounce the American republic a failure, to abandon politics altogether, or else to opt for a politics that sought to replace the American system of government with an entirely new system. But none of these options appealed to Pelchat. After a year of bitter economic hardship, a year of futile letter writing to NRA officials and Roosevelt, Pelchat could still proclaim: "I believe in the New Deal and the N.R.A. . . . I have traveled in several states in the South. . . and I find that the people especially the laboring class believe and have faith that you Mr. President will pull this country out of the slump. I am a Democrat and proud of it."[41]

By "Democrat" Pelchat meant his party affiliation, but in the context of his argument to the President, we can interpret the word to mean as well his belief that the democratic principles of the republic were still worth fighting for. Had he been in Woonsocket in 1935 and thereafter, he no doubt would have found considerable truth in the ITU claim that "economic royalists" violated the principles of 1776 and stripped workers of their rights, and he would no doubt have seconded the ITU radicals' proposition that "a powerful trade union movement" could yet "make democracy in the United States an everlasting reality."[42]

The progressive dimension

ITU radicals easily, if somewhat incongruously, interwove their backward-looking nationalist perspective with Americanism's progressive dimension. Despite the ruin of the economic system, the "royalist" tendencies of capital, and the impoverished, dependent condition of the nation's workers, Schmetz and Spitz portrayed indus-

---

[40] Albert Pelchat to President Roosevelt, September 14, 1934, and January 18, 1935, Woonsocket Rayon Co. file, Record Group 9 (hereafter RG 9), Entry 402, National Archives (hereafter NA), Washington, D.C.

[41] Ibid., September 14, 1934.

[42] What became of Pelchat after 1935 is not known. The Textile Labor Relations Board finally did, in April 1935, notify Pelchat that they were going to investigate his complaint. But the post office returned this notification to the TLRB: Pelchat had moved and had not left a forwarding address. It had taken two years and six letters (including the original complaint) from Pelchat to move the board to action. Pelchat's letters (as well as the TLRB bureaucratic responses) can be found in Woonsocket Rayon Co. file, RG 9, Entry 402, NA. His original complaint, filed on January 24, 1934, has been preserved in Woonsocket Rayon Co. file, RG 9, Entry 398, NA.

Figure 5.8. "Labor's awakening!" *ITU News*, May 1937 (cover). (Reproduced by permission of The Rhode Island Historical Society.)

trial society – its massive productive power, ingenious machinery, and its mastery of the natural world – as one of America's great achievements. They paid tribute to workers as the group most responsible for bringing this industrial world into being. "The high buildings, the fine machinery, the fertile fields," Schmetz remarked on one occasion, "are the REAL accomplishments of labor."[43] Starkly realist and somewhat crude representations of supermanlike American workers towering over their workplaces and cities appeared frequently on the covers of their newsmagazine (Figure 5.8).[44] By emphasizing the "awesome" workers who had built "awesome" industry ITU radicals clearly hoped to imbue the union movement with the same inexorably progressive trend that most Americans of the time attributed to their technological civilization. Just as the "modern aeroplane speeds towards its destination...a product of industrial progress," the editors wrote in a caption of a cover illustration (Figure 5.9), so too "the ever-growing labor movement races on towards its goal...a product of industrial progress. Both are modern and indispensable! Both, products of our time."

[43] *ITU News*, August 1940, 5.
[44] See also the following *ITU News* covers: August 1936, September 1937, September 1939, and July 1940. Similar images, executed in the popular socialist-realist style of the day, appeared in countless labor and radical journals as well as in the murals and frescoes that WPA artists painted on the walls of post offices and other public buildings.

Swiftly and surely the modern aeroplane speeds towards its destination . . . . a product of industrial progress.

With equal accuracy the ever-growing labor m o v e-ment races on towards its goal . . . PEACE . . . LIBERTY . . . and ECONOMIC SECURITY . . . a product of social progress.

Both are modern and indispensable! Both, products of our time!

Figure 5.9. The inexorability of industrial and social progress. *ITU News*, September 1938 (cover). (Reproduced by permission of The Rhode Island Historical Society.)

The radicals' progressivism was in part tactical: They hoped to reassure their averaged-sized unionists (who were in reality dwarfed by the industrial society around them) that they collectively possessed the necessary muscle to triumph over their feared opponents. But the radicals' progressivism also expressed their own long-standing convictions concerning the inexorable forward march of labor and the inevitable triumph of socialism. ITU radicals were themselves deeply committed to the widely held progressive belief that American industrial society of the 1930s represented an extraordinarily advanced state of civilization. Humanity, one wrote, had mastered "the forces of nature" and could "organize a constant flow of goods which would satisfy everybody's needs with nobody compelled to go without food, clothing or shelter." They further believed, like virtually every socialist of the day, that "not until labor has the authority to apply its principles to our common life, will that other Conquest of Power –

scientific and industrial – be a creative, instead of, as is now the case, a destructive force."[45]

Such a progressive faith in the forward march of labor meshed neatly with the progressive streak imbedded in the radicals' nationalist rhetoric. The very notion of an irrepressible conflict between kings and commoners, between slavery and freedom, was a progressive one. It implied that the conflict would repeatedly break out until the people and the ideal of freedom triumphed. ITU radicals did not view American history in strictly linear, Whiggish terms; they did not see in it the unobstructed development and diffusion of freedom to all Americans. The people and their democratic ideals had suffered shattering defeats. But the quest for freedom – like the forward march of labor – simply could not be stopped. In such ways did the ITU's nationalist and progressive perspectives both fuel a tremendous optimism about the future.

The democratic dimension

The democratic dimension of Americanism, in the hands of ITU radicals, likewise evoked the past while pointing to the future. Like generations of American radicals preceding them, ITU radicals constructed their democratic vision around the eighteenth-century republican principle that the greatest threat to liberty lay in the accumulation of power in the hands of a few.[46] Eighteenth-century revolutionists had feared primarily the accumulation of power in government; following the lead of nineteenth-century radicals, ITU radicals identified industrial enterprises as the principal sources of autocracy. The great concentrations of economic power such enterprises represented would, if unchecked, radicals maintained, undermine the democratic and libertarian basis of the republic. Workers, dependent on powerful, self-interested employers for their survival, would lose the capacity for independent thinking so critical to the maintenance of a republic's citizenry. For democracy to prove successful, the ITU leaders asserted, "there must first be the opportunity for all to live and learn, free from either economic or political repres-

---

[45] Ibid., May 1937, 12.

[46] The seminal works on eighteenth-century republicanism are J.G.A. Pocock, *The Machiavellian Moment: Florentine Political Thought and the Atlantic Republican Tradition* (Princeton, N.J., 1975); Bernard Bailyn, *The Ideological Origins of the American Revolution* (Cambridge, Mass., 1967); Gordon Wood, *The Creation of the American Republic, 1776–1787* (Chapel Hill, N.C., 1969); Joyce Appleby, *Capitalism and a New Social Order: The Republican Vision of the 1790s* (New York, 1984).

sion."[47] Such freedom from repression could only be predicated on the economic independence of all Americans. "Until the millions of farmers and industrial workers of America have reached a status of economic independence, the work launched by Washington and Lincoln cannot be considered complete," they wrote, echoing the theme that nineteenth-century radicals had made so central to political debate.[48]

When ITU leaders discussed the meaning they attached to the phrase "economic independence," however, they revealed not their proximity to but their distance from nineteenth-century radicals. The latter considered wage labor a disgraceful form of dependence, and argued that independence in its many forms was predicated on eliminating or transcending an economic system based on wage labor. They differed in their visions of what would supersede capitalism, some looking backward toward a Jeffersonian nation of artisans and yeoman farmers and others looking forward to a nation of small worker-run cooperatives.[49] In the 1930s, the huge industrial structures and armies of wage labor that dominated the land rendered a Jeffersonian vision obsolete, and fifty years of bruising, often violent relations between capital and labor made a vision of numerous worker-run cooperatives, heavily dependent on a benign state, virtuous citizens, and a spirit of commonwealth, seem hopelessly utopian.[50] The phrase "wage slavery" ran like a trope through union discourse,[51] but, in reality, ITU radicals had accepted the concentration of industry and the wage-earning status of millions of Americans as unalterable realities of the twentieth century. Economic independence

---

[47] *ITU News*, January 1939, 4.
[48] Ibid., February–March 1941, 15.
[49] See David Montgomery, *Beyond Equality: Labor and the Radical Republicans, 1862–1872* (New York, 1967); Eric Foner, *Reconstruction: America's Unfinished Revolution, 1863–1877* (New York, 1988); Sean Wilentz, *Chants Democratic: New York City and the Rise of the American Working Class* (New York, 1984); Nick Salvatore, *Eugene V. Debs: Citizen and Socialist*; Steven Hahn, *The Roots of Southern Populism: Yeomen Farmers and the Transformation of the Georgia Upcountry* (New York, 1983); Lawrence Goodwyn, *Democratic Promise: The Populist Movement in America* (New York, 1976).
[50] On the dissolution of the republican vision, see David Montgomery, "Labor and the Republic in Industrial America, 1860–1920," *Le mouvement social* 111 (1980), 201–15, and Sean Wilentz, "Against Exceptionalism: Class Consciousness and the American Labor Movement, 1790–1920," *International Labor and Working Class History* 26 (Fall 1984), 1–24. On the bruising, violent history of class conflict, see Montgomery, *The Fall of the House of Labor: The Workplace, the State, and American Labor Activism, 1865–1925* (Cambridge, U.K., 1987), passim.
[51] See, for example, *ITU News*, October 1936, 10.

would be achieved not through an escape from wage-earning status, but through the empowerment of wage earners.

The leaders of the ITU told their members that the path to empowerment lay in the exercise of their constitutional rights. "As a worker in America you are a free man in a free country. You have certain rights which others must respect." One of those rights was the "sacred right of voting." Workers could use it to insure that politicians honored the Constitution and enforced the Bill of Rights; and they could remove "from public office. . . those individuals who make a mockery of the rights our forefathers so valiantly fought for."[52]

Exercising these electoral rights may appear, in retrospect, a rather tame tactic for radicals to have advocated. But ethnic workers in Woonsocket, like their counterparts elsewhere in the North and West, had only begun to think of themselves as American citizens with the full complement of rights that such citizenship entailed. To them, casting a ballot to determine who would govern and what policies would be implemented constituted a bold, even radical, political act. Fewer than 2,500 Woonsocket residents had voted in the presidential election of 1912. This figure had more than quadrupled to 11,500 by 1924; it then almost doubled again, to 21,000, by 1940.[53] Part of this increase reflected the extension of electoral rights to women in 1920 and the addition to the electorate of increasing numbers of Woonsocket immigrants who had completed their naturalization proceedings. But the extraordinary increase in voter participation – up more than eightfold from 1912 to 1940 – reflected also the decisions made by an increasing number of long-enfranchised ethnics to exercise their voting rights. A number of factors influenced such decisions: the increasing tendency of ethnics to regard America as their home and to believe that they might share in the government of their country; the determination of ethnic communities to elect legislators who would not use the state to undermine ethnic cultural life; and, in places like Woonsocket, an increased desire among poor ethnic Americans to elect politicians who would use the state to promote the economic and social welfare of workers and other groups of relatively powerless citizens. For all these reasons, the use of the ballot in the 1920s and 1930s, in cities like Woonsocket, signified a profound political awakening among millions of ethnic Americans. Its significance for national politics was every bit as great as the

---

[52] Ibid., March 1938, 15; November 1936, 1; June 1938, 4.

[53] *Providence Journal Almanac: A Reference Book for the State of Rhode Island* (Providence, R.I.), 1913, 45–6; 1917, 42–3; 1921, 134; 1925, 165; 1929, 160–1; 1933, 173; 1937, 186; 1941, 225.

dramatic growth of black Americans' electoral participation in the 1970s and 1980s.[54]

The ITU radicals had more than a political awakening in mind when they called on their members to exercise their voting rights. They also thought that massive labor electoral support for Franklin Roosevelt and the Democratic Party would push the New Deal in a social democratic direction. Schmetz, of course, had been carrying around his dreams of social democracy since his Belgian youth, and in Sweden's political experience of the early 1930s he found the concrete social democratic programs that might actually work in American society. "Gradually under socialist [Swedish] leaders, who preach evolution and reform rather than revolution," Schmetz wrote admiringly in October 1936, "the country vanquished her depression and made the living standards one of the world's highest." The Swedish socialists, Schmetz noted, had eliminated unemployment through a massive public works program financed by death and property taxes. They had nationalized essential resources like forests and iron mines, essential services like railways and electric power generation, and certain manufacturing plants like sawmills. Through these and other measures, they had effected, in Schmetz's opinion, "a happy compromise between socialism and capitalism."[55]

What made the Swedish policy successes so intoxicating to an American radical like Schmetz was the realization that a portion of Roosevelt's New Deal administration favored, by the mid-1930s, the implementation of similar social democratic policies in the United States. These left-wing New Dealers played a crucial role in designing and then operating the rambling collection of state agencies that comprised the New Deal welfare state: the Departments of Labor and Interior, the Works Project Administration, the National Labor Relations Board, the National Resources Planning Board, the Rural Elec-

---

[54] The mobilization of millions of new voters in the 1920s and 1930s has been well documented by political scientists and the new political historians. See, for example, Kristi Andersen, *The Creation of a Democratic Majority, 1928–1936* (Chicago, 1979); Paul Kleppner, *Who Voted? The Dynamics of Electoral Turnout, 1870–1980* (New York, 1982), 83–111; and Richard Jensen, "The Last Party System: Decay of Consensus, 1932–1980," in Paul Kleppner, ed., *The Evolution of American Political Systems* (Westport, Conn., 1981), 203–41. The ramifications of this mobilization, however, require further study.

[55] *ITU News*, October 1936, 5. Schmetz and fellow radicals also followed closely the experiments of Léon Blum's government in France; ibid., August 1936, 1. On the Swedish experience see Margaret Weir and Theda Skocpol, "State Structures and the Possibilities for 'Keynesian' Responses to the Great Depression in Sweden, Britain and the United States," in Peter B. Evans, Dietrich Rueschemeyer and Theda Skocpol, eds., *Bringing the State Back In* (Cambridge, U.K., 1985), 107–63.

trification Agency, and the Federal Reserve Board. Their ranks included such figures as Frances Perkins, Harold Ickes, Harry Hopkins, Henry Wallace, Beardsley Ruml, Morris Cooke, and Marriner Eccles. They were not, in any strict sense, anticapitalist. Rather, they were guided by a proto-Keynesian philosophy that saw the state as an institution capable of stabilizing a capitalist economy and restoring its prosperity. They viewed the stimulation of the people's purchasing power as the key to stabilization and prosperity. They favored the redistribution of income (via progressive taxation, welfare spending, and public works projects) and the regulation of financial and labor markets. Although these policies sought capitalism's restoration, they threatened to intrude on the capitalist economy – and especially its capital accumulation mechanisms – on a scale never before seen in American society. Further, the proto-Keynesians couched their policy proposals in the sort of anticapitalist rhetoric not heard in government circles since the age of Jackson. They depicted laissez-faire capitalism contemptuously, as a decrepit economic system that could no longer manage its own affairs or bring the American people a good life.[56]

This rhetorical assault resembled, in many ways, the socialist critique of capitalism. It allowed radicals like Schmetz to identify wholly with the direction that the New Deal of 1935, 1936, and 1937 seemed to be taking. And who could say, in those years, whether the state's activist role would restore the capitalist system to its earlier vigor and independence or lead instead to social democracy, that "happy compromise between socialism and capitalism?" To Schmetz, the radical reform energies whipping through Washington made the mid-1930s seem like a propitious historical moment for changing the character of the American economy and with it the experience of the American working class. Schmetz and fellow radicals thus perched themselves on the left wing of the New Deal, hailing its actual reforms, excoriating its opponents (like the Supreme Court justices), and calling repeatedly for its extension.[57] The existence of such an unprecedented

---

[56] In their "State Structures" article, Skocpol and Weir have labeled these New Dealers "social Keynesians"; see pp. 108, 132–48. See also Steve Fraser, "The 'Labor Question,'" and Alan Brinkley, "The New Deal and the State," in Steve Fraser and Gary Gerstle, eds., *The Rise and Fall of the New Deal Order, 1930–1980* (Princeton, N.J., 1989), 55–121; Dean L. May, *From New Deal to New Economics: The American Liberal Response to the Recession of 1937* (New York, 1981); Herbert Stein, *The Fiscal Revolution in America* (Chicago, 1969); George McJimsey, *Harry Hopkins: Ally of the Poor and Defender of Democracy* (Cambridge, Mass., 1987); Arthur Schlesinger, Jr., *The Age of Roosevelt: Years of Upheaval, 1935–1936* (Boston, 1960).

[57] *ITU News*, July 1936, 1; August 1936, 5; October 1936, 10, 17; January 1939, 4; January 1940, 3; March 1940, 3.

political opportunity makes sense, then, of the ITU's emphasis on the exercise of political rights. Those rights, if exercised by enough working-class voters, might actually thrust the progressive labor movement into control of the American state.

It was but a short ideological leap from the assertion of familiar political rights to the elaboration of new industrial rights: to jobs, to a fair share of the nation's wealth, and to a voice in the direction of the nation's economic institutions. ITU radicals were always prodding rank and filers to extend the discourse on rights to economic affairs. They bundled together particular industrial rights under the elastic label "industrial democracy" which, they repeatedly insisted to their membership, was but the logical, modern extension of political democracy.[58]

It is difficult to know how many Woonsocket workers interpreted industrial democracy as a grand plan for the reconstruction of the nation's economy. But the discussion of industrial rights and industrial democracy had a quite concrete meaning for workers in Woonsocket and elsewhere, speaking to the conditions of their employment and the character of their working experience. Industrial democracy, as union radicals discussed it, promised workers a very tangible kind of empowerment: control over their hours, their wages, their jobs, their chances for promotion, and even their employers' pricing and investment decisions. "Our forefathers stated their rights in the Declaration of Independence and set up a free government to protect them," union radicals asserted. "But to have a free government you must have recognition and respect of your rights in the workshop as well as the polls. . . . Can you really be free if they are not recognized and respected?"[59] Workshop rights would not be respected unless industrial democracy reigned. Industrial democracy, at the level of the individual workshop, denoted the system of industrial government set up under the National Labor Relations Act (or Wagner Act) passed in 1935. The act allowed workers the right to campaign and to vote for union representation without interference from their employers. If a majority of workers voted to join a union, the act required the employer to sit down with union representatives and bargain in good faith on all matters pertaining to "wages, hours, and working conditions." A National Labor Relations Board stood ready to supervise elections and bring suit against employers and workers who violated any section of the act.

Two overlapping but distinct visions of social reconstruction under-

[58] Ibid., January 1939, cover, 4; June 1940, 3–4; December 1940, 4.
[59] Ibid., March 1938, 15.

girded this system of industrial government. One focused on the ways in which the organization of labor would give workers the collective strength to raise their wages and limit their hours of work. On a macroeconomic level, rising wages and increasing leisure were expected to stimulate consumption and thereby revive and sustain capitalist production. On a microeconomic level, this vision saw workers as consumers who would increasingly find fulfillment in an exciting array of leisure pursuits, from movies and baseball games to vacations and summer homes, that high wages and ample free time would put within their grasp. The other vision animating the NLRA focused on the empowerment of workers at the workplace. The unionized workplace would become a miniature democratic society, governed by a constitution (the NLRA) that granted to workers basic industrial rights. By granting workers the right to join unions, to protest employer abuses, and to bargain collectively over "wages, hours, and working conditions," the NLRA was meant to dissuade workers – in certain situations it specifically prohibited them – from striking and engaging in other means of extralegal protest. As industrial citizenship replaced industrial serfdom, social peace would replace social conflict.[60]

Both the "consumption" and "citizenship" visions imbedded in the NLRA found expression in the writings of ITU radicals. They understood the relationship between working-class purchasing power and the health of the nation's economy and advertised unionism as a way of promoting both.[61] The radicals themselves yearned for the economic security that high wages and union membership would bestow on their personal and family lives; nothing was more harrowing than job and income insecurity.[62] And they were attracted to the ideal of enlarging the leisure portion of their day and shrinking that portion spent at grimy and wearying textile labor. In fact, they sometimes suggested that the major purpose of trade unions was to bring "com-

---

[60] On these two visions see Fraser, "The 'Labor Question'"; Fraser, "Dress Rehearsal for the New Deal: Shop-Floor Insurgents, Political Elites, and Industrial Democracy in the Amalgamated Clothing Workers," in Michael H. Frisch and Daniel J. Walkowitz, *Working-Class America: Essays on Labor, Community, and American Society* (Urbana, Ill., 1983), 212–55; Fraser "From the 'New Unionism' to the New Deal," *Labor History* 25 (Summer 1984), 405–30; Stanley Vittoz, *The New Deal Labor Policy and the American Industrial Economy* (Chapel Hill, N.C., 1987), 77–96, 137–52: Christopher L. Tomlins, *The State and the Unions: Labor Relations, Law, and the Organized Labor Movement in America, 1880–1960* (Cambridge, U.K., 1985), 99–243.

[61] *ITU News*, January 1937, 1; March 1938, 15.

[62] Ibid., January 1937, 5; November 1937, cover; February–March 1941, 15; November 1940, 5.

fort, leisure, happiness... within reach of every worker."[63] The point of leisure and comfort, however, was not simply – or even primarily – to indulge in the commercial satisfactions made available by department stores, movie palaces, or amusement parks; it was instead to enlarge working men's and women's opportunities for education, contemplation, and moral improvement. "It is good for men to have leisure," ITU radicals wrote, "so that he [sic] may devote some of his time to the enrichment of his soul and to the eventual betterment of humanity."[64] Leisure, in other words, would nurture citizenship qualities as much as it would stimulate consumption.

The main arena for honing one's citizenship qualities in these years was, however, the workshop, and here, the question of what industrial citizenship entailed was not to be approached abstractly or contemplatively. Rather, the meaning of industrial citizenship had to be hammered out in concrete struggles involving workers, employers, and the state. A critical ambiguity in the language of the NLRA gave rise to such struggles. While the NLRA obligated employers to bargain with their unionized workers over "working conditions," it did not specify what the phrase signified, leaving the act open to widely divergent readings. Employers could claim that working conditions involved no more than the cleanliness and proper ventilation of work areas. Radically minded workers could claim with equal justification that such matters as hiring, firing, job allocation, technological change, speed of production, quality control, and perhaps even corporate planning vitally affected "working conditions."[65]

Such ambiguity had long surrounded the term "industrial democracy" itself. To the left-wing New Dealers (who had been industrial democracy's chief proponents since the early 1920s), the establishment of constitutional regimes on the shopfloor had always had the instrumental purpose of improving the operation of industry. The point of granting workers their rights and involving them in workplace governance was to give them a stake in an industry's smooth and prosperous operation. If workers believed that the operation of industry somehow depended on their consent, then they would be likely to cooperate with management in the pursuit of efficiency and productivity. If the exercise of shopfloor rights did not serve efficiency, productivity, and harmony, then the rights themselves could

---

[63] Ibid., January 1937, 5.

[64] Ibid., October 1936, 10.

[65] For an exploration of these critical ambiguities in the NLRA see Karl Klare, "Judicial Deradicalization of the Wagner Act and the Origins of Modern Legal Consciousness, 1937–1941," *Minnesota Law Review* 62 (1977–78), 265–339; Tomlins, *The State and the Unions*, 224–43.

be curtailed. This instrumental reasoning may help explain why the phrase "working conditions" was left so vague in the Wagner Act. The act's framers may have been less concerned to impart a narrow construction to the phrase than to make clear that any working-class voice in working conditions had to contribute to – or at least not obstruct – industrial efficiency and productivity. The experience of industrial relations in the clothing industry – a much-discussed and highly touted model in New Deal circles in the 1930s – had shown that extensive union participation in the determination of piece rates (one of the prime determinants of working conditions in garment shops) had contributed significantly to industrial stabilization. Thus, similar patterns of extensive union participation in production matters could be justified in other industries if they too benefited productivity and stability.[66]

The problem with such reasoning was that it underestimated the subversive potential to be found in such words as "democracy" and "rights." In a country that so valued its tradition of natural, inalienable rights, the discussion of "industrial rights" could not easily be confined to an instrumental, or functional, plane of discourse. In the heady days following World War I, the discussion of rights and industrial democracy did indeed break free of its functionalist trappings and did inspire radical visions of social reconstruction.[67] This period of "100 flowers" did not survive the depression of 1921 and 1922, but Norman Thomas and fellow socialists diligently carried forward – well into the 1930s – the struggle to imbue the phrase "industrial democracy" with a truly radical meaning.[68] Thus when left-wing New Dealers and their labor movement allies passed the NLRA, placing industrial democracy back on the national political agenda,

[66] Fraser, "The 'Labor Question,'" and "Dress Rehearsal for the New Deal"; Tomlins, *The State and the Unions*. See also J. Joseph Huthmacher, *Robert Wagner and the Rise of Urban Liberalism* (New York, 1968), 153–98; Philippa Strum, *Louis D. Brandeis: A Justice for the People* (Cambridge, Mass., 1984), 94–195; W. Jett Lauck, *Political and Industrial Democracy, 1776–1926* (New York, 1926); Edward Filene, *The Way Out* (New York, 1925); John L. Lewis, *The Miners' Fight for American Standards* (New York, 1925).

[67] Daniel T. Rodgers, *The Work Ethic in Industrial America, 1850–1920* (Chicago, 1978), 57–64; Montgomery, *The Fall of the House of Labor*, 370–457; John A. Ryan, *Social Reconstruction* (New York, 1920); Milton Derber, *The American Idea of Industrial Democracy, 1865–1965* (Urbana, Ill., 1970); Steve Fraser, "Industrial Democracy in the 1980s," *Socialist Review* 72 (November-December 1983), 99–122; James Gilbert, *Designing the Industrial State: The Intellectual Pursuit of Collectivism in America, 1880–1940* (Chicago, 1972), 80–124.

[68] See, for example, Norman Thomas, "What is Industrial Democracy?" in Bernard K. Johnpoll and Mark R. Yerburgh, eds., *A Documentary History of the League for Industrial Democracy* (Westport, Conn., 1980), vol. I, 387–446.

the debate on what kind of rights this phrase really entailed quickly revived. This New Deal discussion, in relation to post–World War I discussions, was a narrowed one: The passage of the NLRA put an end to the wide-ranging, imaginative, and often wildly speculative debate that had erupted in the immediate postwar years over the institutional forms (work councils, industrial parliaments, and bicameral legislatures) that industrial democracy might take. Virtually all participants in the 1930s discussion accepted, in broad terms, the labor relations machinery established by the Wagner Act.[69] Discussion, thus, increasingly turned on the definition of key phrases such as "working conditions" and "employee rights." Workers and employers would fight countless battles over these definitions both on the shopfloor and in cases brought before the NLRB, the National War Labor Board, and the federal courts. Only in the mid- to late-1940s did a clear (and limited) interpretation of "working conditions" and "employee rights" gain the status of law.[70]

In Woonsocket, these struggles generally lacked theoretical or ideological acuity. ITU radicals themselves muddled the meaning of "industrial democracy," sometimes casting it in minimalist terms, as simply the freedom of workers to speak their minds and make known their demands without fear of reprisal, and at other times suggesting that the establishment of collective bargaining units was but the first step in labor's efforts to extend its authority to every aspect of the production process.[71] Their insistence on the workers' right to scrutinize the size and distribution of employer profits reveals a determination to gain a voice even in pricing and investment decisions, the areas of most jealously guarded managerial prerogatives. At such moments radicals made plain their desire that labor one day exercise sovereignty over all of industry.[72]

That ITU leaders expressed both minimalist and maximalist views reveals a great deal about the pressures operating on labor radicals in the 1930s. They could not loudly proclaim their socialism or their desire that labor would one day take over all of industry. The successful operation of a union required that they subordinate such ultimate goals to the priorities of the here and now: maintaining solidarity in the ranks, generating enthusiasm for the CIO, gaining support from fearful ethnic leaders and suspicious state legislators. Moreover,

---

[69] The AFL, though, became a sharp critic of the NLRA in the late 1930s. See Tomlins, *The State and the Unions*, 161–96, 213–24.

[70] This denouement will be discussed in Chapter 10.

[71] *ITU News*, June 1940, 3–4.

[72] Ibid., March 1938, 15.

the realization of social democracy in the nation required that the ITU bend all its efforts to support Roosevelt, his New Deal policies, and the legislative majority that Democrats had forged in Congress. In such circumstances ITU radicals were bound, at times, to identify their views of industrial relations with those emanating from Washington; they were bound as well to use phrases like "industrial democracy" as New Deal administrators and politicians used them. Yet imbedded in the phrase "industrial democracy" was the kernel of a truly radical idea – the democratization of industrial enterprise – that helped ITU radicals communicate to Woonsocket unionists their far-reaching plans for social reconstruction. To their minds, the concept could encourage workers of all kinds to put aside the problems of daily toil and contemplate radical visions of a new social order.

That industrial democracy – however ambiguously defined – had become so central to political discussions in the 1930s marked an important achievement for liberals and radicals of the time. It meant that left-liberal forces had managed to extract from the democratic language of Americanism the words necessary to establish capital-labor relations as a political, even moral, issue of cardinal importance. It meant that radicals and liberals had shifted the balance of ideological power between capital and labor in labor's favor after a long period of unchallenged corporate domination. And, finally, it focused the attention of the American polity squarely on the glaring problem of industrial autocracy in a society ostensibly dedicated to democratic principles.

The (missing) traditionalist dimension

The fate of the radicals' campaign for industrial democracy depended first and foremost on how much enthusiasm it could generate among union members, most of whom were French Canadian. One of the most striking features of the Americanist discourse developed by union leaders was the almost complete absence of any references to French-Canadian culture. The heroes of French-Canadian immigrants and their children, the heroes of whom they learned at home and in parochial schools, were not the Pilgrims, Washington, and Lincoln; they were rather the early French explorers of North America, the generals who valiantly fought the English before losing Quebec on the Plains of Abraham, and the saints who enriched their religious lives. Their traditional folk hero was not the American pioneer but the French-Canadian *habitant* – the sturdy peasant who raised his family, practiced his religion, and tilled a piece of land somewhere in rural Quebec. This folk hero and the dream of a homestead in rural Quebec survived well into the twentieth century, even among the children and grandchildren of the original immigrants raised in New England's mill towns. So, too, did the immigrants' reverence for saints. Many French Canadians passionately followed the case of Marie-Rose Ferron, a young Woonsocket woman who was said to have borne, in the 1930s, the stigmata of Christ's crucifixion.[73]

No explorers, saints, ecstatics, or *habitants* appeared on the covers or in the pages of the *ITU News*. At Christmastime, when the union newspaper applauded the holiday's emphasis on unity and harmony and printed, occasionally, French poems extolling the Christmas spirit, the radicals did acknowledge the culture that shaped the lives of so many rank and filers.[74] But even these exceptional moments barely hinted at the intense, all-encompassing religiosity so integral to many areas of Woonsocket life. Figure 5.10, a 1944 picture of a resident and staff member of Woonsocket's Hospice St-Antoine, an old-age home staffed by a religious order, suggests how much the *ITU News* left out; prominently displayed rosary beads, like the ones hanging from the old man's shirt, and flowing robes that all but obscured the nuns who inhabited them were two of Woonsocket's more common sights.[75]

The exclusion of French-Canadian culture from the *ITU News* was so complete that it appears deliberate. In fact, the ITU's use of the language of Americanism may be understood in part as an effort by union radicals to oppose local ethnic culture and liberate French-Canadian workers from their traditional leadership. Union radicals urged French-Canadian workers to feel like Americans, not immigrants, to think of their class needs before the needs of their church or ethnic group, to act to redress the balance of wealth and power in American society rather than meekly accept their earthly lot. The radicals never made their attack on French-Canadian society and culture explicit. Occasionally editors noted how the spirit of Christmas brought few benefits to unemployed or poorly paid workers, and they made sure

[73] Pierre Anctil, "Aspects of Class Ideology in a New England Ethnic Minority: The Franco-Americans of Woonsocket, Rhode Island (1865–1929)" (Ph.D. dissertation, New School for Social Research, 1980), 201; O.A. Boyer, *She Wears a Crown of Thorns: Marie-Rose Ferron (1902–1936) Known as "Little Rose," the Stigmatized Ecstatic of Woonsocket, Rhode Island* (Ellenburg, N.Y., 1939); Gerard J. Brault, *The French-Canadian Heritage in New England* (Hanover, N.H., 1986), 92–7; Richard S. Sorrell, "Kerouac's Lowell: 'Little Canada' and the Ethnicity of Jack Kerouac," *Essex Institute Historical Collections* 114 (October 1981), 276–7.

[74] See, for example, *ITU News*, December 1936, "Le Retour du Christ," 7; December 1938, 3, 5; December 1939, cover.

[75] Federal Writers' Project, Works Progress Administration, *Rhode Island: Guide to the Smallest State* (Boston, 1937), 101.

Figure 5.10. Hospice St-Antoine, Woonsocket, 1944, U.S. Office of War Information, Ruth Ames, photographer. (Courtesy Library of Congress.)

to include in their magazine any report of an American priest proclaiming his support for trade unions.[76] But generally the radicals sought to persuade not through criticism but through a promise: Become American, and you will improve yourselves. They implied that as American trade unionists, ethnic workers could develop the strength and pride – even the size of those awesome proletarians depicted on *ITU News* covers – to change society to better suit their own needs and aspirations.

ITU radicals believed that such an appeal would resonate among French-Canadian workers who felt inferior in America because of their difficulty speaking English, their reputation as cheap labor, and their inability during the Depression to provide for their families. These ethnic workers had begun questioning the vision of their traditional leaders, a vision that had consigned them to a life of hardship.

[76] See, for example, *ITU News*, December 1937, cover; March 1938, 6; April 1938, 7; April 1939, 14.

As union members, they had responded eagerly to notions of independence and democracy. ITU leaders thought that French Canadians would accept a cultural heritage that validated their shopfloor experience. Spitz recalled that they had "strong feelings about being recognized as full-fledged American citizens."[77] He and Schmetz tied the success of their labor movement to the willingness of Woonsocket workers to embrace an American political and cultural heritage and free themselves from the restrictive and conservative ethnic society in which they had grown up.

The radicals' strategy of inducing a rupture between ethnic workers and their traditional culture was in some respects well-considered. What better way for the radicals to overcome an ethnic Catholic community's deep hostility to socialism than by quietly devaluing the ethnic Catholic roots of such hostility? But putting the problem this way also highlights how shortsighted that strategy was: It was simply wildly implausible to think that ethnic workers would – or could, even if they wanted to – jettison their ethnic and religious traditions for the sake of socialism or some other modernist faith.

What saved this Americanization strategy from utter failure was something that radicals only dimly – if at all – understood. Spitz correctly perceived that an American identity was important to French-Canadian workers. They were tired of their powerlessness; they did feel as though they could better defend themselves if they gained the full rights and entitlements that accompanied the status and practice of citizenship. But they were attracted to an American identity for another reason as well: They had begun to realize that the traditionalist dimension of Americanism offered them an opportunity to incorporate – and thus preserve – treasured values of their culture in a new American identity. Traditionalist language valued family, religion, community. It looked backward to a simpler, more virtuous past. To ITU radicals, such traditionalism was anathema; barely a trace of it surfaces in their writings. For a long time such rhetoric repulsed ethnic workers as well. Nativists of the 1920s, after all, had used it as a tool for subjecting Catholics and immigrants to abuse and discrimination. But the waning of nativism in the 1930s allowed Catholic Americans to begin (and in some cases to resume) exploration of the affinities between their ethnocultural values and the traditionalist strain of Americanism. Such an exploration can be detected in the thinking of individuals as different as the radio priest Father Coughlin and the Sicilian-born filmmaker Frank Capra. Coughlin repeatedly stressed the interconnectedness of Christian and American values,

[77] Interview with Lawrence Spitz, September 19–20, 1979.

declaring in 1936, for example, that "America was cradled in the spirit of Christ's doctrine."[78] Capra, meanwhile, won the hearts of millions of Americans with movies extolling America's golden small town past, when life was simple, people were honest, and morally upright individuals commanded respect. The success with which Capra made movies that captured the mythical spirit of small-town life suggests a close affinity between his own Italian background and traditional American values.[79]

Despite the fact that ITU radicals controlled the union and its press in the late 1930s, traditional values of religion, family, and patriarchy occasionally did break into print or illustration. One such occasion was Thanksgiving; in November 1939, union radicals hailed it "as a day of family feasting and pleasure" that had "no equal on our calendar." They were quick to add, of course, that the deeper meaning of the day lay in the opportunity it gave union men and women to offer "thanks for the benefits received during the past year."[80] The radicals no doubt had it wrong. The deeper meaning of the day lay not in the contemplation of union benefits but in the affirmation of family togetherness that the celebrations entailed. This affirmation of family, in fact, may have accounted for the rapidity with which Catholic and Jewish ethnic households in twentieth-century America absorbed into their social calendar a holiday honoring a strange group of seventeenth-century Protestant zealots.

The traditional values of the ITU's many French-Canadian unionists can be further glimpsed in the illustrations that a rank and filer occasionally drew for ITU News covers. This rank and filer, identifiable only by the names "G. Levitre" and "Gus" (probably short for Gaston) with which he signed his art, portrayed the world in images strikingly different from those the radicals preferred.[81] On one occasion (Figure 5.11) he depicted class struggle in Biblical terms, as a struggle to death between a monstrous Goliath ("industrial greed") and a small but valiant David ("organized labor"). Other illustrations

---

[78] Quoted in David O'Brien, *American Catholics and Social Reform: The New Deal Years* (New York, 1968), 162.

[79] See Capra's *Mr. Deeds Goes to Town* (1936), *Mr. Smith Goes to Washington* (1939), *Meet John Doe* (1941), and *It's a Wonderful Life* (1946). For thoughtful analyses of Capra's movies see Leonard Quart, "A Populist in Hollywood: Frank Capra's Politics," *Socialist Review* 68 (March–April, 1983), 59–74; Raymond Carney, *American Vision: The Films of Frank Capra* (Cambridge, U.K., 1986). The relationship of Capra's ethnic background to his film making has yet to receive much attention. For glimpses, see Frank Capra, *The Name Above the Title* (New York, 1971), 3–16, and passim.

[80] *ITU News*, November 1939, cover.

[81] No other background information – occupational, familial, political – has survived on this artist.

Figure 5.11. David and Goliath, cartoon, *ITU News*, April 1939 (cover). (Reproduced by permission of The Rhode Island Historical Society.)

emphasized – in the way that radicals never did – the centrality of families to union life. One (Figure 5.12), framed around a father handing his toddler a big chocolate bunny while an admiring mother looked on, depicted Easter as a time of family togetherness and joy. Radical illustrations of working-class life, by contrast, ignored family life altogether and focused entirely on the relationship of men (and only men) to their work.[82] Gus's depiction of working-class life, though more firmly rooted in Woonsocket's social reality than radical depictions, must itself be seen as a particular kind of ideological construction. Most French-Canadian mothers did more than prepare their husband's lunch and groom their toddler's appearance, and many labored alongside their husbands in the textile mills. Those who did stay at home rarely enjoyed the luxury of caring for only one child. A

---

[82] The radicals did present Pilgrims in familial contexts but never industrial workers.

Figure 5.12. "Happy Easter," *ITU News*, April 1938. (Reproduced by permission of The Rhode Island Historical Society.)

woman surrounded by five or six children ranging in age from five to fifteen would have more accurately caught the reality of Woonsocket's domestic sphere. Gus's illustration did, however, capture the patriarchal spirit so deeply imbedded in French-Canadian home life. His placing a dominant husband in the illustration's center and a diminutive wife off to the side (as well as choosing a factory rather than a home as background) reflected widely shared beliefs about the proper relations between the sexes.

Gus's evocation of the Bible, family, and patriarchy, then, points to the enduring traditionalism of Woonsocket's French-Canadian workers. His drawings further suggest that these values had become detached from a larger cultural context. He made no effort to connect the Bible, the family, or patriarchy to traditional notions of *la survivance*, nor did he make a serious attempt to express these values in the traditionalist language of Americanism. He, like many French Canadians, perhaps, had reached a crossroads. Though he felt ready, it seems, to leave behind the ethnocultural world in which he had been raised, he did not feel comfortable embracing the traditionalist language of Americanism to which he felt drawn. Other French-Canadian unionists, however, had gone further than Gus in adopting the language of Americanism as their own, and many more would transform themselves into flag-waving champions of American values once they had experienced the ideological developments of world war and cold war, and especially the sudden centrality of cultural pluralism and anti-communism in Americanist discourse (the subjects of Chapter 9).

The determination of French Canadians to preserve their traditionalist values would generate sharp conflicts between ethnics and radicals on the place of religion and radicalism in union affairs, on union relations with local political machines, and on ITU relations with the CIO. But the preliminary efforts of these ethnics to formulate their aspirations in the traditionalist language of Americanism strengthened the radical-ethnic alliance on matters of political economy. Moral traditionalism could easily lend itself to militant, even radical, attacks on capitalism. Many French-Canadian workers believed, as a result of the Woonsocket Rayon affair, that capital and community stood in opposition to each other. Gus's metaphorical use of David's mortal struggle with Goliath conveys a powerful sense of the fundamental nature of this opposition. *ITU News* editors underscored this opposition by writing, under the illustration, that employers "in the drive for profits...have forgotten completely the welfare of the workers, their families and the community as a whole."[83] It followed from such an analysis that workers would have to resort to unprecedented measures to insure the safety of family and community. Such measures would necessarily include the curtailment of capital's rights and the augmentation of workers' rights both at particular Woonsocket workplaces and in the nation at large. The traditionalism of French Canadians, in other words, could powerfully sanction the radicals' campaign for industrial democracy. This was all the more likely to occur as French Canadians began finding in the democratic dimension of Americanism language for asserting their communal rights.

The very malleability of Americanism's various dimensions as well as the way in which they contradicted each other, then, enhanced their ability to transcend deep political, cultural, and moral divisions within Woonsocket's working class. Radicals could express their pro-

---

[83] *ITU News*, April 1939, cover.

gressive beliefs in the language of Americanism while ethnics could use the same language to promote traditionalist values. And both groups could find in the words and ideas of Americanism's democratic dimension a justification for limiting the rights of capital and augmenting the rights of labor. Both could portray their struggles as the continuation of battles that had begun in the American Revolution 150 years before. The language of Americanism worked remarkably well in giving ideological and linguistic unity to a working class that was deeply divided over matters of politics, culture, and morals. The irony, of course, was that ITU radicals, who prided themselves on their foresight, their organizational skills, and their strategical acuity did not really understand how the language of Americanism gave their union cohesion and strength. They did not really comprehend how union ethnics were building their American identity around traditionalist values; they did not really understand the process by which traditional values thrown off by a disintegrating ethnic culture were being transformed into American values. They thus were not prepared for the kind of American identity that began coalescing in the ranks of French-Canadian workers: anticapitalist but anticommunist, patriotic but parochial, militant but devout.

6   *Ethnic-style unionism*

Between 1936 and 1941, ITU radicals achieved many of their most sought-after goals. The union doubled in size, becoming ever more inclusive of Woonsocket's working class. Organizing triumphs at the French Worsted and Woonsocket Rayon broke the will of the city's two most bitterly antiunion textile employers. In countless other mills, rank-and-file workers, spurred by talk of industrial democracy, established shopfloor regimes that either eliminated managerial authority altogether or obligated managers to win union assent on all proposed changes in personnel, work assignments, and technology. Away from work, the ITU became the kind of comprehensive labor movement, sponsoring activities as diverse as beach outings, housing projects, and medical clinics, that replicated on a municipal scale the social unionism that Schmetz had known in Belgium.

Yet these years of triumph were hardly, from the radicals' perspective, trouble-free. Efforts to link the ITU with the CIO failed; so, too, did a major campaign to force employers to open their finances to public scrutiny. An internal faction fight, unprecedented in severity and bitterness, tore through union ranks in 1939. Some of these reversals in union fortunes, most notably the failure of the open-books campaign, reflected the belated solidifying of employer ranks and the government's growing inclination to define an area of managerial prerogative beyond the reach of unions. But others reflected the increasing determination of the French-Canadian skilled workers to flex their muscles in union affairs. These years marked the emergence, in the ranks of the skilled, of a distinctive, ethnic-style unionism. Drawing heavily on French-Canadian traditions and experiences, this ethnic unionism would impart a distinctly parochial, communal, and patriarchal character to ITU affairs. French-Canadian unionists would obstruct the radicals' efforts to affiliate with the CIO and strengthen conservative cultural currents, most notably sexist ones, in union affairs. Moreover, the more these unionists played out the implications of their ethnic perspective, the more they felt compelled to challenge the leadership of Schmetz, Spitz, and their supporters. Yet, a simple "conservative" label does not adequately describe this ethnic-style unionism. The very act of elaborating an ethnic union vision inspired

196

the French Canadians to reinterpret ethnic traditions in creative ways, and many began finding in those traditions reasons to support the radicals' dreams of establishing a comprehensive labor movement and of democratizing social relations on the shopfloor. Further, ethnics would remain committed to the restructuring of their community and factories along communal, democratic lines even as they began marshaling their resources to oust the radicals from union power.

Belgian unionism, French-Canadian style

From the moment he left Europe in 1919, Schmetz had nurtured a dream of establishing in America a Belgian-style labor movement. He did not see an opportunity to realize it until the ITU had achieved power and stability in the mid-1930s, and he could not have accomplished it without the administrative skills of Lawrence Spitz. But by the late 1930s and early 1940s, a miniature version of the Belgian labor movement had emerged in Woonsocket. Like the Belgian Workers Party, the ITU was becoming a "state within a state." By late 1941 and early 1942, the ITU provided its members with life insurance, a medical clinic, and a credit union, and it had moved the first union families into its own cooperative housing project, built by ITU labor. Every year the union offered a greater variety of educational programs. Spitz began teaching a course in American labor history in 1937 and arranged for a lecture series that brought prominent government figures, labor leaders, clergymen, and professors to Woonsocket in 1938. The same year the union opened its own library. The following year it arranged with the WPA's Worker Education Program for classes in English, citizenship, trade unionism, journalism, drama, and chorus.[1] How many ITU members attended classes in serious subjects is not known, but the drama and choral classes – and performances – were wildly popular.[2] So, too, were the other union events that involved singing, music, and other forms of entertainment. Every winter the union sponsored a dance at the Joyland Ballroom in Woonsocket that attracted thousands. Each summer the union's annual outing – a festive day of games, singing, feasting, speechmaking, and

---

[1] ITU, *Labor Review, 1931–1942* (Woonsocket, R.I., 1942), 43–46; *Woonsocket Call* (hereafter *WC*), December 21, 1940, and August 30, 1941; Robert Maurice Mooney, "The Origins, Nature, Internal and External Operations of the Industrial Trades Union of America" (M.A. thesis, Catholic University of America, 1947), 49; *ITU News*, October 1939, 8, and November 1939, 7.

[2] *ITU News*, January 1940, 8; April 1940, 7; May 1940, 4; September 1940, 9.

general camaraderie – attracted 5,000 to 6,000 unionists and family members. Huge convoys, involving as many as forty buses and 500 individual cars, were required to transport these unionists to their beach or park destination, and ITU members delighted in the convoys themselves, which wound slowly and deliberately through the city's major streets with motors humming, horns blaring, hands waving, and voices singing.[3]

The rapid development of such a comprehensive labor movement, impressive not just for the range of new organizations and activities established but also for the high level of rank-and-file participation, cannot be understood simply in terms of some "natural" working-class enthusiasm for the Belgian trade-union ideal. What made that ideal so attractive to ITU rank and filers, and especially the French-Canadian majority among them, was the opportunity it gave them to infuse their trade-union movement with the communal spirit so intrinsic to their ethnic culture.

The process by which an old communal spirit infuses new institutional forms is exceedingly hard to trace, especially when it has occurred in an ethnic working class notable for its weak associational life. If French-Canadian workers had had their own (that is specifically working-class) fraternal, ethnic, or political organizations, as did the Italians and Franco-Belgians in Woonsocket, then we could perhaps show how an ethnic lodge served as a meeting place for union activities, and how that lodge's ostensibly ethnic activities (recorded in minutes of meetings and in commemorative publications) contributed to the vibrancy of a labor organization. But French-Canadian workers in Woonsocket, like their counterparts in many other New England communities, had never forged much of an independent associational life for themselves; the independence they did achieve was customarily of an informal, even furtive, sort within elite-controlled institutions like the Church, or in spaces, like bars, homes, and the Maine forests, not already occupied by elite ethnic structures.[4]

Thus, evidence for the invigoration of a labor movement by an ethnic communal spirit must be gleaned from the few glimpses into

---

[3] *ITU News*, July 1938, 6; July 1939, 4; May 1939, 7; April–May 1941, 9; August 1937, 8–9; June 1939, 6–7; August 1939, 6; September 1940, 6. Interview with Lawrence Spitz, October 22, 1976.

[4] C. Stewart Doty, ed., *The First Franco-Americans: New England Life Histories from the Federal Writers' Project, 1938–1939* (Orono, Maine, 1985), passim; Horace Miner, *St. Denis: A French-Canadian Parish* (Chicago, 1939), 61, 63–90; Pierre Anctil, "Aspects of Class Ideology in a New England Ethnic Minority: The Franco-Americans of Woonsocket, Rhode Island (1865–1929)" (Ph.D. dissertation, New School for Social Research, 1980), 251–78.

the informal life of French-Canadian unionists that the historical record affords us. Perhaps the best evidence is the degree to which the festive, family-oriented gatherings that so characterized French-Canadian home life came, in the years 1936 to 1941, to characterize ITU social life. Occasionally, the union would formally sponsor a French-Canadian celebration as it did on Christmas Eve in 1938 when it hosted a réveillon, a midnight supper following Mass.[5] Far more common, however, were instances where French-Canadian unionists spontaneously made their songs, their dances, and their games the centerpiece of union festivals. No union-sponsored dance event at the Joyland Ballroom could end without the assembled crowd engaging in a series of quadrille dances – a distinctively French form of square dancing. French-Canadian unionists would start singing the French songs that accompanied quadrille dancing as soon as they boarded the buses for their annual summer outings.[6] The outings themselves always included long and robust sessions of French singing, ample servings of home-cooked food, and an inexhaustible supply of frolicsome games and contests.

Few of these games had distinctive French-Canadian roots; quoits, running and swimming races, and tug-of-war contests could be found almost everywhere in 1930s America. The French-Canadian spirit was to be found instead in the family-centered, clownish character of many of the games. Not only were many of the races expressly designed for children, but many of the adult races called on their participants to act silly and childlike: There were fat-man and fat-woman races, men and women tub races, men and women three-legged races, potato races, egg races, and so on. The appearance of ITU unionists dressed as clowns and the inevitable water dunking of some admired (and fully clothed) ITU member further contributed to the carnival-like atmosphere.[7] All told, the fun-loving, musical, and imaginative character of these occasions resembled nothing so much as the festive gatherings of family and kin that were so intrinsic a feature of French-Canadian private life.[8] The flow of such familial sociability into union affairs also generated support for the ITU's numerous social welfare institutions such as the medical clinic, credit union, and life-insurance program. In such ways did French-Canadian cultural traditions facilitate the realization of Schmetz's dream of a Belgian labor movement in America.

[5] *ITU News*, January 1939, 7; Sophie-Laurence Lamontagne, *L'Hiver dans la culture québecoise (XVIIe–XIXe siècles)* (Quebec, 1983), 127.
[6] *ITU News*, November 1940, 8; August 1936, 8; April 1938, 6.
[7] *ITU News*, July 1936, 10; August 1936, 11.
[8] Doty, *The First Franco-Americans*, 27–30, 44, 84–87; Miner, *St. Denis*, 141–68.

The importance in union affairs of French-Canadian cultural traditions did not undermine the ITU's panethnic character. As the union more than doubled in size from 1936 to 1941 (from about 6,000 to more than 12,000), it continued to appeal to all the major ethnic groups in the population.[9] Poor membership records have made it impossible to analyze the ethnic composition of the entire rank and file. But surviving information on rank-and-file leaders – those elected by workers in each union local to serve on the ITU's legislative body (the Executive Council) – indicates that each ethnic group was represented in numbers roughly proportional to its numerical importance in the Woonsocket population. Of 179 local leaders who served on the union's Executive Council from 1937 to 1942 and whose ethnic background is known, 133 (75 percent) were French Canadian, and 43 (24 percent) were drawn from other ethnic groups.[10] These percentages, virtually identical to those characterizing the union's leadership group in the years 1931 to 1936, underscore the persistence of the union's panethnic character. Moreover, the non–French-Canadian leadership group had become more diverse. Whereas Franco-Belgian and Italian workers had comprised virtually all non–French-Canadian representation in the years 1931 to 1936, they formed only two-thirds of non–French-Canadian representation in the 1937 to 1942 cohort. Greeks, Portuguese, English, Polish, and Irish workers gained visibility and authority in union affairs. The long history of embittered Irish–French-Canadian relations made the growing participation of the Irish in the ITU an especially potent symbol of interethnic cooperation.

[9] These 12,000 members belonged to thirty-nine locals. Thirty locals represented about 10,000 workers laboring in textile mills; the other nine represented workers in other industries, in various crafts, and on federal relief. Information on new locals entering the union in the years 1936 to 1941 comes from reports appearing in the *ITU News* in those years. There are no published figures on the number of members in each local. But since the ITU established union shops in most of its mills, I have presumed the number of members to be equal to the number employed. The numbers employed by the various mills have been derived from the reports of manufacturers on their employment levels appearing in the *Providence Journal Almanac: A Reference Book for the State of Rhode Island* (Providence, R.I.), 1940, 100–10. These figures must be regarded as approximate because employers reported their average employment levels and not the actual number employed at a given moment in time; they are, however, the best available. See Appendix A for a full listing of the names, industrial sectors, and sizes of locals entering the ITU in these years.

[10] Names of the 179 leaders were compiled from references to their union involvement appearing in the *ITU News*, 1936–1942. Ethnic information was drawn from 1935 Rhode Island Manuscript Census, Rhode Island State Archives, Providence, R.I.; U.S. Department of Justice, "Petitions for Naturalization," Providence Superior Court, Providence, R.I.; and oral history.

Members from all these groups participated in ITU festivals – organizing them, competing in races, dancing quadrilles, and singing French-Canadian folk songs; in the process they partook of the French-Canadian festive spirit. At the same time, they injected their own cultural traditions into union affairs. The union's anthem and most popular song, "Chant d'ITU," drew on radical Franco-Belgian musical traditions.[11] The most popular play put on by the ITU Drama Group was Clifford Odets's *Waiting for Lefty*, an exemplary piece of Popular Front proletarian culture.[12] The frivolous games of ITU outings, as already noted, could be found anywhere in 1930s America as could the more serious baseball, football, basketball, and bowling contests that shaped the busy ITU sports calendar the rest of the year.[13] All these activities seemed to partake of energy generated by French-Canadian festiveness.

The family-based sociability that flowed into the ITU in the 1930s was not, of course, a unique characteristic of French Canadians. Jews and Italians, for example, had long organized a good deal of their social life around family gatherings and celebrations. Unions where these two groups were well-represented, like the International Ladies Garment Workers Union and Amalgamated Clothing Workers, developed the same panoply of social services (medical clinics and housing projects) and the same energetic social life (drama and choral groups, large and frequent outings for union families) as the ITU. Often the initiative for these activities came from radical leaders with dreams of a comprehensive labor movement very similar to those that gripped Schmetz, but it was the interaction of these social democratic blueprints with vibrant traditions of ethnic communalism that made these unions, like the ITU, such notable examples of social unionism. That both men and women, many of them married with children, formed substantial segments of the membership in all three unions may also have contributed to the unions' social character. A family-style union life was a more natural choice for them than it was in unions whose memberships were overwhelmingly male.[14]

---

[11] *ITU News*, July 1936, 18; January 1940, 8; September 1938, 8. Interview with Lawrence Spitz, October 22, 1976. One of the fondest memories of Samuel Angoff, the Jewish labor attorney who served the ITU in these years, was the savory Franco-Belgian food he consumed on ITU outings. Interview with Angoff, November 7, 1976.

[12] *ITU News*, April 1940, 7; May 1940, 11.

[13] Only hockey may have had distinctive ethnic (Canadian) roots. Ibid., August 1937, 8–9; September 1940, 6; July 1936, 6, 10; August 1936, 8; October 1936, 9; July 1937, 12; September 1937, 15; October 1937, 10; December 1939, 7; January 1940, 8.

[14] On the ILGWU and the ACW: Joel Seidman, *The Needle Trades* (New York, 1942); Jesse Thomas Carpenter, *Competition and Collective Bargaining in the Needle Trades*,

As the principal carriers of such home-based traditions of sociability, ITU women participated heavily in the union's social activities, and they also found informal ways to assert powerfully their ethic of togetherness in confrontations with employers. But the very act of infusing a union with the communalism of their home life strengthened patriarchy, another essential characteristic of those homes. The centrality of patriarchal relations to union life is most strikingly apparent in the small number of women unionists who served in official leadership positions. Of the 200 union members serving on the Executive Council in the years 1937 to 1942 whose names are known, twenty-eight, or 14 percent, were women. Though this percentage marked a significant advance over the earlier period when only one woman (out of thirty-three) sat on the Executive Council, it still left women workers, who now formed almost half of the ITU's membership (up from one-third in 1936), severely underrepresented in leadership positions.[15]

Such underrepresentation resulted in part from generalized discriminatory attitudes pervading all aspects of union and community life. Consider, for example, the ITU's published account of its 1937 outing. Despite the fact that women formed roughly half the beach goers, the account of the outing reads at times like a report of a stag party. One unionist, Henri Theroux, "drank as though prohibition was once again going to be enforced." The losing (all male) tug-of-war team "imbibed too freely and as a result could not even stand up let alone pull the other team across the line." Such wild drinking lowered the men's sexual inhibitions, of course, and allowed their sexual fantasies to surface. Thus, Brother Gagne, "sedate old gentleman that he is, deserted his family for the day and was constantly whirling some sweet young thing over the dance floor"; other men,

Footnote 14 (*cont.*)

1910–1967 (Ithaca, N.Y., 1972); Charles Elbert Zaretz, *The Amalgamated Clothing Workers of America: A Study in Progressive Trades-Unionism* (New York, 1934); Steve Fraser, "Dress Rehearsal for the New Deal: Shop-Floor Insurgents, Political Elites, and Industrial Democracy in the Amalgamated Clothing Workers," in Michael H. Frisch and Daniel J. Walkowitz, eds., *Working-Class America: Essays on Labor, Community, and American Society* (Urbana, Ill., 1983), 212–55; Fraser, "*Landslayt* and *Paesani*: Ethnic Conflict and Cooperation in the Amalgamated Clothing Workers of America," in Dirk Hoerder, ed., "*Struggle a Hard Battle*": *Essays on Working-Class Immigrants* (DeKalb, Ill., 1986), 280–303; Irving Howe, *World of Our Fathers: The Journey of the East European Jews to America and the World They Found and Made* (New York, 1976), 287–359.

[15] Gender and ethnic information has been drawn from the same sources listed in note 10; gender breakdown has been computed from data contained in Rhode Island Department of Labor, *Annual Report* (Providence, R.I.), 1935, 200–4.

"looking for their wives...[were] inwardly happy when the search proved unsuccessful." These fantasies, however, usually ended with the brusque return of the dreaded *femme*: Ovila Bourget, "that good natured master of ceremonies," whose "jokes brought blushes to the cheeks of the fairer sex,...ended up by being led by the ear from the Beer Garden by friend wife [sic]." These written comments appeared in columns and half-columns of print that framed a large picture of Ann Mary Tavernier, Miss ITU of 1937, attired in a modest swimsuit – the "sweet young" antithesis of "friend wife."[16]

This report bore only a tangential relationship to the reality of the beach outing for the thousands of people who danced, drank, sang, and ate; many married couples danced happily with each other, and many adults made children's activities the focus of their day.[17] But the fact that the *ITU News* would publish such a masculinist account of a family-centered outing, ignoring altogether the perspective of the union's many women members, starkly reveals the generalized and largely unexamined sexism of the union's men. It is hardly surprising, given such attitudes, that women played a subordinate role to men in union affairs.[18]

But other factors shaped the union experience of ITU women. Rates of female participation on the ITU's Executive Council varied from one ethnic group to another: Franco-Belgian women were the best represented female leadership group relative to their total Woonsocket population, followed by the Irish, the French Canadians, the Poles, and at the bottom the Italians. These differences suggest that gender relations varied somewhat from one ethnic culture to another, and that the opportunities for women to participate in union affairs were determined as much by how those cultures influenced the personal relations between husbands and wives and fathers and daughters in the home as by discriminatory practices on the part of the ITU's male-dominated Executive Council.[19] Thus, it would seem that Franco-Belgian and Irish women received the most encouragement – or encountered the least resistance – in their aspirations toward leadership, while Polish and especially Italian women encountered a stone wall.[20]

[16] *ITU News*, August 1937, 8–9.
[17] Ibid
[18] Interview with Leonel Galipeau, October 22–23, 1980.
[19] These are the numbers and percentages of the twenty-four women representatives whose ethnic identity is known: Franco-Belgians – three (13 percent); Irish – three (13 percent); French Canadians – seventeen (71 percent); Poles – one (4 percent); Italians – none (total exceeds 100 percent due to rounding error). Information drawn from same sources listed in note 10.
[20] The existence of such varying gender relations among the different ethnic groups

Occupying a middle and highly ambivalent ground both in actual rates of leadership participation and in the memories of veteran ITU unionists were French-Canadian women. Forming by far the largest numerical group of women in both the rank-and-file and leadership strata of the ITU, carrying into the union the all-important home-based spirit of French-Canadian sociability, these women gained a reputation for their paradoxical mix of militance and reticence in union affairs. According to union lore, they displayed more spontaneous militancy than any other group. No group was as quick to shut down the machines and walk out over an issue of working conditions; as one man put it, French-Canadian women would "go out at the drop of a hat."[21] But French-Canadian women rarely chose to translate their shopfloor militance into formal union power (in the form of representation at Executive Council meetings, for example). It seems as though these women were relegated to acting (whether by choice or not) as a moral, rather than political, force, expressing outrage at those individual bosses and industrialists who dared violate deeply felt and widely shared community values. It seems, further, that these women resumed their subordinate gender roles once they protested the violation, allowing their men to complete, through sustained strikes and collective bargaining, what they had started: enforcing community values on employers.[22] In such ways, perhaps, did French-Canadian women workers find a way to enlarge their role in union affairs without challenging the larger patriarchal contours of the culture in which they lived. That way, of course, may well have been a working-class variant of the one carved out by earlier generations of middle-class, homebound Yankee women who claimed that the moral purity of their domestic sphere gave them a special – though limited – authority in the world of politics.[23]

One of the union's most militant strikes of this period suggests that the pervasive, Depression-induced shortage of work may actually have strengthened partriarchal values.[24] In early 1938 the city's all-

Footnote 20 (cont.)
   was confirmed unwittingly by veteran male unionists who invariably, in interviews, praised the union activities of Franco-Belgian and Irish women and lamented the refusal of Polish and Italian women to involve themselves more in union affairs. Interviews with Lawrence Spitz, September 19–20, 1979, Angelo Turbesi, October 9, 1980, and Ernest Gignac, June 25, 1981.
21 Interview with Angelo Turbesi, October 9, 1980; see also interviews with George Butsika, September 14, 1984, and Samuel Angoff, November 7, 1976.
22 Interview with Arthur Rock, October 8, 1976.
23 See Nancy Cott, *The Bonds of Womanhood: "Woman's Sphere" in New England, 1780–1835* (New Haven, Conn., 1977).
24 On the effects of the Depression on patriarchy, feminism, and women's work, see

male woolen mulespinner work force went on strike when two of the city's five woolen manufacturers began hiring women to operate newly installed spinning frames. Frames were normally operated by semiskilled women who possessed far less shopfloor power and who commanded far less pay than mulespinners. Local woolen manufacturers clearly intended to use the introduction of these machines as the occasion to begin shrinking the numbers, power, and wages of the mulespinners in their employ. Not surprisingly, the union's response to this assault on mulespinner power was swift and dramatic. The mulespinners of all five woolen mills – including those where no efforts had been made to introduce frames – walked off their jobs, and they enjoyed such widespread support from the ranks of Woonsocket's workers – male and female – that the union made no effort to surround the mills with pickets. But union leaders did not use such a militant display of strength to press a radical demand – namely, the removal of all spinning frames. They merely insisted that men be allowed to operate the frames, and even signaled the men's willingness to work at the customarily low level of frame-spinning wages.

The demonstration of such reasonableness was part of a calculated effort on the union's part to arouse public, male indignation at the employers' unreasonable attack on the breadwinning and family-provider roles of male mulespinners. Already in Woonsocket, Schmetz stressed, there were men "at home, getting the meals, and even escorting small children to school while their wives are making good money in the mills," a scenario that, Schmetz implied, should have troubled the miserly manufacturers who preferred female to male labor on the grounds of economy as much as the emasculated men themselves. On this issue, Schmetz argued, men of all classes should make common cause. "Any real man in any walk of life, as well as his wife and his family should see the far-reaching possibility of such a change [in gender relations], and support the moral side of our cause," Schmetz declared.[25] Any real man, in other words, should

Lois Scharf, *To Work and to Wed: Female Employment, Feminism, and the Great Depression* (Westport, Conn., 1980); Winifred Wandersee, *Women's Work and Family Values, 1920–1940* (Cambridge, Mass., 1981); Ruth Milkman, *Gender at Work: The Dynamics of Job Segregation by Sex During World War II* (Urbana, Ill., 1987), 27–48, Alice Kessler-Harris, *Out to Work: A History of Wage-Earning Women in the United States* (New York, 1982), 250–72.

[25] *Providence Journal* (hereafter *PJ*), March 12, 16, 1937; *WC*, March 1, 1936; *Boston Traveler*, March 8, 1937; *Daily News Record*, March 8, 1937; all these clippings are located in Woonsocket Woolen Mills file, Record Group 9 (hereafter RG 9), Entry 402, National Archives (hereafter NA) Washington, D.C. See also ITU, *Labor Review*, 29.

do his utmost to insure that patriarchy – "the moral side" – would prevail. The woolen mulespinners, union leaders noted on another occasion, must "be permitted to be the bread-winners for their wives and families."[26]

While it is unlikely that many wives would have dissented from the union's support for a family wage, it is significant that no women's or socialist caucus argued the point that women (for not all women were married) deserved the same opportunities to work as men; nor did any union voice of moderation point out – as did two government investigators, James L. Bernard and Carl E. L. Gill – that the union may have exaggerated the threat to male pride implied by the switch to frame spinning. Only two of the five woolen mills, after all, had declared their intention of introducing frames, and a third had demonstrated for some years that frame and mulespinning technologies could easily coexist in the same workplace. The mulespinners affected by the change may have been relatively small in number, then, and they may have been easily absorbed into the work forces of mills that still used mules.[27]

The government mediators thought that Schmetz understood the minor character of the displacement effects but that radical rank and filers prevented him from settling the matter promptly with manufacturers.[28] The mediators were right about the rank-and-file roots of the union's militance on the frame issue but wrong about its radical character. Leading the strike were the French-Canadian mulespinners who had long formed the union's core in each of the five woolen mills. The manufacturers' plan struck at the heart of their identity as family providers and as men of stature in their ethnic neighborhoods. Their protest, then, was rooted in a profoundly conservative desire to preserve their established place in their families and in their community. They sustained their strike for eight weeks until they agreed with the manufacturers to turn the matter over to government arbitration. The arbitrator then handed the ITU a stunning victory by ordering the manufacturers to offer any new frame spinner jobs to displaced mulespinners. The order not only preserved mulespinners'

---

[26] ITU, "Causes of Strike" (typescript, 1938), Lawrence N. Spitz Collection, Mss 31 (hereafter Spitz Collection), Box 8, Rhode Island Historical Society (hereafter RIHS), Providence, R.I.

[27] James L. Bernard to Samuel R. McClurd (executive assistant, Textile Division Conciliation Service, U.S. Department of Labor), February 13, March 1, 4, 11, 1937; Carl E. L. Gill to McClurd, March 8, May 13, 1937; McClurd to Bernard, March 3, 27, 1937; Woonsocket Woolen Mills file, RG 9, Entry 402, NA.

[28] Ibid., Gill to McClurd, May 13, 1937.

rights to their jobs but dampened the manufacturers' enthusiasm for adopting frame technology.[29]

The woolen mills strike of 1937 offers an appropriately complex example of French-Canadian workers insisting that their community values shape the practice of industrial relations in their city. On the one hand such insistence intensified conservative aspects of their community life, most notably the commitment to patriarchy; on the other hand, the very defense of community and patriarchy in a time of economic crisis required ethnic workers to intrude on the prerogatives of capitalist institutions to a degree they had never previously contemplated. The same affirmation of ethnocommunal values that foreclosed the possibility of a union-based campaign for gender equality, in other words, would bring considerable vigor to Schmetz's and Spitz's campaign for industrial democracy.

The transformation of shopfloor life

The campaign for industrial democracy generated enormous enthusiasm in the ranks of the ITU. In five short years, 1936 to 1941, Woonsocket textile workers thoroughly transformed social relations on the shopfloor. They eliminated foremen – as well as all other managerial representatives – from decisions regarding work loads, work distribution, promotions, layoffs, and even discharges; these decisions were now made according to seniority principles or according to decisions collectively made by the workers themselves. Even in such sensitive areas of production as technological innovation, many managements now had to win the assent of their workers before introducing any change.

This portrait of a wide-scale assault on managerial functions emerges from an analysis not of strikes but of the union's first formal collective bargaining agreements, dating from 1941. Though only five of these agreements have survived, three – those with Guerin Mills – Alsace, Bonin Spinning, and Woonsocket Falls Yarn – are representative of the French spinning industry, the woolen industry, and the cotton plush industry respectively. Those three industrial sectors, in 1941, included fifteen textile mills, fully half of the ITU's textile locals.[30] The other agreements with American Wringer (a rubber

---

[29] Ibid., "In the Matter of Arbitration Proceedings Between Belmont Woolen Yarn Mills, Bonin Spinning Co., Falls Yarn Mills, River Mills, Inc., Woonsocket Spinning Co., and the Independent Textile Union, June 2, 1937"; Gill to McClurd, June 30, 1937. See also ITU, *Labor Review*, 29.

[30] By 1941, the ITU had established the practice of industrywide bargaining in each of these industrial sectors. *ITU News*, April 1939, 13; November 1940, 9.

plant) and Woonsocket Brush may not have been representative because they pertained to firms in the "miscellaneous" sector of Woonsocket industry, which did not resemble other production shops in the city. Yet, news of contract achievements in one mill traveled quickly to another in this small industrial city; thus the contracts of American Wringer and Woonsocket Brush workers may either have been inspired by gains made at other locals or else have set a bargaining standard that other workers sought to emulate.[31]

The contract clauses in the five agreements can be divided into two broad categories: those providing union and job security for workers, and those defining the character of work in terms of hours, work loads, technology, and health and safety. The contracts always alluded to but rarely explained in detail the third category of wages. The usual wage phrase simply called for a 5 or 10 percent increase in prevailing wages or else stipulated that the employer should pay the wages prevailing in its sector of Woonsocket industry.

Each of the contracts began with the recognition of the union by the employer "as the sole collective bargaining agency for all . . . employees except bosses, management and office workers." Each of the five contracts stipulated as well that all employees in the bargaining unit and all newly hired employees had to join the union. By 1941, the ITU seems to have established the union shop in most locals.[32] The union also had won the right to post its notices "in conspicuous places throughout the mills" and to collect union dues on employer premises during working hours.[33] Only one of the five contracts provided for dues checkoff (Woonsocket Brush) – a system in which employers deducted union dues from employee wages and transferred them directly to union accounts.[34] The predominant form of dues collection remained that of stewards walking through their departments once a month and asking each member for his or her dues payments. This method was not as efficient as the checkoff – employees who did not favor the union or who disliked parting with

---

[31] Agreements between the ITU and the following corporations and companies: Bonin Spinning Company, April 7, 1941; American Wringer Company, Inc., April 10, 1941; Woonsocket Falls Mills, May 26, 1941; the Guerin Mills, Inc., Alsace Division (hereafter Guerin Mills-Alsace), June 3, 1941; Woonsocket Brush Company, September 29, 1941. Each contract was printed on a 2 foot by 1.5 foot piece of cardboard and posted in a conspicuous location in the mill. Copies have survived in the Spitz Collection, Box 8, RIHS.

[32] Articles A and B in all agreements.

[33] Articles H and I, Bonin Spinning, Guerin Mills-Alsace, and Woonsocket Falls Mills; Articles J and K, American Wringer.

[34] Articles C and H, Woonsocket Brush.

their money could have easily refused payment – but it had the virtue of providing an effective rank-and-file veto over the policies of union leaders. Whatever the union lost in financial security, it gained in rank-and-file participation in union affairs.[35]

Union contracts also provided individual workers with extensive job protection. All of the contracts established the principle of seniority for promotions, and four of the five stipulated its applicability to hiring and firing.[36] The contracts seemed to maintain a voice for foremen in determining whether an individual worker had the qualifications for promotion; all promotions had "to be determined by mutual agreement between the Employer and the Union." But if the two parties could not agree on a candidate's qualifications, then the job went to the employee with greatest seniority "having the approval of one of the parties involved."[37] In other words, when union and management could not agree on qualifications, a system of simple seniority prevailed. The contracts sharply limited foreman input into promotion decisions.

In the three contracts that pertained to the textile industry – Alsace, Bonin, and Woonsocket Falls – seniority principles complemented share-the-work principles guiding work distribution.[38] As previously discussed, share-the-work systems operated on the principle that all regular employees in a mill department had to work the same number of hours in the course of the year. Contracts in the textile mills, then, not only virtually eliminated foremen from decisions regarding promotions, but stripped them of their power to distribute available work.[39]

In other areas, the power of foremen was curtailed by grievance procedures, which subjected most of their decisions to union review. Three of the five contracts called for the union to establish a Local Grievance Committee (LGC) to meet with management to resolve shopfloor disputes.[40] When a dispute occurred, the LGC would first

---

[35] Interview with Angelo Turbesi, October 9, 1980.
[36] Article E, Bonin Spinning; Article G, Guerin Mills-Alsace, Woonsocket Falls Mills, and Woonsocket Brush; Article I, American Wringer.
[37] All the contracts stipulated that seniority would accrue during military service leaves.
[38] Article D, Bonin Spinning; Article F, Guerin Mills-Alsace and Woonsocket Falls Mills.
[39] Share-the-work schemes existed alongside seniority promotion schemes; the latter did not simply supplant the former as they apparently did in the contracts of electrical workers and other industrial unionists. See Ronald W. Schatz, *The Electrical Workers: A History of Labor at General Electric and Westinghouse, 1923–1960* (Urbana, Ill., 1983), 105–36.
[40] Article O, Guerin Mills-Alsace and Woonsocket Brush; Article K, Bonin Spin-

try to resolve it in discussions with the overseer of the department in which the grievance arose. If that conference failed, the LGC would take up the issue with higher levels of mill management. Two of the three contracts stipulated that if the grievance still could not be resolved, it had to go to an arbitration board composed of seven individuals, three chosen by the union, three by management, and one chosen by the other six board members. The decision of the arbitration board would be final and binding on both parties. The cost of arbitration would be shared equally by both parties.[41]

Scholars have criticized such grievance mechanisms for channeling worker dissatisfaction and defusing it through a long process of dispute resolution frequently made even longer by a backlog of complaints.[42] These criticisms were voiced by the workers themselves. When Spitz first introduced his proposal for an arbitration clause at an Executive Council meeting in late 1939, a delegate walked to the front of the hall and communicated his dislike of the proposal by writing one word in large letters on a blackboard: A-R-B-E-T-R-A-Y-T-I-O-N. He represented workers who did not believe in the impartiality of arbitration boards and who wanted to keep the power to resolve disputes on the shopfloor in their own hands.[43] This attitude found expression in the Bonin Spinning contract and presumably in the four other woolen contracts as well. The final step in Bonin's grievance procedure was not binding arbitration but rather the customary "stoppage of work."[44] Clearly, some ITU workers feared that a grievance procedure would be turned against them.[45]

Even granting the potential for abuses of a grievance procedure, however, it is still important to recognize that the initial inclusion in contracts of a grievance mechanism culminating in arbitration sharply

Footnote 40 (cont.)

　ning. The American Wringer contract had a weak grievance procedure and the Woonsocket Falls Mills contract had none.

[41] Article O, Guerin Mills-Alsace and Woonsocket Brush.

[42] See William Serrin, *The Company and the Union: The "Civilized Relationship" of the General Motors Corporation and the United Auto Workers* (New York, 1973); Stanley Aronowitz, *False Promises: The Shaping of American Working Class Consciousness* (New York, 1973), 11–50, 214–63.

[43] Interview with Lawrence Spitz, September 19–20, 1979.

[44] Article K, Section c, Bonin Spinning; conversely, Article D of the Guerin Mills-Alsace and Woonsocket Brush contracts prohibited strikes or lockouts for the life of the contract (usually one year).

[45] The Bonin "stoppage of work" clause actually violated the ITU constitution which, since 1939, required locals to submit their unresolvable grievances to a union advisory board before striking. Bonin workers would no more accept constitutional prohibitions than contractual limits on their right to strike. See ITU, *Constitution and By-Laws* (Woonsocket, R.I., 1939), 21–4.

impinged on the authority of millowners. Woonsocket employers had to submit virtually all unresolved disputes with workers to an arbitration board that they did not control. None of these contracts contained "management rights" clauses specifying managerial prerogatives that workers could not touch, nor did any exempt such crucial managerial functions as the right to institute new technologies from binding arbitration. Woonsocket employers did not yet understand how to use contracts in general and grievance mechanisms in particular to defuse working-class protest. And they received little advice on such matters from the decidedly prolabor National Labor Relations Board. The initiative in this state-administered industrial relations system clearly lay, in these years, with workers.[46]

Further evidence of the workers' upper hand in collective bargaining can be found in contractual rules governing discharges. The ultimate form of job security is the right of a union to veto a firing of one of its members. Two contracts, those of Guerin Mills–Alsace and Woonsocket Brush, gave workers this extraordinary protection by flatly stating that discharges had to "be mutually agreed upon by the Employer and the Union."[47] By contractual law, in other words, managers simply could not fire anyone unless the union agreed to allow it, and if a manager, in defiance of the contract, fired a worker anyway, unionists did not have to wait patiently for a grievance to wind its way through arbitration or through a NLRB hearing. The contracts specifically exempted discharge disputes from arbitration machinery. If managers and workers did not resolve the discharge dispute within a few days, workers gained the right to continue their protest through a strike. Unionists in these two mills had succeeded, in other words, where their employers in these years had failed: namely, in barring the state, a private arbitrator, or some other third party from exercising jurisdiction over a most precious workplace right. It is not known how many union locals enjoyed such employment security; Spitz, however, contended that the union won its inclusion in a substantial number of contracts.[48] The provisions governing

---

[46] On the prolabor character of the NLRB in these years, see Christopher L. Tomlins, *The State and the Unions: Labor Relations, Law, and the Organized Labor Movement in America, 1880–1960* (Cambridge, U.K., 1985), 197–240; Karl Klare, "Judicial Deradicalization of the Wagner Act and the Origins of Modern Legal Consciousness, 1937–1941," *Minnesota Law Review* 62 (1977–78), 265–339; James A. Gross, *The Reshaping of the National Labor Relations Board: National Labor Policy in Transition, 1937–1947* (Albany, N.Y., 1981), 5–23.

[47] Guerin Mills-Alsace, Article L, Sections 1 and 2; Woonsocket Brush, Article P, and Article K, Section 1.

[48] Interview with Lawrence Spitz, September 19–20, 1979.

discharges, in conjunction with the principle of seniority in promotion and share-the-work systems of work distribution, practically eliminated management from personnel decisions. Managers could not fire, promote, or assign workers to particular tasks without the union's agreement.

In many mills, managers could also not change work load, production speeds, technology, health and safety conditions, piece rates (where they applied), and numerous other aspects of production without union approval. Two contracts flatly stated "that any change in the prevailing work load and working conditions throughout the mill shall be mutually agreed upon by the Employer and the Union."[49] A third agreement extended the same protection to weavers and dyehouse workers who formed a large proportion of the Woonsocket Falls work force.[50] A fourth agreement did not contain such a general clause but did stipulate the appropriate work loads for a number of occupations.[51] And a fifth agreement stipulated that "no piece or bonus rate shall be set unless said rates are mutually agreed upon between the Employer and the [union] Price Committee of the department affected."[52]

Such contract clauses reveal how far the union had gone in democratizing the workplace. In mill after mill, unionists sought to replace the managerial unilateralism that had characterized shopfloor governance with management-labor mutualism. Again and again, the ITU's contracts stressed that changes on the shopfloor could not proceed unless they were "mutually agreed upon" by management and labor. Discharges, qualifications for promotion, piece rates and bonuses, work loads and working conditions all demanded the mutual agreement of employers and employees. The contracts under consideration differed in some ways from each other – some were stronger on the regulation of piece rates, others stronger on the regulation of working conditions or the distribution of work – but the uniformity of their challenge to managerial authority outweighed the particular differences. The contracts placed no limits on the issues subject to such negotiation; and in this tightly knit community, news of what one group of workers achieved in their particular negotiations quickly inspired other groups to do the same. To ITU members in 1941, industrial democracy had come to mean equal voices for management and labor on every issue relating to life on the shopfloor.[53]

[49] Article L, Section 1, Guerin Mills-Alsace; Article K, Section 1, Woonsocket Brush.
[50] Articles L and M, Woonsocket Falls Mills.
[51] Article G, Bonin Spinning.
[52] Article D, Section 1, American Wringer.
[53] The contracts dealt with a host of other issues that can only be mentioned here:

The ITU's record of quite radical gains in Woonsocket runs counter to an emerging consensus among labor historians that industrial workers in the 1930s were little interested in workers' control and made few efforts – through strikes or collective bargaining – to democratize relations on the shopfloor.[54] Two factors may account for the divergence of the Woonsocket case. First, Woonsocket workers established a strong union and compelled employers to bargain with them earlier than their counterparts in other sectors of mass production such as auto and steel.[55] At a time when auto workers were still attempting to gain recognition for their unions from such corporate giants as General Motors and Ford, Woonsocket textile workers were busy negotiating with their employers the appropriate division of shopfloor power between labor and management. Because negotiations in Woonsocket had advanced to such a point, unionists there benefited enormously from the open-ended bargaining, encouraged in the late 1930s by the prolabor NLRB. As previously noted, the NLRB had not yet established a realm of managerial prerogatives, which labor could not touch, nor had it clearly established the priority of industrial efficiency or productivity over employee rights. A strongly organized group of workers was able, therefore, to force employer concessions on virtually every managerial function. This open-ended period of bargaining came to a close during World War II, just as most industrial unions were first gaining the institutional security they desperately needed to carry on aggressive bargaining; many of these unions, therefore, never enjoyed the same opportuni-

particularly important, standardizing the work day at eight hours and the work week at forty, guaranteeing workers time-and-a-half pay for overtime and holiday work; premiums for night shifts, and four hours pay for reporting to work; establishing the principle of paid leisure by assuring workers eight hours' pay for Labor Day and, in one instance, giving them one week of paid vacation; and requiring employers to maintain minimal health and safety standards. Article C, Bonin Spinning, Guerin Mills-Alsace, Woonsocket Falls Mills, and American Wringer; Article D, Woonsocket Brush; Article J, Guerin Mills-Alsace, Woonsocket Falls Mills; Article F, Section 3, Bonin Spinning; Article C in all agreements; Article L, Section 3, Guerin Mills-Alsace; Articles L and M, Woonsocket Falls Mills; Article D, Section 3, Guerin Mills-Alsace; Article C, Section 4, Woonsocket Falls Mills; Article N, Section 2, Woonsocket Brush; Article E, Guerin Mills-Alsace, Woonsocket Falls Mills; Article F, Woonsocket Brush; Article E, Section 4, Woonsocket Falls Mills; Article C, Section 3, Guerin Mills-Alsace.

[54] For excellent summaries of this consensus, see David Brody, "The CIO After 50 Years: A Historical Reckoning," *Dissent* (Fall 1985), 457–472, and Robert H. Zieger, "Toward the History of the CIO: A Bibliographical Report," *Labor History* 26 (Fall 1985), 487–516.

[55] Nelson Lichtenstein, *Labor's War at Home: The CIO in World War II* (Cambridge, U.K., 1982), 8–25.

ties as the ITU in the late 1930s and thus never gained the same kind of shopfloor power. Even the ITU, as we shall see (in Chapter 10), was forced to relinquish in the 1940s much of the shopfloor power it had achieved through collective bargaining in the 1930s.

The institutional weakness of most unions in the 1930s followed by the state's decisive limiting of workers' workplace rights in the 1940s, then, made it extremely difficult for many unionists to pursue dreams of worker control. This is not to say that all workers harbored such dreams. The hold of that dream on Woonsocket unionists reflected, no doubt, a second factor shaping the city's industrial life: the unusually large number of skilled workers, especially mulespinners, laboring in the city's mills. Demands for working-class authority on the shopfloor emerged most naturally from skilled workers who were proud of their role in the production process and whose whole personal identity depended critically on satisfactions – of skill, autonomy, control – derived from their craft.[56] To lesser-skilled workers whose perfunctory jobs offered few intrinsic satisfactions, the prospect of controlling the shopfloor was less alluring and thus less likely to galvanize them into action. Indeed ITU locals lacking skilled worker leadership often achieved far less control over the shopfloor than did locals dominated by skilled workers.[57]

It is hardly surprising, given skilled-worker predilections for workplace autonomy and control, that the ITU contract most extensively challenging managerial authority belonged to the Guerin Mills–Alsace, a local led by the union's most entrenched group of European, mulespinning radicals. Maurice Pierre, a French mulespinner, had led the local since its inception in the early 1930s. His political radicalism and craft pride had inspired a powerful movement of self-determination among Franco-Belgians, French Canadians, and other ethnic groups.[58]

By 1941 the industrial democratic campaign had also rooted itself deeply in the woolen mill locals, like Bonin Spinning, where French-Canadian skilled workers occupied leadership positions. Amedée Miclette, who had held the Bonin presidency almost as long as Maurice

[56] Woonsocket's only sit-down strike arose from the skilled worker ranks – the mulespinners of the French Worsted. See *ITU News*, December 1937, 9.

[57] The more moderate shopfloor demands thrown up by the lesser-skilled did not mean that they were incapable of militancy or radicalism; it meant instead that their radicalism would flow into different channels. Semiskilled dye-house workers, as we shall see, would be the first ITU members to raise the union's most radical demand – public scrutiny of corporate finances.

[58] Interview with Lawrence Spitz, September 19–20, 1979, and Angelo Turbesi, October 9, 1980.

Pierre had been president of the Alsace, was an equally powerful figure in union affairs.[59] The French-Canadian skilled workers like Miclette derived as much pride from their mulespinning skills as did the Europeans, and they felt that their skill entitled them to power on the shopfloor. Though they did not share the Europeans' radical creed, many had begun to fuse their quest for workplace autonomy with the ideological injunction, deeply rooted in their ethnic culture, to resist authorities deemed harmful to the welfare of their community. As early as the 1920s, French-Canadian workers had begun reinterpreting that culture to justify resistance to economic authorities. Some of these workers, especially those in the skilled ranks, gradually moved from displays of resistance to demands that their community participate in the management of capitalist institutions. These demands began to coalesce into an ideology in the late 1930s, as local clergy, worried about the loss of their increasingly class-conscious parishioners, began preaching the need to establish the rights of labor in industry. An emerging doctrine of Catholic corporatism lent religious sanction to the union's campaign to democratize relations on the shopfloor. The mutualist principles underlying so many of the ITU's contractual agreements with city employers were now being interpreted as the fulfillment of a Catholic corporatist ideal.

The French-Canadian clergy's sudden recognition of the rights of labor was a stunning development in Woonsocket society that will receive detailed examination in the next chapter. Here we need only note that such a fundamental ideological reorientation resulted in large part from the success of the ITU in transforming the character of class relations both on the shopfloor and in Woonsocket society at large. Union radicals and ethnics, seizing upon the open-ended opportunities for collective bargaining made available by the NLRB in the late 1930s, ended the reign of employer unilateralism and replaced it with an industrial democratic regime based on mutualism. The French-Canadian workers who embraced this regime, and the mutualist principles on which it was based, had not, in their own minds, become radicals; few, if any, would have admitted to finding in their culture the justification for an anticapitalist, socially transformative politics. They viewed the democratization of shopfloor life in familiar terms, as simply the assertion of craft prerogatives on the one hand and of the exercise of communal rights in the sphere of industry on the other. But in the years 1936 to 1941, such views propelled French-Canadian skilled workers down a path similar to the

[59] Interview with Lawrence Spitz, September 19–20, 1979.

one union radicals were traveling, giving the campaign for industrial democracy an unusually broad working-class mandate.

Little of the political language these French-Canadian unionists used in the late 1930s is recoverable. The most important vehicle for such language, the *ITU News*, was controlled by union radicals at this time, and they used it to promote their Americanized radicalism. There thus is little direct evidence that these budding, working-class corporatists expressed their political vision in the language of Americanism. But the evidence that does exist, especially the patriotic iconography on display in the 1937 Labor Day parade, strongly suggests that French-Canadian unionists had begun to express their political vision in Americanist terms.

Americanism on parade

The 1937 parade was the highlight of the first Labor Day celebration in Woonsocket in many years. Few of the city's AFL craft unionists could remember the last time their unions had sponsored Labor Day celebrations, and the ITU had never before organized one. Small groups of ITU members, mostly of Italian, Belgian, and French origin, had celebrated May 1 as the international day of labor and would continue to do so.[60] But only with the rise of the ITU did Labor Day become a central event in the life of Woonsocket's working class. Making the date the most important on its social calendar, the ITU staged, in 1937, the largest Labor Day parade in New England.[61] The union leadership invited each local to contribute a float to the parade. More than 300 ITU members joined the planning committee for the parade, and twenty-six locals submitted their own floats. The floats were extravagant productions. ITU women, serving in their customary support role, made 75,000 artificial flowers for the occasion. Each float developed a particular theme chosen by members of the local. It is not known whether the choice of a theme required the vote of a majority of a local's members or simply the approval of the local's committee. But at minimum, the choice of theme involved ten to twenty workers from each of the twenty-six locals contributing a float.[62] The floats, therefore, constitute an expression of rank-and-file attitudes unmediated by the union's top leadership.

The 35,000 spectators lining the parade route first saw two color

[60] *WC*, May 3, 1938.
[61] *L'Indépendant*, September 4, 1937.
[62] *ITU News*, September 1937, 7. Additional members may have been involved in the construction of the floats.

bearers carrying the American and ITU flags.[63] Then the procession
of floats began, and the first, put together by the staff of the *ITU
News*, set the tone for the parade: The truck carried a huge American
flag painstakingly constructed from 3,000 individual flowers. American symbols appeared prominently in at least five other floats. The
American Wringer local built "a covered wagon, reminiscent of the
pioneering days, declaring that the American Labor Movement was
pioneering today." French Worsted workers hung a "facsimile of the
Liberty Bell...on an arch thoroughly decorated with ferns and
flowers" and "proclaimed Liberty for all workers." Blackstone Cotton
workers presented a "living Statue of Liberty surrounded by beautiful
women in white robes," expressing "the continuance and extention
[sic] of Liberty for the American People." Two other locals constructed floats to express the themes of democracy, liberty, peace,
and justice.[64]

Other floats emphasized that such cherished American political
values could only be realized if workers built strong unions and,
through them, defeated employers. Florence Dye unionists built
an anchor on their float, and surrounded it with banners calling on
workers "to anchor the labor movement solidly in Woonsocket."
Rhode Island Plush workers pictured the ITU as a fortress while
Riverside (formerly Desurmont) workers built a "huge lock set on a
base," symbolizing the union's campaign for a closed-shop town.
From such strength, other floats suggested, flowed the resolve to
struggle against employers, financiers, fascists, and scabs. Workers
on the Blackstone Dye float staged a mock sit-down strike while the
Fairmount Dye entry called on organized labor ("four husky workers")
to struggle against Wall Street ("a stout fellow"). The float of the Falls
Yarn local offered a two-scene drama, the first showing fascist guards
beating a poorly clad worker, and the second depicting a worker,
arms thrust upward with "broken chains dangling from his wrists,"
reaching skyward for some elusive democratic ideal. The Montrose
Worsted float vividly conveyed unionists' low opinion of scabs by
making strikebreakers appear as monkeys and having them scream
and screech while shaking the bars of their cage.

Through these floats ITU rank and filers seemed to be echoing
what their radical leaders had proclaimed in many illustrations and
editorials in the *ITU News*: American political traditions, as symbolized
by the flag, the Liberty Bell, the Statue of Liberty and the pioneers,

---

[63] The following account draws on the description of the floats appearing in the *ITU
News*, September 1937, 6–10.

[64] These were the ITU's official float and the ITU Club's float.

were being subverted by powerful, monied interests; workers must organize, struggle against these interests, and guarantee the future of liberty, democracy, and justice in American society. Since floats made no attempt to define the democratic ideal to which rank-and-file unionists like the Falls Yarn worker who broke his fascist chains aspired, they shed little light on rank-and-file understanding of their leadership's campaign for industrial democracy. But the floats do reveal how traditional values of French Canadians were fueling the French-Canadian struggle against capital and its allies. Woonsocket Spinning workers chose vivid, religious imagery to express their anger at strikebreakers: Amidst "the realistic flames of hell" and under a banner proclaiming, "Mr. Scab, he will never rest in peace!" two devils with forks made the afterlife of a recently arrived scab (still laid out in his black coffin) thoroughly hellish. Commenting on this scene, the *ITU News* drolly remarked, "There is no doubt left in the minds of the Woonsocket workers where the souls of scabs go to." Another float, this one by the workers of the Bell Worsted, dramatized the opposition between the greedy wishes of capital and the needs of innocent children. Under a slogan proclaiming "Abolish Child Labor," an evil man, "Greed," was shown whipping the six undernourished children who pulled his chariot. This float drew a chorus of hisses and jeers from parade onlookers who reacted viscerally and angrily to this depiction of children's enslavement and to the destruction of family life that such enslavement implied.

The fact that floats expressing religious and family values were interspersed with others hailing nationalist symbols suggests that French Canadians were beginning to frame their traditionalist concerns in the words not of *la survivance* but rather of the language of Americanism. It seems equally significant, in this regard, that none of the floats dramatized themes drawn from specifically French-Canadian myths – such as the prowess of the early French explorers, the independence of the *habitant*, or the piety and compassion of saintly French-Canadian monks. The absence of French-Canadian ethnic or fraternal organizations from the ITU parade – in marked contrast to contributions of bands and floats by Italian, Franco-Belgian, and Ukrainian groups – further underscores the gap that had opened up between French-Canadian workers and the organized lay leadership of their ethnic community.[65]

How far French-Canadian workers had gone, on the other hand, in

---

[65] The Ukrainian Band and Sons of Italy Band marched in the parade, and three ethnic societies, the Val di Serchio Club, the Italian Workingmen's Club, and the Club Belge, entered floats.

embracing Americanist discourse is impossible to determine from the parade materials alone. A range of predispositions no doubt existed, encompassing all from those who felt reluctant to define their politics and identities in Americanist terms to those who threw themselves into the task wholeheartedly. The *ITU News* artist Gus Levitre (whose illustrations were discussed in the last chapter) represented those who remained wary of using Americanism's traditionalist language to express their concerns about family and community. On the other hand, two French-Canadian rank and filers gained widespread union fame in 1939 by repeatedly stressing the intrinsic connection between unionism and Americanism. One, Ernest J. Tellier, a thirty-four-year-old city councillor who worked as a dye mixer at the French Worsted, emphasized to a group of applicants for citizenship "the absolute necessity of maintaining unionism as the key factor in Americanism."[66] The other, Oliver Benoit, a forty-seven-year-old mulespinner and local leader from the Alsace Worsted, gained renown for his cry, "Unionism is the Spirit of Americanism," at Executive Council meetings.[67] The centrality of "Americanism" to the consciousness of these French-Canadian rank and filers could not have been more directly stated, and the popularity of these two individuals – their fellow unionists bestowed the honor of "Union Man of the Month" on each – suggests the eagerness with which increasing numbers of French-Canadian unionists sought to enter the discourse on Americanism and to shape it to their own ideological specifications. By the mid-1940s virtually all French-Canadian union activists would frame their political arguments, as did Tellier and Benoit in 1939, in terms of what it meant to be an American and what constituted "the American way."[68]

The limits of industrial democracy

The late 1930s saw a marked convergence in the goals of union radicals and ethnics: Both groups sought to make their union a community within a community, both wanted to establish mutualist shopfloor regimes, and both increasingly expressed their aims in the language of Americanism. Yet the two trade-union visions underlying these particular goals remained distinct and, in at least one critical way, opposed. Radicals regarded their campaign for industrial democracy as a dynamic process that knew few, if any, limits. In their vision, workers had a right to a voice in every aspect of capitalist enterprise,

---

[66] *ITU News*, August 1939, 5.
[67] Ibid., September 1939, 8.
[68] These ideological developments will be discussed in Chapter 9.

from shopfloor power to the most jealously guarded investment decisions. The union's French-Canadian activists, on the other hand,
emphasized the rights of capitalists as much as the rights of workers,
and regarded certain aspects of capitalist enterprise as the province of
management alone. As long as the union's campaign for industrial
democracy remained at the shopfloor level, the differences between
the radicals and the ethnics remained submerged beneath a surface of
cooperation. But once the ITU attempted to gain for itself a voice in
industry's most jealously guarded area – corporate financial structures – those differences emerged in sharp relief and the union found
itself riven with dissension.[69]

Union leadership first revealed the aim of gaining a voice in capitalist
finances in a 1938 strike against the city's dye-house owners. In late
April 1938, dye-house owners announced their decision to cut wages
by 12.5 percent. Dye-house workers, angered by the owners' failure
to discuss the issue with them and skeptical about the owners' need
to cut wages, initiated an industrywide strike. The strikers announced
that they would only accept a wage cut if the mills showed that they
were "not capable of paying prevailing wages." To prove their inability to pay, however, the owners had to allow "an impartial person

[69] Sharp differences between the radicals and ethnics also surfaced over the issue of
affiliation with the CIO. Although French-Canadian activists closely identified with
John L. Lewis, the CIO, and the interests of American labor, they could not bring
themselves to support the radicals' proposal to join this national labor movement.
They traveled with enthusiasm to Lawrence to aid the CIO organizing campaign
there, and they breathed life into the Labor Non-Partisan League of Rhode Island –
the CIO's political arm in the state; but they repeatedly defeated Schmetz's and
Spitz's efforts to affiliate the ITU with the Textile Workers Union of America, the
CIO textile union. The ITU and the TWUA-CIO actually entered merger negotiations
in 1939 but the discussions could not survive French-Canadian suspicions on the
one hand and the insecurity of Emil Rieve, president of the TWUA, on the other.
The TWUA had been stung by the collapse of its southern organizing drive in 1937
and then by the secession of a large number of New England locals (and their
reaffiliation with the AFL) in 1938. These defeats had made Rieve desperate to
acquire the ITU, and he showed no patience with the anxieties of French-Canadian
rank and filers. When negotiations broke down, Rieve took the unpardonable step
(in ITU eyes) of opening a TWUA headquarters in northern Rhode Island to compete
with the ITU for the area's textile workers. See Editha Hadcock, "Labor Problems in
Rhode Island Cotton Mills, 1790–1940" (Ph.D. dissertation, Brown University, 1944),
420–44; Textile Labor, June 1939, 6, February 1, 1941, 6, April 1, 1941, 1, 2; ITU,
"Minutes of Meeting between ITU and TWUA," Spitz Collection, Box 8, RIHS; correspondence between Schmetz, Spitz, and TWUA officials Emil Rieve and George
Baldanzi, February–July, 1939, Textile Workers Union of America papers, Mss 396,
Box 54, Independent Textile Union of America file, Wisconsin State Historical So-
ciety, Madison, Wis.; interviews with Lawrence Spitz, October 22, 1976, and
September 19–20, 1979, Angelo Turbesi, October 9, 1980, and George Butsika,
September 14, 1984.

or committee, preferably government... to investigate the books and financial structure of the dye houses affected by the strike."[70] The owners, in other words, had to open their books to public scrutiny.

The owners refused. The strike continued amidst increasing pressure for a settlement from local spinning mills desperate for more dyestuff. Woonsocket's Mayor Pratt accused the strikers of "ruining the local textile industry" through excessive wage demands. ITU leadership defended its dye-house workers, calling them "civic minded individuals interested in the welfare of our city and thoroughly desirous of seeing our local dye houses retain their orders." But union leaders reiterated their original demand: The strike would continue until the company allowed the union or the government to investigate the owners' "financial structure and ability to pay."[71]

The pressure on the strikers from local political leaders, however, grew too intense. On May 11, only a week after the union insisted it would not back off its demands, strikers returned to work under an agreement that foreclosed the possibility of a government probe of company finances. The agreement called for strikers to work at the old wage rates while the Department of Labor studied Woonsocket wage rates in relation to those prevailing in other dye centers. Woonsocket dye-house owners would be entitled to cut their wages by a percentage equal to the amount their old rates exceeded those paid in other dye centers.[72] Though the union leadership sold the agreement as a compromise solution, in reality it amounted to a double defeat. First, the "compromise" undermined the principle that the ITU had established in 1936 and early 1937: namely, that Woonsocket wages should be maintained at a level higher than those prevailing elsewhere.[73] And second, the "compromise" did not authorize the Department of Labor to investigate the owners' financial structure. Dye-house owners had won their battle to keep their books closed, safe from public scrutiny.[74]

Despite the resistance of employers and local political leaders to

---

[70] *ITU News*, May 1938, 7; *WC*, May 6–7, 1938.

[71] *PJ*, May 4, 1938; *ITU News*, May 1938, 6–7.

[72] *PJ*, May 12, 1938.

[73] It was one thing, of course, for local manufacturers to accede to this principle during the recovery of 1936 and early 1937, quite another for them to continue abiding by it in the wake of the 1937 recession.

[74] Dye-house workers did win some minor concessions such as a guaranteed four hours' pay for reporting to work, and they won back the 10 percent cut the following December. But these victories hardly compensated for the union's defeat on the larger issues. *ITU News*, December 1938, 5.

the open-books demand, the ITU renewed its campaign for public scrutiny of corporate finances in 1939. This time it raised the demand during a strike of Woonsocket Rayon workers who had walked out in February, dissatisfied with wages, work loads, and unhealthy conditions. When management refused most union demands, claiming that they could not afford the increased production costs that meeting the demands would entail, the union asked management to open its finances to public review and offered to withdraw its demands if it found that management would be burdened with excessive production costs. In late April, Manville Jenckes, the parent company of Woonsocket Rayon, released production information purporting to show financial losses suffered by Manville Jenckes the previous five years.[75] The union dismissed the report as insufficient. The union argued that the Rayon Company was systematically undervaluing its production (and thus its ability to afford a wage increase) by selling its yarn to Manville Jenckes at an artificially low rate, and asked for a more detailed look at Manville Jenckes's books.[76] The union demanded to know the price at which Manville Jenckes purchased its subsidiary's rayon, information management refused to disclose. The union then proposed that both parties submit the dispute to arbitration and that the company's financial records "be submitted to an impartial auditor who would be empowered to make a recommendation on the wage question."[77]

Manville Jenckes also dismissed this proposal. The corporation had no intention of opening its finances to third-party scrutiny of any sort. Management rightly understood the radical implications of the

[75] The information was sent to Carl E. F. Gill, commissioner of conciliation, United States Department of Labor, Boston, Massachusetts, May 4, 1939; a copy was then forwarded to the union. Spitz Collection, Box 8, RIHS.

[76] The union's suspicions were well-founded. Woonsocket Rayon was one of Manville Jenckes's most profitable operations, turning net profits in excess of 20 percent of sales even in the Depression's worst years. Manville Jenckes management saw such profits as necessary to pay off its large debts and to modernize its other plants, but it may have felt that to have revealed publicly the size of those profits – regardless of the accompanying rationale – would have further turned community sentiment against the corporation. See Henry F. Lippitt II, "The Financial History of the Manville Jenckes Company, Manville, Rhode Island" (unpublished paper, MIT, 1936), 182, and a ledger sheet detailing Manville Jenckes sales, income, and profits, 1936–1943, in the Manville Jenckes Corporation records; both Lippitt's paper and the corporation's records are located at the RIHS.

[77] U.S. National Labor Relations Board, "In Matter of Manville Jenckes Corporation and Woonsocket Rayon Company and Independent Textile Union of America: Decision and Order," Case No. C-1659 (typescript, 1941) (hereafter NLRB, "Decision and Order"), 16, Spitz Collection, Box 13, RIHS.

open-books demand. Allowing public review of internal corporate finances could have established a dangerous precedent in industrial relations, one that might later have been used to legitimate union demands for public supervision of pricing, marketing, and even investment decisions. The notion of government review would have been liable to a similar kind of expansive interpretation: Its proponents might have begun arguing that a government arbitrator, temporarily appointed and working behind closed doors, should be replaced by a permanent government commission whose deliberations were open to the general public. Such expanded forms of public supervision were precisely the kind of policies favored by the social Keynesians of the mid-1930s and their social democratic supporters in Woonsocket.[78] They were also the kind of policies that Manville Jenckes was determined to oppose.

Manville Jenckes, thus, not only refused to accede to the union's open-books demand but actually intensified its campaign to discredit the ITU and to sow discord in union ranks. Management had already enlisted the Woonsocket Chamber of Commerce in a campaign to portray the ITU as a radical organization bent on the destruction of Woonsocket industry.[79] It had also sent its foremen to the homes of the strikers to explain the company's position and ask the strikers to give up their demands and return to work.[80] These campaigns eventually wore workers down. In late July, the Board of Directors of the Manville Jenckes Corporation settled on a bold tactic to break the strike. The board announced on July 27 that in view of repeated employee refusals to return to work, the corporation had no alternative but to close the mill permanently.[81] Once more the Chamber of Commerce filled local papers with ads accusing the union of ruining Woonsocket industry.[82] The U.S. Congressman from the region, Charles Risk, called the ITU "a communistic organization" that should be destroyed.[83] The mounting intensity of antiunion attacks weakened the resolve of many unionists. One group began to wonder whether the ITU leadership was in fact making excessive demands on the city's industries; perhaps Woonsocket Rayon really could not afford

---

[78] The ITU's open-books demand anticipated a similar, social-Keynesian-inspired demand made by the UAW on General Motors in 1946 (see Chapter 10).
[79] See, for example, ads appearing in WC, April 20, May 3, 9, 1939, and in L'Indépendant, April 20, 1939.
[80] NLRB, "Decision and Order," 12, Spitz Collection, Box 13, RIHS.
[81] Ibid., 16.
[82] Ibid., 17; PJ, August 1, 1939; WC, August 21, 25, 1939; L'Indépendant, August 21, 25, 1939.
[83] WC, August 17, 1939.

an increase in wages. And why should the Rayon plant or its corporate parent be obliged to reveal its corporate finances to the public?

Sometime during the summer, Victor Canzano, an Italian mule-spinner and union activist from the Falls Yarn local, began to meet privately with management representatives of Manville Jenckes to arrange a compromise settlement. The Falls Yarn was a center of the emerging opposition group, and Canzano, as vice president of the ITU, was the opposition's highest-ranking member. Word of Canzano's unauthorized negotiations soon leaked back to Spitz and Schmetz, who immediately repudiated Canzano and rebuked him in front of the ITU membership.[84] The rebuke ended Canzano's effort, but it inflamed the antiradical sentiments of his supporters. On September 16, 1939, these union oppositionists launched a full-scale assault on Schmetz's leadership. A group of fourteen prominent local union leaders issued a statement challenging the recent reelection of Schmetz to the ITU presidency and accusing him of violating the union's electoral process. These insurgent unionists described Schmetz "as a Hitler who rules with an iron hand," and they called his leadership "autocratic and destructive." The shock waves from these denunciations, reverberating throughout the state, prompted the *Providence Journal* to remark that "grumbling has been heard before in the ranks of the union but never has so large a group boldly come out publicly with the denunciation of the union's leadership."[85] Never before had Rhode Island's strongest union allowed itself to appear so divided and so vulnerable.

French-Canadian skilled workers dominated the list of signatories to the opposition statement. Eight of the first ten signers were French-Canadian skilled workers who had led ITU locals since the early 1930s, including Leona Galipeau and Eugene Thibeault of Falls Yarn, Bertrand Boucher of Woonsocket Spinning, Amedée Miclette of Bonin Spinning, and François Gagne of Florence Dye.[86] Many signatories harbored personal grudges against Schmetz or Spitz. Schmetz had once humiliated Boucher, for example, by rudely interrupting a union speech that Boucher had laboriously prepared for an Executive

[84] Testimony of Victor Canzano, "In Matter of Manville Jenckes Corporation and Woonsocket Rayon Company and the Independent Textile Union of America," Case No. I-C-1227, May 24, 1940 (trial transcript), 965–1010, Spitz Collection, Box 13, RIHS; interview with Lawrence Spitz, September 19–20, 1979.

[85] *PJ*, September 17, 1939.

[86] The list included four non–French Canadians as well: Henri Soubricas, a Belgian weaver from the Montrose, Edward Kotfia, a Pole from Rhode Island Plush, Timothy Kittrich, an Irishman from Blackstone Cotton, and, of course, Victor Canzano. *L'Indépendant*, September 18, 1939.

Council meeting.[87] Schmetz had also offended Canzano by denying him the union's endorsement for appointment as the state's commissioner of labor.[88] But personal insults were not sufficient grounds on which to forge a political opposition. What solidified the opposition was a growing conviction that the radicals' campaign for industrial democracy had gone too far. The ITU, the dissenters felt, had to respect capitalists' rights to exercise unilateral control over certain aspects of their business. The radical, confrontational posture of their union not only violated capitalist rights but threatened the very existence of Woonsocket industry. Manville Jenckes had made clear that if the ITU persisted in its campaign to strip capitalists of their managerial prerogatives, capitalists would simply move their enterprises elsewhere and deprive Woonsocket workers of their jobs. The oppositionist ITU members began calling for a more moderate, less confrontational agenda that would respect the rights of capital and replace industrial strife with industrial cooperation. Mutualism, in their eyes, meant genuine cooperation with management, not the progressive diminution of managerial power to the point of collapse.[89]

The French-Canadian opposition, determined to oust Schmetz from his office, gathered enough support in the rank and file to force another election for the union presidency. On October 1 the Executive Council of the ITU met to choose between Schmetz and Henri Soubricas, the opposition's candidate. Schmetz's supporters and opponents yelled at each other for six hours. Only a dramatic plea by Spitz, in which he stressed the utmost importance of unity and warned that "dissension would result only in the weakening and possible destruction of the union," seemed to place the opposition on the defensive. Spitz concluded his speech with an endorsement of Schmetz and then broke down and wept. Soon after, ITU delegates, swayed by Spitz's oratory, voted 404 to 296 to return Schmetz to office.[90]

Manville Jenckes seized on the union's moment of weakness to break union power among Woonsocket Rayon workers. On September 20, only four days after internal turmoil erupted in the union, Manville Jenckes announced the reopening of the Rayon and invited all its "former" employees to return to work under the conditions prevailing before the strike began. Seventy-three of the 150 strikers

[87] Interviews with Lawrence Spitz, October 22, 1976, and September 19–20, 1979.
[88] ITU, *Labor Review*, 35.
[89] Interview with Leona and Leonel Galipeau, October 22–23, 1980.
[90] *PJ*, *Providence Evening Bulletin*, and *WC*, September 17–October 2, 1939; ITU *Labor Review*, 35.

accepted the offer and returned to work. Union leaders shelved their list of specific demands and concentrated their declining strength on one issue: union recognition. Strike leaders collected signatures from a majority of Rayon employees indicating their choice of the ITU as "their collective bargaining agency." Management agreed to hold a NLRB election but immediately sent out foremen to warn workers that the mill would close again if the workers chose the union to represent them. In response, ITU leaders demanded that management post signs stating the plant's future would not be affected by the election's outcome. Management refused and withdrew its consent to hold a union election. Some strikers gamely continued their protest; only on November 21, nine months after the battle against Woonsocket Rayon began, did the last strikers vote to return to work. Management, sensing a complete victory within its grasp, refused to rehire them.[91]

Only the NLRB saved the strikers at Woonsocket Rayon from unemployment and the union from a ruinous loss. The ITU lodged a complaint with the NLRB in the aftermath of the debacle at Woonsocket Rayon, charging Manville Jenckes with numerous violations of the National Labor Relations Act. In May 1940, a team of NLRB examiners arrived in Woonsocket to determine the validity of the union's accusations. After twenty-three days of detailed testimony and heated cross-examination, the trial examiner found Woonsocket Rayon and Manville Jenckes guilty of numerous violations of the Wagner Act, a decision upheld the following year by the national NLRB in Washington. Shortly thereafter the ITU successfully negotiated a contract with Woonsocket Rayon which brought workers a closed shop, vacations with pay, dues checkoff, and, in Spitz's opinion, many other improvements in wages and working conditions.[92]

The ITU had won a tremendous victory, a victory that signaled a new era of labor relations with a corporation whose policies had bedeviled Woonsocket workers for almost twenty years. After signing a contract with the ITU for Woonsocket Rayon employees, Manville Jenckes's management intimated to Spitz its willingness to sign a similar contract for the corporation's other remaining mill in the area – the huge cotton mill in nearby Manville.[93] Negotiations began

[91] NLRB, "Decision and Order," 17–20, Spitz Collection, Box 13, RIHS.
[92] U.S. National Labor Relations Board, "In the Matter of Manville Jenckes Corporation and Woonsocket Rayon Company and Independent Textile Union of America: Intermediate Report," Case No. I-C-1227 (typescript, 1940), and NLRB, "Decision and Order," Spitz Collection, Box 13, RIHS; ITU, *Labor Review*, 43.
[93] Interview with Lawrence Spitz, September 19–20, 1979.

immediately and by the summer's end 3,000 textile workers at the Manville plant had entered the union. Spitz could barely contain his joy over the union's accomplishments. "The ITU stands second to none in its patriotism for American ideals and in its defense of its democratic principles," he exclaimed in the *ITU News* in the summer of 1940. "We have defended. . . [democracy] on every picket line, in every strike and in every conference where collective bargaining was the keynote. We have given to the workers in our union their rights as citizens of a democracy!. . . we have established industrial democracy."[94]

The struggle against Manville Jenckes revealed, however, not the triumph of industrial democracy but its limits. The union again had lost its fight to open corporate books to public scrutiny. The NLRB decision, in its enumeration of the many violations committed by Manville Jenckes, did not fault the corporation for refusing to open its books.[95] The NLRA did not challenge the institution of private property per se, and the NLRB, by 1939 and 1940, was no longer willing to fine or otherwise punish those companies which refused to open their most essential operations to labor's scrutiny. Though the refusal of the NLRB or the Department of Labor to support ITU efforts to open corporate books to public scrutiny did not necessarily render the union's efforts futile, it did diminish chances for success. Woonsocket employers had shown an uncommon determination to resist the union on this issue, especially manifest in their ability to mobilize support from the city's political leadership and to enlist the Chamber of Commerce in their antiunion campaign.[96] Employers were now emboldened by the NLRB's refusal to back the ITU in its open-books demand. Their opposition, moreover, had encouraged the development of an internal union opposition that sought to replace the confrontational, radical agenda with a moderate, cooperative one. The union had survived an open fight between the radicals and the moderates, and Schmetz and Spitz had successfully defended their leadership. But the pressures that the radicals' opponents – employ-

---

[94] *ITU News*, June 1940, 3.

[95] NLRB, "Decision and Order," passim, Spitz Collection, Box 13, RIHS.

[96] Employers' success with the Chamber of Commerce in 1939 reflected a newfound ability to pool their resources and to abide by decisions collectively undertaken. Only in 1937 had they established an organization, the Woonsocket Association of Manufacturers, to exercise their collective will in the city's economic and industrial affairs. Rhode Island Secretary of State, "Original Articles of Association of Non-Business Corporations, 1940–41," Rhode Island State Archives, Providence, R.I.; Edmund J. Brock, *The Background and Recent Status of Collective Bargaining in the Cotton Textile Industry in Rhode Island* (Washington, D.C., 1942), 78–9.

ers, politicians, and increasingly clergy – were bringing to bear on the union would deepen these internal divisions and further frustrate the radicals' ambitions. The union's campaign for industrial democracy had run aground.

Why, then, did Spitz proclaim in June 1940 that the ITU had "established an industrial democracy"? The sheer joy of victory over an employer that, in unionist eyes, had harmed the city's economic welfare more severely than any other, may have led him to exaggerate the union's actual accomplishments. But he may also have felt that the setback experienced in the Manville Jenckes fight was minor in comparison to how much the campaign for industrial democracy had already achieved. In five short years, after all, Woonsocket workers had gained a voice for themselves in almost every aspect of shopfloor life. The campaign for industrial democracy had yielded a degree of worker participation in, even control of, shopfloor regimes that ten years earlier had been unimaginable to all but a handful of Woonsocket radicals. Such rapid progress was, indeed, a cause to rejoice, and Spitz might have felt that he would find some way – perhaps through expansion of the ITU beyond Woonsocket or through the radicalization of Catholic corporatist doctrine – to carry his industrial democratic campaign into management's upper reaches.

For Schmetz, the Manville Jenckes episode was a far more sobering affair. Not only had his own rank and filers accused him of Hitlerlike behavior, but he had been forced to question the premises that had informed his social democratic politics for a quarter century. Schmetz had long believed that the democratic relations learned in union affairs would offer downtrodden workers a glimpse of how different the world might be and generate support for a fundamental social transformation. In his own mind, union democracy was a stepping-stone to industrial democracy. Once ITU rank and filers began embracing Americanist discourse as their own – an embrace so powerfully evident in the 1937 Labor Day parade – and learned the practice of democracy in union affairs, Schmetz had every expectation that they would fully embrace his radical vision. He had never really contemplated the possibility that workers might use a democratic faith for nonradical, even class collaborationist, ends. The sudden emergence of an ethnic corporatist opposition to his leadership thus left him in a state of ideological as well as personal shock.

The ethnic corporatists, in contrast to Schmetz, regarded their union's future with a great deal of optimism. They had all but seized control of their shopfloors; they had begun finding a way to incorporate treasured elements of their traditional culture into an American identity. Their communal spirit infused union activities with great vigor, and their collective power had forced ethnic leaders to make their concerns central to those of the whole French-Canadian community. Their numerical strength within the ITU, moreover, had placed the heights of union power within their grasp. They were experiencing, in other words, a degree of independence in economic, cultural, and political life that they had never previously known.

7   *Ethnic renaissance*

In late June 1939, thousands of French Canadians from all over New England gathered in Woonsocket for a gala, three-day festival honoring their nation's patron saint, Saint-Jean-Baptiste. This celebration of Saint-Jean-Baptiste was the largest held in Woonsocket since 1904, and it attracted more dignitaries, including official delegations from the Quebec and French governments, than had any previous cultural event in the city's history. In addition to a full program of speeches, concerts, and sporting events, the festival's Woonsocket organizers staged a mammoth parade of 10,000 marchers and scores of riding delegations. A dozen elaborately constructed floats dramatized the parade's theme, "The history of the French race in North America," by depicting French men and women (dressed in seventeenth- and eighteenth-century garb) exploring and settling the New World.[1]

Such unabashed glorification of French Canada's past and the overwhelming size of the crowds (reaching 50,000 for some events) suggested that Woonsocket's ethnic community had recovered from the Sentinelle debacle of the late 1920s. Indeed, the speakers dwelled incessantly on the greatness of the French nation and on the importance of *la survivance*. But the ethnic consciousness evident in these festivities differed markedly from that expressed by the Sentinelles in the 1920s. No speaker advocated separatism or demanded a renunciation of Protestant American culture. To the contrary, speakers called for the creation of a distinctive Franco-American identity that would merge the best elements of the two cultures. The Québecois Minister of Agriculture, for example, declared "we are loyal to the crown as you are loyal to the Star Spangled Banner. Let your French civilization be one of the best defenses of American civilization." And the French consul from Boston hailed the raising of the flags of France and the United States, and urged his audience to support "the Constitution of liberty and tolerance in this great society." Several floats in the parade, such as the one depicting generals Lafayette and Rochambeau offering their services to George Washington, testified

---

[1] *L'Indépendant*, June 22–6, 1939; *Woonsocket Call* (hereafter, *WC*), June 26, 1939.

230

to the newly invented long history of friendship binding the French and American peoples.[2]

The more moderate elements of Woonsocket's ethnic leadership had promoted a Franco-American identity since the early years of the century. But never before had this identity generated such widespread support among, and given such common purpose to, Woonsocket's French Canadians. Only ten years earlier, the promotion of Franco-American themes in a French-Canadian festival would have provoked the bitterest disputes in the city's ethnic community. Perhaps the most striking evidence of the distance traveled by ethnic leaders since the late 1920s was the presence on the parade's reviewing stand of an Irish Catholic prelate, Bishop Francis Keough of the Providence diocese. If Keough's predecessor, Bishop Hickey, had made such an appearance in the 1920s, Daignault and his fellow Sentinelles would have boycotted or otherwise disrupted the celebration.

The prominence of an integrationist position in Woonsocket's French-Canadian community reflected in part the triumph of the ethnic moderates over the militants. The threatened excommunication of leading Sentinelles in 1929 had demoralized the ethnic radicals and discredited their separatist doctrine. The moderates, once they recovered from their exhausting fight with Daignault's followers, vigorously promoted the integrationist position they had long advocated. But the widespread enthusiasm for a Franco-*American* identity so evident in the 1939 parade was made possible not only by the recuperation of the ethnic elite's moderate faction but also by the ITU's success in promoting both an American identity and a class consciousness among French-Canadian working-class parishioners. Traditional ethnic leaders felt compelled to accord union goals – most notably economic security, political power, and social justice – a central place in their renascent ethnic consciousness. No longer did these ethnic leaders call on the masses to support the Republican Party simply to preserve the language and faith of the Québecois homeland. Republican Party leaders began offering their party as a vehicle for advancing the material needs of working-class French Canadians, whom they now portrayed as the poorest and most underrepresented Americans in Rhode Island.

The religious leaders in Woonsocket's ethnic community reoriented themselves even more radically. Drawing on two social-activist papal encyclicals, *Rerum Novarum* (1891) and *Quadragesimo Anno* (1931), they began to criticize the evils of laissez-faire capitalism. They advanced the position that wage-earner exploitation resulted from unregulated

---

[2] *L'Indépendant* and *WC*, June 26, 1939.

capitalism and argued that worker grievances often deserved redress. They supported the rights of workers to living wages and secure employment and endorsed their right to form unions and bargain collectively with their employers. They also began to advocate government intervention in the economy to secure the general social welfare.

The emergence of a prolabor stance within the ranks of the French-Canadian clergy reflects the powerful influence of the ITU among French-Canadian parishioners. A clergy that had made Woonsocket a citadel of *la survivance* for fifty years felt compelled, by the ITU's success, to alter substantially its construction of Catholicism and ethnicity. But the very ability of local clergy to reform their ways spelled trouble for the ITU. ITU radicals hoped that their elaboration of a progressive Americanism would further separate an ethnic working class from its Quebec-oriented ethnic leadership. But their ideological campaign produced no final separation, for French-Canadian workers clung to their traditions, and ethnic leaders showed an unexpected capacity for reformation and adaptation. By reconstructing their ethnicity to incorporate American as well as French civilization, and by redefining their Catholicism to legitimate the nascent class consciousness of their parishioners, ethnic leaders built new bridges to their ethnic rank and file as rapidly as the ITU radicals tore down the old ones. They hoped thereby to draw the ITU's French-Canadian majority away from the secular and radical Americanism of ITU leaders and into a religious and conservative Franco-American community. Traditional ethnic authorities first made their influence felt in the election of 1938 when they forced ITU leaders to support Republican candidates rather than opt for third party politics. During the long 1939 strike against Manville Jenckes, they abetted the emergence, in ITU ranks, of the antiradical, French-Canadian skilled-worker caucus. Their influence continued to grow in 1939, 1940, and 1941 as local religious leaders worked systematically to propagate a vision of Catholic unionism antithetical to the radical, secular vision that had infused the ITU throughout the 1930s, and to fashion a rival union leadership that could gain sufficient power to oust the radicals from office.

Republican reformation

Schmetz and Spitz chose 1938 as the year to plunge the ITU into state and local politics. Union members would not simply demand prolabor statements from the candidates put forward by the local Democratic machine. The ITU, through its newly established chapter of the CIO's political arm, Labor's Non-Partisan League (LNPL), would fashion a slate of genuinely prolabor candidates and run a carefully organized campaign to elect them. The ITU had flexed its muscles in the political arena before. It had turned out Woonsocket workers for FDR in 1936 and had contributed to the defeat of local Republican candidates – Alderman Ernest Dupré in 1934 and Mayor Felix Toupin in 1936 – whose antiunion positions had frustrated ITU ambitions.[3] But never had the union involved itself so formally in politics or so risked its reputation on the outcome of a single election.

The motivations of the ITU radicals are not difficult to discern. Schmetz's vision of a social democracy in Woonsocket required a municipal administration and state government which, at minimum, would sympathize with labor's aims, and ideally would initiate social welfare and industrial planning programs.[4] The events of 1937 and 1938 made this goal appear much more elusive than it had initially seemed. In 1936 the ITU had run a low-visibility campaign to help elect a Democratic mayor, Joseph Pratt, and defeat the antiunion Republican, Felix Toupin. ITU members contributed to Pratt's victory, but not in numbers sufficient to make him indebted to the ITU. In fact, Pratt soon began aiding employer efforts to break a sit-down strike at the French Worsted in 1937 and to compel ITU dye-house workers to settle for less than they deemed acceptable in 1938.[5]

Pratt's quick abandonment of the ITU reflected the limited character of his prolabor sympathies. He belonged to an old-style, Irish-controlled Democratic machine that looked askance at any manifestation of working-class radicalism. Pratt believed that all unionists should emulate the AFL building tradesmen, who wanted nothing more than well-paid employment and middle-class respectability. The role of a prolabor city official, in his view, was simply to procure a handful of jobs on municipal construction projects for local AFL unionists. ITU proposals for shopfloor democratization and for public review of corporate finances struck Pratt as dangerously radical, and the ITU's determination to win its demands through bold, public confrontations with employers offended his sense of political decorum. These political antagonisms were overlaid by an ethnic

---

[3] *ITU News*, January 1938, 6; *Providence Journal Almanac: A Reference Book for the State of Rhode Island* (Providence, R I), 1935, 228–9, 1937, 182 214.

[4] Schmetz had already helped establish the Woonsocket Industrial Board, meant to achieve management-labor cooperation in driving out sweat shops and in attracting companies willing to pay decent wage rates. See *Christian Science Monitor*, January 27, 1937, and James L. Bernard to Samuel R. McClurd, January 23, 1937, Woonsocket Woolen Mills file, Record Group 9, Entry 402, National Archives, Washington, D.C.

[5] *ITU News*, October 1938, 3; ITU, *Labor Review, 1931–1942* (Woonsocket, R.I., 1942), 31.

antagonism: Woonsocket's Democratic machine was predominantly Irish while the ITU was primarily French Canadian. Giving too much support to the union, in Pratt's eyes, would necessarily mean ceding a large part of his ethnic group's power to the still despised French Canadians. He and his political cronies, in short, disliked both the politics of the ITU leadership and the ethnic background of the ITU rank and file.[6]

This deep antagonism between local Democrats and industrial unionists was hardly unique to Woonsocket. It arose in virtually every northern city that was home to an entrenched Democratic Party machine on the one hand and a restless, impatient movement of industrial unionists on the other. Both groups saw the local Democratic Party as an instrument of political power. In many cities the two groups tried, as did Pratt and the ITU in Woonsocket, to arrange alliances that preserved urban power in Democratic hands while allowing both labor and the party machine to pursue their respective agendas. But the alliances usually worked to the disadvantage of industrial unionists, who could rarely muster the human or monetary resources necessary to challenge machine power. The Roosevelt Administration might have chosen to aid its new labor and ethnic constituencies in their fights against the entrenched machines, much as the Johnson Administration aided the Democratic Party's new black voters in the 1960s. Roosevelt, however, saw such a strategy as fraught with too much peril. He thus forced on local groups of industrial unionists a series of difficult options: They could continue to fight losing battles against the Democratic Party machines, arrange better deals with local Republican machines, or build a third party.[7]

---

[6] Interview with Lawrence Spitz, September 19–20, 1979; *Providence Journal* (hereafter *PJ*), January 30, 1959 (obituary of James H. Holland, boss of Woonsocket's Democratic Party machine, 1932–1940). On the AFL in Woonsocket, see biography of Martin Van Buren Cass in *WC*, June 1, 1942. Cass was president of the city's Central Labor Union (CLU) almost continuously from 1906 to 1941. In the 1930s the AFL represented small groups of Woonsocket painters, plumbers, steamfitters, barbers, street railway and bus line employees. The CLU's most important function in those years was prevailing on city contractors to hire union tradesmen. Cass and James McGrath, his predecessor as president of the Woonsocket CLU, were both Irish.

[7] On labor-Democratic Party relations in northern cities in the 1930s: Bruce M. Stave, *The New Deal and the Last Hurrah: Pittsburgh Machine Politics* (Pittsburgh, Pa., 1970); Charles Trout, *Boston, the Great Depression and the New Deal* (New York, 1977); Barbara W. Newell, *Chicago and the Labor Movement: Metropolitan Unionism in the 1930s* (Urbana, Ill., 1961); Lyle W. Dorsett, *Franklin D. Roosevelt and the City Bosses* (Port Washington, N.Y., 1977); John Allswang, *Bosses, Machines and City Voters: An American Symbiosis* (Port Washington, N.Y., 1977); Allswang, *The New Deal and American Politics* (New York, 1978); James T. Patterson, *The New Deal and the States* (Princeton, N.J., 1969);

Aware of this range of options, ITU radicals explored the possibility of launching a third party. In April 1936, unionists in the state had toyed with the idea of forming a labor party, prompting state Democrats, fearful of losing an important constituency, to introduce prolabor legislation in the Rhode Island General Assembly.[8] In August 1936, at the first convention of LNPL, John L. Lewis and his supporters further weakened the movement toward third party politics by throwing the full weight of the CIO behind Roosevelt's bid for a second term.[9] And Roosevelt's landslide victory in 1936 in combination with the Socialist Party's disastrous defeat – Norman Thomas's popular vote plummeted from more than 800,000 in 1932 to less than 200,000 in 1936 – confirmed for many radicals the futility of operating outside the conventional two-party structure.[10] Schmetz had remarked on the eve of the 1936 election that labor could not support the Socialist, Socialist Labor, or Communist parties on the grounds that "they were not strong enough to win."[11] Rhode Island unionists, however, did not fully relinquish their hopes for some form of statewide third-party effort. They followed closely political developments in New York, where the American Labor Party allied itself with the Democrats and the New Deal on a national level but ran independent candidates and developed its own political program in state and local elections.

Gary M. Fink, *Labor's Search for Political Order: The Political Behavior of the Missouri Labor Movement, 1890–1940* (Columbia, Mo., 1973); Mike Davis, *Prisoners of the American Dream: Politics and Economy in the History of the U.S. Working Class* (London, 1986), 69–74; Daniel Nelson, "The CIO at Bay: Labor Militancy and Politics at Akron, 1936–1938," *Journal of American History* 71 (December 1984), 565–86; Robert A. Slayton, *Back of the Yards: The Making of a Local Democracy* (Chicago, 1986), 150–223. See also Arthur Mann, *La Guardia: A Fighter Against His Times* (Philadelphia, 1959), and *La Guardia Comes to Power: 1933* (Philadelphia, 1965). On Lyndon Johnson's 1960s strategy of aiding blacks, see Allen J. Matusow, *The Unraveling of America: A History of Liberalism in the 1960s* (New York, 1984), 97–127, 243–71.

[8] *Labor News*, April 1935–April 1936, passim.

[9] Editha Hadcock, "Labor Problems in Rhode Island's Cotton Mills, 1790–1940" (Ph.D. dissertation, Brown University, 1944), 392–96; Eric Leif Davin and Staughton Lynd, "Picket Line and Ballot Box: The Forgotten Legacy of the Local Labor Party Movement," *Radical History Review* 22 (Winter, 1979–80), 43–63; Hugh T. Lovin, "The Fall of Farmer-Labor Parties, 1936–1938," *Pacific Northwest Quarterly* 62 (January 1971), 16–26; Millard L. Gieske, *Minnesota Farmer Laborism: The Third Party Alternative* (Minneapolis, Minn., 1979); Melvyn Dubofsky and Warren Van Tine, *John L. Lewis: A Biography* (New York, 1977), 248–53.

[10] David A. Shannon, *The Socialist Party of America: A History* (New York, 1957), 227–48; Bernard K. Johnpoll, *Pacifist's Progress: Norman Thomas and the Decline of American Socialism* (Chicago, 1970), 135–77; Irving Howe, *Socialism and America* (New York, 1985), 49–86.

[11] *ITU News*, September 1936, 17.

Schmetz and Spitz explored the possibility of launching a similar venture in Rhode Island.[12]

When ITU members convened in January 1938 to establish a local chapter of LNPL, it seemed possible they might actually do so. They listened to the keynote speaker, Frank Manuel, address them "on the necessity for independent political action on the part of organized labor," and for "building. . .a political machine that can carry out the desires of labor and guarantee the maintenance of civil liberties, industrial democracy and the further strengthening of the union movement."[13] But one critical factor argued against independent political action – the revived appeal of Woonsocket's Republican Party among its traditional, French-Canadian, working-class constituency. The long-standing relationship between French Canadians and Rhode Island's Republican Party, dating to 1900, had atrophied in the 1920s and early 1930s, as French-Canadian workers found the Democratic Party more sympathetic to their economic and cultural interests. The extent of the group's newfound enthusiasm for the Democratic Party first became apparent in 1934, when Woonsocket voters elected an all Democratic City Council, and again in 1936, when more than 70 percent of the city's voters cast their vote for FDR.[14]

The magnitude of these Democratic sweeps, however, prompted local Republican Party leaders to search for ways to win back the hearts and minds of Woonsocket's French-Canadian working class. Ernest Dupré, perennial aldermanic representative of the Fifth Ward, the heart of French-Canadian society in Woonsocket, led the Republican reformation. His constituents had rejected him after his failure to defend their interests in the general strike of September 1934, an especially painful defeat for someone like Dupré who styled himself a "man of the people." He had long cultivated a plebeian – some would say demagogic – image, dressing flamboyantly, behaving brazenly in public, and filling his political appearances with song, humor, and bombast. His political persona angered many people in the city, not only his political opponents but also many of his fellow French-Canadian Republicans who were accustomed to the staid, patrician leadership of Aram Pothier and disdainful of Dupré's flamboyance. But Dupré's working-class constituents adored his defiance of political convention and his thinly veiled caricatures of the refined, delicate,

---

[12] WC, November 5, 1937, interview with Lawrence Spitz, July 15, 1983. On the American Labor Party, see Kenneth Waltzer, "The Party and the Polling Place: American Communism and the American Labor Party in the 1930s," *Radical History Review* 23 (Spring 1980), 104–29.

[13] *ITU News*, February 1938, 6.

[14] *Providence Journal Almanac*, 1935, 228–9; 1937, 186.

and sober sensibility cultivated by the local elite. In these and other ways Dupré closely resembled Boston's most famous and outrageous politician of the time, Mayor (and later Governor) James Michael Curley.[15]

Dupré's downfall lay in his failure to anticipate the rise of a labor union in the midst of his ward, a union that had far more substantive political appeal to the masses than he thought possible. Dupré's failure cost him more than his pride; it cost him as well his central place in a lucrative web of graft and corruption. His position as city councillor brought him sizable kickbacks on city contracts and allowed him to arrange necessary protections for his extensive gambling operations in the Fifth Ward. Although officially earning only $300 a year as an alderman, he assembled a stunning wardrobe, rode around in luxurious cars, and built a mansion on the large property he had purchased outside town.[16] With so much revenue riding on his ability to represent the people of Woonsocket, he lost no time, in the aftermath of his 1934 defeat, in fashioning a new Republican Party that would win back his constituency and return him to office.

Dupré first gained control of the local Republican committee in 1934, positioning himself to dispense party patronage and to design the party's political program. He then effected a rapprochement with his rival, Felix Toupin, who in the 1920s had led many French Canadians out of the Republican and into the Democratic Party. After six years as the Democratic mayor of Woonsocket, from 1930 to 1936, Toupin renounced his party membership and rejoined the Republicans. This abrupt switch cost him dearly in the short term, as he lost the mayoralty in 1936 to his Democratic opponent, Joseph Pratt. But Toupin hoped that the regrouping of all French Canadians into the Republican Party and the fostering of a renewed determination to press their demands with a single political voice would eventually bring him a large share of political power in Woonsocket and the state.[17] After 1936, even Eugene Jalbert, a lawyer, industrialist, and heir apparent to Pothier, put aside his old antipathy for Dupré (who

---

[15] *PJ, Providence Evening Bulletin* and *WC*, December 7, 1949; Richard Sorrell, "The Sentinelle Affair (1924–1929) and Militant 'Survivance': The Franco-American Experience in Woonsocket, Rhode Island" (Ph.D. dissertation, State University of New York at Buffalo, 1975), 254, 307, 313, 340, 454. On Curley: Joseph Francis Dinneen, *The Purple Shamrock: The Honorable James Michael Curley of Boston* (New York, 1949); James Michael Curley, *I'd Do It Again: A Record of All My Uproarious Years* (Englewood Cliffs, N.J., 1957); Trout, *Boston, The Great Depression, and the New Deal*, 27–74.

[16] *PJ*, December 7, 1949; interview with George Butsika, September 14, 1984.

[17] Aaron F. DeMoranville, "Ethnic Voting in Rhode Island" (M.A. thesis, Brown University, 1961), 51–123.

had been a Sentinelle in the 1920s) and threw Dupré the support of his faction.[18] By 1938, the French-Canadian ethnic leadership stood united for the first time since the Sentinelle Affair had begun more than fifteen years before.

This reunified ethnic leadership saw the 1938 election as its moment of opportunity. FDR had overreached his popular mandate by tinkering with the Supreme Court, and he lost more support in the wake of the stinging recession of 1937. Rhode Island Democrats had discredited themselves in an infamous racetrack scandal of 1937, when the Democratic governor, Quinn, called out the National Guard to seize a racetrack owned by a rival in his own party.[19] And Woonsocket Democrats like Mayor Pratt had made themselves politically vulnerable through a series of antiunion statements and actions.

Dupré, who had sharpened his political antennae in his years out of office, realized that only by making the Republican Party a champion of labor could Republicans hope to regain power in Woonsocket. Dupré's shameless opportunism helped him effect the necessary political transformation. He had no difficulty embracing the ITU and labor's cause, and never felt compelled to explain his Sentinellism in the 1920s and his antiunionism in the early 1930s. He talked about a Republican triumph as though it would mean a victory for the masses. His populist style enabled him to make his new political line sound convincing, at least to French-Canadian voters. French Canadians, whose attachment to ethnic traditions remained profound, could not easily resist a political organization that offered them an opportunity to join their ethnic affections with their class sentiments. Other leaders in the French-Canadian community, even those far removed from the masses, followed Dupré's lead. The editors of L'Indépendant, the French weekly that replaced La Tribune, told its readers to view the election as an opportunity to bring the masses of French Canadians the economic opportunity and political power they deserved but had been so long denied.[20]

Schmetz and Spitz, fearing that this Republican message would resonate deeply in their own rank and file, began denying the third-party rumors that were in the air. "Labor's Non-Partisan League is not a third party movement at the present time," they announced in March 1938. Rather LNPL sought "to support only those candidates" – Democratic or Republican – "who are acting as the friends of labor

[18] L'Indépendant, November 7, 1938.
[19] Zachariah Chafee, Jr., State House Versus Pent House: Legal Problems of the Rhode Island Race-track Row, Dorr Pamphlet 1 (Providence, R.I., 1937), 1–19.
[20] See, for example, editorials appearing in L'Indépendant, November 2–6, 1938.

and not as the 'Charlie McCarthys' [the name of ventriloquist Edgar Bergen's popular dummy] of the employers in Rhode Island."[21] Given the ITU's determination to punish state and local Democrats for their antiunion behavior, this statement seemed to indicate that union leaders had decided to vote a Republican ticket in November.

But if this strategy seemed appropriate for galvanizing the French-Canadian majority in the union, it would likely outrage all those in the union who feared French-Canadian control and who felt committed to building a political program that would never compromise political principles. These union members, including the bulk of the non–French Canadians, regarded the probable Republican candidates as hopelessly opportunistic and corrupt. How could Schmetz continue to talk about a vision of a new society built on honesty and democracy if he joined forces with those individuals prominent in the old society, like Dupré, who had built a career on personal avarice, dishonesty, and flagrant contempt for democratic procedure?

In August 1938, a union member eloquently expressed his doubts about the ITU's emerging political strategy and proposed a compelling alternative. "How long are our leaders going to advocate the replacement of one nonlabor man by another?" he asked. "Why don't we build Labor's Non-Partisan League strong enough or wait until it is strong enough and then go out and take over and give Woonsocket real clean government?" The writer speculated that union leaders intended to show Woonsocket workers the futility of working with the two parties and "so prepare them for the days to come" – a third-party movement. But, he concluded, "I personally think that we should spend some time in building the movement for 1940 and at that time throw out the phoney politicians and pull away from the two parties, for all time. I strongly favor unity of the workers on all fronts and feel that this is the way to get it."[22]

Such sentiments did not gain sufficient force to deter Spitz and Schmetz from their chosen strategy. At the city's LNPL convention on October 15, 1938, the union endorsed thirty candidates, most of them Republicans. Spitz immediately found himself thrown on the defensive by a storm of criticism coming from both inside and outside the union. "Republicans were endorsed," Spitz insisted, "in order to aid in the purge of those officials on the Democratic ticket who have betrayed the trust of the workers."[23] He emphasized that the move

---

[21] *ITU News*, March 1938, 12.
[22] Letter from W. B., *ITU News*, August 1938, 13. See September 1938, 7, for other letters protesting endorsement of Dupré and Toupin.
[23] *WC*, October 17, 1938.

implied no affinity for Republican Party principles. The union would not support individuals like William H. Vanderbilt, Republican candidate for governor, who represented the state's "reactionary Republican machine" and whose "past record marks him as being opposed to progressive legislation and certainly not a friend of labor."[24] The union was voting Republican in this election solely out of the "necessity for electing men who will aid…[labor's] campaign to better conditions instead of frustrating them."[25]

Spitz's defense failed to explain how Dupré and Toupin, whose records of antiunionism were as long as Vanderbilt's, would aid labor's campaign. The more compelling explanation for the ITU's strategy was the leadership's recognition of the French-Canadian majority's attachment to their ethnic heritage. Although Spitz would not publicly discuss this, evidence to support it could be found in the list of candidates endorsed by the ITU. In addition to Dupré, Toupin, and a host of other familiar Republican politicians, the names of four political novices appeared on the list: Ernest Gignac, candidate for state representative; Victor Canzano, candidate for state senator; and Ernest Tellier and Louis Picard, candidates for city council.[26] All four were long-standing members of the ITU; all four were running as Republicans. Three of the four were French Canadians. One, Ernest Gignac, came from the group of French-Canadian mulespinners that had played such a critical intermediary role in launching the union. All four, including the Italian Canzano, were closely tied to this mulespinning group. From the first they had made clear that unionism would not force them to renounce their ethnic traditions, and the union's Americanization campaign did little to alter their perspective. When presented with an opportunity to express their interests both as French Canadians and as workers, they responded with enthusiasm. Moreover, they could already taste the rich desserts of appointments and kickbacks likely to flow from a Republican sweep.

Schmetz and Spitz wanted to encourage neither renascent ethnic consciousness nor the politics of patronage. They had spent years trying to diminish the significance of French-Canadian ethnicity in union affairs and criticizing the salience of patronage issues in local politics. But they could not risk alienating the skilled French-Canadian workers who were so important to union solidarity. Once Dupré convinced this caucus of unionists that a refurbished Republican Party

[24] Letter from Lawrence Spitz to L'Indépendant, n.d., Lawrence N. Spitz Collection, Mss 31 (hereafter Spitz Collection), Rhode Island Historical Society (hereafter RIHS), Providence, R.I.
[25] ITU News, October 1938, 3; WC, October 17, 1938.
[26] ITU News, October 1938, 6–7.

would offer them a political vehicle to advance their class, ethnic, and personal interests, Spitz and Schmetz felt they had to go along. It was too late to change course, either by advocating independent labor politics or by returning to the Democratic Party's fold. They simply hoped that the ranks of the ITU would be solid enough to withstand the internal struggles that this strategy would undoubtedly provoke, and that the political power of the ITU in the November elections would be impressive enough to compel Toupin, Dupré, and the other Republicans to fulfill their pledges to advance labor's interests.

"A New Deal in municipal affairs"

News of the ITU's political endorsements exploded with the force of a bomb in Woonsocket's Democratic Party headquarters. Although tensions between the ITU and local Democrats had long simmered, none of the Democratic leaders expected the ITU to renounce its Democratic allegiance for a Republican one. Sheriff James Holland, aldermanic candidate of the Fourth Ward and Irish boss of the city's Democratic machine, lost no time attacking the "unholy combination."[27] He accused ITU leaders of making a deal for themselves that sold out the rank and file. "The three highest ranking officials of the Woonsocket Independent Textile Union," he alleged, "will be named to the most important posts in the municipal government if the Republican candidates endorsed by the labor leaders are elected." Schmetz would be appointed city clerk, Spitz city treasurer, and Bert Boucher city auditor. "It only goes to show," he continued, "that the leaders of the union are interested in themselves...that they are traitors of [sic] the working people and that they sold out their thousands of good union members."[28]

Democrats played the "sellout" theme to good effect, and quickly bolstered it with another – communism. Labor's Non-Partisan League, charged Alphonse G. Leblanc, a Democratic state representative running for reelection, "does not represent the laboring class.... It is the first branch of communism. I know because I joined to find out its inner workings."[29] Labor's opponents had frequently hurled charges of communism at ITU leaders; this time, as usual, the accusers could muster little evidence. They pointed repeatedly to a minor incident in June 1938 when Ann Burlak, a Communist Party organizer in New England, had tried to hold a meeting in Woonsocket. The police and

---

[27] *PJ*, January 30, 1959, and October 30, 1938.
[28] *PJ*, October 16, 1938.
[29] Ibid.

city administration had broken up the meeting on the pretext that Burlak and two fellow Communists had profaned the American flag by printing it on their leaflets and flyers. Schmetz's Communist involvement amounted to protesting the charge as false, calling the police action a violation of American civil liberties, and defending Burlak's right to speak.[30]

The Democrats hammered away at the twin themes of corruption and communism throughout the campaign. They produced a booklet of clippings from local newspapers showing how Schmetz, Dupré, and Toupin had vilified each other in past political encounters. Much to the delight of the Democrats, Schmetz had once described Dupré as an "enemy of labor" and Toupin "as worthless to the working man." Mayor Pratt repeatedly read from a statement Toupin had made in 1934 in which he called Dupré "the bad apple of city government" who bore responsibility for all dishonesty in Woonsocket's political affairs.[31]

The Republicans rarely responded to these embarrassing charges, preferring instead to hurl the charge of corruption back at the Democrats.[32] The ITU leaders directed their fire at Pratt's failure to support the union during its difficult French Worsted and dye-house strikes. The union also exploited the apparent class differences separating Democratic politicians from Woonsocket workers. At a rally of 1,000 LNPL supporters on October 30, Victor Canzano, vice president of the ITU and Republican candidate for state senator, contrasted the hard work and small income of Schmetz with the easy job and high income of Sheriff Holland. Schmetz, Canzano told the crowd, "had led working people for five years and his hair is gray today because he has fought constantly for the workers and he has found time to sleep only four or five hours a night in his fourth floor tenement on Diamond Hill Road.... Schmetz gets forty dollars a week for watching out for the workers of Woonsocket, and Holland gets five thousand a year for watching out for his own job."[33]

Louis Picard, union member and city council candidate, also stressed the class differences of ITU workers and Democratic Party politicians. "Holland and Pratt know nothing," Picard charged on one occasion, "about women with children in their arms waiting in line for a pittance at the relief headquarters." "Holland is too busy

---

[30] WC, July 9, 1938.
[31] PJ, October 20, 30, 1938.
[32] Dupré offered as proof the exorbitant prices paid by the city for paint and other materials used to maintain municipal bridges. WC, August 23, 1938.
[33] PJ, October 31, 1938.

strutting around with his ten gallon hat and checkered shirt," Picard went on, "and Pratt is too busy selling the homes of the poor."[34] Schmetz echoed the same theme when he told a huge rally on election eve how proud he was that "the richest man in the hall is a cop."[35]

Unnerved by this portrayal of themselves as fat cats, Holland and Pratt intensified their campaign to portray ITU leaders as communists. The campaign's last days witnessed a fierce contest between ITU leaders and Democratic politicians for the votes of Woonsocket's working class. "In the maze of issues that always arise" in a municipal election, wrote a reporter for the *Providence Journal*, "the struggle between the Democratic city administration and the officers of the Woonsocket Independent Textile Union who are allied with the Republicans has easily become the most prominent." Mayor Pratt told a large rally a few days before the election that "your choice next Tuesday is between orderly government and law and order in Woonsocket, or a communistic form of government that will do you harm and not good." He charged that ITU leaders had betrayed the rank and file and that Ernest Dupré had betrayed his fellow Republicans. "The opposition which bears the title Republican," he insisted, "is only a disguise for a communist ticket which is one of the worst enemies of a city like Woonsocket."[36]

The Democratic charges failed to take hold among the working-class voters of Woonsocket. On November 8, they swept a Republican slate into office. Twenty-three of the thirty candidates endorsed by the ITU triumphed at the polls, including two of the four ITU members who ran on the Republican ticket. Felix Toupin defeated Pratt for mayor by more than 1,000 votes. Sheriff Holland clung to his aldermanic seat in the Fourth Ward by a mere 179 votes and found himself on a Republican-dominated Board of Aldermen. The biggest winner was Ernest Dupré of the Fifth Ward, who received 63 percent of 5,000 votes cast. The city council remained nominally Democratic by a nine to six margin. But Woonsocket's LNPL had supported the three Democrats who won election in the Third Ward and expected them to cast their votes with the Republicans on matters of concern to the ITU.[37]

The ITU had engineered a stunning electoral victory. The Republican victors, ITU leaders predicted, would recognize their indebted-

[34] Ibid.
[35] *WC*, November 5, 1938.
[36] *PJ*, November 4, 1938.
[37] *Providence Journal Almanac*, 1939, 208–18; *ITU News*, October 1938, 8.

ness to labor's political muscle and implement the ITU's municipal program. Indeed, Toupin's victory speech revealed how much the ITU had forced the Republican Party to abandon – at least rhetorically – the elitist, procapitalist orientation characteristic of the party in Pothier's era. "Let the masses know the truth and the light," Toupin proclaimed, "and the masses will be for truth and the right. Let it be known that during the next two years, the city government will be of benefit not to a few and not to the job seekers and job dealers but a definite advantage to the masses and people who made this victory possible."[38] Similarly, the editors of the elitist *L'Indépendant* interpreted the election results as "La Victoire du Peuple."[39] The ITU, through its LNPL chapter, had put a mayor for the masses into office. The editors of the *Woonsocket Call* commented that the "victory of Mayor Toupin and his Republican associates cannot be underestimated. It surely means that Woonsocket citizens have expressed their desire for a New Deal in municipal affairs."[40]

But what was the substance of this New Deal? The two major Republican constituencies, Woonsocket's working-class and French-Canadian communities, offered significantly different answers. To the ITU radicals, a New Deal meant a municipal administration that would respect labor's right to organize, picket, and strike, and eventually sponsor municipal welfare and industrial planning programs. To the leaders of the French-Canadian community, however, the victory meant that French Canadians would finally enjoy the kind of political power in the city and state to which their numbers in the state population had long entitled them. The French-Canadian perspective did not preclude support for prolabor legislation, since so many French Canadians would benefit from municipal and state efforts to improve working conditions in Rhode Island's industries. But the protection and augmentation of the rights of labor was secondary, in the minds of many victorious French-Canadian politicians, to the accumulation of wealth and power, pure and simple.[41] Two days after the election, the *Woonsocket Call* remarked that "already there is activity among aspirants for lucrative city positions, now occupied by Democrats, and more of 'the faithful' among the Republicans are being numbered daily in the ranks of deserving applicants."[42]

[38] *WC*, November 9, 1938.
[39] *L'Indépendant*, November 9, 1938.
[40] *WC*, November 9, 1938.
[41] *L'Indépendant*, November 9 and 12, 1938.
[42] *WC*, November 11, 1938.

The mad scramble for patronage appointments in the new Dupré–Toupin administration confirmed the worst fears of many ITU unionists that the Republican victory would merely reestablish Dupré's machine. A significant number of union members had already expressed their disagreement with the union's Republican strategy during the campaign. In October, the predominantly Irish local of the Blackstone Cotton Company threatened to secede from the ITU if Schmetz and Spitz persisted in their Republican strategy.[43] ITU leaders quelled this minirebellion but found the rank-and-file dissatisfaction that emerged after the election harder to dispel. On November 21, the *Providence Journal* reported that the members of the Rhode Island Plush local had demanded the resignation of Schmetz and threatened to secede if he refused to leave office. "It is understood," the newspaper reported, "that the members were concerned about an alleged loss of prestige and alleged loss of membership because of the [ITU's] political activity. At the heart of the matter was the ITU's decision to favor a party which ... was unfavorable to the interests of labor on its past record."[44]

ITU leaders reacted furiously to the *Providence Journal*'s report of developments at Rhode Island Plush. Schmetz emphatically denied that union members at the Plush had asked for his resignation or threatened to withdraw from the ITU, and filed forthwith a $50,000 libel suit against the newspaper.[45] His subsequent decision, however, to drop the suit quietly without explanation and without claiming an out-of-court settlement suggests that the *Journal*'s reportage had grasped at least a portion of the truth: The Republican strategy of 1938 had generated deep dissension within the union's ranks. Spitz admitted in 1942 that "repercussions of this campaign were severe and...felt long after it was over."[46] In the short run, it forced the union leadership to shy away from the Republicans they had elected in order to defend themselves against the charge that they had made a deal to "get well-paid jobs."[47]

This retreat, however, did little to end the union's internal turmoil. If it placated one group of unionists, it antagonized another that viewed the triumph of Dupré as a great victory for both the union and the French-Canadian community. Members of this second group were not offended by Dupré's desire to reward his friends and punish

[43] ITU, *Labor Review*, 46; *PJ*, October 30, 1983.

[44] *PJ*, November 21, 1938.

[45] Ibid., November 22, 1938; ITU, *Labor Review*, 33.

[46] ITU, *Labor Review*, 33.

[47] Ibid.

his enemies through his control of patronage strings. They rather liked the idea of patronage politics, especially since the power of the ITU was likely to bring them some of the choicest political prizes. This group, led by French-Canadian skilled workers, soon clashed with Schmetz over whether the ITU should endorse Victor Canzano, vice president of the ITU and a narrow loser in his race for state senator in 1938, in his new campaign for appointment as the Rhode Island director of labor. Schmetz insisted that the union could not support him because "the charge would once again be levelled that union officials were using the union for the purpose of getting good jobs for themselves."[48] Schmetz pressed his case with sufficient force to win the Executive Council's support for his position and deny Canzano the endorsement. In the process, however, he insulted his vice president and the pro-patronage unionists who surrounded him, and thus fueled their opposition to the radicals' leadership and vision.

The internal dissent and factionalism that erupted after the victory in November 1938 diminished but did not destroy the ITU's position in local politics. Schmetz and Spitz used their access to the mayor's office to intervene in local government. In 1939 and 1940, for example, they played a decisive role in the establishment of a local housing authority to funnel federal money into low-cost-housing construction.[49] In 1940, the ITU shied away from the partisan involvement of 1938, confining its electoral energy to efforts to reelect FDR and defeat northern Rhode Island's antilabor congressman, Charles Risk.[50] In 1942 the union resumed its campaign to make its influence felt in the local political arena. Not only did it throw its resources behind Ernest Dupré's campaign for the mayoralty, but it demanded that Dupré pledge himself to a nine-point platform. Dupré won easily and kept his faith. On the occasion of Dupré's premature death in 1949, political observers noted that 1942 marked an important change in the chameleon's career. He began to turn away from the corruption and opportunism of his youth, making honesty and principled actions hallmarks of his municipal administration.[51] The electoral strength of the ITU eventually wrought a major change in the character of local politics.

But the internal divisions that flared in 1938 did not die. The Re-

---

[48] Ibid., 35.
[49] WC, August 2, 21, 29, September 13, December 7, 1940.
[50] WC and PJ, October–November, 1940, passim; ITU, Labor Review, 37, 39, 41.
[51] WC and PJ, October 16–November 4, 1942; WC, December 11, 1942; Providence Journal Almanac, 1943, 256; PJ, December 8, 1949.

publican, pro-patronage unionists maintained and deepened their antagonism to union radicals. The direct intervention of local clergy in labor issues, beginning in 1939, widened the internal split. Clergy helped French-Canadian unionists develop a vision of unionism toward which their experience had moved them but that they had not yet articulated. This vision, like that of the radicals, began expressing itself in the language of Americanism; but it was rooted in religion and ethnicity, not socialism.

Christian democracy

The American Catholic Church responded to the Depression with an unprecedented commitment to social reform. The Papacy had declared its concern with the problems arising from the poverty and class divisions characteristic of industrial society as early as 1891, when Pope Leo XIII, in his encyclical *Rerum Novarum*, condemned the "greed and exploitation" so central to "economic liberalism and unchecked individualism" and called for the alleviation of economic distress and the reintroduction of Christian morality into the realm of political economy.[52] At the same time, however, the Pope established the Church's implacable opposition to the solutions advocated by socialists. Their godlessness and their opposition to private property violated, in his view, all that was essential to the workers' spiritual and material well-being.[53] From the 1890s through the First World War, only *Rerum Novarum*'s critique of socialism gained a prominent place in the writings and teachings of American priests and bishops, as few attempted to construct a positive political and social program from Pope Leo's teachings.[54]

Some priests, increasingly concerned with the task of social reconstruction necessitated by the social upheavals of World War I, turned toward the 1891 encyclical for guidance in 1918 and 1919. But not until

---

[52] Joseph M. Corrigan, ed., *Two Basic Encyclicals: On the Condition of Workers, Leo XIII, and Forty Years After, On Reconstructing the Social Order, Pius XI* (hereafter *Two Basic Encyclicals*) (Washington, D.C., 1943).

[53] Ibid.

[54] Marc Karson, *American Labor Unions and Politics* (Carbondale, Ill., 1956), 212–84; Mel Piehl, *Breaking Bread: The Catholic Worker and the Origin of Catholic Radicalism in America* (Philadelphia, 1982), 25–56; David O'Brien, *American Catholics and Social Reform: The New Deal Years* (New York, 1968), 29–46. David Montgomery has modified this view somewhat by showing the importance of Catholic teachings to building trades unionists in the early years of this century. See his *The Fall of the House of Labor: The Workplace, the State, and American Labor Activism, 1865–1925* (Cambridge, U.K., 1987), 306–10.

the Great Depression first caused immense suffering to millions of parishioners and then triggered massive protest movements among working-class Catholics did the American Church show sustained interest in issues of social reform.[55] Its interest, in part, was stimulated by Pope Pius XI's 1931 encyclical, *Quadragesimo Anno*, meant to commemorate the fortieth anniversary of *Rerum Novarum* and impress on Catholic clergy the imperative of involving the Church in social issues. The twin evils of capitalism and communism had seriously weakened the social order; clergy, the Pope argued, had a vital role to play in social reconstruction. Pius XI advocated a middle way between the laissez-faire of the right and the collectivism of the left. Such a way had to address the grievances of wage earners, increase their stake in society, and encourage them to look beyond their own interests to the general social welfare. The social doctrine of corporatism, Pius XI suggested, should guide clergy in their efforts. Corporatism meant a humane and regulated capitalism made possible by the organization of society's main occupational groups – capitalists, workers, farmers, professionals, and small businessmen – into guild-like bodies that would simultaneously promote the interests of their members and enlarge each group's consciousness of its dependence, for its own well-being, on the welfare of other groups. In this doctrine a substantial role was accorded the state; it would both promote the self-organization of various occupational groups and negotiate and resolve group conflicts.[56]

In the 1930s the willingness of some European religious leaders to use corporatism as justification for support of Mussolini's regime led European liberals and radicals to label the doctrine fascist. But there was nothing intrinsically fascist about corporatism. Papal corporatist theory did not glorify the state or justify the subordination of society's corporate groups to its will. The state was merely an instrument for resolving group conflicts; it was an artificial, human creation that could never achieve the status accorded those occupational groups

---

[55] The still indispensable work on this subject is O'Brien's *American Catholics and Social Reform*.

[56] *Two Basic Encyclicals*, 83–195; O'Brien, *American Catholics and Social Reform*, 3–28. On the secular theory and practice of corporatism, see Charles S. Maier, *Recasting Bourgeois Europe: Stabilization in France, Germany and Italy in the Decade After World War I* (Princeton, N.J., 1975); Philippe C. Schmitter, "Still the Century of Corporatism?" in Philippe C. Schmitter and Gerhard Lehmbruch, eds., *Trends Toward a Corporatist Intermediation* (Beverly Hills, Calif., 1982); Wyn Grant, *The Political Economy of Corporatism* (New York, 1983); Alan Cawson, ed., *Organized Interests and the State* (Beverly Hills, Calif., 1985); Suzanne Berger, ed., *Organizing Interests in Western Europe: Pluralism, Corporatism, and the Transformation of Politics* (Cambridge, U.K. 1981).

that sprang naturally (and thus divinely) out of society's social division of labor. Thus clergy could easily find in *Quadragesimo Anno* a justification for a more limited kind of state intervention than the sort Mussolini and other fascists advanced. Indeed, a significant group of American clergy, inspired by the writings of Monsignor John Ryan, believed that Roosevelt's New Deal conformed to corporatist theory far better than Mussolini's fascist state. They became unabashed supporters both of the new industrial unions and of the state's efforts, through the Wagner Act, to procure order and stability in capital-labor relations.[57] Other clergy believed that even the New Deal represented too great an exercise of state power, as it threatened unacceptable interference with such essential underpinnings of the social order as the family and private property. Such disagreements within the Church made it impossible to link papal corporatism to a single political vision. What made the theory so important was the impetus it gave clergy to participate in secular political debates and social movements seeking to define a new social order. Even those Catholics, like Peter Maurin of *The Catholic Worker*, who rejected the corporatist paradigm altogether found in the papal encyclicals a powerful spur to Catholic social activism.[58]

Clerical activism was motivated not only by a noble vision of heaven on earth but also by a fear of the social degeneration that would result from communism's triumph. Pius XI spoke of laissez-faire and communism as comparable evils, but communism, with its atheism and collectivism, clearly was the greater evil. Increasingly,

---

[57] O'Brien, *American Catholics and Social Reform*, 47–69, 120–49; John A. Ryan, *A Better Economic Order* (New York, 1935), 148–90, and *Social Doctrine in Action: A Personal History* (New York, 1941); Francis L. Broderick, *Right Reverend New Dealer, John A. Ryan* (New York, 1963), 211–43.

[58] For the range of clerical positions in political debates and of clerical involvement with social movements, see O'Brien, *American Catholics and Social Reform*, 150–211; Alan Brinkley, *Voices of Protest: Huey Long, Father Coughlin, and the Great Depression* (New York, 1982), 124–42; Piehl, *Breaking Bread*, 57–144; Robert P. Ingalls, *Herbert Lehman and New York State's Little New Deal* (New York, 1975), 118–19. For clerical involvement in labor questions and labor movements, see Ronald W. Schatz, *The Electrical Workers: A History of Labor at General Electric and Westinghouse, 1923–1960* (Urbana, Ill., 1983), 188–221; Schatz, "American Labor and the Catholic Church, 1919–1950," *International Labor and Working-Class History* (Fall 1981), 46–54; Schatz, "Connecticut's Working Class in the 1950s: A Catholic Perspective," *Labor History* 25 (Winter 1984), 83–101; Douglas P. Seaton, *Catholics and Radicals: The Association of Catholic Trade Unionists and the American Labor Movement, from Depression to Cold War* (Lewisburg, Penn., 1981); Neil Betten, *Catholic Activism and the Industrial Worker* (Gainesville, Fla., 1976); Thomas Becnel, *Labor, Church, and the Sugar Establishment: Louisiana, 1887–1976* (Baton Rouge, La., 1980).

through the 1930s, he threw the considerable energies of the Church into opposing communist propaganda and infiltration. A 1937 encyclical, *Divini Redemptoris*, sounded the tocsin against international communism and called on clergy to join an anticommunist crusade. This militant anticommunism, though stimulated by such European events as the establishment of successful Popular Fronts in Spain and France, quickly crossed the Atlantic and powerfully influenced American Catholics.[59] American clergy moved easily from condemning communist participation in the antifascist, loyalist forces in Spain to lashing out at the CIO for accommodating communists in its ranks. Some became so obsessed with identifying and condemning individuals with any connection, apparent or real, to the Communist Party, that they lost sight of the larger goal of social reconstruction. Many proved too willing to dismiss the dangers of fascism in Europe and embrace uncritically the views of anticommunist conservatives at home. Only relatively small groups involved with *The Catholic Worker*, *Commonweal*, and Monsignor Ryan steadfastly refused to allow anticommunism to shape their world view and dictate their agenda.[60]

The Church's social activism and anticommunism appeared in Woonsocket in the late 1930s. Setting aside a fifty-year tradition of antiunionism, local clergy and their lay allies began to speak in support of the rights of labor and to argue for the positive role that trade unions would play in a reconstructed corporatist social order. *L'Indépendant*, the city's French weekly with close ties to local clergy, introduced readers in 1940 to the concept of corporatism and emphasized its endorsement by the Pope. The newspaper approvingly reported the statement by a group of American bishops that laissez-faire capitalism "exploited workers and violated their human rights." It hailed the Wagner Act as legislation that would reduce exploitation, protect human rights, and thus procure the social stability so central to a corporatist vision. Never before in this ethnic community's

---

[59] On Catholic Church and anticommunism in Europe, see Richard A. Webster, *The Cross and the Fasces: Christian Democracy and Fascism in Italy* (Stanford, Calif., 1960); A. D. Binchy, *Church and State in Italy* (London, 1941); Guenter Lewy, *The Catholic Church and Nazi Germany* (New York, 1964); Martin Blinkhorn, *Carlism and Crisis in Spain, 1931–1939* (New York, 1975); Arno J. Mayer, *Why Did the Heavens not Darken? The "Final Solution" in History* (New York, 1988), 216–17, 222, 225–6.

[60] Piehl, *Breaking Bread*, 122; O'Brien, *American Catholics and Social Reform*, 70–119. See also George Q. Flynn, *Roosevelt and Romanism: Catholics and American Diplomacy, 1937–1945* (Westport, Conn., 1976); Leo V. Kanawada, *Franklin D. Roosevelt's Diplomacy and American Catholics, Italians and Jews* (Ann Arbor, Mich., 1982); Donald F. Crosby, "Boston's Catholics and the Spanish Civil War: 1936–1939," *New England Quarterly* 44 (March 1971), 82–100; J. David Valaik, "Catholics, Neutrality, and the Spanish Embargo, 1937–1939," *Journal of American History* 54 (June 1967), 73–85.

history had its leaders shown such a willingness to align themselves with capitalism's critics. For the first time as well, they advocated collective bargaining and worker organization into unions. Such developments, the editors of *L'Indépendant* pointed out, would restore rights to workers, guarantee their liberty, and permit the reconstruction of the social order.[61]

Changing conceptions of spirituality reflected local clergy's new concern for labor as well. To mark Labor Day in 1940, *L'Indépendant* published a piece entitled "La Noblesse du Travail." The author, a Montreal Jesuit, emphasized that the fate of labor under capitalism was "to become an instrument of degradation" and to resemble "the ancient slavery from which Christ delivered us." He rejected the view of Christian pessimists that work was inevitably drudgelike and alienating, yet another price paid by humans for their sins. Earthly labor, he contended, could be ennobling. Labor that expressed the "original personality" of the worker, produced a worthy, spiritual object, and fulfilled both divine and social purposes would serve as a providential bond linking a person to the universe, society, and God. Through the noble labor of the individual, society could become like a single, harmonious city.[62]

The expression of such views in Woonsocket's French newspaper revealed how much the orientation of the local Catholic churches vis-à-vis labor had changed. The rise of organized labor in the city had compelled the local religious leaders to take the material concerns of their parishioners to heart and develop a view of the social order that accorded unions a prominent place. Some clergy went so far as to talk about the spirituality of labor and how fulfilling work brought men closer to God and brought the divine project on earth closer to completion. "La Noblesse du Travail" began to compete with *la survivance* for a central place in the Church's self-definition.

Local clergy also began to speak out, in ever more insistent terms, on the evils of communism. Clergy naturally had to oppose an ideology that denied the existence of God. And the Church's conception of the individual as simultaneously sacred and flawed had long made it a sharp critic of the omnipotence that communists wanted to confer on the state and the faith they expressed in human perfectability. But in places like Woonsocket, the Church's anticommunism reflected more than a fear of communism itself. Rather, communism became, in clerical hands, an evocative representation of the secularist evil that had befallen the modern world. Priests in Woonsocket worried about

---

[61] *L'Indépendant*, February 9, 1940.
[62] Ibid., September 3, 1940.

their parishioners' waning commitment to ethnic survival and the consequent erosion of their own power and authority. They feared the success of a union in their midst, led by radicals who cared little for religion and who advocated an unabashedly secularist message. For some priests, anticommunism became a way of justifying attacks on radicals, communist or not, who had done the most to promote the secularization of society. The sudden involvement of clergy in union affairs in the late 1930s, then, was in part a calculated effort to oust the radical leaders of the ITU from their authoritative positions in the community and to reestablish the power of the Church over its communicants' lives.[63]

Local clergy tried first to undermine the European-born radical leaders of the ITU by denouncing them in sermons. This strategy backfired: In 1938, union members attending Mass at St. Anne's, the city's largest parish, walked out en masse in the midst of one Father Morin's antiradical sermons.[64] Church leaders turned quickly to a more covert strategy. They organized a Catholic workers' league, La Ligue Ouvrière Catholique, comprised of individuals selected for their leadership potential and their status in the working-class community, with the goal of reinjecting Christian values into the labor movement and reestablishing the importance of the parish as the institution best equipped to offer Catholic workers guidance in the problems of daily life. So successful was the Church's covert strategy that union radicals knew nothing of this organization.[65]

The inspiration and direction of this Ligue came from Quebec.[66] Québecois Jesuits helped select for membership in the Ligue individuals who occupied strategic positions in the community and who had demonstrated leadership potential. Those selected were taken on retreats to Quebec and given brief but intense bursts of instruction in subjects ranging from theology and papal encyclicals to organizational skills to family economics. This education was meant to enrich their religious lives, improve their effectiveness as lay leaders in parish affairs, and prepare them for the task of infiltrating Woonsocket's labor movement, propagating religious values, and ousting the radicals.[67]

---

[63] Ibid., January 27, 1938, May 1–3, 1939, February 8, 10, 1940.

[64] Interview with Lawrence Spitz, October 22, 1976, and Angelo Turbesi, October 9, 1980; Lawrence Spitz to author, December 21, 1976.

[65] Interview with Lawrence Spitz, September 14, 1984.

[66] Quebec clergy drew their inspiration from developments in France. On French origins, see Joseph Debès, *Naissance de l'action Catholique ouvrière* (Paris, 1982), 23–62.

[67] No written records on this organization have been found. This account is based on interviews with Arthur Fortin and Phileas and Yvonne Valois, leading members of

The Ligue took elaborate measures to disguise its counterinsurgency. It was designed not as a mass membership organization but as a vanguard group that would succeed (like the Communist Party) through the intelligence, dedication, and charisma of its cadre. Only a few individuals who demonstrated unshakable religious convictions were invited to join the organization. There were perhaps fifty members altogether spread out among the city's six French-Canadian parishes. Each parish group, called a cell, accepted directives from the federation, the Ligue's governing council. The leaders of the federation, the secretary and chief propagandist, worked closely with a local priest, Father Bienvenue, to develop plans to Christianize the labor movement in their midst. The two men who held these positions for much of the Ligue's ten-year existence, Arthur Fortin and Phileas Valois, were drawn from the ranks of the city's petite bourgeoisie. They occupied strategic positions at the crossroads of social intercourse in Woonsocket, one at a service station and the other at a grocery store. They orchestrated plans by Ligue members to make themselves available to Catholic workers in need, to inject their religious values into the currents of daily discourse, and to stimulate opposition in the ranks of the union to its radical leadership. They considered Spitz a communist and viewed Schmetz as the leader of a radical clique of European workers who had gained an unacceptable dominance of union affairs.

The Ligue first took on the radical leadership of one of the union's largest locals, the Alsace Worsted. The local's leadership, consisting of such individuals as Maurice Pierre, Josephine Proulx, and Maurice D'Hondt, formed one of the most solid groups of Franco-Belgian radicals. A young and energetic Italian, Angelo Turbesi, solidified this radical nucleus that had made the Alsace one of the earliest and strongest ITU locals. The Ligue's chief propagandist, Phileas Valois, recalls how a "whole bunch...maybe 15 or 20" European workers "were controlling...everybody there," making the local one "we really wanted to go into."[68] The Ligue wisely chose a sensitive religious issue to galvanize French-Canadian rank and filers into action. The radicals, Valois recalled, had scheduled a meeting on Easter Sunday when "all of our people were at Mass." This issue involved much more than religious freedom; it involved democracy as well. "I wanted to have the [French-Canadian] people working together, to have some part in the administration of the union – not just a little bit

the Ligue, all on July 5, 1983, and with Charlotte LeBlanc, a 1940s member of Woonsocket's Jeunesse Étudiants Catholique, July 16, 1981.

[68] Interview with Phileas Valois, July 5, 1983.

of it," Valois recalls.[69] The Ligue, in other words, intended to use the ITU's most potent ideological tool – democracy – against the radical leadership. By pushing their religious demands, French-Canadian workers would actually strengthen union democracy and thus fulfill the ideal most central to their union experience.

The Ligue's method of operation, however, was hardly a model of democratic procedure. Ligue cadre did not acknowledge their own role in the campaign to oppose the Easter Sunday meeting. They chose the brother of a Ligue member who was also a representative of management – an overseer – to "pass the word" to ITU members in his department and to overseers in other departments. This overseer operated effectively, and quickly mobilized sufficient support to force the meeting's cancellation.[70]

The episode was minor but significant, revealing a great deal about an alternative conception of unionism taking shape in Woonsocket. Most obviously, this conception put religion at the very center of union affairs; the religious habits of ITU members, the Ligue insisted, were to be respected, not merely tolerated or, at worst, subject to the radicals' contempt. But the Ligue did not intend to substitute religion for democracy as the union's guiding principle. It argued, rather, that Catholicism and democracy were intimately linked and that French Canadians, who formed the majority of union members, should shape union development and practice. The introduction of religiosity into union affairs, it asserted, represented the will of the majority and thus the fulfillment, not the denial, of the democratic ideal.[71]

This new conception of unionism also called for a vastly different set of relations between employer and employee. The fact that the Ligue was willing to work through an agent of management, as in the case of the Easter Sunday affair, is indicative of its members' desire to replace the radicals' commitment to class struggle with one of class harmony. Ligue members believed that the ties of religion could overcome the divisions resulting from class. Employers and employees would best serve their own interests by working together for the general welfare of their enterprise. The Ligue's perspective on industrial relations fit well with the mutualist ethic emerging from the shopfloor experience of many French-Canadian workers.

The emergence of this alternative conception of unionism posed a

---

[69] Ibid.

[70] Ibid.

[71] The intimate link between Catholicism and democracy emerged repeatedly in interviews, not only with Ligue members but with French-Canadian ITU activists. Interviews with Leona Galipeau, October 22–23, 1980, and with Arthur Rock and Lionel Harnois, both on October 8, 1976.

serious problem for union radicals. The strength of their union had long depended on an alliance with a group of French-Canadian skilled workers. The radicals had never seen eye to eye with these skilled ethnics. The latter were committed to the union and believed in the practice of democracy at the workplace and in the union. But they also wanted to reconcile their class and American identities with their ethnic heritage. Once local politicians and clergy began to respond positively to the union in their midst, reconciliation with their traditional ethnic leaders became possible. Dupré's reformation of the Republican Party offered one avenue of reconciliation, and the emergence of the proworker and pro-union Ligue Ouvrière offered another.

The precise relationship between Ligue members and French-Canadian ITU members is difficult to establish. Arthur Fortin of the Ligue recalled that a number of ITU French-Canadian officials wanted to join, but the Ligue refused to accept them. The Ligue wanted as members unobtrusive infiltrators who seemed to spring naturally from the rank and file, not prominent union officials known throughout the city. The Ligue's prohibition of formal links with union officials, however, did not prevent Fortin from developing close friendships with leaders of the French-Canadian skilled worker caucus. He became especially close to Eugene Thibeault and Leona Galipeau of the Falls Yarn Mill.[72] The emergence of Galipeau and Thibeault as leaders of an anti-Schmetz movement in 1939, the year the Ligue was founded, suggests that Ligue leaders helped French-Canadian unionists develop an effective critique of union radicals and mount a coherent opposition. Indeed, the manner in which this opposition group first tried to end the long, debilitating strike against Manville Jenckes in the summer of 1939 and then to oust Schmetz from the presidency that fall point to Ligue involvement.

Victor Canzano, the unionist who initiated the secret, unauthorized negotiations with Manville Jenckes management, knew Thibeault and Galipeau well. The three men worked alongside each other at the Falls Yarn and shared a growing dissatisfaction with the radicalism of the union's leadership. If the Ligue's influence had spread to Thibeault and Galipeau, it almost certainly had reached Canzano too. Indeed, Canzano's growing conviction that Schmetz and Spitz did not truly want a peaceful settlement with Manville Jenckes was one interpretation of the Ligue's line that a dangerous group of radicals bent on the destruction of Woonsocket labor and industry controlled union affairs. Canzano's initiation of informal negotiations with Manville Jenckes management accorded with another Ligue belief

---

[72] Interview with Arthur Fortin, July 5, 1983.

that employers and unionists, if freed from the dishonest and un-reasonable dogmas spread by agitators like Spitz and Schmetz, could resolve all outstanding differences between capital and labor and secure class harmony. Schmetz's public repudiation of Canzano's initiatives, as previously noted, induced Canzano's supporters to launch an all-out challenge to Schmetz's leadership. The strategy used by Canzano's group to discredit Schmetz before the rank and file – the depiction of him "as a Hitler who rules with an iron hand" and the labeling of his leadership as "autocratic and destructive" – was virtually identical to the Ligue's effort, as revealed in the Alsace episode, to stigmatize the ITU leadership as an authoritarian, Euro-pean clique. The similarity in tactics and language between the Ligue and the ITU oppositionists cannot establish that the former created, or even controlled, the latter; the actual relationship between the two groups is impossible to document. But the similarity is nonetheless telling, suggestive that the Ligue was influential because it gave the skilled French-Canadian workers a way of expressing and acting upon sentiments that they had long felt but could only partially articulate.

In the short term the Catholic opposition movement failed to dis-lodge the radicals from power. Spitz and Schmetz rallied their sup-porters and gained a stirring endorsement for their leadership. But the opposition had won its spurs in this fight and continued to gain in strength. Local clergy, emboldened by the appearance of a strong opposition caucus in the union, went public with their denunciations of the radicals. Early in 1940, the Rev. Stephen Grenier, pastor of the Holy Family Church, charged "that a communistic organization mas-querading as an agency for the promotion of the industrial worker's welfare has established itself in Woonsocket and is working to sow the seeds of discord among employers and their employees." He assured parishioners of his belief in "the banding together of workers under a union standard" but declared his implacable opposition to "workers' organizations that looked to communists for leadership." He warned against supporting movements dedicated "to under-mining...those principles on which this nation was founded."[73] He then instructed his parishioners on typical communist tactics, which gave him the opportunity to launch a thinly veiled attack on the union's long, bitter, and, from his perspective, wrong-headed strike against Manville Jenckes. The communist plan of action, Grenier claimed, lay in "bringing misery to a thriving community. Their first step is to precipitate strikes for unreasonable wage increases which manufacturers are unable to meet. The employers, realizing that if

[73] WC, February 5, 1940.

they grant the rates of pay asked they will not be able to compete with factories in other communities paying lower wages, are forced to close their plants. Then the strikes go on indefinitely until the starved worker is unable to resist any longer and is ripe for the teaching of communism and for the violence which Communists crave."[74] A grim scenario, indeed.

Fortunately for ITU radicals, the NLRB ruling in June 1940, that Manville Jenckes and the Woonsocket Chamber of Commerce, not the ITU, had violated American law and thus the "principles on which this nation was founded," did much to discredit Grenier's anti-union fusillade. The ITU's victory over Manville Jenckes effectively silenced the conservative opponents within the union and brought the ITU a stretch of internal peace. But the opposition did not go away. Galipeau, Thibeault, and their supporters bided their time and waited for another opportune day.

The opposition to radicalism that cohered in the late 1930s, both within the ITU and in Woonsocket society at large, can be viewed as part of a rising conservative tide that everywhere in America placed radicals and New Deal liberals on the defensive. Congressional defeat of Roosevelt's ill-conceived court-packing scheme, the failure of New Deal policies even to moderate the steep economic recession of 1937, and a growing middle-class backlash against organized labor in the wake of the sit-down strike wave of 1936 and 1937, emboldened Roosevelt's critics and made criticism of the New Deal respectable, even appealing, among broad sectors of the population for the first time.[75] What has remained somewhat elusive in this familiar tale, however, is the precise social base and political orientation of this New Deal opposition, especially that segment located in the North. The Woonsocket story, in this regard, offers some interesting insights.

Late 1930s events in Woonsocket confirm, first, the commonly held view that the rise of labor alarmed and mobilized middle-class Americans. But, in Woonsocket, these middle-class Americans were not, as is often assumed, Protestants of old Yankee stock protesting ethnic America's bid for political power or fulminating against the New Deal's alleged erosion of such fundamental Yankee beliefs as "rugged individualism" and "self-reliance." Rather, they were ethnic Americans themselves – French-Canadian clerics, politicians, newspaper editors, lawyers – who were desperate to regain political author-

[74] Ibid.
[75] See James T. Patterson, *Congressional Conservatism and the New Deal: The Growth of the Conservative Coalition in Congress, 1933–1939* (Lexington, Ky., 1967).

ity in their own ethnic communities. That authority had so eroded by the late 1930s that the only path to rehabilitation lay in wholesale concessions to the prolabor and pro-New Deal vision of their working-class parishioners. Thus, Republican politicians in Woonsocket advocated the rights of the masses and brought them a "New Deal" in municipal affairs. Local clergy lent religious sanction to the ITU's campaign to connect bread-and-butter union struggles to a larger vision of social reconstruction. Much of the ITU's campaign for industrial democracy – to gain a substantial voice for workers in their jobs and places of work – suddenly found a place in Church doctrine; so did the ITU's demand that the federal government assume responsibility for the general social welfare. Political demands and critiques of the social order that had been regarded as dangerously radical as late as the early 1930s had gained, by the end of the decade, widespread acceptance.

Woonsocket conservatism of the late 1930s was thus of a distinctly limited sort. It dared not attack the fundamental reforms of the New Deal already in place. It dared not question the primacy of a working-class agenda in local politics. It sought merely to avert further reform and to kill any chance ITU radicals might have had of realizing their most ambitious dreams.

Middle-class French Canadians could claim to have achieved these goals, at least in the short term. Most French-Canadian unionists did not want to abandon their ethnic community. They desired instead to reconcile their new class and American identities with their traditional ethnic and religious ones, and they seized upon the opportunity for reconciliation that the rise of a Franco-American orientation within Woonsocket's lay and religious elites offered them.

But the long-term success of this conservative campaign was far from certain. Woonsocket's French-Canadian middle class paid dearly for the legitimacy it accorded working-class rebellion. What began as a change in local clergy's labor doctrine culminated in profound alterations in their religious self-definition. When faced with the need to make some accommodation to the powerful union in their midst, Woonsocket clergy had turned reflexively to authorities in their ancestral Québecois home for advice and expertise.[76] But their involvement in labor questions drew them inexorably into the world of American Catholicism. The Ligue was a statewide federation which

---

[76] They turned to Quebec despite the existence of an American Catholic organization, the Association of Catholic Trade Unionists, far more experienced than the Ligue in dealing with American industrial unions. See Schatz, *The Electrical Workers*, 167–221; Betten, *Catholic Activism and the Industrial Worker*; Seaton, *Catholics and Radicals*.

increased contacts between Woonsocket clergy and priests of the Providence diocese. Within a few years, French-Canadian clergy would be drawing on the resources of the Social Action Institute of the Providence diocese and welcoming Irish-American priests into their community to discuss the labor question with their parishioners. Priests like Father Grenier suddenly found themselves referring to the intentions of the Founding Fathers and to the character of American law to defend their positions on union questions. Woonsocket's clerical community, in order to regain authority over its parishioners, had relinquished the primacy it had long accorded to *la survivance*. To counter the influence of the ITU, the Woonsocket Church found itself accepting what its clergy had resisted for fifty years – separation from Québecois Catholicism and incorporation into an American Catholic Church.

Such incorporation would undoubtedly diminish the stature of local priests vis-à-vis diocesan and archdiocesan Church officials; worse, it might provoke a spiritual crisis among devout French-Canadian Catholics, who had always defined their faith in ethno-religious terms. The combination of declining clerical stature and spiritual crisis, in turn, could quickly wipe out whatever gains in political and moral authority that Woonsocket's ethnic elite had achieved during the years of its renaissance.

Such elite vulnerability made the outcome of the looming battle between the union's radicals and its ethnic corporatists exceedingly hard to predict. Would the radicals, perhaps, recover the initiative? Would the ethnic corporatists, if they came to power, remain beholden to their troubled ethnic elite? If not, how might they revise their political beliefs and refashion the language of Americanism?

Such uncertainty about which working-class faction would hold union power and what political vision it would elaborate undoubtedly worried Woonsocket's chief political contestants, for all knew the stakes were high. But the uncertainty that so troubled these contestants can be interpreted more positively, as an indication of how much the Depression experience, and especially the rise of the ITU, opened up the local political process to new groups and new ideas. Indeed, Woonsocket's working-class citizens were being called upon – as they never had been – to make a series of weighty decisions about the political future of their union and their community. Even before the experience of sustained, global warfare triggered dramatic changes in American society and international relations, the 1940s were becoming, for Woonsocket workers, the crucial decade.

Part IV

The crucial decade – and after,
1941–1960

8   The struggle for union power, 1941–1946

That liberalism of the 1940s was fundamentally continuous with that of the 1930s is still a commonplace among American political historians. Though allowing for liberalism's changed tenor from one decade to another, epitomized in FDR's transformation from "Dr. New Deal" to "Dr. Win-the-War," historians have generally viewed the 1940s as a time when liberals consolidated the essential reform initiatives of the 1930s and in some cases (such as the GI Bill of Rights and the Fair Deal) extended the reform impulse into new areas. Liberalism appeared imperilled for a few years when Senators Joe McCarthy and Robert Taft were ascendant in the Republican Party, but by 1955, as Eric Goldman argues in his classic book, *The Crucial Decade – and After*, the American people and their wise Republican president decided that the critical changes wrought in American life by the New Deal must endure.[1]

Organized labor seems a perfect case in point. Still fledgling in 1940, uncertain of whether its Wagner Act–inspired gains would survive, the labor movement doubled in size during the war and enjoyed by 1946 unprecedented institutional and political security. And though it lost its 1947 fight to defeat the Taft-Hartley Act and suffered significant membership losses as a result of its expulsion of Communist-led unions in 1949, the labor movement entered the 1950s with enormous economic and political muscle. Labor's leaders had become men of power.

Such a story could be told about the ITU in Woonsocket. It increased its membership substantially during the war years, it vanquished the remaining antiunion employers in Woonsocket, and it negotiated dramatic increases in wage and benefit levels that lifted thousands of Woonsocket workers out of their historic poverty. Such a tale, however, would be neither the most illuminating nor the most accurate. The union experience in 1940s Woonsocket was, in several critical ways, discontinuous with that of the 1930s. The radicals lost

---

[1] Eric F. Goldman, *The Crucial Decade – and After: America, 1945–1960* (New York, 1960); originally published as *The Crucial Decade: America, 1945–1955* (New York, 1956).

263

their grip on ITU leadership; the union lost the ideological independence that had enabled it to use the language of Americanism in ways that suited working-class needs; and Woonsocket workers lost the political advantage they had enjoyed, vis-à-vis employers, in the state-regulated system of collective bargaining. These three losses (which will be discussed, in turn, in this and the following two chapters) doomed both the ITU radicals' social democratic agenda and the surprisingly assertive corporatist campaign unveiled by the French-Canadian skilled workers when they came to power in 1945.

The 1940s, then, were a crucial decade for these unionists, though not quite in the manner outlined by Goldman and others. These were not the years when Woonsocket workers consolidated the tentative gains of the 1930s. They were instead the years in which workers relinquished the political dreams and ideological independence that had propelled their Depression-era movement to power. That a good part of this defeat occurred at the hands of a liberal state, and under the same president who in 1935 approved a labor relations law giving workers considerable access to federal power, suggests that liberalism itself had changed in some essential way. Indeed, an analysis of the propaganda that agencies of this liberal state were disseminating to Woonsocket workers during the war years (a subject taken up in the next chapter) reveals a marked weakening of liberal engagement with the labor question and an increasing absorption with the problems of racial prejudice and religious bigotry. This incipient transformation in liberal thought would profoundly affect organized labor in Woonsocket and elsewhere.

Spitz's bid for power, 1941–1943

This story must begin, however, on a more mundane note: the struggle between ITU radicals and ethnic corporatists for control of union affairs. The first year of the war gave little hint of the furious internal struggle that would soon engulf the union. A beneficiary of the industrial mobilization that brought a level of economic activity and employment that the city had not experienced in fifteen years, the ITU added ten new locals and thousands of members in 1942 alone. Unionists accustomed to chronic underemployment now encountered an inexhaustible demand for their labor. The combination of long hours and slowly rising wages brought to many quite dramatic increases in income; the union, too, found its coffers beginning to fill with funds, especially once the government's no-strike/union security deal with unions in June 1942 made union membership and dues payments virtually mandatory in every workplace where a union had won collective bargaining rights.[2]

The improving economic circumstances of individual members and of the union as a whole strengthened the labor movement in Woonsocket and enhanced its prestige. To many participants and observers, the day when the ITU would complete its transformation of northern Rhode Island society must have seemed near indeed. On Labor Day in 1941, the union staged a six-division parade of marchers, bands, and floats that surpassed its 1937 parade in size and extravagance. In April 1942, it moved into a spacious new headquarters where union leaders hoped to expand the services of their medical clinic and credit union. In November, unionists and their allies swept Ernest Dupré back into the mayor's office (he had been defeated in 1940), having extracted from him a public commitment to a widely circulated union agenda for municipal reform. And the ITU published a lavishly produced book celebrating its first decade, *Labor Review, 1931–1942*, bulging with photographs of ITU leaders and rank-and-file activists, containing a detailed history of the union's rise and accomplishments, and generally conveying to the public an image of strength, vigor, and vision. It was the most impressive document that the union had ever produced, befitting its dramatically increased size and confidence.[3]

Unity was central to the history of the union as it appeared in *Labor Review*. Unity was the ITU's "most precious factor"; it could account for the organization's remarkable past success, and it held the key to future progress.[4] Lawrence Spitz, who wrote the history, was careful to show how its absence at various times had weakened union power and resolve. Offering a surprisingly frank and grudge-free account of past internal conflicts, including those in which he had taken sides, Spitz appeared to be holding out an olive branch to the ethnic corporatists who now presented the most serious threat to the radicals'

---

[2] Interviews with Arthur Riendeau and Ernest Gignac, both on June 25, 1981. For the dramatic increases in union revenues see Christiansen and Company, "Report on Financial Statements of the Industrial Trades Union of America," June 30 and December 31, 1940, June 30 and December 31, 1941, and June 30 and December 31, 1942, Lawrence N. Spitz Collection, Mss 31 (hereafter Spitz Collection), Box 8, Rhode Island Historical Society, Providence, R.I. The ITU changed its name to Industrial Trades Union in 1941 on account of the growing number of nontextile workers in its ranks.

[3] ITU, *Labor Review, 1931–1942* (Woonsocket, R.I., 1942); *Woonsocket Call* (hereafter *WC*), August 30 and September 2, 1941, June 1, 1942; *L'Indépendant*, August 30, 1941; *Providence Journal* (hereafter *PJ*), November 4, 1942.

[4] ITU, *Labor Review*, 46.

power.[5] An outsider might plausibly have concluded from such evidence that the radicals and ethnics had decided to patch up their differences or at least declare a truce for the war's duration. Any such conclusion, however, could not have been further from the truth. If Spitz were indeed holding out an olive branch, it was only to buy time to prepare his own offensive. He saw the war years not as a time for rapprochement with ethnic corporatists but rather as the radicals' last opportunity to realize their social democratic vision.

Spitz believed more fervently than ever that affiliation with the CIO was a precondition to the realization of his radical ambitions. The cohering of a French-Canadian union opposition on the eve of war meant that the thousands of new wartime recruits could choose an ethnic corporatist future for the union and give men like Leona Galipeau and Eugene Thibeault the votes to oust the radicals from power. The union seemed headed in precisely such a direction when the 2,500 member Manville Jenckes local, the prize awarded the ITU in 1941 for its NLRB victory at Woonsocket Rayon in 1939 and 1940, fell under the control of a conservatively minded French-Canadian leadership.[6] CIO affiliation was necessary, to radicals' minds, to dilute French-Canadian strength.

The rise of a corporatist opposition was not the only factor pushing Spitz to affiliate the ITU with the CIO. He understood that the war years would be a decisive period in the history of the CIO – and thus in setting the course for the American labor movement as a whole – and he wanted to play a role in that coming drama. Spitz had opposed American involvement in a European war throughout the 1930s. Like most American labor leaders at the time, he saw war as a strategy capitalist elites used to increase their profits and to deflect attention from inequality and conflict on the home front. The fall of France in June 1940, however, made labor leaders' antiwar stance untenable, for they knew of the systematic destruction of rights and liberties that Hitler had visited upon his "enemies" and realized that Germany's expansion threatened the rights and freedoms of workers everywhere. The question that increasingly absorbed their attention was how to fight a war abroad without losing the fight for industrial democracy at home.[7] The answer, put forward most forcefully by CIO chieftain Philip Murray and UAW leader Walter Reuther, was that domestic mobilization had to be handled democratically. Murray and Reuther

[5] Ibid., 33, 35, 37.
[6] Interview with Lawrence Spitz, September 19–20, 1979.
[7] The turnaround in the *ITU News*'s attitude toward war dates almost precisely from June 1940. See *ITU News*, July 1940, cover. See also Spitz's article, "Dollar Patriots," December 1940, 4.

called for the establishment of industrial councils, which they envisioned as tripartite boards of businessmen, unionists, and government appointees representing the public, that would take charge of
the economy and supervise industrial relations. Such councils, if
established in wartime, would not only preserve but expand labor's
gains and set a precedent for a democratic form of national planning
in the postwar world.[8]

It is clear in retrospect that it was unlikely these ambitious plans
would have been adopted. The left-wing New Dealers whose support
was so critical to progressive labor's ambitions had lost the initiative
and power that they had enjoyed in administrative circles in 1936 and
1937. Even before the war, Roosevelt had begun to turn away from
social-Keynesian proposals calling for extensive government intervention into the economy's capital, labor, and resource markets and
to favor advisers who argued that the government should maintain a
healthy macroeconomic environment without interfering in the management or regulation of particular capitalist enterprises. Such arguments led to the elaboration of what Robert Lekachman has called
"commercial Keynesianism" – the government's use of its fiscal and
monetary powers to stimulate economic growth.

Although this ideological variant of Keynesianism had not yet
emerged as Democratic Party orthodoxy by 1941 and 1942, it clearly
influenced Roosevelt's approach to wartime mobilization. In particular it persuaded him to rely almost entirely on capitalist institutions to
supply the nation's war matériel. The government would seek to
stimulate such production by offering capitalists hefty contracts with
guaranteed profits, but it would otherwise sharply limit its economic
role. It would not build its own production facilities, nationalize
existing ones, or even seek for itself a partial managerial role. The
ascendancy of such economic views at the center of Roosevelt's administration dramatically narrowed the opportunities for the social-
Keynesian experimentation that left-wing New Dealers and their
labor allies favored. But their imaginations were still fired by the

[8] See Nelson Lichtenstein, *Labor's War at Home: The CIO in World War II* (Cambridge,
U.K., 1982), 26–43; Lichtenstein, "From Corporatism to Collective Bargaining: Organized Labor and the Eclipse of Social Democracy in the Postwar Era," in Steve
Fraser and Gary Gerstle, eds., *The Rise and Fall of the New Deal Order, 1930–1980*
(Princeton, N.J., 1989), 122–52; Ronald W. Schatz, "Philip Murray and the Sub-
ordination of the Industrial Unions to the United States Government," in Melvyn
Dubofsky and Warren Van Tine, eds., *Labor Leaders in America* (Urbana, Ill., 1987),
234–57; Philip Murray and Morris Cooke, *Organized Labor and Production* (New York,
1940); Clinton Golden and Harold Ruttenberg, *The Dynamics of Industrial Democracy*
(New York, 1942).

exhilarating political successes of 1935 and 1936; they still believed that their political program could triumph. Such a belief led these American social democrats to view mobilization for war as their second – the heady days of the Second New Deal had been their first – great political opportunity. Spitz was among them.[9]

By 1942 Spitz had eclipsed Schmetz as the ITU's most important radical. The internal union upheaval of September 1939, though resolved in favor of the radicals, had begun a subtle but steady transfer of power from Schmetz to Spitz. Spitz, who played the role of mediator in 1939, pleading with all union factions to restore the organization's unity, emerged from the fracas with a better reputation than Schmetz, who had had to cope with charges of "Hitleresque" behavior. The mobilization for war further enhanced Spitz's power relative to Schmetz, since it intensified ITU involvement in state and federal agencies charged with organizing the war effort. Although Spitz and Schmetz were equally committed to such involvement, Spitz, with his language and legal skills, was far more adept. This power shift from master to protégé would eventually prove too painful for Schmetz to accept, and would lead to a debilitating split between the two.

Spitz's growing power was apparent in the strategy ITU radicals chose to restore their power and enhance their social democratic vision in the early 1940s. No longer would the radical faction be content, as it had been in the 1930s, to educate Woonsocket workers on the benefits of CIO affiliation; rather, it would throw its resources into expanding the union beyond Woonsocket, not only into textile mills but also into other industrial sectors such as machine tools, clothing, and rubber. Sound reasoning stood behind this decision. If successful, such a campaign would bring large numbers of non–French Canadians into the union and perhaps even forge a non–French-Canadian ma-

---

[9] See Alan Brinkley, "The New Deal and the Idea of the State," in Fraser and Gerstle, *The Rise and Fall of the New Deal Order*, 85–121; Lichtenstein, "From Corporatism to Collective Bargaining." On the idea of commercial Keynesianism, see Robert Lekachman, *The Age of Keynes* (New York, 1967), 287; on its relationship to social Keynesianism, see Margaret Weir and Theda Skocpol, "State Structures and the Possibilities for 'Keynesian' Responses to the Great Depression in Sweden, Britain, and the United States," in Peter B. Evans, Dietrich Rueschemeyer, and Skocpol, eds., *Bringing the State Back In* (Cambridge, U.K., 1985), 185, 151n. On the government's approach to wartime mobilization, see also John M. Blum, *V Was for Victory: Politics and American Culture During World War II* (New York, 1976), 90–146; Paul A. C. Koistinen, "Mobilizing the World War II Economy: Labor and the Military–Industrial Alliance," *Pacific Historical Review* 42 (November 1973), 443–78; Bruce Catton, *The War Lords of Washington* (New York, 1948).

jority. Further, a successful campaign would diminish the ITU's dependence on textiles and thus enable it to survive the likely resumption of textile capital flight at the war's end. Finally, expansion would create opportunities for the ITU to cooperate with CIO unions like the rubber workers, clothing workers, and steel workers. Such cooperation, in turn, might bolster the CIO's image in Woonsocket and generate support in ITU ranks for an ITU-CIO affiliation.[10]

But Spitz may also have viewed expansion as a way to complete his triumph over Schmetz. It would magnify Schmetz's limitations – his lack of fluency in English, his lack of familiarity with industries other than textiles, his lack of ease in the burgeoning industrial-relations world of federal bureaucracies and intricate labor law – and thus erode his support among both his old allies in Woonsocket and the new members to come from the outside.[11]

The radicals' strategy bore fruit immediately. Six of the ten locals that came into the union in 1942 were located either in Mansfield, Massachusetts, an industrial town of 7,000 twenty miles to the northeast, or in Providence, twenty miles to the south. None of the six was a textile mill: The three in Mansfield – Bay State Tap and Die, S. W. Card, and New England Drawn Steel – were metal-working plants; and the three in Providence – Textile Finishing Machinery and Adolph Meller plants 4 and 7 – were machinery and gem-cutting plants respectively. These six locals brought 2,205 workers into the ITU, representing nearly 15 percent of the total union membership of 15,449. Textile Finishing Machinery in Providence and S. W. Card in Mansfield together accounted for nearly 80 percent of the new, non-Woonsocket membership.[12] French Canadians were conspicuously absent from the leadership of these new locals; Italians, Armenians, Irish, and Yankees – the ethnic spectrum usually associated with industrial

---

[10] The actions of the CIO's textile union, the Textile Workers Union of America – publicly condemning the ITU for its determination to remain independent, opening up a headquarters in northern Rhode Island to compete with the ITU – had done much to damage the CIO's image in Woonsocket. Interview with Lawrence Spitz, September 19–20, 1979. See also newspaper clippings and TWUA press releases in Textile Workers Union of America papers, US Mss 129A, File 10A, Box 13, Independent Textile Union folder, Wisconsin State Historical Society, Madison, Wis.

[11] Interview with Lawrence Spitz, October 22, 1976. Spitz has disputed this interpretation, arguing that his growing opposition to Schmetz was in the best interests of the ITU and did not reflect a personal desire to oust Schmetz from power.

[12] ITU, Executive Council Meeting, Minutes and Income Statements, 1943–44, passim, Spitz Collection, Box 8, RIHS; Spitz to author, May 11, 1977; *Providence Journal Almanac: A Reference Book for the State of Rhode Island* (Providence, R.I.), 1940; Rhode Island Division of Industrial Inspection, *List of Industrial Establishments* (Providence, R.I., 1944), 74–9. See Appendix A, sections IX, X, and XI, for names, locations, and sizes of these new ITU locals.

unions in the 1930s and 1940s – predominated. For the ITU, with its overwhelming French-Canadian majority, the emergence of such leaders signified a real change in union affairs.[13]

For Spitz the addition of these new locals represented only the beginning of his bid for greater union power. By early 1943, he had organizing campaigns well under way at a number of locations: at a Mansfield storage tank manufacturer, at two metal-working plants in adjacent Wrentham, at a rubber products plant in Warwick, Rhode Island, at a clothing manufacturer's shop in Pawtucket, Rhode Island, and at another metal-working plant in North Attleboro, just north of Pawtucket in Massachusetts.[14] He hired two full-time organizers, the first in the union's history, who were more loyal to him than to Schmetz: Gaston (Gus) LeBlanc, a French-Canadian union activist and communist sympathizer from Boston who had been recommended by the ITU lawyer, Samuel Angoff, a close friend of Spitz's; and Paul Ryan, who came out of the Taft Pierce machinery plant in Woonsocket, one of the few local industrial establishments that the ITU had failed to organize.[15] Spitz further solidified his hold on union administration by winning membership approval for an expanded Executive Board in which two vice presidents would be elected directly by the pro-Spitz workers of Mansfield and Providence.[16]

Spitz's successes in organizing outside Woonsocket and in internal union politics brought to a head his confrontation with Schmetz. The ITU expansion had indeed cut into Schmetz's support, both by adding many members committed to Spitz and by forcing an increasingly desperate Schmetz into making several poor decisions. The declining quality of his leadership became distressingly apparent in his attempts

13 Italians predominated in the first local committees of Adolph Meller and New England Drawn Steel; a mixture of Italians, Irish, Yankees and eastern Europeans comprised the first local committees of Bay State Tap and Die, S. W. Card, and Textile Finishing Machinery. Of those who would play prominent roles in ITU affairs, Frank Cinelli (S. W. Card) was Italian, Richard Arzoomanian (Textile Finishing Machinery) was Armenian, Herbert Marshall (Textile Finishing) was a Yankee, and Stanley Donlon (S. W. Card) was an Irishman. *ITU News*, August 7, 1942; September 18, 1942, 2, 5; December 18, 1942; March 5, 1943, 6; May 21, 1943; May 12, 1944. The lack of full membership or employment lists of these non-Woonsocket locals makes it impossible to analyze the overall ethnic composition of these various work forces.
14 Lawrence Spitz to author, May 11 and 19, 1977; *ITU News*, May 21, 1943.
15 Interview with Lawrence Spitz, September 19–20, 1979, and July 15, 1983.
16 *ITU News*, April 20, 1943. The change was not a complete victory for Spitz and his supporters. The union added six vice presidents altogether; in addition to the two from Mansfield and Providence, one was to be elected by the French-Canadian stronghold in Manville, and three were to be elected by Woonsocket unionists. The careful geographical balancing suggests a delicate compromise had to be struck between the radicals and the ethnics.

to bail out a small and inconsequential woolen mill, Tarkiln Woolen, located some miles outside Woonsocket. A friendship – perhaps an affair – with an ITU Council delegate whose husband worked at the financially troubled Tarkiln drew disproportionate amounts of Schmetz's attention. When the ITU's Executive Council rebuffed his request for union money to bail out the Tarkiln, Schmetz secretly invested his own meager savings.[17]

Why Schmetz embarked on such a foolhardy venture, risking not only his money but his integrity as a union man, remains unclear. But the consequences of his action unfolded quickly, and tragically. When news leaked out that Schmetz had invested his money in Tarkiln, becoming, in effect, part owner, a movement to oust him from the presidency flared into the open once more.[18] This time, unlike in 1939, Spitz was prepared to see him go. On August 16, 1943, Spitz publicly broke with Schmetz, declaring that in the upcoming election for union president, he would support Henry Heroux, a French-Canadian weaver from the Woonsocket Falls plush mill.[19] Spitz avoided any discussion of the Tarkiln incident and gave no hint that the opposition to Schmetz had shifted from the ethnic corporatists to Spitz's loyalists. Casting himself as an impartial observer acting in the best interests of the union, Spitz simply noted that "old wounds... against Schmetz's tactics and type of leadership" dating from the ethnic corporatist revolt of 1939 "have not healed and will not heal."[20] ITU welfare therefore demanded that Schmetz be replaced. The ethnic corporatists were themselves perplexed by this split in radical ranks, though by the time of the election a month later, they seemed to be swinging to Schmetz's support. Still, Schmetz suffered his first electoral defeat at the hands of ITU unionists, losing by eighteen votes

---

[17] Interviews with Lawrence Spitz, October 22, 1976, September 19–20, 1979, and July 15, 1983.

[18] Spitz believed that Schmetz, feeling outclassed by his (Spitz's) organizing successes, became desperate to prove that he, too, could organize mills outside Woonsocket. Interview with Lawrence Spitz, October 22, 1976.

[19] WC, August 16, 1943. Little is known of Heroux's background. He was forty-one in 1943, married, and father to at least four children. From 1932 to 1935, he worked as a weaver at Manville Jenckes in Manville, R.I. and became president of a UTW local there. He was fired in 1935, allegedly because of his inferior work but probably because of his union sympathies. He then found another weaving job at Woonsocket Falls, organized an ITU local there, and became its president in 1940. Textile Labor Relations Board, "Report of Examiner, In the Matter of Manville Jenckes Corporation, Manville, Rhode Island, and Local Union No. 1560 of the United Textile Workers of America, Manville, Rhode Island, 13–8," Manville Jenckes Corporation file, in Record Group 9, Entry 402, National Archives, Washington, D.C.

[20] WC, August 16, 1943.

out of 270 Executive Council ballots cast.[21] The next day a dispirited Schmetz gamely faced reporters and tried to find a positive meaning in his devastating loss. The defeat "was a surprise and a disappointment," he admitted, "but I feel that a great weight has been lifted from my shoulders, a great responsibility has been transferred.... I have had only seven days' rest in the past twelve years, now I'm going to settle down to take a well-earned vacation."[22] A year later he was dead, at age fifty-one, from stomach cancer.[23]

Spitz must have had mixed feelings about the September 1943 election results. He knew that the president-elect Henry Heroux, though well-intentioned, was no match for Schmetz in terms of intelligence or leadership ability.[24] He also knew – as did everyone else in Woonsocket – that he, Spitz, had lost his draft deferment and would be leaving for army service in a matter of days.[25] Spitz knew, in other words, that the ITU was about to lose its two most important radical leaders. He nevertheless persisted in his opposition to Schmetz, suggesting that he had come to two conclusions regarding internal union politics: first, that relations with Schmetz could no longer be salvaged; and second, that, because he had placed a number of his loyalists in important union positions, the ethnic corporatists could be kept at bay until he returned from his tour of duty. Following the September election, Spitz and his supporters did indeed control a majority of positions – six of ten – on the restructured Executive Board.[26] But their hold on the board was tenuous, and they would quickly lose it if the ethnic corporatists were to elect one of their own to occupy the general-secretary position that Spitz would soon vacate. Spitz, whether out of exaggerated self-confidence or desperation, had committed himself to a huge gamble: that the ITU radical faction, bereft of its crucial leaders, could hold onto power.

The ethnic corporatists' triumph, 1944–1946

That the ethnic corporatists would view the Schmetz-Spitz breakup as an unprecedented opportunity to seize union power was certain.

---

21 *PJ*, September 12, 1943.
22 *WC*, September 13, 1943.
23 *ITU News*, November 10, 1944, 2; *WC*, November 13, 1944; Schmetz died on November 11.
24 Interview with Lawrence Spitz, September 19–20, 1979.
25 *WC*, October 10, 1943; Helen Joly to Normand (last name unidentified), an ITU member, February 27, 1943, Spitz Collection, Box 8, RIHS.
26 Henry Heroux, president; Spitz, general secretary; and Angelo Turbesi, Paul Moussas, Herbert Marshall, and Stanley Donlon, vice presidents. *WC*, September 12, 1943; *ITU News*, April 20, 1943.

Their faction had undergone none of the internal turmoil that had afflicted the radicals. Rather, Spitz's expansionist strategy – and its ultimate goal of overturning the French-Canadian majority in union affairs – had had the unintended consequence of making their ranks more cohesive.[27] The roster of ethnic corporatist activists had changed somewhat since the group first coalesced in 1939. Victor Canzano had left the ITU for the CIO, and Bert Boucher had left mill and union work altogether to open a liquor shop.[28] Herve Gagnon of the French Worsted and Raoul Vandal of the Lafayette Worsted, minor players in 1939, increasingly committed themselves to the opposition's cause. Three new recruits, Gaetan Hemond of the Sidney Blumenthal local, Joseph Bell of the Joan Plush local, and Eugene Joly of the Manville Jenckes local, became especially active after 1943. The heart of the 1939 group, however, remained the same: Eugene Thibeault and Leona Galipeau of the Falls Yarn local. Born in the late 1890s, they were too old to be drafted. Unlike Schmetz, they remained healthy through the 1940s and thirty years beyond. They organized the assault on the radical leadership.[29]

They would execute no swift coup d'état; victory would elude them for two years after Spitz's departure. Spitz had left in place a skillful and hard-working staff, consisting primarily of his handpicked organizers, LeBlanc and Ryan.[30] He had developed a surprising depth of support among a large number of French-Canadian unionists who had come to treasure his honesty and effectiveness as a union leader.[31]

---

[27] Splits would later tear them apart, especially as it became clear that one of their top leaders, Eugene Thibeault, was an opportunist who had used the ethnic corporatist faction first to empower and then enrich himself; but few if any French Canadians understood Thibeault's true intentions in 1943. Interviews with Lawrence Spitz, September 19–20, 1979, and Leona Galipeau, October 22–23, 1980. Thibeault refused to be interviewed for this project.

[28] Interview with Lawrence Spitz, September 19–20, 1979.

[29] Letters to Lawrence Spitz from Gus LeBlanc, May 19, 1944, Henry Heroux, September 18 and November 30, 1944, and Angie Arturo, ITU office secretary, January 15, 1945, Spitz Collection, Box 8, RIHS.

[30] They were assisted by Henry Anderson, a CP-leaning *ITU News* writer and union educator who had come to Woonsocket through the WPA, and Sam Angoff, the Boston attorney intimately involved in ITU affairs since Spitz's arrival in 1937. This group was probably most effective among the union's non–French Canadians and in administering to the needs of the locals beyond Woonsocket. Letters to Spitz from Gus LeBlanc, May 19, 1944, Paul Ryan, September 14, 1944, Sam Angoff, November 28, 1944, and May 3, 1945, Angie Arturo, January 15, 1945, Spitz Collection, Box 8, RIHS. Interviews with Lawrence Spitz, September 19–20, 1979, and July 15, 1983, and with Sam Angoff, November 7, 1976.

[31] The leader of this pro-Spitz French-Canadian faction was Henry Heroux, the ITU's new president. See his letters to Spitz, September 14 and 18, November 2, 15, and 30, and December 18, 1944, Spitz Collection, Box 8, RIHS.

And his loyalists benefited from a series of blunders made by the ethnic corporatists in their bid for power. Most notably, the latter hired an incompetent lawyer to represent the union and elected to the union's general-secretary position in the fall of 1944 a politically naive man who, unable to handle the pressures of the office, suffered a severe nervous breakdown. Nevertheless, by the end of 1944, the ethnic corporatists had managed to capture four crucial staff posts – the two organizing positions, the editorship of the *ITU News*, and a newly created business agent job – and by September 1945 they controlled three of the top elective offices as well. The election of Herve Gagnon to the union's presidency that month – and the defeat of Heroux, the candidate of the Spitz loyalists – completed the ethnic corporatist ascension to union power.[32]

The ethnic corporatists moved quickly to remake the ITU in their religious and ethnic image. Before the month was out, these ITU leaders proudly announced the opening of the Woonsocket Labor School, a diocesan-sponsored effort to teach workers the principles of Catholic unionism.[33] That same month, articles written in French began appearing in the *ITU News*.[34] In October and November, President Herve Gagnon and General Secretary Raoul Vandal began unveiling, in speeches at the Woonsocket Labor School, the corporatist ideology that would now guide union affairs.[35]

The ethnic corporatists still had to deal with Spitz, however; their triumph was not yet complete. Five days after his honorable discharge from the army on March 18, 1946, Spitz marched into ITU headquarters demanding his old job back, arguing that the ITU Executive Council had passed a resolution when he left promising to reinstate him as general secretary for a period of up to ninety days after his discharge from the service. The corporatist leadership argued back that the union's obligation to reinstate Spitz ceased when his term in office expired in March 1944. Spitz managed to force this leadership to submit

---

[32] Letters sent to Spitz by his loyalists chronicle the ethnic corporatist bid for power in great detail. See those from Gus LeBlanc, May 19, 1944, Paul Ryan, September 14, 1944, Henry Heroux, September 18, November 2 and 15, and December 18, 1944, Sam Angoff, October 13, 1944 and May 3, 1945, Angie Arturo, January 15, 1945, Spitz Collection, Box 8, RIHS. See also letter from Helen Joly, February 5, 1945, Spitz Collection. An interesting aspect of Woonsocket factional developments in wartime was the relative unimportance of new faces. The battles were fought between veteran members and old enemies. New faces did appear, but they were generally integrated into the old factions without substantially changing the overall political configuration.

[33] *ITU News*, September 14, 1945, 2.

[34] The first actually appeared in ibid., August 3, 1945. See also the October 5, 1945, issue.

[35] Ibid., October 19, 1945, 1, and November 16, 1945, 1.

the issue to the Executive Council meeting scheduled for April 13.[36]

Still the tireless and meticulous organizer of his prewar days, Spitz threw himself and a band of loyalists into an energetic canvassing operation designed to reach every one of the over four hundred Executive Council delegates who would determine his fate.[37] He distributed a broadside on April 9 asking Executive Council members to honor the pledge made to him when he entered the Armed Forces in 1943.[38] He gathered endorsements from pivotal union figures like Henri Soubricas, a Belgian-born weaver who commanded considerable support among French-Canadian unionists.[39] And he tried to dig up dirt on the new corporatist leadership, coming up with a damning affidavit from a woman in which she admitted to having carried on a two-year affair with Eugene Thibeault (who was married) that had resulted in a child whom Thibeault had acknowledged but had refused to support.[40]

The ethnic corporatist leadership responded to Spitz's campaign with the most powerful and reliable weapon in its ideological arsenal: the charge that Spitz was a communist. They admitted in their own widely distributed broadside that the Executive Council motion of September 1943, did, in a strict legal sense, entitle Spitz to resume his duties as general secretary, but that he had forfeited his right to due process on account of the undemocratic, un-American, and unethical manner in which he had run the union during his years of incumbency. "Those who follow the Communist Party line do not like our American way of doing things," the ethnic corporatists announced. "They prefer, like Spitz, to invade a peaceful Union, split its membership, make unwarranted claims, lie and use every means, good or bad, to show that they are on the side of justice, smear the good name of anyone who dares to oppose their plot to exercise a virtual dictatorship over good Union members by calling their opponents Fascists." Since the corporatists could not prove Spitz's membership in the Communist Party, they dredged up old, unsubstantiated allegations from the 1930s, most of them made by the

---

[36] Lawrence Spitz to Herve Gagnon, March 29, 1946; Lawrence Spitz, "To All Executive Council Members," April 9, 1946; both in Spitz Collection, Box 8, RIHS.

[37] Spitz and his loyalists compiled complete lists of the local officers and Executive Council delegates of all ITU locals to aid them in their canvassing. Copies survive in ibid.

[38] Ibid., Lawrence Spitz, "To All Executive Council Members," April 9, 1946.

[39] Ibid., "Statement of Henry [sic] Soubricas," n.d. See also a two-page memo detailing the character endorsements Spitz had picked up over the years from Woonsocket politicians and businessmen as well as from his military superiors, n.d.

[40] Ibid., "Affidavit of Helen Cournoyer," copy, n.d.

Americanism Committee of the American Legion's Rhode Island Department. A rash claim concluded the broadside: "Spitz is the first American man in history to threaten that Great American Tradition: – Freedom of Vote.... DO NOT PERMIT SPITZ TO KID YOU – He is out to ruin your ITU because he cannot rule it."[41]

Spitz lost his bid for reinstatement at the April 13 Executive Council meeting by a mere four votes out of more than two hundred cast.[42] The inflammatory anticommunism of the ethnic corporatists, deployed in an incipient Cold War environment among a Catholic population deeply fearful of the communist evil, may well have spelled the difference between victory and defeat.[43] Spitz, though shaken, refused to concede defeat. He threatened lawsuits. He collected petitions from local after local demanding that the issue be referred to a mass meeting of all ITU members.[44] The corporatist victors, still fearing the outcome of Spitz's appeal, kept their anticommunist crusade, in public and private, at a fever pitch. Sometime in mid-June Spitz finally gave up the fight and accepted a standing offer of a staff job in the Providence subregional headquarters of the United Steel Workers of America (USWA), the most solidly anticommunist union in the CIO federation.[45] After a few months spent trying to raid ITU machine-tool locals, in part out of loyalty to workers whom he had once organized and in part out of revenge, Spitz concentrated instead on building USWA locals from scratch. Freed from the endless charges of communism that swirled around him in Woonsocket, he would become one of the state's most important CIO leaders over the next twenty years. When I. W. Abel defeated David

[41] Ibid., "To You Whom We Consider a Loyal Member of the ITU and a Good American Citizen," n.d.

[42] Interview with George Butsika, Angelo Turbesi, Ernest Moretti, and Livio Gramolini, all on September 14, 1984.

[43] The ethnic corporatists were aided in their anti-Spitz campaign by members of the Ligue Ouvrière Catholique and by Father Henry Crépeau, a priest appointed by the Providence bishop to teach the principles of Catholic unionism to northern Rhode Island workers. Crépeau wrote Bishop Keough on the occasion of Spitz's defeat, "With the use of every medium of publicity at our command and with the cooperation of the L.O.C. members in the different parishes we were able to muster enough strength to defeat Mr. Spitz.... We tried to organize our campaign of opposition as secretly as possible so as not to bring the Church openly into an issue which is considered by many as being a purely internal affair of the Union. I feel that we have been successful." Crépeau to the Most Reverend Francis P. Keough, April 22, 1946, Social Action Institute Papers, File 19–194, Folder 1, Providence Diocesan Archives, Providence, R.I.

[44] Seventeen such petitions, signed by the locals' leadership sometime between April 14 and May 31, 1946, survive in the Spitz Collection, Box 8, RIHS.

[45] WC, June 17, 1946.

McDonald for the USWA presidency in 1964, he selected Spitz to accompany him to USWA's Pittsburgh headquarters as the director of the union's Wage Division. As a USWA leader in Rhode Island and staffer in Pittsburgh, Spitz would enjoy a far more successful and rewarding union career than the Woonsocket unionists who ran him out of town in 1946.[46]

A good deal of backslapping must have gone on among the ITU's ethnic cadre in the early summer of 1946. Some interpreted their fifteen years of union membership as a struggle to oust the "outsiders" and to turn control of the union over to its rightful French-Canadian majority. The more thoughtful members of this group, schooled in the principles of Catholic trade unionism by members of the Ligue Ouvrière Catholique and more recently by clergy representing the prolabor Social Action Institute of the Providence Diocese, were eager to implement corporatist ideas in union affairs. But the period of corporatist experimentation would prove remarkably short. A number of the new leaders used corporatist principles of labor-management cooperation to legitimate their rise out of the labor movement and into management. Those who stayed in labor's ranks never enjoyed the independence that Spitz's ouster was to have brought them, for they had, in a sense, exchanged one set of "outside" masters for another. The new master, a powerful liberal state that emerged from its wartime mobilization in control of the language of Americanism and of the conduct of industrial relations, would increasingly determine the course the labor movement in Woonsocket would take.

[46] "Biographical Data of Lawrence N. Spitz," typescript, 1976 (prepared on the occasion of Spitz's receipt of an honorary degree from Brown University, June 1976), Spitz Collection, Box 2, RIHS. Interviews with Lawrence Spitz, October 22, 1976, September 19–20, 1979, August 27, 1980. Almost nothing has been written about the post-ITU period of Spitz's career. See "'We Want Integrity': An Interview with Al Sisti," *Radical History Review* 17 (Spring 1978), 181–190, and John Herling, *Right to Challenge: People and Power in the Steelworkers Union* (New York, 1972), 179–97. Considerable material on Spitz and his USWA activities survive in the Spitz Collection Boxes 2, 9–11, 15, RIHS, and in the USWA papers at Pennsylvania State University.

9 "Be American!": refashioning a political language, 1944–1946

As early as 1940, Spitz had worried that war mobilization might give capital and its allies the opportunity to regain the ideological offensive and reappropriate Americanism for their own uses. Spitz thus called on ITU members to make "the conservation of democracy" as central a component of National Defense as the "production of guns and butter." Conserving democracy "means guaranteeing to the people of America the right to work, the right to join unions of their own choosing, the right to speak freely and the right to share the nation's wealth." Americanism, Spitz continued, "must not become synonymous with suppression of people's rights. Americanism must still continue to mean to the average man the right to 'life, liberty, and the pursuit of happiness.'"[1]

Despite determination to oust Spitz from the union, the ethnic corporatists were as ideologically vigilant as he had urged, as patriotic as the radicals, and just as passionate in their commitment to democracy. Drawing on Catholic corporatist doctrines, they kept the union's Americanist discourse focused, for a time, on the industrial rights of workers and the pursuit of economic justice. They even began advancing, in words plucked from Americanism's traditionalist dimension, an aggressive, at times radical, critique of capitalism. But their radicalism, and the ideological independence from which it stemmed, proved fleeting. Increasingly they allowed anticommunism and cultural pluralism to dominate their discussions of what it meant to be an American. The sudden appearance of cultural pluralism in ITU discourse – apparent in the redefinition of democracy in terms of "brotherhood of man" themes – reflected the influence of the federal government in defining the meaning of the war and spreading the definition to every American city and town. Anticommunism, of course, had deep roots in Woonsocket Catholic culture, but events in Washington, especially the mobilization for the Cold War that began in 1946, would profoundly shape its local expression. The Americanist language of the triumphant ethnic corporatists, as a result, would increasingly depend on ideas and words emanating from outside

---

[1] *ITU News*, December 1940, 4.

Woonsocket and outside the working class. Less able to control the political language they embraced, Woonsocket workers would find it more and more difficult to fashion an American identity that truly served their needs.

Catholic corporatism

The union's French-Canadian leadership began disseminating its corporatist vision soon after securing its position in September 1945. The place accorded labor in this vision differed significantly from that which labor enjoyed in the corporatist vision ethnic insurgents put forward in 1939. In 1939, they had stressed the limitations on labor's rights, the existence of managerial prerogatives that labor could not touch, and the importance of harmonious relations with employers. In 1945, by contrast, these insurgents-turned-leaders compiled a long list of labor's rights, made few references to managerial prerogatives, and seemed little interested in industrial harmony. The rights of labor that the ethnic corporatists now stressed included the usual list: to choose freely a union, to bargain collectively with employers, and to strike. But they also included a more contested set of substantive rights, such as the right to a job, to a living wage, and "to a measure of ownership and control of the nation's economic system." Although no rights entitled workers to claim industry outright, the corporatists left ambiguous what exactly they meant by the worker's right to "a measure of ownership and control." This right might involve securing national legislation to raise the minimum wage, to improve social security and unemployment benefits, and to strengthen in other ways the nation's welfare system. But control might also involve curbing, eliminating, or redistributing employer profits. The leaders called at numerous points for profit-sharing plans, "taxing [employer] profits to the limits," and "a leveling off process" that would redistribute employer dividends "to provide those who labor and produce the wealth with the things they need to survive."[2]

The corporatists' emphasis on profits reflected the convergence of three lines of thinking. The first was the conviction that employers had profited enormously during the war because the government had, in effect, allowed them to charge whatever they wanted for their products. Wartime corporate profit taking was especially galling to workers whose wages were sharply controlled by the Little Steel formula of 1942, which had allowed only modest increases in wages beyond the wage rates already in place on January 1, 1941, before

---

[2] *ITU News*, May 17, July 20, August 17 (1,8), October 17, and November 16, 1945.

war mobilization and inflation began. The second line of thinking centered on the now widely shared Keynesian belief that the Great Depression had been caused by inadequate demand for the products of American industry. If the government, through some combination of profit taxes and wage increases, placed more money in the hands of America's workers, it would bolster demand and thus avoid a return after reconversion to the depressed conditions of the 1930s.

The third line of thinking, rooted not in the experience of war or in economic theory but in religious doctrine, focused on the immorality of excessive profit taking. Herve Gagnon, newly elected president of the ITU, spoke to this point in a November 1945 speech in which he said that "labor produces wealth and to deprive labor of its share is not only economically unsound, it is also immoral." Gagnon argued that labor gave rise to capital both historically and economically and thus was superior to it. Labor had conceded the right of capital to exist and manage its own property, but this right was a conditional one that capital would retain only as long as it was "just" in its management and protected "its people." He then warned that unless "American management wakes up and appeases the people" – by which he meant giving them a better share of the profits – the people would throw out capital's management, as they had done in Russia, and substitute their own. Gagnon did not want such an event to occur "in this grand and glorious nation of ours" but feared that it would unless management reformed its ways.[3]

Gagnon's aggressive impatience toward management – his demand that they "shape up" – was indicative of as striking a change in the ethnics' thinking as were their criticisms of the evils of profit taking. This aggressiveness, so different from the conciliatory temperament of ethnic corporatists in 1939, reflected in part changes that Woonsocket's economy had undergone since 1939. Corporatism had taken shape in the late 1930s as a response to the feared collapse of Woonsocket's economic base through mill shutdowns and to the recklessness of the ITU's radical leaders, who seemed hell-bent on bringing that collapse on. Corporatist advocates, as a result, had stressed the moderate nature of labor's demands, the realm of managerial prerogative that labor would not touch, and the desire for industrial peace at almost any price. The corporatists of 1945, by contrast, had seen Woonsocket industry invigorated by war orders and industrialists made rich by cost-plus government contracts. Prodded, moreover, by a restless rank and file, they were in no mood to empower industry further while continuing to accept government-

---

[3] Ibid., November 16, 1945, 1, 4–5.

imposed limits on labor's earnings and right to strike. They thus began to stress, at the war's end, the rights that corporatist doctrine accorded labor rather than capital.

Corporatists' aggressiveness reflected not only the changed economics of the postwar world, which set wartime government largesse toward corporations in sharp, and unflattering, relief against labor's sacrifices. It also reflected the diminishing authority of Woonsocket priests among the new ITU leaders and the growing influence of the diocesan Social Action Institute and especially of its director, Father Edmund Brock. The new union leaders turned to the Social Action Institute primarily because priests like Brock were more learned and enthusiastic about the labor movement than anyone in their city. Woonsocket priests' embrace of the labor movement had always had a negative quality to it: By supporting labor they hoped to bolster the campaign to oust the European radicals and Spitz from the ITU. They had never mustered much enthusiasm for establishing programs in labor education, on such topics as the principles of Catholic unionism or the history of industrial relations. Even the Ligue Ouvrière Catholique, which devoted a good deal of time to helping working-class families draw up budgets, seemed little interested in training Catholic union leaders to handle union finances or negotiations with management.[4] These tasks, as a result, fell increasingly to Brock and his associates.

Brock belonged to a younger generation of priests who came to religious and political maturity during the Great Depression. A significant number of these individuals, including Brock, came to view the condition of labor as the central moral issue in modern, industrial society. This perspective arose from their experience of Depression-era poverty, their dealings with the psychological scars of unemployment, and their exposure to the violence of labor–capital conflict. As a young seminary student in Paris, where he encountered the followers of the Belgian Cardinal Cardijn,[5] Brock first envisioned the social role that a priest could play. Cardijn had established several Catholic youth groups, including Young Christian Workers, Young Christian Students, and Young Christian Industrialists, to nurture in talented young men and women a Catholic perspective on social and political issues. These groups were not meant primarily to attract individuals to the priesthood or religious orders; rather they were meant to prepare devout Catholics for leadership positions in the lay community, where they could bring their religious perspective to bear on social problems. These programs in religious-political education had, by

[4] Interviews with Arthur Fortin and Phileas Valois, both on July 5, 1983.
[5] Interview with Mons. Edmund Brock, July 7, 1983.

the 1930s, attracted considerable interest in Catholic circles, not only in France and in Belgium but also in Quebec. The inspiration for Woonsocket's Ligue Ouvrière Catholique lay in Cardinal Cardijn's educational philosophy.[6]

These programs offered young priests like Brock an opportunity to play a much more direct role in addressing the world's social problems than traditional parish duties would have allowed. Brock would not, upon his return to the United States, seek to reproduce the same groups he had encountered in Europe, but he would embark on a quest to find a socially active role for himself within the Church. He enrolled in an M.A. program in social work at Catholic University of America and wrote a thesis on the sources of juvenile delinquency among the youth of Olneyville, an Irish and Italian working-class section of Providence.[7] He then enrolled in Catholic University's School of Social Science Ph.D. program, where he wrote a dissertation, under the direction of Monsignor John Ryan, on the development of collective bargaining in Rhode Island's cotton textile industry.[8]

Brock knew he would return to Rhode Island, the state of his birth, upon completion of his Ph.D., and looked forward to playing an active role in the state's labor affairs. Bishop Keough assigned him to teach Latin and Greek at the Providence Seminary instead. Undaunted, Brock sought out other young priests like himself who deemed the labor question more important than the teaching of classics. They met regularly to study the three papal encyclicals that addressed the question of labor in modern society and to make them "living" documents that would be relevant to the situation of labor and capital in Rhode Island. Out of their study group the Social Action Institute of the Providence diocese eventually emerged.[9] One of many founded nationwide in the 1940s, their institute, like the others, looked to Monsignor Ryan, the towering figure in Catholic social thought from the 1920s through the 1940s, for inspiration and guidance. The national prestige of Ryan was crucial to the establishment of these institutes, since many, like the one in Providence, ran into opposition from the older, more traditional priests in diocesan

---

[6] Interviews with Charlotte LeBlanc, July 16, 1981, and Arthur Fortin, July 5, 1983; see also Joseph Verhoeven, *Joseph Cardijn: prophète de notre temps* (Brussels, 1971).

[7] Edmund Joseph Brock, "A Study of Some Aspects of the Economic, Social and Religious Life of a Selected Group of Young Catholic Workers" (M.A. thesis, Catholic University of America, 1938).

[8] Brock, *The Background and Recent Status of Collective Bargaining in the Cotton Textile Industry in Rhode Island*, Catholic University of America, Studies in Sociology, vol. VIII (Washington, D.C., 1942).

[9] Interview with Mons. Edmund Brock, July 7, 1983.

hierarchies. Brock was long considered a dangerous radical, even a communist, by many Catholics both inside and outside the Church because of his progressive views on the labor question.[10]

Brock's fundamental principle was that economic relationships were moral relationships. He rejected the fiction that the market was a self-regulating mechanism that would tolerate no human intervention and the notion that scientific considerations of efficiency or technological considerations of productivity were paramount in determining the economic health of an industrial system. What mattered was how well labor and management could cooperate, which depended on how able they were to respect each other's God-given rights. Capital's rights consisted chiefly of the right to own property and the right to "receive a reasonable return for the productive use of one's property." Labor's rights, according to Brock, consisted of the right to a just wage which would allow a worker's family to live "decently, with a reasonable amount of security and freedom," the right to associate freely with workers and bargain collectively with one's employer, and the right of a worker to "share in a responsible, effective way in control over his economic and political destiny."[11]

Brock's reflections on the parameters of this last right – the most ambiguous and most threatening to capitalists' prerogatives – were cast in terms reminiscent of nineteenth-century republicanism. Private property, he argued, "is the material basis for...[man's] independence, and freedom. Psychologically, it is the most effective way of engaging his interest, and initiative, and of developing his sense of responsibility. Therefore the more widely it is distributed, the more wholesome, healthy and genuinely prosperous society will be."[12] But when property became concentrated, as it had, in the hands of a few, the right to private property was no longer absolute.[13] Rather, he argued, "it must be controlled and used so as to promote the independence and well-being of all members of the community." Though Brock preferred that workers and employers decide, independently of the government, how to control private property in the interests of the community, he believed that "the government has a positive

---

[10] Ibid.
[11] Father Edmund Brock, draft of radio address (WPRO, Providence, R.I.), September 25, 1947, 6, Mons. Edmund Brock Collection, in Brock's possession.
[12] Brock, draft of radio address (WPJB, Providence, R.I.), March 5, 1949, 3, Brock Collection.
[13] "The key problem [of the nation's economic system]," Brock commented in 1948, was "the concentrated control of our industrial resources in the hands of a relatively few men." Brock, draft of radio address (WPRO, Providence, R.I.), September 29, 1948, 2, Brock Collection.

obligation to protect the personal rights of workers and employers, especially those most in need, and to promote those institutions and policies which will bring about public well-being."[14]

Brock was equally committed, in theory, to the protection of workers' and employers' rights. But he felt that as a group, workers needed more protection. "Some would have you think that labor unions have employers over a barrel, that they are now in the driver's seat," he commented in a radio address in September 1948. "But consider, is control over wages and some working conditions of as much economic significance as control over prices, profits, and production schedules?" Had workers, he asked rhetorically, much to say on these issues? "We boast of our political democracy but we make light of our economic dictatorship," he pointed out, leaving no doubt as to his belief that a severe imbalance of power afflicted industry.[15] This was a bold, even radical stance to take in 1948, with Cold War passions reaching a feverish pitch and with large numbers of Americans favoring a rollback in labor's rights.

Brock was aware that his religious vision of economic relationships dovetailed neatly with an older American political vision, and he sought to make this connection explicit. In 1949 he remarked, "How glibly we repeat the immortal words of the declaration of independence: [']We hold these truths to be self evident that all men are created equal; that they are endowed by their Creator with certain unalienable rights.['] . . . But how slow we are to give practical effect to them in our everyday economic relationships. This is the challenge, however, which our generation faces, plagued as it [is] by wars, depressions, bitterness, and unparalleled tyranny."[16]

Brock's religious-political vision influenced the thinking of the new ethnic leadership in Woonsocket's ITU. He had established contacts with the ITU as early as 1940 and 1941 when he was researching his doctoral dissertation.[17] He formalized contact with the union when he established a labor school in Woonsocket in 1945 under the auspices of the Social Action Institute. The school was directed by Father Henry Crépeau, a priest who shared the ethnic background of the new ITU leaders but whose approach to industrial relations had been decisively shaped, like Brock's, by his Ph.D. work with Monsignor Ryan at Catholic University.[18] Crépeau conferred often with ITU

[14] Ibid., WPJB address, March 5, 1949, 4.
[15] Ibid., WPRO address, September 29, 1948, 2.
[16] Ibid., WPJB address, March 5, 1949, 6.
[17] Interviews with Mons. Edmund Brock, July 7, 1983, and Lawrence Spitz, September 19–20, 1979.
[18] Interview with Mons. Edmund Brock, July 7, 1983.

leaders, expounded his labor philosophy on local radio, and was even given a column of his own in the *ITU News*.[19] When Raoul Vandal, ITU general secretary, spoke in 1945 of labor's right "to a measure of ownership and control of our economic system" – the precise words used in a Social Action Institute brochure to publicize the diocesan labor school – he was revealing the influence that Crépeau, Brock, and their associates had come to have on the political vision of the ITU corporatists.[20]

The influence of the Social Action Institute on organized labor in Woonsocket was, in many ways, a remarkable development. Had an Irish labor priest like Brock attempted to minister to the needs of Woonsocket's French-Canadian Catholics in the 1920s or even early 1930s, he probably would have been run out of town and sent back to Providence. That Brock was embraced in the 1940s testifies to the declining significance of *la survivance* in the lives of working-class French Canadians, a decline attributable at least in part to their enthusiasm for an American, working-class identity. Such enthusiasm, in turn, reflected the realization among French-Canadian unionists that an American identity could accommodate their moral tradition-alism. Brock couched his economic critique in a religious sensibility that was profoundly appealing to Woonsocket's French Canadians: Economic relationships were *moral* relationships; a worker had the right to a *just* and *living* wage; a worker should share *responsibly* in controlling his own economic destiny. Brock argued that these words belonged not to any moral language; they were part of an American moral language that was rooted in the Declaration of Independence itself, in particular the phrase that asserted that "the Creator had en-dowed men with certain unalienable rights." Brock had placed God exactly where French-Canadian unionists felt he belonged – at the very center of American history. He demonstrated that a working-class Catholic could build an American identity – as well as a radical economic critique – around the traditional values of God, family, and religion. Many of Woonsocket's French Canadians wholeheartedly threw themselves into the task.

Anticommunism

Not surprisingly, Woonsocket's ethnic unionists also began to express their anticommunist sentiments in Americanist terms. Anticommunism had been partner to Catholic corporatism from the start of the Church's

[19] See, for example, his column in the *ITU News*, January 31, 1947, 1.
[20] Diocese of Providence, Social Action Institute, "Workers of Rhode Island Attention!" and "A Labor School in Your Community," 1946, Brock Collection.

involvement in labor matters in the 1930s. Pius's *Quadragesimo Anno*, which appeared in 1931, had portrayed corporatism as a response in part to the communist threat, a point that the Vatican reaffirmed and deepened in its 1937 encyclical, *Divini Redemptoris*. In the late 1930s, few issues occupied as much space in diocesan newspapers as the Spanish Civil War, which the Church portrayed as a struggle to the death between Christianity and communism.[21] Anticommunism, by 1939, had become as deeply felt a sentiment in Catholic communities as had devotion to Roosevelt and his New Deal. It broke upon Woonsocket society in the bitterly contested political election of 1938, fueled the ethnic-insurgent assault upon Schmetz and Spitz in 1939, and inflamed priestly sermons in 1940. World War II drove anti-communism underground for a time, as Roosevelt's Grand Alliance strategy demanded a positive portrayal of the Soviet Union and of its dictator, Josef Stalin. Some groups of liberals and radicals, discerning in the antifascist alliance the embryo of a new world order to be built on the principles of democracy and peace, readily interpreted the benign, smiling images of Josef Stalin as indicative of the Soviet Union's genuine interest in friendship with the West.

But in Catholic communities like Woonsocket, the accommodation with Stalin could never be more than a tactical maneuver, an evil that would be tolerated only as long as the war against the fascists had to be fought. This reservoir of anticommunist sentiment helps explain how quickly Cold War hysteria came surging forth in places like Woonsocket in 1946 and 1947 once the Truman Administration turned on the tap.

This resurgence in 1946 and 1947 does not mean, however, that anticommunism, or those who espoused it, were unaffected by the ideological crosscurrents of World War II. To Catholics, the evil of communism was to be found in its militant atheism, in its commitment to the perfectability of society, and in its relentless materialism. Communism's evil, in other words, lay in the challenge it posed to Christian theology, in which an all-powerful creator, the fallen state of man, and the primacy of the spiritual over the material were central tenets. These were the terms in which the ethnic leadership of Woonsocket had first presented the dangers of communism to Catholic parishioners in the late 1930s. The ITU ethnic insurgents, with the help of their Ligue Ouvrière Catholique advisers, had begun to transform this religious anticommunism by grounding it in secular democratic principles. War hastened this transformation to completion. By 1946, ethnic corporatists spoke of the communist threat not

---

[21] See, for example, *Providence Visitor*, April 1938, passim.

in terms of its godlessness but in terms of its threat to the American way of life. Americans had shed too much blood and made too many sacrifices to allow nefarious Reds to seize power and obliterate American values.

Americanist anticommunism made its public debut in October 1945, when the editors of the *ITU News* warned the membership that a "sprinkling of Labor Benedict Arnold's [sic]" had crept into the ITU's ranks.[22] But it did not emerge full-blown until Spitz returned from the army in early 1946. Then the ITU leadership began speaking in near-hysterical tones about the coming battle for the very soul of the American republic. On one side, the ethnic corporatists explained, stood the communists (represented in Woonsocket by Spitz) and their master plan for gaining control of American labor and then the American government. On the other side stood American democracy, American freedom, and the rights, privileges, and liberties guaranteed by the Constitution.[23] "A well organized minority," *ITU News* editors informed their readers in April 1946, "is trying desperately to rob you of all those liberties for which your boys have recently given their blood, including the freedom of organizing into an independent union.... You have got to be actively interested in preserving our American democratic way of life if you want to be a free workingman." The editors then offered readers a detailed analysis of Soviet society where a murderous "clique of Bureaucrats" kept "millions of good workers in slavery," denying them their rights to strike, to earn a living wage, to bargain collectively with their employers, and to choose their political representatives. Josef Stalin made America's most "'hard boiled' capitalists" look tame. His American representatives – members of the American Communist Party – posed as friends of the American workingman but were, in fact, his worst enemies. "Communist Phonies" in the ranks of American labor made the rats who are labor spies for the capitalists" look like angels. If they were to come to power they would quickly install a Stalinist "Workers' Paradise" – more accurately a "Workers' Hell" – in the United States.[24]

In view of "the danger of Communism to Unionism and American democracy," the editors advised, "it is absolutely necessary for every good American working man to find out the real Communists in his Union." Readers should demand that all self styled radicals in the ITU denounce communism and the Soviet Union. Call on them, the editors wrote, to "follow the example of one of our greatest leaders,

[22] *ITU News*, October 17, 1945, 2.
[23] Ibid., April 12, 1946, 1.
[24] Ibid., 1, 4–5.

the late President Roosevelt," who in 1936 repudiated "'the support of any advocate of communism or any other 'ism' which would by fair means or foul change our American democracy.'"[25]

References to God, Christianity, and materialism were conspicuously absent from this anticommunist broadside. Religion came up only once, in reference to the Soviet Union's denial of religious freedom to its people.[26] This was a secular, Americanist anticommunism, cast in terms of the danger it posed to American democracy, liberty, freedom, and way of life, that set the pattern for the many anticommunist tirades that appeared in the spring and summer of 1946. In discussing anticommunism, ITU leaders deliberately ignored the religious basis on which their sentiments rested. This was particularly striking in light of the fact that many of Woonsocket's French-Canadian Catholics still saw communism as the devil incarnate and feared that its advocates were determined to destroy all that godly men and women held dear. ITU ethnics could easily have incorporated religion into their anticommunism. They might have argued that communism was both un-Christian and un-American, or, alternatively, that the spirit of Christianity was closely tied to the spirit of American democracy. In early 1947, an ITU unionist fused patriotism and Christianity in precisely such a manner when he declared that ITU labor leaders "are not hell-bent on pulling down the pillars of our Republic. They are, instead, simple, God-fearing, good Americans, intent only upon justice for themselves and their children. Their philosophy is written in the Gospels of Jesus Christ, their objectives are inscribed in the preamble of our American Constitution."[27] But such frank associations of the Gospels and the Constitution were relatively rare. Among the ethnic corporatist leaders of the ITU in 1946, anticommunism had become a thoroughly secular, democratic creed, and they had become its apostles.

This particular construction of an American identity represented an ominous development in Woonsocket's working-class culture. In earlier renderings, in those initiated both by radicals and by ethnic corporatists, the Woonsocket workers' class and ethnic experiences had found expression in the language of Americanism. But the advocacy of this particular construction seemed as intent on denying a central aspect of that experience – the religious aspect – as on affirming the whole of it. The ethnic corporatist leaders may have been acting instrumentally, trying to downplay their religion for fear

[25] Ibid.
[26] Ibid.
[27] Ibid., February 13, 1947, 3.

of igniting another nativist attack (like that of the 1920s) on the Catholics as popish, authoritarian, and thus un-American. A too-direct affirmation of Catholicism, in other words, could have led others to question the civic loyalty of these ethnic Americans and their capacity for responsible citizenship. But if the ethnics' approach promised protection to Woonsocket's French Canadians against nativist censure, it also signaled their vulnerability to ideological manipulation by outside authorities who were using the language of Americanism for their own ends. This issue assumed a special urgency in the mid-1940s as the federal government began using the language of Americanism to shape local political culture and, in the process, to kindle nationwide support for world war. The sudden prominence, in 1944, of cultural pluralism in the thinking of the ITU ethnics, was a mark of how thoroughly the government's ideological preoccupations had penetrated local discourse.

Cultural pluralism

Cultural pluralism in the 1940s signified a belief in the right of every individual, in the United States and around the world, to life, liberty, and the pursuit of happiness, irrespective of creed, color, or nationality. The doctrine had drawn some support from intellectual, reform, and labor circles since the Progressive era, but it only moved to the forefront of popular political consciousness as a result of the nation's plunge into a world war against nations preaching racism and religious prejudice. Hitler's rise to power in one of the world's most technologically and culturally advanced societies forced many radicals and liberals to reconsider crucial assumptions that had long informed their politics: the absolute superiority of Western civilization, the intrinsic connection between industrial progress and moral progress, the preeminent role of capital–labor relations in determining the quality of social life. One could no longer assume that industrial progress, defined either in terms of the spread of economic abundance or in terms of the resolution of capital–labor disputes, would solve such "secondary" problems as religious bigotry or racial hatred. These problems were themselves primary; their distinctive roots had to be exposed, their baneful influence combated. This rapidly changing intellectual climate triggered an outpouring of books on racial problems and the fallacy of racist ideologies.[28] It triggered as well an

---

[28] The most popular work, of course, was Gunnar Myrdal, *An American Dilemma: The Negro Problem and Modern Democracy* (New York, 1944), 2 vols. Other important works: Ashley Montagu, *Man's Most Dangerous Myth: The Fallacy of Race* (New York,

intellectual (and increasingly popular) embrace of a creed, cultural pluralism, that insisted on the absolute equality of all people regardless of their racial or cultural character. The government, as part of its efforts to mobilize a polyglot population to fight a distant war (and to enlist intellectual talents and passions in the ideological dimension of war making), mounted a concerted propaganda campaign that stressed the centrality of cultural pluralism to the nation's war aims. Cultural pluralism quickly became the very essence of American democracy.

ITU ethnics did not actually use the term "cultural pluralism," preferring to express their support for the doctrine in such words as "a belief in the principles of equality and the brotherhood of man."[29] Accustomed to rummaging through American history for heroes who could be claimed as ideological forefathers, ITU leaders regularly invoked Thomas Jefferson and Abraham Lincoln as the champions of racial and cultural equality. Jefferson displaced Washington in the pantheon of nationalist heroes, becoming the preeminent Founding Father, for no phrase better embodied the cultural pluralist ideal than his "all men are created equal."[30] And the greatness of Lincoln, who had been the union's most revered hero from the first, was now to be found not in his prolabor sympathies but in his determination to make the tenets of Jefferson's Declaration applicable to all Americans, irrespective of color.[31]

The ethnic corporatists interwove their cultural pluralist ideal with American history just as the radicals had rooted their quest for industrial democracy deep in the nation's past. In late 1944, for example, they exhorted union members to "go back to the wisdom of Lincoln, and see where we made our mistakes" in order to understand why war was again raging. "We let a world of many peoples, of many faiths, races and nationalities become a 'house divided against itself,' nation against nation, White against Negro, Catholic against Protestant, Christian against Jew. And now, before we can put that house together again, many millions of the world's finest young men must die."[32]

The ethnic leaders offered no explanation for how such hatred had

Footnote 28 (cont.)
     1942); Ruth Benedict, *The Races of Mankind* (New York, 1943); and Gunnar Dahlberg, *Race, Reason and Rubbish* (New York, 1942).
[29] *ITU News*, August 21, 1944.
[30] Ibid., July 12, 1944, 8.
[31] Ibid., May 26, 1944, 2. Tom Paine was also cast as one of America's champions of "the struggle for Brotherhood and the building of a better world of free peoples." Ibid., June 21, 1946, 6.
[32] Ibid., May 26, 1944, 8.

been unleashed. They were confident, however, that they knew the antidote – democracy. "We shall protect and amplify. . .democracy in America and in every peace-loving nation of the world, so that the soldiers of every race, creed and color – the Colin Kellys and the Meyer Levins and the Dorie Millers, the black men and the white and the yellow, the Catholic, the Protestant and the Jew, 'SHALL NOT HAVE DIED IN VAIN.'"[33]

The invocation of Lincoln and his Gettysburg Address to support the cultural pluralist ideal may seem a rather straightforward attempt to borrow the moral force of one crusade in support of another. But there is more at work here. This passage, though admittedly failing to define its central ideal, democracy, surrounds it with associations very different from those used by the radicals of the late 1930s. No mention was made of industrial democracy; nor did the authors of this passage even hint that the democratization of the workplace was an important component of the democratic ideal. This passage was no aberration. In June 1946, for example, ethnic leaders declared that "one hundred and seventy years ago, the thirteen American colonies laid the cornerstone of American democracy with the stirring dec-laration that 'all men are created equal.'" Such a statement was very much in line with the nationalist efforts of the radicals in the late 1930s to identify their cause with the cause of the Republic. So too was a subsequent declaration that "American labor has always recog-nized its special stake in keeping democracy strong." But in defining the substance of that democracy, the unionists of 1946 veered in a sharply different direction from the unionists of 1936: "In the march toward a peaceful and secure future, workers of every faith, of every color and every national background stand side by side. The Spirit of '76 created a new and glorious nation. The Spirit of '46 – all races and creeds united for freedom – will carry us forward to an even greater tomorrow."[34] The radicals had not been unmindful of racial prejudice and religious discrimination, but they also believed that those prob-lems could not be solved unless the principles of American freedom and American democracy were extended to the workshop.

The ITU's new ethnic leaders did not forget about the workshop. Under the tutelage of priests like Father Brock, they fashioned an aggressive corporatism that aimed at a far-reaching redistribution of power in industry. It could be argued that the reconstruction of Americanism's democratic dimension to express themes of cultural rather than economic freedom was more semantic than substantive,

33 Ibid.
34 Ibid., June 21, 1946, 1.

that the union's fight for industrial democracy continued in spirit if not in name. It is certainly possible for a union to commit itself equally to the elimination of all forms of discrimination and to the extension of political freedoms to the shopfloor. But the last evidence of such a dual commitment comes from the fall of 1944 in the waning days of the radicals' union leadership. The proradical *ITU News* editors then advanced the proposition that only when labor was strongly represented in the regulation, even ownership, of essential industries and services, would the words "'life, liberty, the pursuit of happiness' become vital and meaningful." In the same issue they reprinted a 1939 editorial, written by Spitz, declaring that "democracy cannot succeed without economic as well as political freedom." In another article they condemned prejudice of all varieties – an early gesture in the cultural pluralist direction[35] – but hastened to add that "it will disappear from the earth" only when "political justice and economic security are guaranteed to all people." Union radicals, clearly unwilling to allow the government's wartime ideology to define union aims, were attempting, in these pieces, to make the wartime emphasis on fighting prejudice a part of their overarching commitment to economic democratization.[36]

Set against these radical efforts, the ethnics' tendency to equate "life, liberty, and the pursuit of happiness" with religious and racial equality appears a relinquishing of the union's oppositional stance. Part of the ethnics' acquiescence to the government's line was no doubt witting, a mark of how enticing the cultural pluralist message could appear to an ethnic group that had experienced as much discrimination as the French Canadians. From the start, French Canadians' attraction to unionism had been, in part, a manifestation of their desire to overcome the second-class treatment that their ethnic identity had conferred on them. The nation's decision to attach so much importance to the fight against religious discrimination appeared to them an unprecedented opportunity to integrate themselves into American life. This was the time, therefore, to embrace the government's mission as their own, not to sit on the sidelines suspiciously scrutinizing American war aims. French Canadians were not alone in their wartime embrace of a pluralist interpretation of democracy. To millions of ethnic Americans, especially Jews and Catholics whose families had come from eastern and southern Europe

[35] For the earliest gestures in this direction see ibid., September 1939 (cover) and December 1939, 4, 18.
[36] Ibid., October 13, 1944, 1, 2.

since 1880, the war was the historic moment when they felt fully accepted as Americans.[37]

But acceptance exacted a price. It required ethnics to subscribe – at least outwardly – to the moral relativism that lay at cultural pluralism's core. The doctrine held that Judaism and Protestantism were as valid as Catholicism, atheism as valid as theism, a secular, modern life-style as valid as a religious, traditionalist one. The pressure to embrace publicly such relativism may account for the absence of religious and theological referents from the ITU's anticommunism, for what defined the American way of life was not its Christian but its pluralistic spirit. All Americans, in contrast to the Germans, enjoyed the same free-doms, regardless of whether they were Jewish or gentile, black or white; Americans, in contrast to their Russian counterparts, enjoyed the freedom to embrace or reject a God-centered existence. The life of freedom and toleration that cultural pluralism promised no doubt appealed to many of Woonsocket's French Canadians, but others may have worried that such a modernist perspective would wreak moral havoc by displacing God, the Gospels, and the Church from the center of human consciousness.

Widespread embrace of cultural pluralism threatened to undermine not only the primacy of religion in the lives of Woonsocket's French Canadians but also, with its focus, in the 1940s, on the rights of individuals, the ethnic enclave's communalist orientation. Cultural pluralism had not focused, historically, on the individual at the expense of the group. Indeed, Horace Kallen, the country's leading exponent of cultural pluralism in the 1920s and 1930s, had first proposed this doctrine as a way of preserving ethnic *group* life. Seeing in cultural pluralist doctrine a dramatic alternative to the "100 percent Americanism" identity that the government and its allied American-izers wanted to impose on the country's diverse ethnic populations, Kallen envisioned American society as a federation of culturally autonomous ethnic communities, each maintaining its own language and customs while pledging its political loyalty to the federal govern-ment and constitutional system. Kallen never specified how such a federal system might work over the long term, nor did he expend much energy proving that it could work. Its importance was more symbolic than real: It served as a rallying point for those intellectuals

---

[37] John M. Blum, *V Was for Victory: Politics and American Culture During World War II* (New York, 1976), 147–81. The experience of American blacks and Japanese Americans was, of course, quite different; see Blum, 182–220, and John W. Dower, *War Without Mercy: Race and Power in the Pacific War* (New York, 1986), 3–190.

and ethnics who deplored the centralizing and homogenizing tendencies in American life.[38] By the 1940s, however, the exponents of cultural pluralism no longer talked in terms of creating a federal republic of autonomous ethnic *communities*. They talked, rather, in terms of bestowing a full complement of rights on every ethnic *individual*. The earlier ideal of endowing ethnic communities with autonomy was never directly attacked, but it was generally assumed that granting ethnic individuals equal rights and equal opportunities would pull them out of their parochial ethnic worlds and into a cosmopolitan American society.[39] This message was subtly but powerfully conveyed in those famous World War II scenes, appearing in numerous advertisements, movies, and novels, of ethnically and racially mixed groups of soldiers sharing barracks in basic training, quarters on troop ships, and fox holes close to the front lines. These images are rightly known for their espousal of ethnic diversity and tolerance, but equally significant is the fact that the tolerance and rapport they portray are invariably located in new milieus far away from the soldiers' ethnic homes.[40]

Many of Woonsocket's French Canadians – especially the enclave's youth – may have enthusiastically embraced this message of "ethnic escape." Among the thousands who saw many parts of the United States and the world during the course of military service, some undoubtedly began to imagine a more exciting and glamorous life for themselves than work in a textile mill and residence in a plain working-class neighborhood would have allowed.[41] Among the youth who stayed behind, especially girls, the appearance of furloughed

[38] See Kallen's "Democracy Versus the Melting Pot," *The Nation*, February 18, 25, 1915; *Culture and Democracy in the United States: Group Psychology of the American Peoples* (New York, 1924); *Cultural Pluralism and the American Idea* (Philadelphia, 1956).

[39] On this transformation see John Higham, *Strangers in the Land: Patterns of American Nativism, 1860–1925* (New York, 1975), 234–330, and *Send These to Me: Jews and Other Immigrants in Urban America* (New York, 1975), 196–230; Arthur Mann, *The One and the Many: Reflections on the American Identity* (Chicago, 1979), 136–48; Milton Gordon, *Assimilation in American Life: The Role of Race, Religion and National Origin* (New York, 1964), 132–159; Philip Gleason, "American Identity and Americanization," in Stephan Thernstrom, ed., *The Harvard Encyclopedia of American Ethnic Groups* (Cambridge, Mass., 1980), 31–58; Gleason, "Americans All: World War II and the Shaping of American Identity," *The Review of Politics* 43 (October 1981), 483–518.

[40] See, for example, John Hersey, *A Bell for Adano* (New York, 1944); Harry Brown, *A Walk in the Sun* (New York, 1944); and Ernie Pyle, *Here Is Your War* (New York, 1943) and *Brave Men* (New York, 1944). On the popularity of the mixed-platoon motif in World War II movies, see Thomas Cripps, "Racial Ambiguities in American Propaganda Movies," in K. R. M. Short, ed., *Film and Radio Propaganda in World War II* (London, 1983), 125–45.

[41] Such excitement is a recurring sentiment in the numerous letters of servicemen from

sailors from Newport, Rhode Island, strolling the streets of the Social District aroused similar sorts of romantic, escapist fantasies.[42]

But to substantial numbers of Woonsocket's French Canadians, especially of the older generation and the new ITU leadership, ethnic escape was anathema. They sought an autonomous communal life for their ethnic group, and they hoped that espousal of cultural pluralism would bring them closer to that goal. Yet they failed to incorporate these traditionalist communal concerns into their discussion of the pluralist ideal, focusing on the rights of individuals rather than groups. As in the case of their anticommunist broadsides, their political language came increasingly to reflect the ideological preoccupations of the government and of other groups outside Woonsocket.

Thus the ITU ethnic leaders' embrace of cultural pluralism cannot be understood simply in terms of the doctrine's intrinsic appeal to their ethnic instincts. It must also be seen in terms of the success of government propaganda in wearing down their ideological independence. The intensity that characterized the government's efforts to shape popular political discourse can be gleaned from the rabid "Be American!" government war-bond advertisements that appeared in the *ITU News* in the fall of 1944. Their appearance reflected the increasing government pressure being brought to bear on workers to give themselves wholeheartedly to the war effort.

Most striking about the advertisements is their inflammatory portrayal of the American people as full of "saboteurs," "snipers," and "Nazi agents" all working to deepen religious and racial hatred and thus aid Hitler's cause. These traitors were neither German soldiers nor spies infiltrating American life, nor were they American mercenaries servicing Hitler for the sake of money. They were, rather, average Americans who spread distrust and hate in casual conversations with friends and neighbors. One advertisement, entitled "Invitation to Commit Suicide," gave readers a sampling of the sorts of bigoted statements that friends so often and so casually uttered across lunch tables: "'Look out for the Protestants.' 'Hate the Catholics.' 'Attack the Jews'...'The workers are loafing.' 'Capital is profiteering.' 'The Negro is rebelling.' 'Refugees are taking the best jobs.' 'The farmers are trying to rob you.'" Such bigotry, the advertisement warned, aided Hitler's cause: "The more Americans fighting each other at

Woonsocket and Manville published in *The Manville Eagle*, the Manville Jenckes Corporation's monthly newsletter, from September 1944 to December 1945; Slater Mill Historic Site (hereafter SMHS), Pawtucket, R.I.
[42] Interview with Charlotte LeBlanc, July 16, 1981.

home, the fewer he will have to meet on the field of battle." Americans realized the harm that such internal bickering caused in other lands. But, the advertisement admonished its readers, "are you *keen* enough to recognize it here in America... in your own intimate circle? Are you *smart* enough to reject this invitation [to self destruction]? Are you *patriotic* enough to see that your family, your neighbors, the people you work with, reject it too? If you do this... *and not unless you do*... then you will help America rise to its full stature as a nation fighting for the rights of all humanity." "Be American!" the advertisement concluded in an exhortatory tone, followed by the command, "Buy War Bonds Regularly."[43]

The same admonitions to desist from casual bigotry and the same exhortations to "Be American!" structured the other four advertisements in this series.[44] One accused the mother of two servicemen of spreading "hatred and distrust among groups of Americans" even as she diligently knitted sweaters for her sons in the service, sent them chocolate cakes, and urged her husband to purchase more war bonds. This she did by making "thoughtless remarks" about neighbors "who go to a different church," and "about folks whose skin is a different color, or whose names are hard to pronounce." "As surely as though you landed on these shores in the dark of night from a submarine, bent on blowing up factories and burning bridges," the advertisement charged this witless mother, "in spite of your charming manner and your 'all-out' war record, lady, *you* are a saboteur."[45]

These advertisements and their insistence on the necessity of eliminating all forms of bigotry from American life can be seen as admirable responses to the distressingly heightened level of racial tension between black and white workers both on the shopfloor and in cities, like Detroit and Philadelphia, where large numbers of black migrants had recently settled; persistent anti-semitism was another disturbing sign of prejudice during the war years.[46] Moreover, the

---

[43] *ITU News*, September 15, 1944.

[44] Ibid., Labor Day, September 30, October 13 and 27, 1944.

[45] Ibid., September 30, 1944.

[46] August Meier and Elliott Rudwick, *Black Detroit and the Rise of the UAW* (New York, 1979) 108–74; Joshua Freeman, "Delivering the Goods: Industrial Unionism during World War II," *Labor History* 19 (Fall 1978), 574–91; Blum, *V Was for Victory*, 182–220; Richard Polenberg, *War and Society: The United States, 1941–1945* (Philadelphia, 1972), 99–130; Allan M. Winkler, "The Philadelphia Transit Strike of 1944," *Journal of American History* 59 (June 1972), 73–89; Harvard Sitkoff, "The Detroit Race Riot of 1943," *Michigan History* 53 (Fall 1969), 183–206; Robert Shogan and Tom Craig, *The Detroit Race Riot: A Study in Violence* (Philadelphia, 1964). On anti-Semitism, see the following: Higham, *Send These to Me*, 174–95; Leonard Dinnerstein, *Uneasy at Home: Antisemitism and the American Jewish Experience* (New York, 1987); David Gerber, ed., *Anti-Semitism in American History* (Urbana, Ill., 1986).

advertisements' recognition that private conversations among family members, friends, and neighbors were crucial to the maintenance of racial and religious stereotypes reflected a sophisticated understanding of the transmission of bigotry. In light of the idealistic message these advertisements promulgated and the psychological knowledge of race hatred they reflected, it seems somewhat incongruous that their creators should have chosen to transmit the message through hysterical accusations of disloyalty, betrayal, and backstabbing. They might have shown more respect for the intelligence and goodwill of average Americans by conveying the same message in a calmer, more sober manner, letting the grim facts indicative of rising racism and religious bigotry speak for themselves. The advertisements' rabid tone may have been the consequence of superheated war patriotism run amok, or it may reflect a deliberate effort by the advertisements' creators – probably working out of the War Advertising Council and U.S. Treasury Department offices – to challenge the loyalty of individual Americans as a way of intimidating them into ever more reflexive devotion to the cultural pluralist ideal (and, in the bargain, to purchase war bonds). In either case, the government was playing on loyalty and betrayal, honor and dishonor – among the most powerful of human emotions – in its attempt to deepen the American people's commitment to the war effort and, just as importantly, to the government's definition of the war's aims.[47]

These advertisements were one part of a larger government-sponsored loyalty campaign that involved extensive use of newspapers, radio, and agents of the various federal bureaucracies, such as the War Labor Board, the Treasury Department, and branches of the armed forces, to present the government's goals to various publics. The government, in other words, was exerting extraordinary ideological pressure on individual Americans to support a particular set of war aims.[48] Union leaders of the 1940s, regardless of their political

[47] A war ad appearing in the *Woonsocket Call* on September 13, 1943, noted that it had been "prepared under auspices of the War Advertising Council in cooperation with the U.S. Treasury Department." On the government's decision to rely on the advertising industry to make the case for war bond purchases see Frank W. Fox, *Madison Avenue Goes to War: The Strange Military Career of American Advertising* (Provo, Utah, 1975). See also Blum, *V Was for Victory*, 16–21, and Richard Polenberg, *One Nation Divisible: Class, Race, and Ethnicity in the United States since 1938* (Harmondsworth, U.K., 1980), 49–50.

[48] Few works have tried to grasp the government's propaganda campaign in all its manifestations. See Allan M. Winkler, *The Politics of Propaganda: The Office of War Information, 1942–1945* (New Haven, Conn., 1978); K. R. M. Short, ed., *Film and Radio Propaganda in World War II* (London, 1983); and Blum, *V Was for Victory*, 15–52. Detailed and suggestive work has been done on particular aspects of the government's campaign, especially in connection with its effort to define a wartime

beliefs, were particularly vulnerable to that pressure. The govern
ment, in return for offering unions an unprecedented degree of institutional security during World War II, expected union leaders to
secure from their memberships the maximum productive effort and
maximum war-bond purchases. If union leaders refused to uphold
their part of the bargain, they risked the withdrawal of government
support for their unions. In their own minds, no doubt, it became
increasingly difficult to separate the government's political demand
for uninterrupted production from the government's ideological
demand for unquestioning adherence to its war aims.[49] Thus, as the
ITU leaders urged their members to adhere to the no-strike pledge
and to meet their assigned quotas for war-bond purchases, they increasingly portrayed their nation as threatened by the same kind of
internal dissension that the war-bond advertisements had so hysteri-
cally dramatized. In their 1944 Christmas message, for example, the
ITU leadership noted that "one of the toughest battles of all" had
been fought by American workers on American soil "against the self-
seeking few in our midst who have played the enemy's game of 'divide
and conquer,' . . . dividing us into warring groups – Christians against
Jews, Protestants against Catholics, Whites against Negroes, management against labor." Fortunately, the message continued, "those
who tried to spread discord in America have been thwarted," and the
American people "still remain a proud nation of free men working
together to preserve and strengthen our liberties. That is the way our
forefathers planned America. And that's the way we intend to keep
her, in spite of the rabble-rousers, labor baitors, anti-Semites and race
supremacy addicts who would like to work Hitler's racket over here."[50]
Whether consciously or not, ITU leaders had made the government's
construction of Americanism's democratic dimension their own.

Although the wartime sentiments of rank and filers are, for the
most part, unrecorded, the weight of evidence suggests that, like
union leaders, many subscribed to the cultural pluralist ideal. The
French-Canadian majority had experienced the same bitter history of
discrimination and second-class citizenship as had its ethnic leader-

Footnote 48 (cont.)
    role for women in a way that did not permanently alter established gender roles. See
    Karen Anderson, *Wartime Women: Sex Roles, Family Relations, and the Status of Women
    During World War II* (Westport, Conn., 1981); Maureen Honey, *Creating Rosie the
    Riveter: Class, Gender, and Propaganda During World War II* (Amherst, Mass., 1984);
    Leila J. Rupp, *Mobilizing Women for War: German and American Propaganda, 1939–1945*
    (Princeton, N.J., 1978).
[49] Nelson Lichtenstein, *Labor's War at Home: The CIO in World War II* (Cambridge, U.K.,
    1983), 178–202.
[50] *ITU News*, December 15, 1944 (misspellings and typographical errors corrected).
    Women had no place in the ITU's pluralist vision of "a proud nation of free men."

ship; so, too, had the union's several other ethnic groups – Poles, Slavs, and Italians. Although these rank and filers may not have felt the same government pressures for conformity as their leaders, they nevertheless had a deep, personal stake in the war effort. Fifteen hundred ITU members – one of every ten unionists – served in the armed forces during the war.[51] Woonsocket sent 6,000 servicemen and women – more than 10 percent of the city's population – to war, and many of them were the children or relatives of union members.[52] No single union activity in the years 1941 to 1945 occupied more time or involved more members than war-bond drives and servicemen support committees. Several union locals regularly oversubscribed the war-bond quota assigned them.[53] In February 1944, Woonsocket became the nation's first city to surpass its bond quota in the government's Fourth War Loan Campaign.[54] The next month ITU members received the news that they had made Woonsocket into the American city with the second highest per capita contributions to the Russian War Relief Society.[55] Servicemen committees in virtually every local raised money through dances or through the profits of plant vending machines and cooperative cafeterias to send checks, gift packages, and letters to their members in the armed forces.[56]

Participation in the war effort was common to all locals, irrespective of their particular ethnic or political orientation. It was as strong in the Falls Yarn, the ethnic corporatists' base, as in the French Worsted and Lafayette Worsted, where Franco-Belgians still occupied important local leadership positions. It was as evident in the locals in Providence and Mansfield where few French Canadians worked as in the Manville Jenckes mill with its large French-Canadian majority.[57] Anecdotal

---

[51] Ibid., May 11, 1945, 1.

[52] Woonsocket Chamber of Commerce, Planning Commission, "Survey of Industry in Woonsocket," reprinted in ibid., July 28, 1944, 1, 4.

[53] See, for example, reports in ibid., on the following locals: Masurel Worsted, September 18, 1942 and January 9, 1943; U.S. Rubber, February 15, 1944, and July 12, 1944, 6; Woonsocket Falls and Clinton Plush, March 10, 1944, 3, July 28, 1944, 4, and December 15, 1944, 3.

[54] Ibid., February 23, 1944, 2.

[55] Ibid., March 24, 1944.

[56] See, for example, reports in ibid., on following locals: Alsace, December 4, 1942; American Wringer, June 18, 1943; Sidney Blumenthal, March 24, 1944; Dunn Worsted, March 5, 1943, and April 27, 1945; Masurel Worsted, March 10, 1944; Montrose Worsted, January 28, 1944, September 15, 1944, 4, October 13, 1944, 6, October 27, 1944, and August 3, 1945, 6; Riverside Worsted, August 21 and September 4, 1942; and Woonsocket Spinning, September 29, 1944.

[57] See reports in ibid., on the following locals: Falls Yarn, August 21, 1942, and October 24, 1942; French Worsted, September 18, 1942, February 11, 1944, and March 10, 1944; Lafayette Worsted, April 7, 1944, and May 11, 1945; Adolph Meller (Providence),

testimony adds to the weight of evidence suggesting a profound rank-and-file commitment to the war effort. Pat Murphy, an Irish skilled lathe operator in the Textile Finishing Machinery Local, impressed his union steward one day, turning out five pieces rather than the assigned four, saying it was a birthday gift to his son in the armed forces.[58] Phillipe Plante, a French-Canadian watchman at Woonsocket Spinning, achieved union recognition for solemnly saluting the mill's American flag every day before lowering it.[59] A score of French and Belgian union members, many of whom fought the Germans in World War I, began morale-boosting, short-wave radio broadcasts to the forces of resistance in their native lands.[60] Emily Hart of the Lafayette Doubling Department, a French-Canadian woman with a husband in the navy and a brother in the army, donated five pints of blood to the Red Cross plasma drive.[61] And Mary Bednarchuk, an aging Polish gill-box operator at the Rosemont who wanted to retire from mill work, was determined to "keep going until the war is over" as a demonstration of support for her son, a much decorated aerial gunner, and his fellow soldiers.[62]

It is likely that many rank and filers cared less about the government's stated war aims than about getting a loved one home alive. Some no doubt grew perturbed at the endless appeals to patriotism that always concluded with a request for more money.[63] Rank and filers, as we shall see, would demonstrate a greater capacity than their leadership for challenging the government's wartime authority. Still, cultural pluralism's intrinsic appeal, together with the average worker's personal investment in the war, made a skeptical, detached attitude toward the country's war aims difficult to maintain. Mary

Footnote 57 (cont.)
February 11, 1944; Textile Finishing Machinery (Providence), April 20, 1943; S. W. Card (Mansfield), March 5, 1943, February 28, 1944, and November 30, 1944; and Manville Jenckes, August 21, 1942, January 9, 1943, March 10, 1944, April 7, 1944, July 12, 1944, and July 30, 1944.

[58] Ibid., May 21, 1943.

[59] Ibid., December 18, 1942.

[60] Providence Journal, October 25, 1942. See also photograph of Franco-Belgian Relief Club. This club aided French and Belgian refugees in the United States and sent packages to allied nations abroad. U.S. Office of War Information (hereafter OWI), "French Americans and Their Activities During the Second World War," 1944, Lot 3895, Prints and Photographs Division, Library of Congress, Washington, D.C.

[61] ITU News, April 27, 1945. A remarkable number of women – 10,000 – volunteered for Woonsocket's Red Cross chapter. See photograph of three Woonsocket Red Cross volunteers in U.S. OWI, "French Americans and Their Activities," Lot 3895, Prints and Photograph Division, Library of Congress.

[62] ITU News, July 12, 1944.

[63] See, for example, ibid., March 10, 1944, 7.

Rednaichuk, whose stated loyalty was to her son, not her nation, nevertheless lavished great attention on her son's many medals and diligently collected the newspaper and magazine clippings describing his heroic acts. In such ways did loyalty to kin merge imperceptibly with patriotic feeling.

The danger of internalizing a government-sponsored patriotism lay in the possibility that Woonsocket workers might, as a result, lose control of the language of Americanism and of defining what it meant to "be American." Since the early Depression years, ordinary working-class Americans like those in Woonsocket had enjoyed a period of ideological independence characterized by their ability to use the language of Americanism to express the inequality between capital and labor and the corresponding need to elaborate for themselves a new series of industrial rights. The government's campaign for cultural pluralism could erode this class-based construction of Americanism. It challenged, on the one hand, the notion that the relations between capital and labor formed the central political and moral question of modern American life and obscured, on the other, the fundamental inequality in capital-labor relations that had been so central to progressive Americanism of the 1930s. The subjugation of labor to capital that 1930s radicals had viewed as the great, overriding injustice of modern life became, in the hands of 1940s ethnics, just one of several kinds of deplorably unethical behavior. Thus, the sentiment that "Capital is profiteering" expressed bigotry no different from that imbedded in such inflammatory, groundless exhortations as "Hate the Catholics" and "Attack the Jews."[64] In a "Be American!" advertisement intended to counter Hitler's claim that "America is weak because American blood is tainted by many strains," the text proudly noted the range of individuals – "Catholic and Protestant, Jew and Gentile, laborer and capitalist, Democrat and Republican" – that had donated blood to save a hypothetical American soldier, one Private Parkins. As in cultural pluralist thought in general, capital–labor conflict here became one of several forms of prejudice arising from malicious, racist doctrines. Adherence to the American creed of the equality of all men would lead capital and labor, as it would Catholics and Protestants, Jews and Gentiles, whites and blacks, to respect each other, mend their differences and live harmoniously. No fundamental inequality, in other words, inhered in relations between any of these two groups.[65]

[64] Ibid., "Invitation to Commit Suicide," September 15, 1944.
[65] Ibid., "Whose Blood Saved Private Parkins?" October 13, 1944.

Cultural pluralist thinking, as we shall see, in Chapter 10, contributed to the triumph of a pluralist model of industrial relations in the postwar years. But there was another, more general danger implicit in the government's wartime campaign to shape the American people's patriotism. Those Americans who accepted the government's patriotic vision whether by reason of persuasion or intimidation, might find themselves increasingly acquiescent to other exercises of the government's ideological authority. This subservience could prove especially dangerous to workers and union leaders in the scramble for political and economic power that peace abroad would undoubtedly unleash at home. American capital had restored its productive system and its public image during World War II and would move aggressively to maintain its profits and popularity in the postwar period. Labor would thus have to fight tooth and nail to wrest from the government the major role in the nation's political economy that CIO leaders had long dreamed about. Labor, therefore, could not afford to acquiesce to the exercise of governmental authority.

Resistance and capitulation to national authority

For a brief period in the summer and fall of 1945 the ITU seemed to be holding government authority at bay. Rather than allow cultural pluralism to encroach on its practice of industrial relations or allow the government to dictate its political approach to reconversion, the ITU began brandishing an aggressive corporatism that would return the union to the fiercely independent course it had set in the prewar years.

One impetus for this aggressive corporatism came from the teachings of Father Brock, another from rank-and-file unionists who were increasingly determined to wrest wage and benefit improvements from employers even if that meant disregarding the government's labor relations administration and violating the union's no-strike pledge. In this respect, ITU unionists were expressing the same sentiments as their counterparts across the country. Wildcat strikes, increasing in frequency, size, and duration throughout 1943 and 1944, reached massive proportions by the summer of 1945. This militancy reflected the strain of extremely long work weeks, the arbitrary way in which many foremen exercised their shopfloor authority, and the persistent refusal of the government, obsessed by fears of unleashing an uncontrollable inflationary spiral, to reward employee efforts with significant wage increases. As the perception spread that the War Labor Board was not responsive enough to employee grievances, refusing to grant demands for wage adjust-

ments and to handle cases with dispatch, workers increasingly resorted to their most traditional and powerful weapon – the strike.[66]
The ITU leadership, fearing, like most other industrial union leaders, that such strikes endangered their union's standing with the
government, did not like to own up to strikes, actual or threatened,
by their members.[67] News of strike actions nonetheless began creep-
ing into the local press. The workers of Verdun Worsted successfully
struck for union recognition in 1943; a crew of rubber-boat assemblers
walked off the job at the local U.S. Rubber plant in April 1944 and did
not return until the company granted them a piece-rate increase; and
a threatened strike by Woonsocket Rayon workers in late 1944 forced
the War Labor Board to award them a two-week vacation with pay.[68]
The ITU leadership portrayed these incidents as isolated and exceptional. But when the 3,500 "fighting mad" workers of the French
spinning mills served their employers with a thirty-day strike notice
on June 3, 1945, the leadership could no longer pretend that the
membership was still honoring the no-strike pledge. When the regional
War Labor Board, desperate to avoid a strike, capitulated in July to
French spinning locals' demands for two-weeks' paid vacation, an
increase in the minimum wage, and employer-paid Blue Cross hospitalization insurance for all employees, ITU leaders hailed the militance
of their rank and file.[69]
Militant rank-and-file activity continued apace, despite the climactic
battle for union power between the radicals and ethnics in September
1945. When the newly organized Sydney Worsted workers struck for
a month, beginning in late September, to demand that their employer
grant them a union shop, all ITU factions closed ranks behind them.[70]
Soon thereafter, Raoul Vandal and Herve Gagnon set forth their
aggressive corporatist vision in speeches to the Church-sponsored
Woonsocket Labor School. They warned of "a new era of capitalist
domination if management through the abolition of excess-profit
taxes is allowed once more to build up a financial power that may
erase all gains of the past decade."[71] They called for a series of
measures, including price regulation and a guaranteed annual wage
for every worker, that would have required the government to
maintain, and even increase, the extensive array of economic controls

[66] Lichtenstein, *Labor's War at Home*, 110–35.
[67] See, for example, *ITU News*, May 11, 1945.
[68] *Providence Journal*, March 16, 1943; *Woonsocket Call*, March 20, 1943; *ITU News*, April
21, 1944, and May 25, 1945.
[69] *ITU News*, June 29, July 20, and August 3, 1945.
[70] Ibid., October 17, 1945.
[71] Ibid.

it had instituted during the war.[72] When President Harry Truman began wavering in his determination to extend such controls in the fall of 1945, ethnic leaders went so far as to call on the ITU rank and file to do "some serious thinking" about "independent political organization by labor." "Should a period of contemplation and discussion of the possibilities of a third party – independent political action – develop into something really concrete on a national scale, it might hold the balance of power in 1948."[73]

These bold declarations in the fall of 1945 not only stood in sharp contrast to the ethnics' rejection of independent political action in the prewar years; they also called for as fundamental a restructuring of the economy and of political alignments as any plan being discussed by noncommunist unionists elsewhere.[74] These sentiments suggested that the ITU's new leaders had managed to maintain their ideological independence from the Truman Administration and that they were fashioning an effective political vision to guide the ITU through the difficult period of reconversion. These new leaders even demonstrated a surprising ability to absorb the seductive cultural pluralist philosophy into their aggressive corporatism, as when they called on Congress in October to lift out of poverty the vast army of American poor, "men, women and children, Negro and White, Native and Foreign-born, Americans all, deprived of privileges due all Americans."[75]

But by the spring of 1946, the ethnic corporatist display of ideological independence had vanished. Two seismic shifts in national politics in the winter of 1946 revealed how fragile their ideological independence had been and how dependent on national political authority they had in truth become. The first shift was a dramatic increase in antilabor sentiment, articulated by a brash and supremely confident group of right-wing industrialists and espoused by ever-broader sections of the nation's middle class. Among these groups the belief that American unionists had grown too arrogant and too powerful had been brewing at least since the sit-down strike wave of 1936–37, but it took the massive strikes in the auto, steel, and

---

[72] Ibid., October 5, 1945, 8, October 17, 1945, and Christmas 1945, 3.

[73] Ibid., Christmas 1945.

[74] David Brody, "The Uses of Power II: Political Action," in *Workers in Industrial America: Essays on the Twentieth Century Struggle* (New York, 1980), 215–57; Robert H. Zieger, *American Workers, American Unions, 1920–1985* (Baltimore, 1986), 100–36; Lichtenstein, *Labor's War at Home*, 203–32. See also Norman D. Markowitz, *The Rise and Fall of the People's Century: Henry A. Wallace and American Liberalism, 1941–1948* (New York, 1973).

[75] *ITU News*, October 17, 1945, 3.

electrical industries in January 1946, and those of the coal miners and railwaymen in April and May, to push antilabor sentiments to the center of national politics.[76] The second shift was a resurgence of anticommunist sentiment, as Republicans and then increasing numbers of Democrats rejected the notion that the wartime alliance between the United States and the Soviet Union should be maintained during peacetime. George Kennan's famous "X" telegram emphasizing the futility of a conciliatory policy toward the Soviet Union arrived in Washington in late February; Senator Arthur Vandenberg of Michigan blasted, in a speech on the floor of the Senate that same week, the Truman Administration's efforts to maintain cordial relations with the Soviet Union; and Winston Churchill, after consultations with and then a tacit endorsement from the Truman Administration, delivered his famous "Iron Curtain" speech in Fulton, Missouri, in early March.[77]

These ideological explosions reverberated in Woonsocket.[78] In late February the ITU's ethnic leadership denounced one of labor's most crucial postwar struggles, the United Auto Workers' ill-fated attempt to force General Motors to grant its employees a wage increase without raising automobile prices. When General Motors refused the demand, Walter Reuther led out GM UAW members on a strike that would last for 113 days.[79] The strike represented a crucial test of labor's ability to subject corporate pricing policy – and other managerial functions – to collective bargaining, but ITU leaders could only see it as a publicity ploy, by "a lot of so-called and self-appointed leaders," that would drive public support, so crucial in any strike situation, "to the side of management."[80] In these words ITU leaders admitted the sting they felt from the backlash of public opinion. Seeking to regain the favor of that public, these leaders sought to put as much distance

---

[76] Lichtenstein, *Labor's War at Home*, 203–32; Howell John Harris, *The Right to Manage: Industrial Relations Policy of American Business in the 1940s* (Madison, Wis., 1982), 105–27; Mike Davis, *Prisoners of the American Dream: Politics and Economy in the History of the US Working Class* (London, 1986), 81–2.

[77] John Lewis Gaddis, *The United States and the Origins of the Cold War, 1941–1947* (New York, 1972), 282–315.

[78] On reverberations elsewhere in the labor movement, see Bert Cochran, *Labor and Communism: The Conflict That Shaped American Unions* (Princeton, N.J., 1977), 248–71.

[79] On the GM strike, see David Brody, "The Uses of Power I: Industrial Battleground," in *Workers in Industrial America*, 173–214; Lichtenstein, *Labor's War at Home*, 221–28; Barton Bernstein, "Walter Reuther and the General Motors Strike of 1945–1946," *Michigan History* 49 (1965), 260–77; Irving Howe and B. J. Widick, *The UAW and Walter Reuther* (New York, 1949), 136–48.

[80] *ITU News*, February 22, 1946.

as possible between their own organization and that of the allegedly irresponsible and ineffective CIO: "CIO's failure in this area is typical of failures elsewhere. The whole organization is wrong, the leadership is weak, the accomplishments far less numerous than the failures."[81]

This blanket condemnation of the CIO was perhaps understandable in light of public opinion but puzzling nonetheless, for many CIO leaders (including its president, Philip Murray) were schooled in the same religiously inspired corporatism that guided Woonsocket's ethnic leadership. Further, such condemnations would undoubtedly limit the ITU's own freedom of action by impelling its leaders to distance themselves from all CIO policies. The damaging consequences of this approach quickly became apparent. When the ITU steel workers in Mansfield went out on strike in May to protest management's refusal to grant them an hourly wage increase of 18.5 cents that CIO steel and machine-tool workers were gaining across the country, the ITU leadership refused to rush staffers, strike funds, and other union resources to their support.[82] By September 1946, the ITU had lost the strike, and by December it had lost the local as well. Disgusted workers repudiated the union in a December NLRB election in favor of the United Steel Workers of America (CIO).[83]

The repercussions of the national shift in attitudes toward the Soviet Union were as damaging to the ITU as those resulting from the rise of antilabor sentiment. News of Lawrence Spitz's impending return to Woonsocket had already, by early 1946, inflamed anticommunist sentiment among the ethnic corporatists. Fanned by winds of national opinion, this anticommunism raged out of control in April, May, and June. Not only did it induce the ITU leaders to hurl unsubstantiated allegations at Spitz and demand loyalty oaths from all candidates for union office, but it also made them eager to articulate an industrial relations philosophy that would pass muster with the most strident anticommunists in the land.

Union leaders revealed the influence of anticommunism on their industrial relations philosophy in a long essay on class cooperation as

---

[81] Ibid.

[82] *ITU News*, May 17, 1946.

[83] The course of this losing strike and the resentment toward the ITU leadership brewing among S. W. Card workers can be followed in the numerous letters sent by Frank Cinelli, secretary-treasurer of the S. W. Card local, to Lawrence Spitz in the period from June through December 1946; Lawrence N. Spitz Collection, Mss 31, Box 8, Rhode Island Historical Society, Providence, R.I. Cinelli was a Spitz loyalist who, fed up with the policies of the ethnic corporatists, began the secessionist movement at S.W. Card. See also *ITU News*, September 1946 (date and page numbers are missing).

the American way that appeared in the *ITU News* at midyear.[84] The piece began with a detailed discussion of the communist doctrine of class struggle and of the disastrous consequences of its "successful" application in Russia. It turned then to a discussion of the American "democratic way of life," and how such offered an alternative to the class struggle model. "Americans are known the world over for their fairness in dealings with others," the article claimed. "We are always ready to give a guy a break. We are always willing to lend a hand to any fellow in distress and we insist that justice be done. Moreover we are all for the idea of give-and-take, of not taking advantage of others." Thus American labor and American management should make every effort to get along, to air their differences in a spirit of goodwill, to achieve "production under fair and equitable working conditions for the welfare of all concerned in the enterprise."

The article's authors admitted that working together for the general welfare would not simply happen spontaneously in a factory, like the apparently spontaneous communal raising of a barn in Amish country. Rather, the shop steward was a figure critical to the realization of harmony on the shopfloor. The shop steward was responsible for the welfare of all union members, and he was to see that their rights were properly protected. But, the authors' maintained, "his main job is to see to it that the relationship between the workers and the employer is harmonious, smooth and orderly. He has the obligation of co-operating with management for the proper functioning of the plant." "Steady employment, steady income and general satisfaction with conditions prevailing in the plant" would result. "That is what is meant by class co-operation," the authors explained. "It is essentially democratic."[85]

Although this call for class cooperation and mutuality had deep roots in Catholic corporatism, it virtually reversed the aggressive stand the ethnic leadership had taken the previous fall. Ethnic leaders had then argued that there could be no labor peace, no industrial partnership, unless capital did a better job of recognizing labor's rights. The idea that the union's shopfloor cadre should act as management's agents did not even merit discussion. In the interim, neither the ITU nor the national organizations of American labor had made the sorts of dramatic gains that would have justified a new emphasis on class cooperation. To the contrary, the success of the nation's industrialists – more confident and aggressive than they had been in a decade – in ushering in "that new era of capitalist domina-

---

[84] *ITU News*, June 21, 1946.
[85] Ibid.

tion" about which the ethnic corporatists had warned the previous fall, arguably demanded a rejection of the class cooperation approach. The ITU could point to local industrialists, like Manville Jenckes, whose willingness to settle into harmonious, cooperative relationships with the union after years of bitter conflict seemed to vindicate a class cooperation approach.[86] But for every industrialist so inclined there seemed to be two – like the owners of Sydney Worsted and S. W. Card – looking to break the union's power in their mills.

The ethnic corporatists' call for class cooperation was in this instance not a consequence of their corporatist philosophy but, rather, a defensive expression of their fears – for their own survival and for the labor movement's survival – in the wake of rising antilabor and anticommunist sentiment. These national political developments prompted the union's ethnic leaders to drop their aggressive corporatism, to advance their religiously inspired anticommunism in exclusively secular, Americanist terms, and to recast their unionism in terms antithetical to communism. If communists believed in class struggle, then American unionists believed in class cooperation. By constructing such a Manichean world of cooperation versus struggle, good versus evil, Americanism versus communism, these Woonsocket unionists hoped to gain the moral leverage to banish Spitz from Woonsocket and, at the same time, to help restore labor's favorable image in domestic politics. In the process they drastically narrowed the ideological space in which a militant, noncommunist union could operate.

That this fear surfaced so quickly after the turnaround in national political opinion in 1946 reveals how much the ethnic leadership's wartime experience had tied them to the authority of the federal government and to currents in national politics. As national public opinion turned against them, they had become desperate to curry that public's favor. Such dependence would only deepen through the remainder of 1946 and 1947 as antilabor and anticommunist sentiment increased in intensity, producing in 1947 both the Congressional rollback, in the Taft-Hartley Act, of labor's rights and the administration's declaration, in the Truman Doctrine, of the Cold War. ITU unionists, already calling in the spring of 1946 for the United States to "wave a Big Stick" in foreign affairs to make the American way "the way of the world," would eagerly don the ideological armor being issued to aspiring cold warriors.[87]

---

[86] Manville Jenckes's new spirit of class cooperation suffused the pages of its employee magazine, *The Manville Eagle*. See, for example, vol. 1 (September 1944), 2, SMHS.

[87] *ITU News*, May 17, 1946.

The ITU's ethnic leaders may well have thought, of course, that this incipient language of Cold War Americanism they began speaking in 1946 more truly expressed their ideas and values than had the progressive Americanism of the late 1930s. They may have viewed the centrality of anticommunism to postwar constructions of Americanism as an indication of the degree to which crucial elements of their Catholic sensibility were now shared by a majority of Americans. They may have thought that the government's embrace of cultural pluralism gave matters of cultural and religious freedom the kind of priority in the life of the nation that French Canadians had long felt they deserved.

There was some truth to each of these lines of thought, but, equally true, the language of Americanism had slipped out of the ITU's control. The union's ethnic corporatist leaders did not feel able to attack communism on religious grounds or to make Christianity part of their definition of the American way; nor did they find a way to confront the individualism and relativism that were such intrinsic parts of 1940s pluralism and that, as such, threatened their ethnic communalism and moral traditionalism. Their growing inability to express their religiosity, communalism, and traditionalism in the language of Americanism meant that these critical values were dropping from the plane of political debate. Charlatans like Joe McCarthy would pretend to be fashioning an Americanism that spoke to traditionalist concerns when they were, in fact, only giving such conservatism a bad name. For a period of twenty to thirty years following the end of World War II, ethnic workers in Woonsocket and elsewhere would take satisfaction in their staunch American identity, in their ability to "speak American" with confidence and swagger, while feeling a gnawing sense that some of their deepest concerns seemed irrelevant to the nation's polity and inexpressible in the political vocabulary made available to them.

10 The failure of two dreams, 1946–1960

Two political dreams animated working-class politics in Woonsocket from the onset of the Depression to the conclusion of World War II. One dream, entertained by Joseph Schmetz, Lawrence Spitz, and their supporters, looked forward to the democratization of American capitalism. The other dream, entertained by Leona Galipeau, Eugene Thibeault, Herve Gagnon, Raoul Vandal, and other ethnic corporatists, envisioned a spirited ethnic community bound together by a common heritage and religious principles, democratically governed by its working-class members in partnership with employers and religious authorities. Both dreams were couched in the language of Americanism. For the radicals, appropriating Americanist language was the only way to introduce their socialist visions into American political debate. The same language became an indispensable vehicle of liberation from the industrial and ethnic subordination that had long been the French-Canadians' lot. That both groups managed to articulate these dreams in the 1930s and early 1940s reveals the extent to which they had achieved their ideological independence from both national and local authorities. Their independence allowed them to exert extensive influence over political debate for a period of years. From such influence came political and economic power.

But that independence, reliant on the same symbols and words that fueled other, often conservative, political visions, was always fragile. The war witnessed the recasting of Americanist language, both by liberal elites and by an aggressively ideological wartime state. That recasting produced a sea change in American politics, evident in the rise of anticommunism and cultural pluralism and the decline of the labor question as crucial issues in American politics. That sea change, in turn, drastically narrowed the political space in which a working-class movement could operate. Working-class radicals were the most obvious casualties; their plan for democratizing capitalism would not survive in the postwar world. But the ethnic corporatists were casualties of sorts too. Their wartime experience had propelled them toward an aggressive corporatism that, in the hostile climate of 1946,

310

they felt forced to repudiate. Moreover, the ethnic-religious milieu that had nurtured their corporatist ideas had been substantially weakened by the assimilative pressures of war. As that milieu disintegrated, the ideas that had been so important to the ethnic corporatists in their confrontations with modernity slipped away. This loss may not have mattered so much had Woonsocket's workers enjoyed, like their counterparts in steel, auto, electrical, and rubber manufacture, a postwar, twenty-five-year period of unprecedented job security at middle-class wages. But this cultural loss occurred in conjunction with the city's economic ruin, as countless textile mills either folded or moved their operations south. By 1960, then, Woonsocket's workers had lost the textile industry and ethnic culture around which they had organized their lives for almost 100 years.

From industrial democracy to industrial pluralism

The changing pattern of collective bargaining in 1945 and 1946 strikingly reveals the collapse of the radicals' dream. The government, during the war, had not only moved decisively to shape the language of Americanism in ways that would support its war aims; it also was determined to control the interpretation and application of the National Labor Relations Act. From the passage of the act in 1935 to the beginning of war in 1941, its interpretation was up for grabs. Radicals in the factories, supported by prolabor administrators on the NLRB, sometimes managed to define the Wagner Act's vague goals of industrial democracy and collective bargaining on "wages, hours, and working conditions" in the most expansive possible manner. "Working conditions" could entail matters ranging from the availability of lavatories, to workers' control of the labor force and technological change, to participation in corporate finance. The ITU had established in most Woonsocket mills an industrial democratic regime in which virtually every change in technology, labor force structure, work distribution and assignments, and piece rates had to be mutually agreed upon by management and the union. The union had failed in its attempt to force employers to open their books to public scrutiny – a technique that anticipated Walter Reuther's GM strategy of 1946 – but these employers, as late as 1941, had still not sealed off that area of management, or any other, from future union encroachments.

The onset of war brought the open-ended period of collective bargaining to an end. The National War Labor Board (NWLB), which effectively replaced the NLRB as the primary administrative body in labor relations for the war's duration, deliberately sought to narrow the scope of collective bargaining and to restore to management more control over their industrial enterprises.[1] Four members representing the public on the twelve-member board set its wartime course, for not only did they cast deciding votes on issues that split the board's four management and four labor representatives, but they also gave the board its distinctive ideological cast. These members, mostly labor lawyers and economists, believed in labor's right to organize and thought that strong, industrial unions would benefit not only American workers but all of American society. They also sought, however, to reconcile workers' rights of representation with industrialists' needs for order and efficiency in the management of their enterprises.[2] This they did in two ways: first, by exempting a series of managerial functions, such as investment and pricing decisions, the opening of new factories and the closing of old ones, from the realm of collective bargaining; second, by insisting management had the right to initiate business decisions affecting general working conditions without the union's prior consent. The first strategy affirmed the principle that the ownership of private property – in this case an enterprise – entitled the owner to a significant measure of unilateral control over that property. The second strategy affirmed a different principle, that the continuity and profitability of production was as important a goal of industrial relations law as the right of workers to participate in decisions affecting their jobs. Therefore, business should be allowed to implement changes in production as it saw fit. The right of workers to protest these changes was, in theory, protected by the grievance procedures the NWLB wanted to see instituted in all collective bargaining agreements. In practice, though, this right of protest was limited in two important ways. First, certain changes initiated by management,

[1] On developments in industrial relations during World War II, see Howell John Harris, *The Right to Manage: Industrial Relations Policies of American Business in the 1940s* (Madison, Wis., 1982), 41–89; Harris, "The Snares of Liberalism? Politicians, Bureaucrats, and the Shaping of Federal Labour Relations Policy in the United States, ca 1915–1947," in Steven Tolliday and Jonathan Zeitlin, eds., *Shop Floor Bargaining and the State: Historical and Comparative Perspectives* (Cambridge, U.K., 1985), 145–91; Christopher L. Tomlins, *The State and the Unions: Labor Relations, Law, and the Organized Labor Movement in America, 1880–1960* (Cambridge, U.K., 1985), 197–281; Katherine Van Wezel Stone, "The Post-War Paradigm in American Labor Law," *The Yale Law Journal* 90 (June 1981), 1511–25; National War Labor Board, *Termination Report* (Washington, D.C., 1947–49); Fred Witney, *Wartime Experiences of the National Labor Relations Board, 1941–1945* (Urbana, Ill., 1949); and James A. Gross, *The Reshaping of the National Labor Relations Board: National Labor Policy in Transition, 1937–1947* (Albany, N.Y., 1981).

[2] The National Labor Relations Act had intended such a reconciliation but the pre-1940 NLRB had failed, in practice, to establish it. See Karl Klare, "Judicial Deradicalization of the Wagner Act and the Origins of Modern Legal Consciousness, 1937–1941," *Minnesota Law Review* 62 (1977–78), 265–339; James A. Gross, *The Making of the National Labor Relations Board: A Study in Economics, Politics, and the Law* (Albany, N.Y., 1974).

such as the right to institute new technologies, were exempted from binding arbitration; workers therefore had no guarantee that their grievances would be redressed. Second, binding arbitration, when it did apply, barred workers from taking any action, such as a slowdown or strike, that interrupted production. Rather, they had to wait patiently for their protest to wind its way through a bureaucratic grievance system. The NWLB did its best to insure that grievance systems operated with a minimum of red tape, demanding that they be limited to a few clearly delineated steps and that strict time limits be imposed on how long a grievance could remain at one step before moving to the next. But the system remained vulnerable to extensive delays arising from an overload of grievances. Just as importantly, it made the resolution of workers' protests dependent not on the mobilization of working-class power at the point of production but on the judgments rendered by "disinterested" arbitration experts.

The War Board's "industrial pluralism" was premised on the belief that capital and labor constituted two fundamentally equal interest groups, each with its particular set of rights and responsibilities.[3] If each group's rights and responsibilities were clearly set forth, then differences between the two groups could be rationally discussed and peacefully settled. Industrial pluralism closely resembled cultural pluralism not only in name but also in substance. Both doctrines recognized a diversity of legitimate interests in the world, and both looked to the possibility of a social order that could accommodate such diversity and peacefully resolve the disputes that arose from it. The doctrines differed in their mechanisms of dispute resolution: Cultural pluralism relied on neighborly goodwill and understanding; industrial pluralism elaborated a set of institutions and practices – representation elections, collective bargaining, and arbitration – that would establish a system of representative government in the realm of industry. But individuals could easily have subscribed to both, especially since they shared the same ultimate goal – democracy. The industrial pluralists of the 1940s were the decade's chief proponents of industrial democracy much as the cultural pluralists were advocates of cultural democracy.

How greatly the NWLB and its industrial pluralist philosophy shaped the character of industrial relations in Woonsocket is evident in twelve ITU collective-bargaining agreements negotiated in 1945 and 1946.[4] These contracts solidified many of the union's earlier achieve-

---

[3] See Stone, "The Post-War Paradigm in American Labor Law," 1511–17; Tomlins, *The State and the Unions*, xi; and Harris, *The Right to Manage*, 91–104.

[4] ITU, Agreements with the following: Masurel Worsted Mills (1946); Bell Company of

ments: union shops; eight hour days and forty hour weeks; overtime and report pay; premium pay for second and third shift work; seniority for promotions, shift changes, better jobs, and layoffs; share-the-work procedures to insure equitable work assignments; and health and safety protections. They also incorporated dramatic new gains in such areas as hospitalization insurance and paid vacations, reflecting the NWLB policy of "slipping" workers more compensation in ways that would not raise hourly wage rates (which, in the government's eyes, would have triggered the much-feared inflationary spiral). Finally, more and more union locals won dues-checkoff clauses, reflecting another NWLB policy of bolstering union strength through financial security.[5]

But in a number of significant ways the contracts of 1945 and 1946 revealed a serious erosion of the control that ITU unionists had enjoyed in 1941. The appearance of management rights clauses in nine of the twelve contracts hinted at this erosion.[6] Such clauses were phrased something as follows: "The Union recognizes that the Management of the plant and direction of the personnel, subject to the provisions of this agreement, shall be vested exclusively in the Em-

Footnote 4 (cont.)

Rhode Island, Lowland St. Plant (1946); Argonne Worsted Company (1946); Bonin Spinning Company (1945); Belmont Woolen Yarn (1946); Brighton Woolen Mills, Inc. (1946); Dale Worsted Mills, Inc. (1946); Handicraft Woolen Mills (1945); Guerin Mills, Inc., Rosemont Plant (1946); Manville Jenckes Corporation (1945); Star Carbonizing Co. (1945); and Adolf Meller Company (1945). All but two of these contracts are located in the George Butsika Collection (in author's possession; hereafter Butsika Collection); the two exceptions, the Belmont Woolen and Guerin Mills Rosemont agreements, are located in the Industrial Relations Collection, Littauer Library, Harvard University.

[5] On NWLB policy, see Harris, The Right to Manage, 47–89. The contracts themselves, of course, do not mention NWLB policy or pressure, but evidence from other sources reveals the extensive ITU involvement with the NWLB, especially its regional headquarters in Boston. Disputes in at least seventeen ITU locals came before the War Labor Board between 1942 and 1945: S. W. Card, Lloyd Manufacturing, Adolph Meller, U.S. Rubber, ITU firemen, Rhode Island Plush, Joan Plush, Woonsocket Falls, Woonsocket Rayon, Airedale Worsted, and Woonsocket's seven French spinning mills. See ITU News, March 24, 1944, April 7, 1944, May 12, 1944, June 23, 1944, 3, October 13, 1944, 3, December 15, 1944, 8, April 27, 1945, 8, June 15, 1945, July 20, 1945, and October 17, 1945; "Decision of Regional Board I (Boston) In re Union Twist Drill Company [Mansfield, Mass.] and Industrial Trades Union of America (Ind.), Case No. 111–4536-D, February 22, 1944," War Labor Reports, Salary and Wage Stabilization 14 (Washington, D.C., 1944), 315–18; and "Decision In re Rhode Island Plush Mill, Joan Plush Mill and Woonsocket Falls Mill and Industrial Trades Union of America (Ind.), Case No. I-886, April 12, 1941," War Labor Reports, Salary and Wage Stabilization 7 (Washington, D.C., 1943), 650.

[6] The three without such clauses were Dale Worsted, Manville Jenckes, and Adolph Meller.

ployer."[7] None of the 1941 contracts had included such a statement, and its appearance in 1945 and 1946 was one sign of the broad reassertion of managerial prerogatives that the NWLB meant to encourage and that local employers were determined to enact. This reassertion made itself felt most dramatically in the elimination from the French spinning mill contracts of management's obligation to win union consent before discharging an employee or before instituting a change in work load or any other aspect of working conditions. The 1946 French spinning contracts stipulated that management still had to notify the union of its intention to fire a union member, but that it no longer needed the union's agreement to do so; rather, management could act unilaterally. The union, if it objected to the action, could grieve.[8] Similarly, the 1946 agreements stipulated that while management had to notify the union of impending "changes in equipment, processes, or methods of production," the union had no right to halt the implementation of these changes. The union did retain the right to file a grievance if it felt that the work loads on the new machinery were too great or the wages too low.[9] But this right appeared rather feeble alongside the bold assertion in 1941 French-spinning contracts "that any change in the prevailing workload and working conditions throughout the mill shall be mutually agreed upon by the Employer and the Union."[10] This 1941 clause had made it impossible for management to institute any change in production without the union's prior agreement.

This change was so significant that the management-labor teams negotiating the 1946 contracts took the unusual step of including a justification for it in the text of the contract. The justification reflected the influence of NWLB thinking: changes in "equipment, processes, or methods of production" were periodically necessary, one 1946 contract explained, "in order to meet competition and to lead to better

---

[7] ITU, *Agreement with Masurel Worsted Mills, Inc.*, March 11, 1946, Article A, Section 3, 5.

[8] Ibid., Article M, Section 1, 25–6. The Masurel contract was identical in all key respects to those of two other French spinning locals, the Argonne Worsted and Bell Worsted locals; see ITU, *Agreement with Argonne Worsted Company*, March 11, 1946, Article M, Section 1, 25–26; and ITU, *Agreement with Bell Company of R.I., Lowland St. Plant*, March 11, 1946, Article M, Section 1, 25–26.

[9] ITU, *Agreement with Masurel Worsted*, 1946, Article K, Section 1, 19–21; the same stipulations appeared in the Argonne Worsted and Bell Worsted contracts.

[10] ITU, "Agreement with the Guerin Mills, Inc., Alsace Division," June 3, 1941, Article L, Section 1; see also Article L, Section 2, which stipulates that discharges had to "be mutually agreed upon by the Employer and the Union." Lawrence N. Spitz Collection, Mss 31 (hereafter Spitz Collection), Box 8, Rhode Island Historical Society (hereafter RIHS), Providence, R.I.

and more economical operation of the plant." Since such changes were a matter of running an efficient and profitable business, management had the right to enact them in a unilateral fashion.[11]

The premium placed on running an orderly and efficient business also accounts for the crucial substitution in the 1946 woolen mill contracts of arbitration for the right to strike as the final step in the grievance procedure. The 1941 contracts stated that workers were entitled to strike if management had not satisfactorily redressed their grievances;[12] by 1945 they no longer were entitled to this residual right to strike. The woolen locals were now subject to the same three- or four-step grievance procedure, which culminated in binding arbitration, that prevailed in all other Woonsocket contracts. Workers were expected to perform their assigned tasks and otherwise carry on business as usual while the grievance wound its way through the system.[13]

None of these changes signaled a collapse of union power on the shopfloor. The ITU retained the right to be consulted on a wide range of workplace issues and to submit many of them to an umpire independent of managerial control. These rights were a mark of the dramatic and enduring improvement in shopfloor life that the union had achieved for its members since it had first appeared on the scene in the early 1930s. But the changes of 1945 and 1946 did signal the decisive defeat of the union's quest for complete mutuality, or joint sovereignty, in the operation of Woonsocket industry. Moreover, the fact that this defeat coincided with the augmentation of workers' monetary rights (in the form of insurance and vacation benefits) set in motion a bargaining pattern of unions trading collective shopfloor power in return for increases in their members' individual purchasing power that would continue, even intensify, in the postwar years.[14]

---

[11] See, for example, ITU, *Agreement with the Masurel Worsted,"* Article K, Section 1, 25. The same explanation appeared in the Argonne Worsted and Bell Worsted contracts. Only one of the twelve 1945 and 1946 contracts maintained the prewar insistence that "there shall be no change in the workload and working conditions unless such change shall be mutually agreed upon by the Employer and the Union"; that contract belonged to the Handicraft Woolen workers, a small and marginal local. See *Agreement Between Handicraft Woolen Mills and Industrial Trades Union of America*, December 1, 1945, Article J, Section 1, 14.

[12] ITU, Agreement with Bonin Spinning Company, April 7, 1941, Article K, Section C.

[13] ITU, *Agreement with Bonin Spinning Company*, August 1, 1945, Article K, 19–23; ITU, Belmont Woolen Yarn Local, *Agreement with Belmont Woolen Yarn Mills*, September 12, 1946, Article K, 26–30.

[14] All the 1945 and 1946 contracts offered paid vacations, usually on the principle of one paid week after an employee had completed one year of work and two paid weeks after an employee completed five years of work. Ten of the twelve offered Blue Cross hospitalization insurance, and four of the twelve offered reimbursements for medical and surgical fees as well as life insurance. These provisions would be-

At what point these changes in collective bargaining transpired in Woonsocket is unclear. No contracts from the period 1942 through 1944 survive, nor do any notes or other testimony from negotiating sessions. It is therefore unclear how closely the change in the contracts corresponded with the ethnics' rise to power. The ethnics' corporatist philosophy could easily have justified the reassertion of managerial prerogatives and the curtailment of the union's quest for shopfloor power, but we have seen how this corporatist philosophy legitimated, in the fall of 1945, a broad attack on capitalist power. It would be wrong, therefore, to attribute this change in collective bargaining solely to the ethnic leaders' ascension. The fact, moreover, that the changes in the balance of shopfloor power were so dramatic in the French spinning mills where the union radicals were strongest suggests that the power that the state was willing to exercise in industrial relations forced all groups to capitulate – at least for the war's duration.[15]

The ethnic corporatists perhaps can be held more responsible for perpetuating these wartime trends in the postwar world when, in the face of hostile public opinion, they hastily retreated to the meeker version of their corporatism and a hysterical version of their anticommunism. ITU radicals, had they recovered union power sometime in these years, might have been able to return the union to a more independent and radical course. They undoubtedly would have supported Reuther's effort to force GM to open its books to public scrutiny and thus make corporate pricing policy a matter of collective bargaining.[16] And they might have reinvigorated a rank-and-file fight for shopfloor democracy. But it would not have been an easy task. The rise of antilabor and anticommunist sentiment made the redistribution of power in industry a risky project for any unionist to propose. Moreover, the pluralist philosophy that had suffused government prop-

come standard in virtually all contracts by 1948. See ITU, *Agreement with Masurel Worsted*, 1946, Articles P and R, 32–7, for the language and details of these provisions.

[15] We cannot know, unfortunately, how closely industrial relations practice conformed to the contractual language. The penalties for violating the terms of the contracts were not yet draconian: Only one contract from 1945 and 1946 contained an employer security clause requiring union officials to order unauthorized strikers back to work and allowing employers to fire those who refused. See ITU, *Agreement with Manville Jenckes Corporation*, January 1, 1945, Article L, 17–18. The absence of such harsh punitive measures in other contracts may have allowed workers to use their wildcat strike weapon to preserve de facto joint workplace sovereignty now that their contracts no longer established that sovereignty de jure. Such loopholes were gone by 1948, however, as employer security clauses had found their way into thirteen of the fourteen ITU contracts dating from 1947, 1948, and 1949. These contracts are in the Butsika Collection. See, for example, ITU, *Agreement with Masurel Worsted Mills, Inc.*, February 16, 1948, Article P, 33–5.

[16] Interview with Lawrence Spitz, September 19–20, 1979.

aganda and industrial-relations practice during the war increasingly dominated liberal thinking after the war. Thus even labor's staunchest supporters in government agencies and the Democratic Party had come to believe in the need to defend management's right to operate factories in an efficient, orderly, and profitable manner. Liberal economists and labor lawyers – and, in turn, the federal courts – increasingly turned to the NWLB ideology to guide them in their interpretation of labor law and the regulation of industrial relations.[17] At the same time, the liberal fascination with the cultural pluralist ideal that the war had spawned diminished the stature that the labor question had long occupied in the minds of American reformers. More and more liberal energy began flowing toward the most egregious violation of the cultural pluralist ideal in American life – the discrimination to which America subjected its black citizens. A revivified campaign for industrial democracy, therefore, would have had to withstand a far more hostile reception from the public on the one hand and a less enthusiastic embrace from labor's liberal supporters on the other.[18]

It is hard to escape the conclusion, in other words, that ITU radicals would have failed in their efforts, however intense, to renew their campaign for industrial democracy. The dramatic increase in the power of the state combined with the far-reaching changes in the character of American politics – evident both in the growing power of conservatives vis-à-vis liberals and in liberalism's new pluralist agenda – greatly diminished the autonomy of any group of local unionists, irrespective of their political ambitions. The ITU's period of ideological independence had come to an end.

Economic decline, union collapse, 1949–1960

National political developments rendered differences between union radicals and ethnics inconsequential in the area of shopfloor power. But in other respects, internal union divisions crucially affected the

---

[17] See Stone, "The Post-War Paradigm in American Labor Law," 1511–80.

[18] On the declining significance of the labor question among reformers, see Steve Fraser, "The 'Labor Question,'" and Alan Brinkley, "The New Deal and the Idea of the State," in Steve Fraser and Gary Gerstle, eds., *The Rise and Fall of the New Deal Order, 1930–1980* (Princeton, N.J., 1989), 55–121. On rise of pluralist thinking see Daniel T. Rodgers, *Contested Truths: Keywords in American Politics Since Independence* (New York, 1987), 176–211. Other works illuminating the dramatic changes in the character of American liberalism occurring in the 1940s, include Alonzo L. Hamby, "The Vital Center, the Fair Deal, and the Quest for a Liberal Political Economy," *American Historical Review* 77 (June 1972), 653–78; Richard Pells, *The Liberal Mind in a Conservative Age: American Intellectuals in the 1940s and 1950s* (New York, 1985), 1–182;

postwar character of the ITU. The ethnic corporatist triumph would be decisive in determining the size, regional scope, and ethnic composition of the union. The most immediate consequence of the ethnics' triumph in 1945 and 1946 was a cessation of union growth followed by a gradual membership decline. The ethnic corporatists refused to contemplate any kind of affiliation with the CIO or to organize workers outside Woonsocket. They also, it seemed, had little intention of servicing the union's existing non-Woonsocket locals in a way that would make the latter desirous of maintaining an ITU affiliation. By later 1946 all but one of the non-Woonsocket locals that Spitz and his organizers had brought into the union in 1942, 1943, and 1944 had left the ITU. From the beginning of Spitz's expansion campaign in 1942 until its end in late 1944, twenty-one new locals and 5,787 new workers entered the ITU. Ten of these locals and 3,050 (53 percent) of these members were located outside Woonsocket and outside the textile industry. By late 1944, two of these locals had already disaffiliated with the ITU, the Textile Finishing Machinery plant in Providence leaving soon after Spitz' departure and New England Drawn Steel withdrawing after Paul Ryan, Spitz's last loyal organizer, quit in November 1944. Still, the union entered 1945 with a net gain of nineteen locals and 4,162 members in the previous two years and a total membership reaching 15,000.[19]

The ethnic corporatists reversed this pattern of growth in the next two years as they consolidated their hold on the union. The union added only seven locals and 586 members in 1945 and 1946, with four of these locals being marginal establishments of fifty or fewer workers. At the same time, the union lost twelve locals and 4,215 members including nine of its ten remaining non-Woonsocket locals (only Manville Jenckes remained) and three nontextile locals in Woonsocket. The ITU, in sum, suffered a net loss of five locals and 3,629 members during the years of ethnic corporatist triumph.[20] In this context, the S. W. Card local that bolted from the ITU in September 1946 in disgust over the ethnic corporatist handling of its strike was more notable for how long it maintained its tie to the ITU than for its eventual severing of it.[21]

---

and Howard Brick, *Daniel Bell and the Decline of Intellectual Radicalism: Social Theory and Political Reconciliation in the 1940s* (Madison, Wis., 1986).

[19] ITU, Executive Council Minutes and Dues Income Statements, 1943–47, Spitz Collection, Box 8, RIHS, and Butsika Collection; Lawrence Spitz to author May 11, 1977; Rhode Island Department of Labor, *List of Industrial Establishments* (Providence, R.I., 1944), 74–9. See Appendix A for more details on the locals entering and leaving the ITU in the 1940s.

[20] Ibid.

[21] The fact that an important ethnic corporatist leader, Edwin Van Den Berghe, came

It would be wrong to interpret this run on locals, however, as evidence of an impending collapse of the ITU. The ethnic leadership was engaged in a strategic retreat, not in an act of wanton self-destruction. As the ITU lost its beachheads outside Woonsocket, it was strengthening its control of that part of industry that had always formed its core: Woonsocket's textile industry and especially its woolen and worsted sector. The ethnic corporatists not only maintained the five new woolen and worsted locals that Spitz had brought into the union in the years 1942 to 1944, but added four more in 1945 and 1946. Table 10.1 compares the degree of organization in the textile industry at three points in time: 1941, on the eve of wartime mobilization, 1944, at the end of Spitz's influence on ITU organizing, and 1946, when the ethnic corporatists consolidated their triumph. The percentage of Woonsocket textile mills organized increased from 71 percent in 1941 to 76 percent in 1944 to 79 percent in 1946; the percentage of textile workers organized increased accordingly from 75 percent in 1941 to 83 percent in 1944 and dipped slightly to 81 percent in 1946. The 1946 dip reflects the defection of the Blackstone Cotton local and its 1,100 workers from the ITU in the fall of 1945.[22] If this mill is excluded from the 1946 calculations (the French-Canadian leadership treated the local, with its Polish and Irish majority, like the "foreign" locals in Providence and Mansfield), then the percentage of organized Woonsocket textile workers in 1946 reaches a remarkable 84 percent. The ITU had made the organization of their city's textile industry virtually complete.

This achievement, though impressive, carried with it grave dangers for the future of the ITU. The northern textile industry would likely resume its decline upon war's end as manufacturers found the comparative labor advantages of the American South or foreign lands too alluring to pass up. Thus a union confining itself to textile production in Rhode Island seemed doomed to extinction. Even a cursory examination of industrial statistics relevant to Woonsocket's economy in the 1940s would have yielded ominous predictions for the future.

Footnote 21 (*cont.*)
out of the S. W. Card local probably explains that local's "long affiliation" with the ITU. The ethnic corporatists liked him because he shared their Catholic principles but spoke an eloquent, unaccented English. Van Den Berghe replaced Herve Gagnon as ITU president in the fall of 1946 (Gagnon had accepted a job in management) after only ten months experience as a union staffer, and stayed with the ITU after his S. W. Card local had bolted the ITU for the CIO. See *ITU News*, October 25, 1946, 1, 2, and 7. See also Frank Cinelli to Lawrence Spitz, August 3, 1942, Spitz Collection, Box 8, RIHS.

[22] *ITU News*, November 30, 1945.

Table 10.1. Degree of organization in Woonsocket's textile industry, 1941, 1944, 1946

Textile Sector	1941		1944		1946	
	Mills Org.[a]/ total mills	Emp. Org.[b]/ total emp.	Mills Org.[a]/ total mills	Emp. Org.[b]/ total emp.	Mills Org.[a]/ total mills	Emp. Org.[b]/ total emp.
French spinning[c]	6/7	2,643/3,093	8/8	3,155/3,155	8/8	3,155/3,155
Bradford spinning[c]	1/8	450/3,002	2/8	370/2,309	4/9	765/2,454
Woolen spinning	4/4	750/750	4/4	861/861	4/4	861/861
Woolen and worsted weaving	3/6	890/1,150	5/8	1,076/1,174	7/9	1,156/1,224
Woolen and worsted dyeing	8/8	771/771	8/9	862/922	8/9	862/922
Cotton and rayon[d]	3/3	4,375/4,375	3/3	3,825/3,825	2/3	2,725/3,825
Cotton plush	4/4	570/570	4/4	727/727	4/4	727/727
Cotton knitting	1/2	25/225	1/2	30/233	1/2	30/233
Total:	30/42	10,474/13,936	35/46	10,906/13,206	38/48	10,281/13,401
%	71.4	75.2	76.1	82.6	79.2	80.8

[a] Short for mills organized.
[b] Short for employees organized.
[c] Produced worsted yarn.
[d] Includes the Blackstone Mill in adjacent Blackstone, Mass., and the Manville Jenckes Mill in adjacent Manville, R.I.

Source: ITU, Executive Council Minutes and Dues Income Statements, 1943–1947, and Christiansen and Co., "Report on Financial Statements of the ITUA," 1941–43, both in Lawrence N. Spitz Collection, Mss 31, Box 8, Rhode Island Historical Society, Providence, R.I.; Lawrence Spitz to author, May 11, 1977; Rhode Island, List of Industrial Establishments (Providence, R.I., 1944), 74–9; Providence Journal Almanac: A Reference Book for the State of Rhode Island (Providence, R.I.), 1945.

Despite the invigorating effect of war orders, overall employment in Woonsocket's textile industry did not grow during the war years. Table 10.1 shows that employment actually declined from 13,936 in 1941 to 13,206 in 1944. Two factors explain this phenomenon. First, Woonsocket's labor supply was simply not large enough to support a significant expansion. In an industry that already depended so heavily on female labor, there were not enough women in "household reserve" to pick up the slack from the thousands of departing men.[23] Moreover, textile wages were lower than those in shipbuilding, steel, and airplane and truck manufacture, and thus could not attract a significant stream of in-migrants.[24] In fact, this imbalance in wage structures prompted some Woonsocket textile workers to leave their homes for more lucrative work in shipbuilding and airplane manufacturing centers like Boston and San Diego.[25] These labor-market circumstances imposed on Woonsocket a chronic labor shortage: The Chamber of Commerce calculated in 1944 that the city's industries needed 1,561 more workers than the 15,555 already employed.[26]

The other factor explaining the failure of textile employment to grow was the heavy investment of local manufacturers in new machinery. Such investment was prompted only in part by the chronic labor shortage. In many instances the investments were meant to procure long-contemplated productivity improvements that textile owners had repeatedly delayed making in the gloomy Depression years. As is so often the case, such improvements meant reducing management's reliance on highly skilled and highly paid workers by introducing automatic machinery that could perform the skilled workers' tasks while being tended by semiskilled workers. Management could not only pay each semiskilled worker much less than his or her skilled predecessor, but could also reduce the overall number of such workers required for a production run. The most notable example of such production changes occurred in Woonsocket's woolen mills where

[23] Female employment in Woonsocket industry rose from 4,815 (34 percent of the industrial work force) in 1940 to 7,397 (48 percent) in 1944. Woonsocket Chamber of Commerce, Planning Commission, "Survey of Industry in Woonsocket," reprinted in ibid., July 28, 1944, 1, 4.

[24] Nelson Lichtenstein, *Labor's War at Home: The CIO in World War II* (Cambridge, U.K., 1983), 210–21; U.S. Department of Labor, Bureau of Labor Statistics, "Wage Structure, Woolen and Worsted Industry, April 1946," *Monthly Labor Review* 64 (March 1947), 461–8.

[25] The Woonsocket Chamber of Commerce estimated that 1,200 Woonsocket workers left the area for more lucrative industrial jobs; Woonsocket Chamber of Commerce, "Survey of Industry in Woonsocket." These statistics were confirmed in interviews with Ernest Gignac and Arthur Riendeau, both on June 25, 1981.

[26] Woonsocket Chamber of Commerce, "Survey of Woonsocket Industry."

the mules were increasingly torn out and replaced with spinning frames.[27] The French spinning mills, which had long attributed the superiority of their product to mulespinning, were more loath to rip out their mules. Nevertheless, they began to introduce an increasing number of spinning frames into their plants.[28]

In the short term, these changes would benefit Woonsocket industry by lowering overall production costs and thus making Woonsocket goods more competitive in the national market. But in the long term, these changes would undoubtedly release Woonsocket manufacturers from the single most important bond that tied them to the area: their reliance on skilled textile labor. If all they needed was unskilled and semiskilled textile labor, why stay in Woonsocket? No matter how much these manufacturers saved in Woonsocket wages through technological improvement, more savings awaited them in the American South or abroad, where wage structures were much lower than in the Northeast.[29]

The ethnic corporatist leaders ignored these long-term trends. Noting in late 1945 the fine products produced by northern Rhode Island and southern Massachusetts textile workers, they sanguinely declared that "the quality [of these products] cannot be duplicated elsewhere, for the skill has come through generations of workers, from parents to children."[30] They were able to sustain this illusion for the next three years as their city's textile industry reaped the benefits of its wartime investments and enjoyed a splendid Indian summer. With employment and profits running at high levels, the masses of textile workers in Woonsocket enjoyed the kind of economic security they had never previously known. Dramatic improvements in their economic conditions dated from wartime when the long overtime hours demanded by the war effort – all paid at time-and-a-half or double the

[27] Interview with Arthur Riendeau, June 25, 1981.
[28] See summary of discussion regarding technological change in French Worsted and Bell Worsted spinning mills in ITU, Executive Board Meeting Minutes, January 13, 1949, E, and October 28, 1949, 2, Butsika Collection. See also Manville Jenckes's modernization plans discussed in The Manville Eagle 1 (November 1944), 6, Slater Mill Historic Site, Pawtucket, R.I.; interview with Robert Guerin, November 3, 1980.
[29] On declining competitiveness of New England's woolen and worsted industry, see National Planning Association, the Committee of New England, "The Textile Industries of New England," Staff Memorandum #10, prepared by William H. Miernyk and Arthur A. Bright (August 1952), Serial Files, Littauer Library, Harvard University; Kurt B. Mayer and Sidney Goldstein, Migration and Economic Development in Rhode Island (Providence, R.I., 1958); Donald Norton Anderson, "The Decline of the Woolen and Worsted Industry in New England, 1947–1958: A Regional Economic History" (Ph.D. dissertation, New York University, 1971).
[30] ITU News, October 17, 1945.

regular wage rates – brought most Woonsocket workers significant increases in their weekly incomes. When the mills resumed a more normal production schedule at the war's end, ITU members preserved and even expanded their economic gains by winning ample increases in wage rates through collective bargaining.[31] The minimum wage throughout Woonsocket's textile industry increased from fifty-two, sixty, and sixty-five cents per hour in 1945, to seventy-five and eight cents in 1946, to one dollar and five cents in 1948.[32] By 1948, moreover, most ITU workers were covered by a cost-of-living adjuster: Any unusual inflationary increase allowed the union to reopen wage negotiations and demand a corresponding increase in hourly rates.[33] Woonsocket unionists also enjoyed one to two weeks' paid vacation

[31] The following analysis is based on an examination of twenty-six collective bargaining agreements between the ITU and local employers in the years 1945 to 1949. The twelve from 1945 and 1946 are the ones identified in the "From industrial democracy to industrial pluralism" section of this chapter. The fourteen from 1947, 1948, and 1949 are as follows: ITU, Agreements with Woonsocket Rayon, Inc. (1947); American Wringer Co., Inc. (1947); Masurel Worsted Mills, Inc. (1948); Riverside Worsted Co., Inc. (1948); Argonne Worsted Co., Inc. (1948); Verdun Manufacturing Co., Inc. (1948); Woonsocket Spinning Company, Inc. (1948); Sidney Blumenthal and Co., Inc. (1948); Murray Worsted Company (1948); Spring Grove Spinning Company (1948); Rhode Island Plush Mills (1948); Joan Plush Mills (1948); Star Carbonizing Company (1948); and American Paper Tube Company (1949). All are located in the Butsika Collection.

[32] ITU, *Agreement with Manville Jenckes Corporation*, January 1, 1945, Article E, Section 1, 11; ITU, *Agreement with Manville Jenckes Corporation Succeeded by Textron Mills, Inc.* October 26, 1945, Article E, Section 1, 11; ITU, *Agreement with Adolph Meller Company*, August 1, 1945, Appendix A, 23; ITU, *Agreement with Masurel Worsted Mills*, March 11, 1946, Article D, Section 1, 8; ITU, *Agreement with Dale Worsted Mills Incorporated*, February 18, 1946, Article Q, Section 1, 26; ITU, *Agreement with Brighton Woolen Mills, Inc.*, November 20, 1946, Schedule A, 48; ITU, *Agreement with Masurel Worsted Mills, Inc.*, February 16, 1948, Article D, Section 1, 8. Only two of the 1947-1948-1949 batch of contracts did not provide a $1.05 minimum, American Wringer and American Paper Tube: American Wringer (sixty-five cent minimum) and American Paper Tube (seventy-five cent minimum). These contracts increased the actual hourly pay rates to $1.03 and $1.05 respectively, however, through ample cost-of-living additions: forty-two cents/hour for American Wringer workers and thirty cents/hour for American Paper Tube workers. See ITU, *Agreement with American Wringer Co., Inc.*, December 1, 1947, Article E, Sections 1 and 3, 11–12; and ITU, *Agreement with American Paper Tube Company*, September 1, 1949, Article D, Section 1, 10–11.

[33] Nine of the fourteen 1947–1949 contracts contained these cost-of-living adjusters. See, for example, ITU, *Agreement with Masurel Worsted Mills, Inc.*, February 16, 1948, Article T, Section 3, 43. The five contracts not containing this provision were those of the Sidney Blumenthal, Murray Worsted, Spring Grove, Woonsocket Rayon, and Star Carbonizing locals. The first three were Bradford spinning plants, suggesting the ITU had failed to extend this provision to that sector of Woonsocket industry. The last two were miscellaneous plants whose contracts were not representative of other locals.

each year (depending on length of employment), received extensive medical benefits in the form of Blue Cross hospitalization and reimbursements for doctors' fees, and protected their families against death or dismemberment through employer-paid life and disability insurance.[34]

These gains, paralleling those accruing to the workers in other powerful unions in the country, marked a historic transition in the character of American working-class life. For generations working-class families, living in conditions of chronic economic instability, were periodically plunged into poverty by an economic downturn or by family illness and death. Industrial unionism had brought them a life of economic security and modest comfort. Workers in most unionized industries would be able to avail themselves of this life for the duration of their working years.[35]

In Woonsocket, however, the era of security and comfort was over nearly as soon as it began. The 1948 contract negotiations marked the last time Woonsocket textile employers and workers would bargain under conditions of economic prosperity. By 1949, in the midst of an economic slump, a pall settled over the city. The huge Manville mill, the ITU's largest local, fatally hurt by the speculative investment practices of its new owner, Textron, shut down production in 1949. The ITU suffered an irretrievable loss of more than 2,000 members.[36] It also began to feel the pressure for concessions as employers argued, ever more insistently, that they were losing the ability to compete

[34] All the contracts contained these provisions. Typically they provided a one-week paid vacation to employees with at least one year of continuous service, one-and-a-half weeks to employees with three to five years of service, and two weeks to employees with at least five years of continuous service. They also provided full Blue Cross hospitalization for the individual employee, a $2 reimbursement for a medical treatment at a hospital or a doctor's office ($3 in case of a doctor's home visit), surgical benefits up to $150, life insurance worth $1,500, and accidental and dismemberment insurance worth $1,500. See ITU, *Agreement with Masurel Worsted, Inc.*, 1948, Articles Q and S, 35–6, 38–42. Two contracts provided Blue Cross hospitalization for the employee's family as well. See ITU, *Agreement with Woonsocket Rayon*, 1947, Article N, Section 1, 56; and ITU, *Agreement with American Wringer*, 1947, Article O, Section 1, 32–3.
[35] See Robert H. Zieger, *American Workers, American Unions, 1920–1985* (Baltimore, 1986), 137–53.
[36] Interviews with George Butsika, Angelo Turbesi, Arthur Moretti, and Livio Gramolini, all on September 14, 1984; Textile Workers Union of America, Research, "The Milking and Closing of Manville Jenckes Corporation" (typescript, 1948), Rhode Island Collection, Vertical File, Providence Public Library, Providence, R.I. See also newspaper clippings and report of U.S. Senate investigation on Textron in Textile Workers Union of America (hereafter TWUA) papers, US Mss 129A, File 10A, Box 21, Wisconsin State Historical Society, Madison, Wis.

with southern manufacturers.[37] The 1950 round of contract negotiations, which yielded a bountiful harvest of wage increases and
generous benefit packages for workers in the automobile and other
prosperous industries, brought ITU unionists no improvements in
their minimum wage or benefit packages, and cost them such important
economic protections as the cost-of-living adjuster.[38] Discussion of
givebacks increasingly dominated Executive Council meetings. The
ethnic corporatist leadership, believing employer tales of economic
woe, favored a strategy of further concessions on such matters as
wages and work loads. They encountered an increasingly stiff opposition, however, led by a revivified group of radicals who seized on this
issue as a way of recouping the union power they had lost to the ethnics
in 1945 and 1946. These radicals doubted the veracity of employer
claims. Even if they turned out to be true, the radicals argued, then all
the concessions in the world would not succeed in keeping textile
employers in Woonsocket.[39]

As these internal fights went on, the economic situation of the union
worsened. Employers cut their work forces, and the union lost
members and revenues. By January 1952, 6,780 Woonsocket workers,
representing almost one-third of the city's work force, were unemployed.[40] By 1953, the ITU, in financial crisis, began contemplating

[37] ITU, "Executive Council Meeting Minutes," February 12, 1949, B–D, Butsika Collection.
[38] See ITU, *Agreement with Argonne Worsted Company*, February 1, 1950; ITU, *Agreement
with the French Worsted Co.*, February 1, 1950; ITU, *Agreement with Falls Yarn Mills*,
February 1, 1950; ITU, *Agreement with Spring Grove Spinning*, March 8, 1950; ITU,
Agreement with American Paper Tube Company, September 1, 1951; and ITU, *Agreement
with Crown Manufacturing Company, Worsted Division*, June 12, 1951. All these contracts are located in the Butsika Collection. The minimum wage in the two 1951
contracts did show an increase over the 1948 levels – $1.17 per hour for American
Paper Tube workers (Article D, Section 1, 6) and $1.19 for Crown Manufacturing
workers (Article E, Section 1, 14). These increases may have been general throughout Woonsocket industry. If so, they were the last increases that Woonsocket
workers received for five years: In two 1955 contracts representative of two crucial
sectors of Woonsocket industry (French spinning and woolen spinning), the minimum wage stood at only $1.21 per hour. See Falls Yarn Mills, *Agreement with
Industrial Trades Union of America*, March 16, 1955, Article G, Section 1, 17; and ITU,
Agreement with French Worsted Company, April 15, 1955, Article D, Section 2, 7. Both
are in the Butsika Collection.
[39] The radical leaders included some veterans like Apostole Moussas, Angelo Turbesi,
and Anatole Goethals who had been active in union affairs since the early 1930s;
other local leaders like George Butsika, Arthur Moretti, and Livio Gramolini, represented a second generation that had become active in union affairs in the 1940s.
ITU, Executive Council Meeting Minutes, January 13 and December 8, 1951; January
12, 1952, and November 14, 1953, Butsika Collection. Interviews with Butsika, Gramolini, Moretti and Turbesi, all on September 14, 1984.
[40] Conference of New England Governors, Report on New England Textile Industry

such drastic revenue-saving measures as firing organizers and office staff, ceasing publication of the *ITU News*, and cutting back the funeral benefits it had diligently paid out for more than twenty years, even through the Depression's worst moments.[41] Union locals were torn apart by arguments about whether to accept employer demands for givebacks.[42] The progressive faction forced through the Executive Council a resolution forbidding a local to agree to any concession without the Executive Council's approval.[43] But, in late 1953, the Guerin Mills, the area's largest textile employer since the shutdown of Manville Jenckes, demonstrated the futility of such union militance. It announced the impending shutdown of all Woonsocket operations unless its workers accepted a reduction in pay exceeding 25 percent. Workers at Guerin Mills–Alsace – still the bastion of ITU radicalism – along with their counterparts at Guerin Mills–Montrose and Guerin Mills–Rosemont – responded defiantly with a strike that shut down all production, whereupon management made good on its pledge to leave Woonsocket.[44] By May 1954, the Guerin Mills, long the heart of the city's woolen and worsted industry and of the ITU, had shut down all local operations. Another thousand textile jobs – and a thousand union members – were lost.[45] By 1955, it became clear that the ITU had no future, except to delay the inevitable shutdowns as long as possible. For this task, the ethnic corporatist leadership, with its desire to work with management and its willingness to accept concessions, proved well suited. The ITU stumbled into the sixties with a few thousand members still in its ranks, hoping to survive long enough to pay out the meager severance and death benefits guaranteed its retired members.[46] But the union had lost its raison d'être. Woonsocket had become little more than an industrial junkyard.[47]

This collapse exposed the folly of the ethnic corporatists' decision in 1946 to limit the ITU to Woonsocket. It is doubtful that Spitz and

(1952), 307, Serial File, Littauer Library, Harvard University.

[41] ITU, Executive Council Meeting Minutes, December 12, 1953, Butsika Collection. The ITU had already suspended publication of its newspaper for one period in 1952 due to insufficient funds. The second suspension in 1954 was its last; it would never reappear.

[42] ITU, Executive Council Meeting Minutes, May 8, 1954, 3–4, Butsika Collection.

[43] Ibid., December 12, 1953.

[44] *Providence Journal*, November 3, 7, 8, 11, 1953; A. P. Thomas, *Woonsocket: Highlights of History, 1800–1976* (Woonsocket, R.I., 1976), 107.

[45] ITU, "Income for the Month of May, 1954," Butsika Collection.

[46] Interviews with Arthur Rock and Lionel Harnois, both on October 8, 1976.

[47] On the effects of textile flight on other mill communities, see William Miernyk, *Inter-Industry Labor Mobility: The Case of the Displaced Textile Worker* (Boston, 1955); W. Stanley Devino, Arnold H. Raphaelson, and James A. Storer, *A Study of Textile Mill Closings in Selected New England Communities* (Orono, Maine, 1966).

his supporters could have stopped textile flight from the area. The futile efforts of the Textile Workers Union elsewhere in the Northeast suggests that affiliating the ITU with the national textile union would have made little difference to the fate of Woonsocket's textile industry.[48] But the radicals under Spitz's leadership might have been able to provide a series of options for union members that could possibly have moderated Woonsocket's decline. Spitz would have continued the diversification of the ITU into steel, rubber, and other regional industries that was well underway in 1942 and 1943. This would have created an opportunity for the ITU to affiliate, at some point, with another industrial union, such as the steel workers.[49] Such affiliation, in turn, might have led to retraining programs for displaced Woonsocket textile workers arrived at through collective bargaining with steel employers or through effective lobbying in the state's General Assembly. Such affiliation, moreover, might also have added the power of a national industrial union to political voices in Rhode Island calling for state legislation either to regulate the process of capital flight or to attract new industry to the state. None of these measures would have preserved the ethnic or union élan of Woonsocket's working-class community. They would simply have offered some individuals within that community a better economic deal than the one so brutally thrust upon them. They might also have speeded the process of economic recovery, a process that even in the late 1980s has barely begun.[50]

The French Canadians in the ITU, had they been presented with such options in the 1950s, might have judged them too meager a reward for the loss of local autonomy and the dispersal of their ethnic community that job retraining and economic redevelopment would undoubtedly have entailed. But here we encounter a final and bitter irony. In truth, little was left of Woonsocket's vibrant ethnic community by the mid-1950s. War mobilization, with its dispersal of thousands of Woonsocket boys around the world and with the ever-increasing intrusion of the state and its patriotic authority into every nook and cranny of American life, completed the disintegration of the mission of *la survivance* that had held Woonsocket's French Canadians together for sixty years. Signs of this disintegration abounded. *L'Indépendant*,

[48] The correspondence between Victor Canzano (state director of TWUA in Rhode Island since 1950 and a TWUA staffer since 1941) and Solomon Barkin chronicles TWUA efforts in Rhode Island to halt textile flight; TWUA papers, Mss 396, Boxes 73–74, Canzano folders 3–8.
[49] Interviews with George Butsika, Livio Gramolini, Arthur Moretti, and Angelo Turbesi, all on September 14, 1984.
[50] Ibid.

Woonsocket's French weekly, stopped publishing in 1942, leaving the city without a French newspaper for the first time in almost fifty years.[51] The Ligue Ouvrière Catholique, abandoned by the ethnic corporatist leaders in favor of the Social Action Institute of the Providence diocese, quietly dissolved itself in 1949 and merged with the Chicago-based Christian Family Movement.[52] Charlotte LeBlanc, a Woonsocket teenager in the 1940s, remembers that decade as a critical watershed in her ethnic community's history. The last child in her family to grow up in the 1930s, she was also the last child to grow up speaking French. Her younger brothers and sisters, who spent their formative childhood years in the 1940s, though able to understand French, never learned to speak it. Part of that development reflected the death of her mother, who had spoken only French to her children. But LeBlanc remembers as well a city saturated with patriotic movies, nuns who encouraged their parochial school students to sing American patriotic songs, and younger priests who, by the early 1950s, preferred using English to French in their discussions with parishioners.[53] In the 1950s, as well, English became the dominant language in Woonsocket's parochial schools, with French now limited to two daily periods in which the French language and Catholicism were taught.[54]

French-Canadian Catholicism and ethnicity survived in pockets among the older generation; a heavily accented English lingers on Woonsocket streets to this day. In a few of the surviving textile mills, Catholic corporatism continued to inform the practice of industrial relations; Leonel and Normand Galipeau, sons of Leona, doggedly sustained the ITU and their father's corporatist vision at the Falls Yarn Mill.[55] But the spirit of French Canada lost the capacity to bind together a working class or to inspire it with visions of social reconstruction. The remarkable cultural flowering that spread so quickly throughout Quebec in the 1960s touched Woonsocket workers little more than did any one of a dozen concurrent Third World movements for cultural or political liberation.[56]

Woonsocket workers, had they been employed in almost any industry other than textiles, still would have enjoyed a release from the poverty

---

[51] Steven R. Williams, "Language and Social Structure: Bilingualism and Language Shift in Woonsocket, Rhode Island" (honors thesis, Brown University, 1976), 60–1.

[52] Interviews with Arthur Fortin and with Phileas and Yvonne Valois, all on July 5, 1983.

[53] Interview with Charlotte LeBlanc, July 16, 1981.

[54] Williams, "Language and Social Structure," 83.

[55] Interviews with Leonel and Normand Galipeau, October 22–3, 1980.

[56] I do not include Vietnam in the dozen Third World movements that made little difference to Woonsocket residents.

and insecurity that had been the staples of American working-class life for one hundred years. And the talented children of economically secure working-class parents would have enjoyed unprecedented opportunities to climb out of their parochial surroundings and into the cosmopolitan, middle-class world of universities, corporations, the professions, and bohemia. Even in economically depressed areas, the cultural pluralist ideal created a space for individual ambition and expressiveness that had not been there before. Thus an individual like Jean-Louis de (Jack) Kérouac, who came of age in the 1940s, found it easier to leave his Lowell French-Canadian enclave and to indulge his creative sensibilities than the kindred, restless souls who inhabited New England's numerous "little Canadas" at an earlier time.

The dissolution of ethnic bonds and the rapid expansion of the realm of individual expressiveness thus clearly benefited society in important ways. But these developments also denied working-class Americans the cultural resources that had been so vital in their struggle to control their own collective destiny. They did not lose their class identity; nor did the moral traditionalism of their ethnic culture vanish. Their residual class and cultural concerns would, with the rise of Reaganism in the 1980s, find a limited expression in Americanist discourse. But they would never regain the confidence and resourcefulness that, in the 1930s and early 1940s, had allowed them to shape and reshape the language of Americanism to suit their political and personal needs. Working-class Americans had lost the ambition and the ability to re-create their world.

Conclusion

This study has tried to demonstrate the centrality of the language of Americanism to the political consciousness of American workers in the post–World War I period. Even in a city like Woonsocket, whose working class was as far removed from mainstream culture as an urban population could possibly have been in 1914, the language of Americanism came, by the 1930s, to dominate working-class discourse. This language did not by itself shape or determine consciousness. Social experience was a critical determinant of consciousness as were ideas rooted in the ethnic and political cultures of particular groups of workers. But in the realm of politics – the realm in which contending groups fought for power and dominance – experience and ideas only mattered if they found expression in the words of this nationalist language.

The centrality of this language to working-class movements undoubtedly made such movements susceptible to cooptation and containment. Political contestants of all stripes were always trying to define such critical words as "democracy" in terms that suited their own ends. Amidst such competition, working-class groups often lost the control over the language they had battled so hard to gain. These battles over the definition of key words and phrases required an ideological vigilance that insurgent movements could rarely sustain indefinitely. Sometimes the ideological defeat was apparent for all to see; other times, particular constructions of the language seemed to slip away almost unnoticed.

The American state played a crucial role in such conflicts, both by abetting the spread of the language of Americanism to every region and group in the country and by seeking, at various moments (especially during war), to use that language for its own ends. The state's efforts to reappropriate Americanism in the 1940s, I have argued, aimed at stabilizing industrial relations and at whipping up support for the war effort in ethnic communities, cost American labor a good deal of its ideological independence. In particular it undermined working-class efforts to make capital–labor relations the true test of the nation's democratic character.

It will be tempting for some to interpret this argument as yet further

331

evidence of the debilitating effects of the labor movement's dependence on the state. That temptation should be resisted. It must be remembered that no labor movement would have successfully arisen in the 1930s without federal support. Even in 1930s Woonsocket, with its unified working class and divided capitalist class, there would have been no union movement worth writing about had not the state intervened at crucial moments – in 1933 with 7(a) of the NIRA, in 1935 with the NLRA (and the active enforcement of that law against Woonsocket Rayon in 1939) – to save the ITU from ruinous defeats. The argument some labor historians are now inclined to make, that the labor movement should have resisted its dependence on state power, is akin to arguing that American blacks, in their twentieth-century fight for freedom and equality, should have refused federal assistance.[1] In the best of all possible worlds, it might be better for social movements to achieve their goals on their own, but the actual distribution of power between blacks and whites, between workers and capitalists, prevalent in *our* society renders such visions utopian. For workers and blacks alike, entanglement with a large bureaucratic state, with all its attendant perils, has been essential to the survival of their movements and dreams.

Though a local study such as this necessarily views an institution like the state from afar, I hope it nevertheless suggests something about the complex, even malleable, character of that critical twentieth-century institution. The state certainly cannot be regarded as a capitalist tool, nor as a mechanism that invariably reinforces society's prevailing distribution of power.[2] It should be regarded instead as a political arena in which society's social conflicts and tensions are themselves fought out. Groups like capitalists usually have the advantage in such conflicts, simply because they are more powerful than most, if not all, opponents. But capitalists have lost key battles for control of the American state, usually in moments when they have been weakened as a result of the economy's poor performance or as a result of ideological divisions within their own ranks. One such moment came in the 1930s when popular insurgency and capitalist disarray not only caused the state to pass the National Labor Relations Act but also allowed workers, in places like Woonsocket, to gain the upper hand

---

[1] A notable example of this kind of argument (that labor should have resisted its dependence on state power) is Christopher L. Tomlins, *The State and the Unions: Labor Relations, Law, and the Organized Labor Movement in America, 1880–1960* (Cambridge, U.K., 1985).

[2] For trenchant criticism of these neo-Marxist theories of the state see Theda Skocpol, "Political Response to Capitalist Crisis: Neo-Marxist Theories of the State and the Case of the New Deal," *Politics and Society* 10 (Spring 1980), 155–201.

in the state-supervised industrial relations machinery that was then established.[3]

The 1940s loss of that working-class advantage in state institutions occurred not simply as a result of the natural or inevitable righting of America's capitalist ship, nor can the role of cultural pluralism in state-sponsored war propaganda be understood simply as a plot to contain and roll back the labor movement, and especially the radically minded insurgents in its ranks. Cultural pluralism must be viewed as a form of modernism which, by World War II, had been fifty years in the making. For much of that time its appeal was confined to small groups of philosophers and anthropologists, but when the horrors of nazism and Stalinism plunged the Western intellectual world into crisis and forced reconsideration of cherished notions of "Western" superiority and of the inextricable link of technological progress and moral progress, cultural pluralism became a most popular creed. Its insistence on the common humanity of all individuals and on the validity (even desirability) of cultural difference suddenly made this creed the most appropriate, most moral, lens through which to view and judge the world. Its rise could not help but diminish the importance that many intellectuals and reformers had long bestowed on the labor question. This fact, however, should not be stretched to mean that cultural pluralism's advocates devised the creed simply to contain and then disarm the radicals in labor's ranks. It had a life, a dynamic, of its own.

Nowhere was this clearer than in the impetus cultural pluralism gave to the civil rights movement. The emphasis that liberals began placing on "brotherhood of man" themes, on eliminating all racial and religious hatred from American life, forced the issue of racial discrimination into the public, political eye as never before. The Democratic Party, which had long ignored the issue for the sake of unity, could no longer escape it: Democratic liberals insisted on including a civil rights plank in the 1948 party platform despite knowing that it was going to trigger a revolt of southern Democrats that the party could ill afford. Repeated clashes between party liberals and conservatives on the race issue would severely weaken the Democratic Party and its presidents over the next thirty years. The pluralist creed that a Democratic administration had so skillfully used to tame the labor movement in World War II, in other words, upset the ideological and

---

[3] For a suggestive interpretation of the post-1935 federal industrial relations system as a "contested terrain" on which capital and labor fought out their class antagonisms see David Abraham, "Individual Autonomy and Collective Empowerment in Labor Law: Union Membership Resignations and Strikebreaking in the New Economy," *New York University Law Review* 63 (December 1988), 1268–340.

organizational equilibrium of the Democratic Party in a most unexpected and uncontrollable way.[4]

The rise of the civil rights movement was only one manifestation of
the ideological transformation that the pluralist creed would effect
on American political consciousness. Its emphasis on equal rights for
all individuals inspired protest movements among women, Hispanics
and other ethnic minorities, and homosexuals. Its message of freedom
from racial and religious discrimination was expanded by 1960s radicals
to include freedom from all the arbitrary constraints imposed by
families, universities, corporations, and the nation-state.

For a long time, the continued dominance of the language of
Americanism hid this profound transformation from view; as late as
the mid-1960s most Americans viewed the ideological preoccupations
of their era as a simple outgrowth of the politics ushered in by FDR
and his New Dealers in the 1930s. But then the social movements that
the pluralist creed had helped inspire turned, in the late 1960s, against
patriotism and against their nation-state. For the first time since 1919,
significant groups of Americans refused to speak the language of
Americanism. Black nationalists and student radicals turned their
earlier reverence for American ideals into their hatred of a "totalitar-
ian" *Amerika*. Young men, angry about the military draft that would
send them to Vietnam, burned American flags while high school
students across the country refused to utter the Pledge of Allegiance.
Deliberately spurning their country's own revolutionary heroes, tens
of thousands of university students turned toward Che Guevara,
Mao Zedong, and Frantz Fanon for political inspiration.[5]

Such explicit renunciation of Americanism's nationalist dimension
was accompanied by a widespread rejection of the premises underlying the democratic and progressive dimensions as well. Radical

---

[4] On the Democratic Party's changing attitude toward the civil rights question, see
Alonzo L. Hamby, *Beyond the New Deal: Harry S. Truman and American Liberalism* (New
York, 1973), 209–65. On the dilemmas which the "race question" caused the Dem-
ocratic Party from the 1940s through the 1970s, see Nelson Lichtenstein, "From
Corporatism to Collective Bargaining: Organized Labor and the Eclipse of Social
Democracy in the Postwar Era," Jonathan Rieder, "The Rise of the 'Silent Majority',"
and Thomas Byrne Edsall, "The Changing Shape of Power: A Realignment in Public
Policy," all in Steve Fraser and Gary Gerstle, eds., *The Rise and Fall of the New Deal
Order, 1930–1980* (Princeton, N.J., 1989), 122–52, 243–93.

[5] On the origins and development of the New Left, see Todd Gitlin, *The Sixties: Years of
Hope, Days of Rage* (New York, 1987), and Maurice Isserman and Michael Kazin, "The
Failure and Success of the New Radicalism," in Fraser and Gerstle, *The Rise and Fall of
the New Deal Order*, 212–42. The critical story of cultural pluralism's rise and of the
role it played in transforming modern American liberalism and radicalism awaits its
historian.

students viewed American society as fundamentally antidemocratic, its ideals but a clever cover for the racism, imperialism, and authoritarianism that formed the ideological core of the American "system." More and more radicals and liberals, meanwhile, began challenging (in the 1970s) the progressive belief that industrial society could deliver humanity to a state of abundance, harmony, and individual freedom.

This radical and liberal revolt against the language of Americanism allowed conservatives to monopolize its use and thus to control its meaning. Conservatives, in fact, have made the control of this political language a brilliant component of their quest for national power. They have understood that a majority of Americans, throughout the 1960s and beyond, continued to think of themselves and of their society in Americanist words, terms, and phrases. They have reinvigorated the nationalist dimension with their flag waving, Pledges of Allegiance, and proclamations of American greatness. They have constructed from the democratic dimension a faith in "free enterprise" and "individual rights" and successfully merged that faith with a progressive belief in the prosperity that a market-oriented capitalist economy could deliver to all Americans. And, most remarkable of all, they have interwoven this forward-looking faith in market forces (and the hostility to traditional forms of community which such a faith implies) with a revivified traditionalist reverence for the authority of God, the sanctity of the patriarchal family, and the moral superiority of Western, Christian civilization.

This conservative Americanist creed, especially its heavy emphasis on traditionalist concerns, profoundly appealed to millions of ethnic Americans who had been Democrats, unionists, and patriots since the days of the New Deal. The Reagan Democrat phenomenon was as strong in Woonsocket as elsewhere: Reagan actually won this city in 1984, receiving more than 8,000 votes (out of a total of 16,000) at a time when fewer than 300 Woonsocket citizens had registered themselves as Republicans.[6] A good deal of Reagan's success rested on his ability to speak in the traditionalist idiom that had been so central a component of ethnic Democrats' Americanism since the late 1930s.

But as much as Reagan did to restore the voice of long-silent Democratic constituencies to national political discourse, he could not recapture the resonance that had so characterized the traditionalist dimension of Americanism during industrial unionism's heyday. Then, ethnic unionists in Woonsocket and elsewhere had found in this traditionalist dimension not only the words to challenge the claims of secularism, materialism, and communism; they also found the

---

[6] Interview with Lino Brunetti, Woonsocket Board of Canvassers, November 21, 1988.

language to challenge the prevalent power relations governing economic life in their city and in the nation at large. To the claims of capital they had counterposed the claims of their community. As an alternative to the reckless individualism of the market they had offered the communalism of their ethnic life.

It may be that such ideological formulations were the product of a particular historical moment – when tightly bonded communities were lived experiences and not just worthy ideals – that has long since passed away. It may also be that the very hope that labor could transform society rested on a set of historical experiences that also belongs to the past, rendering the hope irrelevant to the politics of today. Still, the passing of a distinct era of ethnic and labor solidarity does not mean that the current construction of Americanism is somehow the only "true" Americanism. The language of Americanism remains supple and malleable, capable of introducing a variety of experiences and ideas into the nation's political discourse. To the extent to which liberals and radicals want to attain political power, they must learn, or relearn, how to speak this language. Those who set themselves such a task might begin their education with a consideration of how an earlier generation of political insurgents – those active in Woonsocket and elsewhere in the 1930s – constructed a "new, progressive Americanism" and made it an instrument of their empowerment.

Appendix A: Locals organized by ITU, 1932–1955

Local	Location	Members[a]	Entry/exit years
I. Textiles/French spinning			
Alsace Mill, Guerin Mills	Woonsocket	524	1933/1954
Argonne Worsted	Woonsocket	375	1942
Bell Co. of R.I.	Woonsocket	156	1938
Jules Desurmont Worsted (Riverside Worsted)	Woonsocket	329	1932
French Worsted	Woonsocket	450	1933
Lafayette Worsted	Woonsocket	350	1939
Masurel Worsted Mills	Woonsocket	200	1939
II. Textiles/woolen spinning			
Belmont Woolen Yarn Mills	Woonsocket	78	1934
Bonin Spinning	Woonsocket	246	1934
Falls Yarn Mill	Woonsocket	141	1933
River Mills	Woonsocket	177	1934/1937
Woonsocket Spinning	Woonsocket	113	1934
III. Textiles/Bradford spinning			
Sidney Blumenthal	Woonsocket	250	1942
Onawa (Premier) Spinning (Murray Worsted)	Woonsocket	450	1941
Philmont Mill, Guerin Mills	Woonsocket	285	1934/1935
Spring Grove Spinning	Woonsocket	145	1946
Sydney Worsted	Woonsocket	250	1945/1947
Woonsocket Worsted Mills	Woonsocket	250	1938/1938
IV. Textiles/wool top dyeing			
Blackstone Dye Works	Woonsocket	95	1933
Enterprise Dye Works	Woonsocket	143	1934
Fairmount Dye Works	Woonsocket	75	1934
Florence Dye Works	Woonsocket	81	1934
Model Dyeing and Printing	Woonsocket	30	1940
Rosemont Mill, Guerin Mills	Woonsocket	184	1933/1954

Local	Location	Members[a]	Entry/exit years
Woonsocket Dyeing and Bleach	Woonsocket	72	1937
V. Textiles/woolen and worsted weaving			
Airedale Worsted Mills	Woonsocket	145	1942
Brighton Woolen	Woonsocket	50	1946/1948
Dunn Worsted Mills	Woonsocket	300	1941
Empire Woolen Mills	Woonsocket	?	1948/1950
Lippitt Woolen (Dale Worsted Mills)	Woonsocket	249	1935
Montrose Mill, Guerin Mills	Woonsocket	303	1933/1954
Verdun Manufacturing[b]	Woonsocket	160	1943
Yorkshire	Woonsocket	?	1953
VI. Textiles/cotton and rayon spinning			
Blackstone Cotton	Blackstone, Mass.	1,100	1937/1945
Lawton Spinning	Woonsocket	11	1933/1935
Manville Jenckes (Textron)	Manville, R.I.	3,000	1940/1949
Woonsocket Rayon (Synthetic Yarn)	Woonsocket	275	1939/1948
VII. Textiles/cotton plush			
Joan Plush Mills	Woonsocket	40	1938
Rhode Island Plush Mills	Woonsocket	140	1935
Woonsocket Falls Mills (includes Clinton Plush)	Woonsocket	330	1938
VIII. Textiles/miscellaneous			
B. Cohen and Sons (wool waste)	Woonsocket	60	1943
Arthur I. Darman (wool sorting)	Woonsocket	57	1943
Dauray Textiles (specialty knitting weaving)	Woonsocket	?	1949
Handicraft Woolen Mills (handwoven woolens)	Woonsocket	30	1945/1951
E. P. Hebert Knitting Mill (cotton knitting)	Woonsocket	25	1938
Star Carbonizing (wool scouring & carbonizing)	Woonsocket	50	1933
Textile Coning (synthetics)	Woonsocket	?	1946/1948
Woonsocket Garnetting (picking, carding, and garnetting)	Woonsocket	?	1949

Local	Location	Members[a]	Entry/exit years
IX. Rubber manufacture			
American Wringer	Woonsocket	518	1935
Lloyd Manufacturing	Warwick, R.I.	100	1943/1945
United States Rubber	Woonsocket	1,500	1944/1945
Woonsocket Rubber and Plastics	Woonsocket	?	1954
X. Machine, tool, and steel manufacture			
American Ball Bearing	Providence	35	1944/1946
Bay State Tap and Die	Mansfield, Mass.	250	1942/1945
Diamond Foundry	Woonsocket	?	1946/1948
New England Drawn Steel	Mansfield, Mass.	125	1942/1944
S. W. Card (taps and dies)	Mansfield, Mass.	330	1942/1946
Textile Finishing Machinery	Providence	1,400	1942/1944
Wrentham Brothers (dies and punches)	Wrentham, Mass.	250	1944/1945
Winter Brothers (machine tools)	Wrentham, Mass.	100	1944/1945
XI. Miscellaneous manufacture			
Adolph Meller Nos. 4 & 7	Providence (2 locals)	100	1942/1946
American Paper Tube (mule cardboard tubes)	Woonsocket	400	1941/1955
Bakeries	Woonsocket	75	1934
Breton Cigar	Woonsocket	?	1944/1945
M. Diamond Mattress	Woonsocket	11	1950/1954
Unemployed (WPA)	Woonsocket	1,000	1938/1941
Woonsocket Brush	Woonsocket	100	1942
XII. Construction, service, and trade			
Barbers	Woonsocket	70	1936/1948
Electricians	Woonsocket	110	1937/1938
Newspapermen	Woonsocket	20	1943/1945
New York Cleansing & Dyeing (Parisian cleaners)	Woonsocket	11	1945/1948
Office Workers	Woonsocket	?	1937/1943
Painters	Woonsocket	?	1943/1946
Plumbers	Woonsocket	70	1942
Sheet Metal Workers	Woonsocket	90	1937
Store Clerks	Woonsocket	235	1936/1942
Shoe Repairers	Woonsocket	?	1937/1938

[a] No direct membership figures are available; since the ITU established union shops in virtually all its locals by the late 1930s, the number of members is as-

sumed to be equal to the number of employees. Employment figures have been derived from state reports (see below for specifics). The figures chosen reflect employment levels prevailing at the moment of union organization and thus do not reflect – for those mills organized in the 1930s – the growth in employment and membership occurring in the full employment conditions of the 1940s.

[b] One of the Verdun mills spun worsted yarn on the French system.

Sources: ITU News, 1936–1955; Christiansen, Murphy, and Company, "Report on Audit of the Independent Textile Union of America," September 30 and December 31, 1937, March 31, June 30, and December 31, 1938, June 30 and September 9, 1939, June 30 and December 31, 1940, June 30 and December 31, 1941, and June 30 and December 31, 1942, Lawrence N. Spitz Collection, Mss 31, Box 8, Rhode Island Historical Society, Providence, R.I.; ITU, Dues Income Statements, 1943–1946, Spitz Collection, Box 8; ITU, Dues Income Statements, 1949–1955, George Butsika Collection, in author's possession; Lawrence Spitz to author, May 11, 1977; Rhode Island Department of Labor (hereafter R.I. DOL), *Annual Report* (Providence, R.I.) 1935, 200–4; R.I. DOL, *List of Industrial Establishments* (Providence, R.I., 1944), 74–9; R.I. DOL, *List of Industrial Establishments* (Providence, R.I., 1950), 38–41, 79–80; *Providence Journal Almanac: A Reference Book for the State of Rhode Island* (Providence, R.I.), 1930, 1935, 1940, 1945, 1950.

Note: A number of mills – such as the Cherry Brook Worsted, Branch River, and Contrexeville – that were listed as locals on the ITU's dues income statements in the late 1930s have not been included in this appendix. The dues payments were always small relative to the size of the mills in question. No other evidence suggests, moreover, that the ITU actually won elections in these mills. Union supporters in these mills had probably begun paying dues as an expression of their enthusiasm for the ITU or else in anticipation of an imminent union NLRB victory.

Appendix B: A note on union sources and a list of interviewees

For more than thirty years, Lawrence Spitz preserved the largest and most critical collection of extant ITU documents (covering the years 1936 to 1946) in the garage of his summer home. He generously allowed me frequent and unrestricted access to it and then donated its entire contents to the Rhode Island Historical Society (RIHS). George Butsika stored in his home a far smaller but still significant collection of ITU documents consisting chiefly of ITU collective bargaining agreements and Executive Council Meeting minutes for the years 1945 to 1955. He graciously lent them to me to use in my research, and I hope to have them transferred soon to the RIHS. I shall always be in both men's debt.

Though all of this book had been researched and much of it written before Spitz donated his collection to the RIHS, I have changed virtually all my references to the Spitz Collection to accord with the manuscript and box numbers that RIHS archivists have assigned to it. In a few instances when I could not determine how a particular document had been catalogued, I have simply identified its source as the Spitz Collection without specifying the relevant box number.

Some issues of the *ITU News* in the years 1936 to 1941 have found their way to various libraries but the only complete run survives in the Spitz Collection; all my references to the *ITU News* in these years are to copies in this collection. For the years 1942 to 1946, I used the substantially complete collection located at the U.S. Department of Labor Library in Washington, D.C., and for the years 1947 to 1951, I relied on a run preserved at Harvard University's Littauer Library.

Material contained in the *ITU News* allowed me not only to reconstruct the history of union activities and of working-class encounters with the language of Americanism, but also to begin the complicated process of identifying the crucial occupational, ethnic, and familial characteristics of the union's pioneers and early rank-and-file leaders. I constructed a list of these cadre from references to them (usually in stories honoring their pioneering roles) appearing in the *ITU News* in the years 1936 to 1942, and then searched for information on each in the 1935 Rhode Island Manuscript Census (located in the Rhode Island State Archives, Providence, Rhode Island) and the U.S. Department of Justice's Petitions for Naturalization for Providence County (located in Providence Superior Court, Providence). Fortunately, for my purposes, the 1935 state census officials filled out a separate card for each Rhode Island resident and then arranged the cards alphabetically; the Providence County naturalization petitions are indexed alphabetically by name. These circumstances made the process of linking union cadre to their census cards and naturalization petitions rather straightforward.

These two sets of records contain a wealth of information. Each 1935 census card has the country (or state) of birth, date of birth, current address, marital status, number in family if head of household, occupation (for adults), number of months unemployed in previous year, school (for children), citizenship status, and so on. Each naturalization petition has the country and city of birth, date of birth, spouse, date and place of marriage, date and place of birth of children, last foreign residence, port of entry into the United States, years in Providence County, occupation, and so on. This information proved crucial to understanding the formative social experiences of the ITU's two groups of pioneers – the Franco-Belgian radicals and French-Canadian Catholics.

I found the National Archives' National Recovery Administration records (Record 9, Entries 398 and 402) extremely useful for reconstructing the history of industrial relations in Woonsocket in the years 1933 to 1937. These records contain not only letters written by ordinary workers to FDR, Secretary of Labor Perkins, NRA administrators (and so on) describing and protesting their conditions of work (the same sort that Jacquelyn Dowd Hall, James Leloudis, Robert Korstad, Mary Murphy, Lu Ann Jones, and Christopher B. Daly used so effectively in their *Like a Family: The Making of a Southern Cotton Mill World* [Chapel Hill, N.C., 1987]); they contain as well detailed reports filed in Washington by government investigators sent out by labor boards to investigate the complaints and issues raised by workers (and sometimes companies) in their letters. The amount of bureaucratic effort poured into such investigations was, quite simply, staggering, especially in view of the limited statutory power of these labor boards to effect change. This ineffectual effort, however, left behind a wealth of deposits that historians have only just begun to discover and to mine. Most of the complaints and investigations are organized alphabetically by employer (e.g., Manville Jenckes Corp., Manville, R.I.) or by regionally based employer groups (e.g., Woonsocket Woolen Mills, Woonsocket, R.I.). Scholars focusing on a particular community or region will thus find the relevant complaints and investigations relatively easy to locate.

I have already noted in my acknowledgments how much I owe to the many individuals who agreed to be interviewed and to share with me their memories of the ITU, of textile mill work, of Woonsocket social and cultural life, and of various aspects of radical politics and Catholic activism in the period from 1920 to 1950. Table B.1 contains the names of the forty-four interviewees as well as their former occupations and union affiliations, the dates of my interviews with them, and the locations of the interview tapes.

Table B.1. *Interviews*

Name	Former occupation and/or union affiliation[a]	Date	Tape[b]
Samuel Angoff	Boston-based labor lawyer	11/7/76	RIHS
Rose Boudreau	R.I. worsted worker	10/14/80	SMHS
Lino Brunetti	Woon. Bd. of Canvassers (current)	11/21/88	nt
Edmund R. Brock	labor priest	7/7/83	GG
George Butsika	ITU weaver, Montrose Worsted	9/14/84	RIHS
Leo Cloutier	paymaster, French Worsted	6/26/81	nt
Heliodore Comeau	ITU barber	6/24/81	nt
James Cullen	Woon. worsted weaver	9/8/80	SMHS
Irene Cullen	Woon. resident	9/8/80	SMHS
Herve Duhamel	ITU weaver, Montrose Worsted	10/27/80	RIHS
Harry Fleischman	Socialist Party activist	11/9/84	nt
Arthur Fortin	Ligue Ouvrière Catholique leader	7/5/83	GG
Cecile Galipeau	Woon. cotton frame spinner	9/8/80	SMHS
Hector Galipeau	Woon. cotton worker	9/8/80	SMHS
Leona Galipeau	ITU mulespinner, Falls Yarn	10-22-3/80	RIHS
Leonel Galipeau	ITU cardstripper, Falls Yarn	10/22-3/80	RIHS
Normand Galipeau	ITU woolen worker, Falls Yarn	10/22-3/80	RIHS
Harriet Gaudet	R.I. worsted worker	10/14/80	SMHS
Ernest Gignac	ITU mulespinner, French Worsted	6/25/81	nt
Livio Gramolini	ITU weaver, Rhode Island Plush	9/14/84	RIHS
Robert Guerin	Woon. industrialist, grandson of Joseph Guerin	11/3/80	RIHS
Lionel Harnois	ITU treasurer (1970s)	10/8/76	nt
Charlotte LeBlanc	Woon. youth, granddaughter of French Worsted superintendent	7/16/81	RIHS
Oscar Legendre	R.I. silk weaver	9/8/80	SMHS
William McNeill	R.I. cotton weaver	10/7/80	SMHS
Arthur Moretti	ITU mulespinner, Lafayette Worsted	9/14/84	RIHS
Apostole Moussas	ITU mulespinner, French Worsted	10/20/80	nt

Table B.1. *Cont.*

Name	Former occupation and/or union affiliation[a]	Date	Tape[b]
Mrs. Carl Oberg	R.I. cotton framespinner	9/9/80	SMHS
Harvey O'Connor	radical labor journalist	6/17/85	GG
Michael Parlak	ITU weaver, Clinton Plush	6/24/81	nt
Eva Proroczok	ITU worsted finisher, Desurmont	6/22/81	nt
Arthur Riendeau	ITU mulespinner, Bonin Spinning	6/25/81	RIHS
John Robinson	R.I. cotton mulespinner	10/7/80	SMHS
Arthur Rock	ITU dye worker, Florence Dye, and ITU president (1970s)	10/8/76	nt
Stanley Rypsyc	ITU dye worker, Blackstone Dye	10/30/80	nt
Joseph D. Schmetz	Woon. worker, son of ITU president	10/15/76	RIHS
Harry Shallis	R.I. cotton loomfixer	10/8/80	SMHS
Warren Slaney	R.I. cotton mill clerk	10/14/80	SMHS
Lawrence Spitz	ITU general secretary	10/22/76	RIHS
		9/19–20/79	RIHS
		8/28/80	GG
		7/15/83	nt
A.P. Thomas	Woon. historian (1970s)	10/22/80	nt
Mrs. A. P. Thomas	Woon. resident	10/22/80	nt
Angelo Turbesi	ITU mulepiecer, Guerin Mills-Alsace, and ITU vice-president	10/9/80	RIHS
		9/14/84	RIHS
Phileas Valois	Ligue Ouvrière Catholique leader	7/5/83	RIHS
Yvonne Valois	Ligue Ouvrière Catholique member	7/5/83	RIHS

[a] "R.I. . . ." refers to someone who worked in Rhode Island textile mills outside Woonsocket; "Woon. . ." refers to someone who worked (or lived) in Woonsocket but who did not belong to the ITU; "ITU . . ." refers to someone who belonged to the ITU and worked in a Woonsocket mill or trade.

Unless otherwise specified, information in this column refers to the occupations and union affiliations of these individuals in the years 1920–50. In those instances in which an individual, in these years, worked in more than one occupation and belonged to more than one union local, I have only identified that occupation and union affiliation most relevant to this study. Many of the unionists I interviewed were rank-and-file leaders who held elective office in their union locals; I have only identified, however, the leadership positions of those unionists elected to the four top union-wide offices: president, general secretary, general vice president, general treasurer.

[b] "RIHS" means the tape is located at the Rhode Island Historical Society, Providence, R.I.; "SMHS" means the tape is located at the Slater Mill Historic

Site, Pawtucket, R.I. (I conducted these interviews for the Slater Mill as part of its effort to create an oral history archive of Rhode Island textile workers.); "nt" means no tape exists either because the interviewee refused me permission to record or else because I conducted the interview by phone; "GG" means the tape is in author's possession.

Index

Alsace spinning mill, 72, 145, 327
  ITU at, 106, 108, 207, 209, 211, 214, 253–4
Amalgamated Clothing Workers, 201
Amalgamated Textile Workers of America, 75–8, 79n40, 80, 85, 156
American Federation of Labor (AFL), 1, 43, 82, 153
  in Woonsocket, 42, 216, 233, 234n6
Americanism, language of, 5–15, 45, 216–18
  centrality of, in 1920s and 1930s, 5–8, 14, 331
  defined, 8
  democratic dimension of, 9, 10, 177–87, 334–5; see also cultural pluralism
  French Canadians and, 86–7, 154, 187–95, 218–19, 247, 287–8, 310
  malleability of, 9–13, 14, 194–5, 336
  nationalist dimension of, 9, 166–74, 334–6
  progressive dimension of, 9, 10–11, 12, 86, 174–7, 334–5
  traditionalist dimension of, 9, 11–12, 190–5, 335–6
  use of, by radicals in ITU, 6, 166–72, 174–8, 180–4, 188–91, 195, 310; by Joseph Schmetz, 84–8, 90, 156, 157, 174–5
Americanization campaigns, 3–4, 8, 46–7, 75, 77, 134
  by radicals within ITU, 87–8, 155, 188–90
American Legion, 46, 276
American Paper Tube Company, 64, 96
American Woolen Company, 32

American Wringer, 207–8
  ITU local at, 217
Amoskeag Manufacturing Company, 32, 36–7
Anderson, Henry, 273
Angoff, Samuel, 141, 270, 273
anticommunism, 285–9, 305
  of Catholic Church, 122, 249–57
  of ethnic corporatist leaders in ITU, 275–6, 286–8, 306–9
arbitration, 210–11, 313
Armenian workers, 269–70

Bednarchuk, Mary, 300–1
Belgians, See Franco-Belgians
Belgian Workers Party, 70, 74, 84, 197
Bell, Joseph, 273
Bell Worsted local, 218
benefits, 324–5
Benoit, Oliver, 219
Bernard, James, 142–3, 206
Bernon district, 67, 71
Bienvenue, Father, 253
Blackstone Cotton local, 217, 245, 320
Blackstone Dye local, 217
Bodnar, John, 125
Bonin Spinning mill, 118, 207, 209, 214–15
Bordes, Charlotte, 67–9, 329
Bordes, Fernande, 66–8
Boucher, Bertrand, 224, 241, 273
Boucher, Henry, 34–5, 36n43, 37, 49
Bouvier, Joseph, 38
Branch River Wool Combing Company, 105, 110
Brock, Father Edmund, 281–5, 291, 302
Browder, Earl, 5–6
Burlak, Ann, 241–2